T0385498

THE I TATTI
RENAISSANCE LIBRARY

James Hankins, General Editor

ALBERTI

DINNER PIECES

VOLUME I

ITRL 97

LEON BATTISTA ALBERTI
• • •
DINNER PIECES
VOLUME I

INTRODUCTION, TEXT EDITION, AND NOTES BY

ROBERTO CARDINI

TRANSLATED BY

DAVID MARSH

THE I TATTI RENAISSANCE LIBRARY

HARVARD UNIVERSITY PRESS

CAMBRIDGE, MASSACHUSETTS

LONDON, ENGLAND

2024

Series design by Dean Bornstein

First printing

Library of Congress Cataloging-in-Publication Data

Names: Alberti, Leon Battista, 1404–1472, author. | Alberti, Leon
Battista, 1404–1472. Intercenales. Latin (Cardini) | Alberti, Leon Battista,
1404–1472. Intercenales. English. | Cardini, Roberto, editor. |
Marsh, David, 1950 September 25– translator.
Title: Dinner pieces : Leon Battista Alberti ; introduction, text edition,
and notes by Roberto Cardini ; translated by David Marsh.
Other titles: I Tatti Renaissance library ; 97–98.
Description: Cambridge, Massachusetts : Harvard University Press, 2024. |
Series: The I Tatti renaissance library ; ITRL 97–98 | Includes bibliographical
references and index. | Contents: v. 1. Book One. Book Two. Book Three.
Book Four. Book Seven — v. 2. Book Eight. Book Nine. Book Ten.
Book Eleven. Appendix I. Appendix II. Appendix III. |
Text in Latin with English translation; introduction and notes in English.
Identifiers: LCCN 2023022614 | ISBN 9780674295742 (v. 1 ; cloth) |
ISBN 9780674295759 (v. 2 ; cloth)
Subjects: LCSH: Dialogues, Latin (Medieval and modern) —
Translation into English. | Satire, Latin (Medieval and modern) —
Translations into English. | Fables, Latin (Medieval and modern) —
Translations into English. | Humor in literature.
Classification: LCC PA8450.A5 I5813 2024 |
DDC 878/.04 — dc23/eng/20230915
LC record available at https://lccn.loc.gov/2023022614

Contents

꙳

Introduction

❦❧❦

Leon Battista Alberti's *Intercenales* (*Dinner Pieces*) is his most innovative literary work and surely stands as an absolute masterpiece both of Italian Renaissance and of modern European letters. This Introduction discusses the character, evolution, and ultimate design of the work as a whole, Alberti's relationship to the humanist movement of his time, and the key role the work played in the history of humor writing. The dating of the individual *Dinner Pieces* is also discussed and, for context, a short sketch of Alberti's life to 1443, the *terminus ante quem* of the work, is offered. For the interpretation of the fifty-three individual pieces included in the collection, the reader is referred to the headnotes for each piece in the Notes to the Translation, to be read (for those who read Italian) along with the fuller commentary in Cardini 2022. For the various manuscripts and redactions mentioned in this Introduction, the reader may consult the Note on the Text.

Character, Evolution, and Design of the Dinner Pieces

As Alberti himself explains, the title means texts to be read while dining and drinking, thus clearly situating the work in the tradition of symposial, or banquet literature. This was a genre that, while vigorous in many ages, enjoyed a significant rebirth in 1425 with Antonio Panormita's *Hermaphroditus*, a scandalous collection of elegiacs and epigrams. Alberti was surely familiar with the work; in fact, Panormita dedicates three epigrams in it to him. Composed only a few years later, Alberti's *Dinner Pieces* stand in opposition to the *Hermaphroditus* in many ways, beginning with their comic elements.

Symposial literature is a sort of *satura lanx*, or abundant platter, that luxuriates in thematic, stylistic, and linguistic variety. Indeed, besides their varied themes, the *Dinner Pieces* explore the most diverse intellectual spheres, ranging from *ekphrasis* to astrology, from philosophy to religion, from physiognomy to cryptic puzzles; they discuss every sphere of life, from household management and marriage to the state. The literary genres employed are nearly countless, and the stylistic palette astonishingly broad. Even so, it is the lesser genres of fable and comedy, written in their humbler style, that generally predominate in the work.

Alberti's title, itself a neologism, offers a foretaste of his supreme linguistic experimentation, among the most fascinating and fecund offered by the Neo-Latin literature of the Quattrocento. The Latin of the *Dinner Pieces* is a delicious mélange. It blends every age of Latin style, if with uneven emphasis: archaic, golden, silver, late-classical, Christian, and medieval. Especially impressive is the author's gift for creating names. Neologisms and resemantizations of traditional vocabulary are strewn abundantly throughout the text. They permeate the symbolic naming of Alberti's characters and are emblazoned within particular titles, from that of the entire collection to those of single pieces, such as *Debate on Marriage* (*Uxoria*) and *Enigmas* (*Convelata*), thus catching the reader's attention by their originality.

The gateway to the work is clearly marked by two paratexts at the beginning of Book 1: the dedication-preface to Paolo Dal Pozzo Toscanelli, and *The Writer* (*Scriptor*). The opening words of the dedication ("I have begun to collect my *Dinner Pieces* into short books so that they may be more easily read over dinners and drinks") demonstrate that the composition, revision, assembly, and the publication of the work took place at different times. Alberti first wrote his dinner pieces, then collected, revised, and organized them in short books, but not all at once—rather, by sections and at different moments. Since he undertook to collect them to make it easier and simpler to read them, they must first have been read — even if less easily and simply — and therefore *published* before they could be collected and organized. Hence, before they were revised and gathered into short books, many texts circulated singly in private circles. This history of their revision and publication is rigorously confirmed by the dedicatory letter to the first version of *Debate on Marriage* (found in Appendix 1 of this edition) and by those dinner pieces (*Virtue* [*Virtus*], *The Deceased* [*Defunctus*], *Debate on Marriage*) whose evolution is completely documented as texts published separately from the larger collection.

Indeed, the *Dinner Pieces* were not grouped in a single arrangement, but in at least three. The first arrangement, as revealed in the headnote to *The Orphan* (*Pupillus*), was almost certainly in two books, evidently those mentioned in the dedication to Toscanelli and found in the Oxford manuscript. In the final arrangement, known to us in the Pistoia manuscript, the work is nearly tripled: the number of books increases from two to eleven, the number of dinner pieces from fourteen to forty-one, and the number of prefaces from one to seven. At the same time, the work has been ruptured: *The Deceased*, which in the Oxford manuscript occupied all of Book 4, has disappeared and is replaced by six brand-new dinner pieces. Furthermore, the intermediate arrangement has not come down to us, but it clearly existed at one time. The manuscript Moreni 2 of the Biblioteca Moreniana in Florence, a group of consolatory texts assembled by Alberti, indicates that *Naufragus*, which makes up Book 9 in the Pistoia collection, made up Book 11 in the intermediate arrangement, but under a different title: not *Naufragus* (*Shipwrecked*), but *Naufragium* (*Shipwreck*).

We thus infer that the *Dinner Pieces* originated as an "open work," on which Alberti worked for more than a decade (from around 1430 to the spring of 1443), a period that he spent mainly in Florence, and that the collection to our knowledge remained an "open work," in the sense of "unfinished." The final arrangement that has come down to us lacks two books and several prefaces.

Now, in the dedication to Toscanelli the author positions his work within the symposial tradition and hints at its complex process of revision and publication. More important, he defines its nature, which is mainly humoristic, and its purpose, which is therapeutic. He intends to remedy mental distress using the therapy of laughter. In this way the *Dinner Pieces* mix and supplement Cicero and Democritus: the Cicero of the *Tusculan Disputations* and the depiction of Democritus in the epistolary novel *Madness and Laughter*, (falsely) attributed to Hippocrates.[1]

As if to make clear the nature of the work, at its entrance we hear the announcement "Lepidus is back." In *The Writer*, the second paratext in Book 1, the author puts on the mask that disguised him in his youthful debut, the *Philodoxeos fabula*, which he circulated under the name Lepidus, supposedly a hitherto unknown comic writer of ancient Rome.[2] For more than a century, at least until the 1582 edition of Aldus Manutius the Younger, this forgery was thought to be authentic; but the twenty-year-old Alberti used it to mock the movement typical of early Quattrocento humanism, the vogue for "discoveries." The *Dinner Pieces* thus revive that comic, parodic, and irreverent experiment, but refashion it with miraculous complexity. In the comedy, Lepidus was in a sense a double oxymoron, whereas in *Garlands* (*Corolle*), he is the first formulation of modern humorism.

Alberti's declaration "I have begun" in the dedication to Toscanelli compels us to ask how this messy "open work" — comprising a few texts composed at intervals and published individually — was planned as an organic corpus in eleven books. In the preface to Book 3 of his *Remedies for Affliction*, Alberti wrote that literary texts are buildings, the "private lodgings" of their authors. And in *De re aedificatoria* (*On the Art of Building*) 9.5, he added that a well-constructed building, regulated by geometric proportions and internal harmonies, is a living organism (*veluti animal aedificium*).[3] Presumably, then, Alberti was guided by the same principles in his numerous attempts to construct the edifice of the *Dinner Pieces*: first to collect into short books a mass of disparate texts, in part separately published and in part unpublished, and then to transform these books into a collection. Not presumably, but certainly, for the individual books of the Pistoia redaction contain frequent internal echoes and additions, and there are numerous links between books, which—as is shown to some extent in the headnotes in the Notes to the Translation and in greater detail in my commentary in volume 2 of Cardini 2022—clearly demonstrate a structural design that is no longer tentative but to a great extent realized. To be sure, the Pistoia redaction is still an open work that lacks the finishing touches: two books and several prefaces are missing, and some of the extant texts are defective. All the same, there is a clear and constant attention to structural design. Most prominent are two elements of "ring composition": the early, partial unity of Books 1 and 2, and the arch that embraces the entire work from *The Orphan* to *The Love Affair* (*Amores*). These demonstrate that the Pistoia redaction, albeit "unfinished," is by no means a disjointed batch of texts, but rather a truly organic corpus that invites our questions, analysis, and judgment.

What is more, the structure as assembled of both the single books and the entire collection does not reflect their chronological development, as two of the dinner pieces make clear. Alberti's autobiography tells us that *The Widow* (*Vidua*) and *The Deceased* antedate the author's thirtieth birthday (February 18, 1434) and are thus among the earliest dinner pieces.[4] If their arrangement were chronological, they would appear in the first books; instead, in the first phase of the collection, represented by the Oxford redaction, *The Widow* is missing, while *The Deceased* by itself constitutes Book 4, and only in the intermediate arrangements. The final phase of the collection, that of the Pistoia redaction, speaks clearly. In it, *The Widow* is transferred to the final book (Book 11), while *The Deceased* is completely absent.

There are, moreover, clear indications that the distribution and the arrangement of the dinner pieces were influenced by considerations of theme, style, and structure. Consider the evidence offered by the Pistoia redaction. Book 1 lends itself to two interpretations. If we accept the authorial gloss that concludes the preface to Toscanelli, the book is a *Bildungsroman*, or coming-of-age story. But if we consider the sequence of texts, it also amounts to a religious breviary with a Stoic coloring, at once both unfamiliar and instructive. Thus, the first dinner piece, *The Orphan*, is about the silence of God; the second, *Religion* (*Religio*), is about prayer; the third, *Virtue*, shows that God Almighty, being subject to fortune, not only pays no attention to Virtue but will not receive her; the fourth, *Fate and Fortune* (*Fatum et Fortuna*), explains the two powers that are superior to divinity; the fifth, *Patience* (*Patientia*), gives the genealogy of the difficult but salutary virtue of tolerance, defined as the daughter of Necessity; the sixth and final piece, *Happiness* (*Felicitas*), illustrates the principle that human affairs are guided by opinion rather than reason. Book 2 examines money and wealth, except for the opening piece, *The Oracle* (*Oraculum*), which acts as a link to the religious themes of Book 1 and shows that in our requests to the gods we foolishly ask for things exclusively within our control. Book 3 illustrates the consequences of envy and ambition, the two mothers from whom descend the family trees depicted in *Paintings* (*Picture*) on the left-hand wall of the temple of Good and Ill Fortune. Book 4 is not on any one subject, but the "Libripeta cycle" runs through it, in *The Dream* (*Somnium*), *Fame* (*Fama*), and even *Garlands*, in which Libripeta is replaced by an analogous Detractor. Book 7 is a diptych about marriage, and Book 8 is a diptych on alternative and dangerous knowledge (Pythagorean enigmas and astrology). Book 9 is consolatory; Book

10 is an organic overview of politics in the form of apologues. Book II, the last book, is another diptych, this time on extramarital love.

With respect to internal symmetries and the general structure of the work, I have already surmised that the first installment of the collection comprised two books that form a ring composition. The first piece in Book 1, *The Orphan*, and the last of Book 2, *Wealth (Divitie)*, are mutually referential. *The Orphan* depicts Alberti himself, and *Wealth* his grandfather Benedetto Alberti, who, in a challenge to Leonardo Bruni's negative judgment of him, is portrayed in a positive light.[5] Benedetto here delivers a deathbed speech that suggests that the illegitimate orphan Battista is his true heir. The strategic placement of *The Orphan* and *The Love Affair* as the first and the last pieces in the collection is also, surely, no accident, but an almost geometrical indication of the work's architecture. In *The Orphan*, the orphan's irresistible literary vocation is thwarted by his greedy kinsmen, while in *The Love Affair*, Friginnius, another *alter ego* of the author, is thwarted by love, that most destructive and deleterious passion, which destroys the spiritual tranquility essential to study. Hence, like the two-book version, the eleven-book version of the *Dinner Pieces* forms a ring composition.

That the literary experimentation and invention of the young Alberti permeates all of the *Dinner Pieces*, with far greater intensity and depth than earlier in his career as a writer, is made clear by the second interlocutor in *The Writer*, Libripeta. When he asserts that culture is disparaged in Florence, he almost literally repeats what we read in *De commodis litterarum atque incommodis (On the Advantages and Disadvantages of Literature)*. The latter was the first work to reveal a lesser-known Alberti, Alberti as the "critical conscience of humanism," a systematic subverter of the myths and illusions of the cultural movement launched by Petrarch, and an unrelenting desecrater of the dominant culture of Florence, the civic humanism of Leonardo Bruni. This accounts for the dim prospects that the author foresees in *The Writer* as inevitable if he chooses to publish his work in Florence: the public reception will be horrible. The internal genesis of the *Dinner Pieces* thus doubly reprises Alberti's recent works: their humorism represents the culmination of the original comic inspiration of his early play, the *Philodoxus* (1424); and the anger of protest and desecration, the unmasking of everyone and everything, including death, develops, extends, and intensifies the brilliant sarcasm of the pamphlet *On the Advantages and Disadvantages of Literature*.[6]

Alberti as a Critic of Humanism

Besides Alberti's internal motivation, there are also external motives: the stimuli of the new cultural pressures of the times as well as the circulation of new texts, and the author's polemical reactions to them. If we recall that the *Dinner Pieces* are almost entirely a work of the 1430s, it is immediately clear how very timely they are. Every literary novelty, every current, debate, or experiment in ideas, taste, or fashion from the first three decades of the Quattrocento has left its mark, often deep and sometimes groundbreaking. Clearly, the *Dinner Pieces* cannot be understood apart from their many stimuli: the dialogues of Lucian, the revolution in the visual arts and discovery of perspective taking place in Florence, the hyperphilosophy of Democritus, the new interest in the Aesopic corpus in Greek, the renewed enthusiasm for comedy and the discovery of new texts by Plautus, the emergence of the Sienese elegiac poets, and the Pythagorean movement — all new elements in the first three decades of the century. The *Dinner Pieces* reveal Alberti as the "critical conscience" with respect to contemporary humanism, opposed not only to Petrarch as the leader of all the humanists but also to the leader of the previous generation, Leo-

nardo Bruni, as well as to the other leading thinker of his generation, Lorenzo Valla.

A single text suffices to gauge the distance that separates the
new ideal of culture and intellectual life, perfectly theorized and
embodied in Alberti, from the solitary, contemplative, literary, and
almost exclusively book-based ideal theorized and embodied by
Petrarch. The dinner piece *Paintings* describes the temple of Good
and Ill Fortune, which is decorated with twenty allegorical frescoes
on its walls. *Humanitas* is depicted as follows: "The first panel
there depicts an extraordinary image of a woman, around whose
neck are gathered various faces, young, old, happy, sad, joyful, serious, and so forth. Numerous hands extend from her shoulders,
some holding pens, others lyres, some a polished gem, others a
painted or carved ornament, some various mathematical instruments, and others books. Above her is written, HUMANITY,
MOTHER" (3.1.28). For Alberti, the peculiar dignity of man thus
resides not in his intellect, but in his hands. As he observes in his
last work, *De iciarchia* (*Ruling the Household*), man speaks and acts,
and reading and writing are actions: they are "personal operations."
Such is the way Alberti understands the active and contemplative
lives.

Just as fundamental is Alberti's reflection on the humanities,
humanae litterae. Humanity, or culture and civilization, does not
coincide with the humanities and cannot be identified with mere
books. Writing and reading are part of it, but equally part of it, as
liberal arts, are painting and sculpture, music and goldsmithing,
astronomy and astrology, mathematics and geometry, and hence
science. This revolutionary, nonbookish concept of humanity at a
stroke destroys a millennial system of knowledge, that of the entire
Middle Ages and that of early humanism as well. In his *Solitary
Life*, Petrarch placed architects, painters, and sculptors among the
practitioners of the "mechanical arts," thus marshaling them indis-

criminately amid perfumers, butchers, cooks, bakers, sausage makers, launderers, and weavers. As for scientific culture, we hardly need to recall that the author of *Invectives against a Physician* was scarcely fond of it. By contrast, Alberti regards the employment of "mathematical instruments" as a constituent part of *humanitas*, to such an extent that, in discussing "public libraries" in *The Art of Building*, he considers these "instruments" just as necessary as books.

If we turn now to Alberti's critique of Leonardo Bruni, we observe that in *The Enemy* (*Hostis*) and *The Owl* (*Bubo*), Cicero's treatise *On Duties*, the Bible of civic humanism, provides no philosophical justification for the intellectual's civic and political commitments — as it had for Bruni — much less an etiquette or model for establishing a just and rational commonwealth. It is rather merely a manual for losers. All of the "political" *Dinner Pieces* in Book 10 deal with the historical crisis of the Italian communes. The author both offers and invites reflections on the focal points of this history: from constitutional devices to the difficulties of democracy, from demagoguery to tyranny (and their causes), from condottieri to bloody and festering partisan conflicts, from the perennially destructive *studium rerum novarum* (the desire for revolution) to arms and mercenaries. The result is a convulsive and dramatic history of Florence and Italy, individualistic and moralistic, but completely devoid of providential outcomes and schemes of legitimation — and thus aimed precisely at overturning the historiographic glorifications and the panegyrics of Florence penned by Bruni. In *Discord* (*Discordia*), Florence is not the Athens of Italy, a free and just republic, but the only city, ancient or modern, in which justice has never set foot. In *The Coin* (*Nummus*), the sole and supreme deity of every priest and every merchant is money — which Leonardo Bruni, Poggio Bracciolini, and previous merchant writers had revalued and were passionately revaluing — and this deity is the target of another bloody and stinging satire. In his 1436 biography of Dante, Bruni appropriated Aristotle's definition of man as "by nature a political animal," and inserted it into his radical manifesto together with a sketch of his own ideology. Refuting Boccaccio and all those like him who had raised doubts about intellectuals marrying, Bruni had celebrated Dante's marriage, alongside his military and political commitments. Indeed, he had posited marriage — viewed as a unique form of "natural, legitimate, and permissible" union — as fundamental to civil society. Now, the *Dinner Pieces* were composed in the same years, published for a Florentine readership, and (as if that were not enough) included a Book 2 dedicated to Leonardo Bruni himself. Yet in the *Dinner Pieces* love is more or less treated as in Boccaccio's misogynistic *Corbaccio*: in *The Love Affair*, the woman is torn apart, celibacy is exalted, and marriage is everywhere mocked and rejected. Even more often, humoristic material dominates, for example, in *Debate on Marriage*, or even "black" humor, almost in the manner of Hitchcock, as in *The Husband (Maritus)*.

Alberti's alternative vision struck at and exposed not only civic humanism but also the very ideology of humanism. It revealed that not a few of its leading concepts, premises, and goals were nothing more than dreams and illusions. During the years when Alberti was working on his *Dinner Pieces* (ca. 1430–43) and even later, Lorenzo Valla was working on the *Elegances of the Latin Language* (ca. 1432–49), which aimed at "restoring classical Latin and all the disciplines" by reviving them in the contemporary world. Alberti dismissed this gigantic project as a mere illusion. In *The Dream*, he contends that such an idea can occur only to a deluded person living "in the world of dreams," the world where everything lost on earth ends up, beginning with the "liberal arts and Latin writings of antiquity," which "never return, once they are lost" (4.1.25–26).

Alberti's Place in the History of Humor

Clearly, one of the two principal contributions of the *Dinner Pieces* to humanist literature and to modern European culture is its critical reconsideration of the intellectual revolution begun by Petrarch. The second, more fundamental contribution lies in the character of its humor.

From the *Dinner Pieces* to his *Momus*, Alberti never regards his comic writings as a pastime or a way to avoid the subject of death, nor as a carnival entertainment or as recreation or as mere mental and physical relaxation. Instead, they aim at therapy and self-help, above all knowledge, self-awareness, and a "certain kind of philosophizing" (*genus quoddam philosophandi*). That is what we read in the dedication to Toscanelli and in the preface to *Momus*. If we are to grasp that Alberti's comic manner is actually mere humorism, three texts are essential: *Garlands* and *The Deceased* in the *Dinner Pieces*, and the "myth of masks" in *Momus*. *Garlands* is an allegorical comedy in one act, in which Praise and Envy award garlands on the basis of the professional merits and talents of various aspirants. Except for the Detractor, only a crowd of unworthy candidates approach Praise. But then in a corner a young man appears, who stands alone without approaching: Lepidus, the figure from *Philodoxeos fabula* now transformed into a humoristic *persona*. Asked what his talent is, he replies, "I take delight in letters, and I always strive to afford merriment and laughter to myself and my friends, without sacrificing my dignity" (4.2.64). By his own declaration, Lepidus should know how to laugh and make others laugh. But when Envy says, "Then go ahead and laugh," he bursts into tears (65). He justifies this behavior by explaining that, ever since he was born, nothing turns out as he wishes: everything goes against his expectations and contrary to his hopes. At this point Praise comments, "You are truly ridiculous!" (71) but nevertheless gives Lepidus the garland that none of the aspirants had deserved. Lepidus thanks her, observing that he has received a double gift: a garland to adorn his head, which, when dried, will serve to scour his pans.

This inspired and impressive declaration of poetics is impressive precisely because it makes clear beyond any doubt how Alberti's comic invention is completely foreign to what, since Aristotle, had usually been considered comic. In the comic art practiced by Alberti, laughter and weeping (to wit, grief) are indissolubly bound together. In fact, the mixture of laughter and weeping is its essence. Battista-Lepidus says that his job is to laugh and make laugh, but then reveals that he is capable only of weeping. If Praise rewards him all the same, it means that the function of the comic writer is precisely both to laugh and to weep at the same time: like a two-faced herm whose one face laughs at the weeping of the other. This laughter-weeping presupposes not just "pain" but a tragic experience of life. Battista-Lepidus laughs and weeps because his life is fractured; he is someone for whom everything has gone wrong. He is a living contradiction, or rather a perfect oxymoron. Indeed, just as Greek ὀξύμωρος means "sharp and foolish," in the first version of *Philodoxeos fabula* Battista-Lepidus is already a double oxymoron: he is both a shrewd madman (*catus demens*) and an ignorant man of learning (*inscitus sapiens*). He is mocking and sarcastic. He laughs at everything and everyone, but primarily at himself. The garland that he is awarded and has long coveted is proof that he has perfectly mastered the art that he professes, namely, comicity. Yet as soon as he receives it, he suddenly laughs and desecrates it. Fundamental in itself and to Alberti's position in the history of the comic is his proviso that Battista-Lepidus must laugh without sacrificing his dignity (*servata dignitate*). His comicity is thus refined, noble, and aristocratic, and gladly rejects the vast comedic resources of sex and of the "lower bodily stratum." This is a conscious and polemical rejection. We have seen that Alberti was very familiar with the *Hermaphroditus*. But it is precisely the type of comic bawdiness embodied in the

Hermaphroditus against which he places himself in direct opposition. In all of his "witty" works — which are numerous, spanning three decades from *Philodoxeos fabula* to *Momus* — appeals to prurience and to the "lower bodily stratum" can be counted on the fingers of one hand, and even those few examples never exceed what is decorous.

It is more than abundantly clear, I think, that none of this constitutes comicity. From the mid-seventeenth century onward, it is more exactly called humorism (*humeur, humor*). Although the term dates from the seventeenth century and apparently has French and English origins, the phenomenon is clearly Italian and is much older. It is one of the principal literary contributions that Latin humanism, born and evolved in Italy, has given to modern European literature.

As noted above, other texts are essential to our understanding of this new and distinctive sense of the humorous. In *The Deceased*, the recently deceased Neophronus decides to attend his own funeral. He nimbly leaps up and perches on the roof of a neighboring house, where he can observe everything inside his house. Before him there unfolds a terrifying spectacle, which he recounts in the rest of the dialogue. From this vantage point, he gets to know himself, and with that knowledge he gets to know two fundamental truths: that life is absurd, and that death is good. To arrive at this knowledge, he must first of all discover that during his entire life he was a naïve simpleton, a hopeless "idealist." His entire account to his friend Polytropus is the story of his disillusion. He lived among masked people without realizing it: a masked wife, a masked steward, masked children, masked relatives, masked servants, and masked friends and acquaintances. Everyone deceived and betrayed him, while he believed himself surrounded by people who were good, sincere, loving, and grateful. As a result, he is a fool, a madman. He says this to himself many times, and each time Polytropus seconds his words. He is a madman because he trusted others, and because (as he later discovers) everything went wrong. Sunk in appearances, he believed that he lived amid realities. He lived on a stage while he believed he was living in real life. From this we may infer that the text examines the radical contrast between *seeming* and *being*, a contrast that is at the heart of all humor. Indeed, as Neophronus discovers this contrast, he laughs with convulsive and uncontrollable laughter. Like Battista-Lepidus, he laughs at his own pain, and laughs at his own horrible misfortunes, at a life in which everything has gone wrong.

The "myth of the masks" positioned in the very middle of Book 4 of *Momus* is a paratext by which the author seeks to aid the reader in properly understanding his text.[7] This means grasping how this work, with masks as a central theme and with the god of calumny as its hero, can be a "certain kind of philosophizing" (*genus quoddam philosophandi*). With its Platonic aura, the myth teaches us to "know ourselves," but teaches it better than the philosophers, who are so bombastic and obscure, so conceited and vacuous. A "certain kind of philosophizing" thus means that Alberti regards his humorism as an alternative philosophy, or rather a hyperphilosophy, like that of Democritus in the epistolary novel of pseudo-Hippocrates. In fact, the first to relate this was a painter who, by dint of portraying bodies, understood more than all the philosophers taken together.

The myth teaches that our social life is no more than a theater, an immense stage, trodden by shady and duplicitous people, each of whom puts on and takes off countless masks. The humorist's task is the same as the painter's: to fix his gaze on the pinholes in the masks and to peer inside (*introspicere*) to view the various monsters lurking within. But since by so doing the humorist strips us naked, his function is identical to that of death. Hence, the humorist is an observer and an analyst: he abhors appearances, and demolishes illusions, deceptions, and self-deceptions. He tears off the masks that people wear in order to seem other than they are, masks worn to become acceptable to oneself and others, masks that are the consubstantial form of our social life, masks that a person assumes at birth and wears constantly until death.

The twin coordinates of the succinct interpretation of the *Dinner Pieces* proposed here suggest two further reflections. First, if humanism can still speak to us, I believe that its most congenial voice resembles that of writers who, like Alberti, make central to their inquiry the incongruity, exposure, and demolition of illusions and myths, who fuse together the two cultures, humane and scientific, and who profess the equal value of all disciplines. This is a concept of *humanitas* in which we can see ourselves reflected today. The second reflection arises from the role Alberti played in the particular realm of literature — the "refounding of the Italian language and literature on humanistic principles," the revival of numerous important literary genres, the decisive contribution to the language of the visual arts and architecture, and the creation of humor in its modern form. The great scholars of the present writer's generation — Eugenio Garin, Paul Oskar Kristeller, Giuseppe Billanovich, Alessandro Perosa — explored, to be sure, the humanist revolution in depth and rightly stressed its significant contribution to many spheres, such as the history of philosophy, theology, and science, the classical tradition, and philology. But they failed to show how that revolution was equally decisive for literature and for literary history. Ernst Robert Curtius studied the role that the Middle Ages played in modern European literature. But he neglected the even more important role played by Latin humanism. In his groundbreaking book on Rabelais, Mikhail Bakhtin devoted a lengthy chapter to the history of the comic during the Renaissance, but he completely overlooked Italian humanism and the Italian writers of the Quattrocento. Had he studied them, he would surely have realized that they are fundamental to the history of the comic: Panormita and Poggio for the "lower bodily stratum," and Alberti's five humoristic works (*Inter-*

cenales, Apologi centum, Canis, Musca, and *Momus*) for an alternative comicity, which is, in my view, far more modern.

Dating of the Individual Dinner Pieces

The chronology of the *Dinner Pieces* in the last extant redaction, that of the Pistoia manuscript, can be dated between ca. 1430 and the spring of 1443. For the *terminus post quem*, the fundamental text is *Rings* (*Anuli*), which in three passages (App. 2.30, 113, 120) refers to Alberti's entrance into the papal Curia, an event datable to 1432, when the young humanist was appointed apostolic abbreviator. But since *Rings* is certainly not the first dinner piece, we may reasonably suppose that the oldest dinner pieces date from a few years earlier. The *terminus ante quem* is the date of the death of Leonardo Bruni (March 9, 1444), to whom Alberti dedicated Book 2. Since passages in the entire work refer to Florence (dedications, *The Writer, The Cock* [*Gallus,* 2.3.7], *Discord* [3.3.3–4], *The Clouds* [*Nebule*]), this *terminus* can be retrodated to the spring of 1443, when Alberti and the papal Curia under Eugenius IV left Florence for Rome by way of Siena.

The "original redaction" in two books, preserved in the Oxford manuscript, was likewise published in Florence — as the dedication to Toscanelli, *The Writer,* and *The Cock* prove — presumably in 1439–ca. 1440. Following the movements of the Council of Florence, Alberti was in fact in Florence in the first days of 1439; and the internal chronology of the two books indicates a dating of February at the earliest. The last piece in Book 2, *Wealth,* is a political vindication of Benedetto Alberti that presupposes Alberti's knowledge of Book 9 of Leonardo Bruni's *History of the Florentine People,* a book that is part of the second installment of the work, published on February 6, 1439.[8]

Except for subsequent revisions, the compositional chronology of single pieces may be assigned as follows:

before 1432: *The Orphan, Virtue, The Love Affair*

1432: *Rings*

before February 18, 1434: *The Widow, The Deceased*

1436/37: *Affliction (Erumna), Debate on Marriage*

1438/39: *The Coin, Pluto*

between 1438 and 1439/40: *Patience*

before 1439/40: *Religion, Fate and Fortune, Happiness, The Oracle, Frugality (Parsimonia), The Cock, Soothsaying (Vaticinium), Poverty (Paupertas)*

from late 1439 to 1440: *Wealth* and the two paratexts in Book 1 (dedication to Toscanelli and *The Writer*)

spring 1440: *The Clouds*

1440/41: *Enigmas, Shipwrecked, The Owl, Stubbornness (Pervicacia), The Temple (Templum), The Lake (Lacus), The Wolf (Lupus), The Spider (Aranea)*

1440/42: *Flowers (Flores), Discord, The Enemy, Stones (Lapides), Ivy (Hedera), Suspicion (Suspitio), The Slave (Servus), The Husband, Fate and the Unfortunate Father (Fatum et pater infelix)*

before October 21, 1441: *Paintings*

between late 1442 and spring 1443: *The Dream, Garlands, The Cynic (Cynicus), Fame*, and the apologue-prefaces to Books 2, 4, 7, 8, and 10

Alberti himself mentions the *Dinner Pieces* on only two occasions. In his fragmentary *Autobiography*, he alludes to their inception. According to Martin McLaughlin, Alberti declares that in 1433–34, roughly contemporary with his draft of the first three books *On the Family*, he had already written several, but had burned many of them: "Besides these works, he wrote before he was thirty numerous *Dinner Pieces*, among them the especially amusing *The Widow* and *The Deceased* and works like them, some of which, because they seemed to him not mature creations, even if very delightful and apt to elicit much laughter, he committed to the flames lest he might give his detractors grounds for accusing him of levity."[9]

In a later work, alluding to a collection already published and appreciated (presumably a redaction intermediate between the Oxford version in two books and the Pistoia version in eleven books), Alberti has Agnolo Pandolfini speak the following words: "Affairs here on earth are governed either by us men or by someone other than us mortals. If someone else governs these affairs, let us trust their care to those who have for so many years governed them well and wisely. But if perchance, as you write in one of your most delightful *intercenali* (dinner pieces), our fortune as mortals doesn't come from heaven, but springs from human folly, let us accept our affairs as created by men like you, who are liable and subject to all passions of the mind and to instability. I like this saying of yours and endorse it."[10] In this passage, as we clearly see, he introduced into Italian, and thus into modern languages, the neologism *intercenali* (dinner pieces).

Biographical Sketch of Alberti until 1443

The composition and successive publications of the *Dinner Pieces* were thus roughly contemporary with the drafting, publications, and final revision of his books *On the Family*, the Italian masterpiece that Alberti worked on from 1433 to the spring of 1443. As is well known, we cannot understand the dialogue if we fail to take into account the author's biography. But, in fact, members of the Alberti family and Battista are also present in his Latin masterpiece. This is confirmed by *The Orphan*, *Wealth*, and *Affliction*, as well as by the countless masks that Alberti wears: Lepidus, Philodoxus, Philoponius, the goat in the preface to Book 4, Micrologus in the preface to Book 10, Friginnius in *The Love Affair*, and the

Cynic in *The Cynic*. Hence, a brief schematic biographical sketch, from his birth to the spring of 1443, will aid us in better understanding these books, meant to be read *inter cenas et pocula*.

Battista Alberti (who only added the pen name Leone in the 1430s) was born in Genoa on February 18, 1404, as he documents in an autograph note on the flyleaf of his personal copy of Cicero's *On Laws*. Battista and his brother Carlo were born from a liaison between the Florentine exile Lorenzo di Benedetto Alberti and an unknown woman. It has long been imagined that she was Bianca Fieschi, widow of a Grimaldi, but the document that is supposed to prove this is in fact a nineteenth-century forgery.

Battista never named his mother, and he mentioned Genoa as his birthplace only in the autograph note. His *patria* was always Florence alone, and all the official documents call him Florentine. The exile of the Albertis, which in *Wealth* he regards as completely unjust, his illegitimate birth, regarded as a serious stain on his reputation, and his difficult relations with his relatives, who after his father's death begrudged him the means to study — all these things caused wounds that never entirely healed and that may perhaps explain the many obsessions of this great writer and intellectual.

As far as we know, Alberti studied in the Paduan school of Gasparino Barzizza. He then entered the University of Bologna, which he attended until ca. 1428, reluctantly enrolled in the faculty of jurisprudence, where he studied civil and canon law. From August 28, 1428, until 1431, the city was torn by bloody fighting between factions, one favoring papal governance and another their opponents. The university was repeatedly closed for long periods. Between 1428 and 1429 several noted professors — Francesco Filelfo, Gaspare Sighicelli, and Ludovico Pontano, teachers respectively of Greek and rhetoric, of moral and natural philosophy, and of civil law — moved to the University of Florence. Among the students that they took with them was Alberti, who moved there in 1429, a year after the ban was rescinded that had forced into exile the male adults of his family. It was in this way that the twenty-five-year-old Battista visited his ancestors' city for the first time. At the time, Florence was a beacon of European culture for its cultural and artistic flowering, due mainly to Leonardo Bruni and to the revolution in architecture and the visual arts promoted by Filippo Brunelleschi, Donatello, Lorenzo Ghiberti, Luca della Robbia, and Masaccio. For the first time, Alberti heard firsthand the spoken language of the Florentines, uttered by the locals and echoing in the shops and squares of the city — the spoken language of which he would write the first grammar and which he would "enrich" like no other writer, as Cristoforo Landino wrote. This decisive threefold experience deeply affected the *scolaris florentinus* (Florentine student), directing him toward the multiplicity of interests and expertise that won him the title of "universal man" and that made him a "classic," not only in the Latin domain of Italian literature but also in the vernacular, in which he began to take an interest during this time, writing two verse elegies and his prose *Deifira*. Other events confirm the absolutely crucial importance of this first residence in Florence. He enrolled in the university, attended Greek classes given by Filelfo, and began his ecclesiastical career. From Pope Martin V he obtained a dispensation that freed him from the humiliating declaration of a "defective birth" and that opened the way to advancement in that career. In January 1430 he took minor orders, and that same year became the secretary of Biagio Molin, the patriarch of Grado and director of the papal chancellery. He obtained the benefice of the priory of San Martino a Gangalandi and the title of apostolic abbreviator. Apparently, he was in no hurry to take his law degree. The first mention of his baccalaureate in civil and canon law is found in the "argument" to the second version of his *Philodoxeos fabula*, that is, a text of 1437.

From 1431 to the first half of 1434, Alberti lived in Rome, where he exercised his official duties. On May 29, 1434, a revolt erupted in the city leading to the imprisonment of Cardinal Francesco Condulmer, the nephew of Eugenius IV, and forcing the pope himself to flee. Eugenius found asylum and hospitality in Florence, where he remained for two years, from June 1434 to April 1436. Like other members of the Curia, Alberti presumably arrived in Florence in the latter half of 1434. During this second, longer residence in Florence, he experienced events of great importance: the decline of the oligarchic regime and the founding of Medici rule in 1433–34, the debate between Leonardo Bruni and Biondo Flavio concerning the spoken language of the ancient Romans,[11] and the inauguration of the prodigious cupola completed by Filippo Brunelleschi, "raised into the heavens and so vast that its shadow covers all the people of Tuscany." From the debate about the Latin language arose the linguistic interests that bore fruit after 1438 in the Vatican *Grammatichetta*, the first Italian grammar, and in the preface to Book 3 of *On the Family*, which is Alberti's manifesto of the "refounding of the Italian language and literature on humanistic principles." His direct experience of the architectural and visual revolution created by the five Florentine "giants" produced a shock that accelerated the opening of a new arena for his interests and activities: the arena of the art theorist and architect. Significantly, the inauguration of the cupola of Santa Maria del Fiore moved him to dedicate the Italian version of *On Painting* to Brunelleschi.

On April 18, 1436, the pope left Florence for Bologna. For Alberti, who soon followed, this was a chance to strengthen old bonds and to establish new friendships, but especially to close one phase of his literary activities and to open another. From Bologna he sent Leonello d'Este the second version of his early comedy *Philodoxeos*; and in Bologna he composed *Pontifex* (*The Bishop*) and *De iure* (*On Law*), but more important his *Apologi centum* (One

Hundred Fables), which by the turn of the sixteenth century had elevated him to the status of a classic, truly an *Aesopus alter*, the Aesop of modernity.

In January 1438, Alberti moved to Ferrara, where the pope had convened the Council of Union between the Greek and the Latin churches. Here, he met the city's future ruler, Leonello d'Este, and could inspect the twelve new plays of Plautus, recently discovered by Nicholas of Cusa and now disseminated from Ferrara. In this same year and city, Alberti's fame as a "universal man" was recognized for the first time in glowing terms. In his dialogue *The Benefits of Papal Employment* (completed in July 1438), Lapo da Castiglionchio sketched a perceptive and lifelike portrait of Alberti that proclaimed him one of the most prominent members of the papal Curia, which at the time was the foremost center of European culture.[12]

In August–September of 1438, an outbreak of the plague forced the pope to transfer the Council to Florence. Thus began the third residence in Florence of Alberti, who lived in this "homeland far more beautiful than any other" practically without interruption until April–May of 1443. By that time, he had completed his *On the Family* and *Dinner Pieces*, had also written the first *Grammar of the Tuscan Language* based solely on spoken Florentine, and had conceived and organized the Certame Coronario, a poetic contest on the theme of friendship, which was held on October 21, 1441, in Florence Cathedral, the culmination of his "refounding of the Italian language and literature on humanistic principles."

On June 6, 1443, we find Alberti in Siena, where he stayed until September, when he departed to rejoin the papal Curia, which had left for Rome in July. He spent most of his later life in Rome, where he increasingly devoted himself to architecture and city planning and produced his two most ambitious works in Latin, the ten books *On the Art of Building* and *Momus*, a prose novel in four books strongly influenced, like the *Dinner Pieces*, by Lucian. He died in 1472 at the age of sixty-eight.

Roberto Cardini would like to express the deepest gratitude to James Hankins for including this book in his important I Tatti Renaissance Library series.

David Marsh would like to acknowledge the many colleagues who have promoted his research in Alberti studies, among them Stefano Ugo Baldassarri, Stefano Borsi, Luca Boschetto, Jeroen De Keyser, Anthony D'Elia, Francesco Furlan, Timothy Kircher, Paul McLean, John Monfasani, Gary Rendsburg, David Rundle, and Hartmut Wulfram. In questions of Latinity, I have relied on the expertise of Robert Kaster. Several libraries facilitated my research, most notably the Biblioteca Apostolica Vaticana in Vatican City, the Biblioteca Medicea Laurenziana and Biblioteca Nazionale Centrale in Florence, and the Rutgers University Libraries. I owe a special debt to James Hankins, editor of the I Tatti Renaissance Library, for his invaluable advice and encouragement. I dedicate this translation to my wife Elizabeth, and to my daughters Diana and Christina.

NOTES

1. Contained in the letters of pseudo-Hippocrates, Letters 10–17 between Hippocrates and Democritus, with the appendix, Letters 18–21, in W. D. Smith, *Hippocrates: Pseudepigraphic writings* (Leiden: E. J. Brill, 1990). For a definition of humorism and the humoristic, see below, xviii.

2. Published in this I Tatti series (hereafter ITRL) in *Humanist Comedies*, trans. Gary L. Grund (Cambridge, MA: Harvard University Press, 2005) = ITRL 18.

3. Leon Battista Alberti, *On the Art of Building in Ten Books*, ed. Joseph Rykwert, Neil Leach, and Robert Tavernor. Cambridge, MA: MIT Press, 1988.

4. See Leon Battista Alberti, *Biographical and Autobiographical Writings*, ed. and trans. Martin McLaughlin (Cambridge, MA: Harvard University Press, 2023) = ITRL 96.

5. Leonardo Bruni, *History of the Florentine People*, ed. and trans. James Hankins, 3 vols. (Cambridge, MA: Harvard University Press, 2001–7), vol. 3 = ITRL 27, at 9.76.

6. Included in *Biographical and Autobiographical Writings* (above, n. 4).

7. Leon Battista Alberti, *Momus*, ed. Virginia Brown and trans. Sarah Knight (Cambridge, MA: Harvard University Press, 2003) = ITRL 8.

8. For the chronology, see James Hankins, "The Dates of Leonardo Bruni's Later Works (1437–1443)," *Studi medievali e umanistici* 5–6 (2007–8), 11–48.

9. Alberti, *My Life* 14, in *Biographical and Autobiographical Writings*, ed. McLaughlin, 219.

10. *Profugiorum ab erumna libri* (*Remedies for Affliction*), in *Opere volgari*, ed. Cecil Grayson (Bari: Laterza, 1966), Book 2: "Le cose di quaggiù sono rette o da noi uomini o da altri che noi mortali. S'altri le regge che noi, lasciànne la cura a chi già tanto numero d'anni le resse con ragione e bene. Ma se forse, come tu scrivi in una delle tue iocundissime intercenali, Battista, la fortuna di noi mortali non viene dal cielo ma nasce dalla stultizia degli uomini, ricevianle fatte come dagli uomini simili a te, proclivi e dati a ogni passione d'animo e inconstanzia. Qual tua sententia mi diletta, e confermola." (Cited from http://www.bibliotecaitaliana.it).

11. On the debate about whether Latin was a natural or an artificial language, see Christopher Celenza, *The Intellectual world of the Italian Renaissance Language, Philosophy, and the Search for Meaning* (New York: Cambridge University Press, 2018).

12. See Christopher Celenza, *Renaissance Humanism and the Papal Curia: Lapo da Castiglionchio the Younger's De curiae commodis* (Ann Arbor: University of Michigan Press, 1999).

LEONIS BAPTISTE ALBERTI
INTERCENALES

LEON BATTISTA ALBERTI
DINNER PIECES

LIBER I

1   ⟨*Prohemium ad Paulum Physicum*⟩

2 Cepi nostras Intercenales redigere in parvos libellos, quo inter ce-
3 nas et pocula commodius possent perlegi. Tu quidem, ut ceteri
physici, Paule mi suavissime, amaras et que usque nauseam moveant egrotis corporibus medicinas exhibes; ego vero his meis
scriptis genus levandi morbos animi affero, quod per risum atque
4 hilaritatem suscipiatur. Ac meis quidem omnibus Intercenalibus id
potissimum a me videri quesitum cupio, ut qui legerint nos cum
facetos fuisse sentiant, tum sibi ad graves curas animi levandas ar-
gumenta apud nos non inepta inveniant.

5   Eam ob rem hic primus liber Intercenalium admonet, uti ab
6 ineunte etate quibusque casibus fortune sit assuefaciendum; in ea
tamen re bene merendo moribus esse et virtute enitendum, ut no-
7 bis superi quam propitii adsint; neque, tametsi virtus ipsa semper
fortune fuerit obnoxia, a virtute tamen uspiam esse discedendum;
8 verum ita vivendum, ut vite quidem cursum bonis artibus et sim-
9 plici virtute reddi commodiorem putemus; at vero, si fata nostras
mortalium vires superent, patientia et tolerantia, quoad ipsa neces-
10 sitas postulet, esse nobis providendum; in omnique vita ita de rebus ipsis admodo censendum, ut nihil felicitatem aut infelicitatem
afferre existimemus, quod ipsum non ab opinione nostra profec-
tum sit.

11   Tu igitur, mi Paule, Leonem Baptistam tuum amabis, ut facis,
nostrumque libellum, cum a ceteris tuis maioribus studiis vacabis,
perleges proque nostra vetere amicitia dabis operam, ut per te
quam emendatior fiat.

BOOK I

Preface to Paolo Toscanelli of Florence   1

I have begun to collect my *Dinner Pieces* into short books so that   2
they may be more easily read over dinners and drinks.[1] You treat   3
diseased bodies as other physicians do, sweetest Paolo, with bitter
medicines which even provoke nausea.[2] But I, through my writings, provide a way of relieving the mind's maladies which works
through laughter and hilarity. In all my *Dinner Pieces*, I want my   4
readers to see how I have sought above all to have them perceive
my wit and find in me arguments not unsuited to relieving their
gravest cares.

Accordingly, this first book of *Dinner Pieces* urges us that from   5
early youth we must steel ourselves against all of fortune's vicissitudes.[3] Yet in this effort, we must also strive to make our character   6
and virtue merit the highest favor of the gods. And even though   7
virtue should forever prove inimical to fortune, still we must never
abandon virtue. Our conduct must be guided by the conviction   8
that life is enhanced by noble accomplishments and disinterested
virtue. Yet should the fates be stronger than our mortal powers,   9
moreover, we must arm ourselves with patience and tolerance, as
necessity dictates. Throughout life we must firmly believe that   10
nothing which does not originate in our judgment can affect our
happiness or misery.

My dear Paolo, continue to love your friend Leon Battista.   11
When you find time from your more important pursuits to read
this book, please emend it, mindful of our long friendship.

Scriptor

1 *Libr.* Eodum, Lepide, ecquid tibi per hosce dies fuit negotii? Mensis admodum est quo apud nos in lucem nunquam prodisti!

2 *Lep.* O litteratorum alumne, salve. Ego quidem apud meos libellos occupatus enitebar aliquam de me famam proseminare litteris.

3 *Libr.* Ha ha he! ridiculum hominem! Isthocne tu in agro Etrusco id tentas, qui quidem tam undique opertus est caligine omnis ignorantie, cuius et omnis humor est penitus absumptus estu ambitionum et cupiditatum quemve qui colunt multo in dies impetu invidie perturbantur, in quo denique multa pestifera

4 obtrectatorum semina vigent? Officiperdi, dormiendum tibi potius quam eo pacto vigilias perdendas censeo, aut omnino irritos istos et futiles labores tuos fugiendos; tum etiam atque etiam admoneo, nequid lucubrationum tuarum temere in vulgus depromas, nam est quidem ad vituperandum pervigil et

5 admodum severus censor vulgus. In primisque metue ipsum me ad quem plus accessit auctoritatis, quod palam omnibus detraxerim, quam si perquam multos collaudassem.

∴ I ∴

Pupillus

1 Quod aiunt, rectis viris fortunam semper esse adversam, id sane in
2 Philoponio minime obscure patuit. Nam is relictus puer, patre defuncto, sine ullis parentibus, proscriptus a patria coniunctissimisque ab affinibus non modo bonis omnibus paternis spoliatus,

The Writer

Libripeta. You there, Lepidus, what has kept you so busy lately? 1
Hasn't it been a whole month since you came outside?

Lepidus. O nourisher of men of letters, hail! I've been busy with 2
my books, striving to sow seeds of fame by writing.

Libripeta. Ha! Silly fellow! Don't try that on Tuscan soil, which 3
lies entirely under the cloud of ignorance, and where all mois-
ture is utterly consumed by the heat of ambitions and desires.
Those who cultivate it are daily assailed by envious attacks, and
in it flourish countless seeds of pestilent detraction. Waster of 4
your own labor, I think you'd do better to sleep than to waste
your nightly vigils in study. You should abandon your vain and
useless toils. I strongly advise you against foolishly publishing
your research, for our vigilant and severely censorious common
people are quick to condemn. And you should especially fear 5
me. For by disparaging everyone publicly, I command more authority than if I were to praise many.

: I :

The Orphan

They say that fortune is always hostile to just men, and such was 1
clearly the case with Philoponius.[4] Orphaned as a boy when his 2
father died, Philoponius was exiled from his homeland, deprived
of his entire patrimony by his nearest relatives, and even excluded

sed etiam a domestica suorum familiaritate exclusus atque omnino
ita abiectus fuit, ut apud extraneos sibi esset mendicandum.

3   Erat istiusmodi fortuna adolescenti gravis quidem, sed illud
longe gravius, quod impiissimi adolescentis affines summopere
elaborabant, ne adolescens Philoponius in his studiis litterarum
posset prosequi, quibus non mediocri cum expectatione civium et
4   litteratorum omnium proficiebat. Ferebat tamen iniquam sortem
atque in ea re affinium suorum iniurias animo, ut poterat, equo;
famamque cuiusque, quoad in se esset, apud omnes dictis factis-
que tuebatur, veluti qui in ea re paupertatem suam leviorem quam
5   suorum ignominiam duceret. Sed cum illi quidem improbi ita se
in adolescentem gererent, ut iam tum apud omnes eorum impietas
esset et nota et plurimum detestanda, plerique viri optimi humanitatis officio commoti ad affines Philoponii accessere, familiaritatem
amicitiamque, qua cum parentibus adolescentis coniuncti fuerint,
edocuere grandiaque ac multa defuncti merita in omnes propin-
6   quos connumeravere; adolescentis Philoponii virtutem, ingenium
7   atque industriam approbavere; iura sanguinis, iura pietatis atque
8   officii expostulavere; impietatem multis modis vituperavere, atque
denique omnibus argumentis multisque precibus conati sunt istos
ipsos improbos affines in Philoponium reddere mitiores.

9   Illi vero nullam impietatis sue in adolescentem criminationem
nullamve culpam reiiciebant ac ne⟨c⟩ contra bonorum expostulationes digna excusatione ulla utebantur, qua commodis et laudibus
adolescentis faveri non oportere quispiam memor humanitatis as-
10   sentiatur, sed inepti illud aiebant: non esse non odiosum eum, qui
sese ob meritum litterarum ditioribus preferri cuperet; in reliquis
vero rebus se satis quidnam conducat familie non nescire, in qua
quidem familia bene morata et bene instituta ab extraneis consilia
11   fuisse nunquam assumenda gloriabantur. Atque, quod magis
odisse possis, duri affines et domestice suorum laudis usque adeo

and cast out of the closeness and company of his own family, so that he was forced to beg abjectly from strangers.

Such misfortune was naturally hard on the youth, but far worse 3 was the fact that his impious kinsmen strove resolutely to prevent young Philoponius from pursuing his literary studies, in which his progress had aroused both the admiration of men of letters and the expectations of his fellow citizens. Still, Philoponius bore his 4 unjust fate and his kinsmen's insults with all possible equanimity, and he tried his best in all he said and did in public to protect their reputation, like one who considered his own poverty more tolerable than their disgrace. But finally, when these reprobates 5 treated the youth so badly that everyone both recognized and deplored their perversity, a number of worthy men were moved by a sense of humanity and approached his kinsmen. They cited the closeness and friendship which had bound them to the youth's parents, recounted his late father's many great services to all his relatives, and lauded Philoponius' virtues, talents, and industry. 6 They demanded that the kinsmen observe the rights of kinship 7 and the rights of piety and duty, and censured their impiety at 8 great length. In short, they strove with every argument and many entreaties to make these unjust kinsmen kinder toward Philoponius.

The kinsmen denied neither their guilt nor the charge that they 9 had mistreated the youth. Nor did they give any reasonable justification, in answer to the worthy men's remonstrances, for not having fostered the youth's well-being and reputation. Yet what person with any sense of humanity would have condoned them? They 10 foolishly asserted that anyone merited disdain who wished his literary achievements to win him more esteem than wealthy men possessed. They added that, as for the other charges, they were not ignorant of what was best for their well-bred and long-established family, and boasted that they had never needed to seek advice from strangers. Even more odiously, these family members 11

invidos prebuere se, ut ad iniuriam hanc indignam quoque crude-
12 litatem adicerent: siquidem ob labores studiorum gravi valitudine
affectum adolescentem ab omnibus esse desertum voluere, nullam
13 neque opem egroto neque pietatem languenti prebendo. Quod
quidem indignissimum facinus forte accidisset, ni honestissimi
aliqui viri, qui Philoponii moribus et ingenio delectabantur, com-
mendatum sibi hunc ipsum miserandum adolescentem habuissent.
14 Ducti idcirco pietate extranei homines egrotum desertum a suis
15 consolatum accessere. Itaque per eos medici adducuntur, hortantur
iacentem afflictumque animum levant, dictis bene sperandum
suadent, affines denique olim minus duros futuros pollicentur,
quandoquidem et virtutem nosse ac diligere et improbitatem
16 odisse suam ceperint; postremo superos nunquam esse non iustos
et piissimos edicunt, easque ob res pronosticantur futurum ut
Philoponium sui omnes affines vereantur.

17 Ac Philoponius egrotans, desertus, egenus, miser adolescens
sibi iampridem induxerat animo hec omnia fortiter perpeti ip-
samque fortunam patientia, hominum vero nequitiam virtute et
18 animi viribus bene merendo superare ac vincere instituerat. Quam
rem dum pro virili ita ageret, mala tamen valitudo atque egestas in
dies supra vires urgebant, ut iam pro vetere proverbio in furorem
19 verti patientia ceperit. Itaque tantis calamitatibus actus ac devictus
adolescens, incenso animo indignatione et iracundia, his verbis inquit:

20 'Quid ego superos in me fore propitios sperem, qui quidem me
21 re ipsa sentio egregie esse perpetuam ad miseriam natum? Si quidem superi iusti sunt, quid tantam erga me impietatem inultam
22 sinunt? Si piissimi, cur tam longum nostras iustissimas preces as-
23 pernantur? Quid, si peterem quotidianas M. Antonii epulas, aut
Dionisii nonaginta dierum potationes, aut Vitellii nonaginta et
novem milium piscium septemque milium avium expositas cenas,
aut cultissimam illam Cimonis familiam, aut bi⟨s non in⟩du⟨t⟩as
Neronis vestes, aut si denique regum Indorum delicias peterem?

8

proved so jealous of his fame that they added base cruelty to this injustice by hoping that, if they offered the sick and languishing youth neither aid nor sympathy, Philoponius' laborious studies would cause him serious illness. This shameful plight might perhaps have befallen him, if certain honorable men, who delighted in Philoponius' character and talents, had not taken up the cause of the unfortunate youth. Thus it was strangers who, moved by compassion, went to console the sick boy abandoned by his own family. They summoned doctors, cheered the bedridden youth, relieved his depressed spirits by their words, and urged him to be of good cheer. They even promised that his kinsmen would soon be less unkind and begin both to discern and cherish his virtue and to detest their own wickedness. Finally they averred that, since the gods are always just and pious, they even foresaw that his kinsmen would someday revere him.

Although infirm, indigent, and wretched, the youth Philoponius had long been determined to bear everything courageously. He had resolved that he would conquer fortune with patience and overcome men's villainy with meritorious virtue and strength of mind. Yet even as he strove to do so, poor health and poverty each day strained him to the limit, until finally, as the old saying is, patience began to turn to rage.[5] Exasperated and overwhelmed by his great misfortunes, the youth burst into speech, his mind aflame with anger and outrage:

"How can I hope that the gods will favor me, when in fact I myself feel how singularly I was born to perpetual misery? If the gods are indeed just, why do they permit such great cruelty against me to go unpunished? If they are merciful, why do they persist in spurning my just prayers? Suppose I asked for Mark Antony's daily banquets, or Dionysius' three-month drinking bouts, or Vitellius' dinners offering courses of 99,000 fish and 7,000 fowl? Suppose I asked for Cimon's elegantly dressed retinue, or Nero's daily new garments, or the luxuries of Indian kings?[6]

24 Quid, si Crassi divitias, aut estivas hibernasque Luculli edes cena-
culave illa distincta impensis, aut Alexandrinas quadringentorum
milium librorum bibliothecas, aut Darii opes et cristallum expos-
25 cerem? Quid, si Lucii Dentati hominis invictissimi coronas Mar-
cique Servilii consularis tris et viginti trucidato hoste victorias, aut
Babilonum, Macedonum, Cesarumve gloriam bellorum et imperia
26 cuperem? Quid, si Ventidii Bassi fortunam, aut tonstrini Argime-
27 nis in Gangaridas ad Gangem felices amores optarem? Quid, si
navem Persei sexdecim remorum ordinibus, aut Marcelli sympho-
niam ad Syracusas, aut in Actalum trium milium et quadringenta-
rum navium classem?

28   'Quid, si reliqua innumerabilia eiusmodi conarer que vos, o su-
29 peri, mortalibus non denegastis? Ea quidem mihi haud animo
sunt; minima atque sane, ut arbitror, iustissima a vobis deprecor,
superi; unum hoc tandem, ut liceat studiis bonis prosequi, amicos
non malos acquirere affinesque non pessimos perferre; aut saltem,
ne nobis perpetuo sit pro victu mendicandum; demum liceat ipsi
30 mihi honeste vivere. Verum quid ago, infelix? Non cesso meis la-
31 chrimis deos lacessere. Orabo quidem que probe audient. Obsecro, piissimi superi, ne quis posthac pupillus commodiorem sibi,
quam ipse pertulerim, fortunam obtigisse gaudeat, nullam pupilli
apud suos cives humanitatem inveniant, nullam inter suos affines
pietatem comperiant, nullam apud coniunctissimos fidem sentiant,
nullam apud fratres caritatem reperiant; sed contra adsint pupillis
omnia plena odii, insidiarum, inimicitiarum, calamitatum et miserie.'

32   Tum amici, cum satis egrotum consolassent, discedentes aiebant: 'O miserande adolescens qui, dum optima secutus sis, ini-
quissimam fortunam subivisti, utinam optimas preces tuas superi
audissent, ut hanc execrationem fortassis non negligent!'

Suppose I begged for Crassus' riches or Lucullus' summer and   24
winter homes and expensively decorated dining rooms, or the Al-
exandrian libraries of 400,000 volumes, or Darius' wealth and
crystal?[7] Suppose I desired the chaplets of the invincible Lucius   25
Dentatus, the twenty-three bloody victories of the consul Marcus
Servilius, the martial glory and empires of the Babylonians, Mace-
donians, or Romans?[8] Suppose I wished for Ventidius Bassus'   26
good fortune, or for the happy loves of the barber's son Aggrames
for the Gangarids by the Ganges, or Perseus' ship with sixteen   27
banks of oars, or Marcellus' battle fanfare at Syracuse, or the fleet
of 3,400 ships launched against Attalus?[9]

"What if I aspired to countless other such things, which you, O   28
gods, have granted to mortal men? But such things do not matter   29
to me. What I pray for is, I believe, modest and just, O gods. In
short, I ask but one thing. Let me continue my liberal studies,
enjoy good friends, and endure less wicked kinsmen, or at the least
not have to beg continually for my bread—in short, let me live
virtuously. (But what am I doing, poor wretch? I continue to pro-   30
voke the gods by my tears. I shall pray for things that they will
hear clearly.) Most pious gods, I beseech you that henceforth no   31
orphan may rejoice in meeting with fortune more pleasant than
mine, and that orphans find no human feeling in their fellow citizens, no compassion in their kinsmen, no faith in their closest
friends, and no affection in their brothers. Rather, let orphans find
the whole world full of hatred, betrayal, enmity, misfortune, and
misery."

Then his friends, having consoled the patient as best they   32
could, left him, saying: "O pitiable youth, although you pursued
noble things, you have suffered the most unjust fortune. May the
gods answer your just and noble prayers—as they will perhaps not
neglect your imprecation."

: 2 :

Religio

1   *Libr.* Hec mihi ficus religiosa profecto et piissima videtur, quod in hac, veluti in illa celebri ac notissima Timonis ficu, complures homines erumnas vite suspendio posuere. — Sed eccum Lepidum, quem dudum expectavi.

2   *Lep.* Salve, Libripeta! Mene fortassis sacrificium diutius in templo detinuit quam voluisses?

3   *Libr.* Sane diutius. Verum tu quidem quid habuisti commercii cum diis, ut isthic sermones tam longos ageres?

4   *Lep.* Num dedecet deos pie colere atque precari, ut votis nostris faveant?

5   *Libr.* Scilicet isthic sub tectis, ubi vulgus ille sacerdotum latrat, belle te superi audiunt!

6   *Lep.* An tu ignoras omnia plena esse deorum?

7   *Libr.* Ergo et hic sub hac ficu apte id ipsum poteras, quod in templo superstitiosa quadam imperitorum consuetudine effecisti.

8   Verum tu dic, queso: tuamne pictos apud deos orabas causam, an interpres aliorum exstitisti?

9   *Lep.* Quid ita rogas?

    Libr. Namque arrogantie ascriberem, ubi te ita superis gratum pre aliis putares, ut magis quam eorum, ꞏqui ope indigeant, verbis

10   moverentur tuis. Ceterum sic censeo: qui ad deos exorandos adeunt, omnes id in primis rogare, ut presentia futurave bona dedant serventque, mala vero tollant atque propulsent. Tu adeo quid hic ais?

    Lep. Isthec eadem mihi sententia est.

11   *Libr.* O igitur ineptissimi! Deos eo pacto vultis satellites atque predones vestros esse, siquidem nulla queant vobis bona

Religion

Libripeta. This fig tree seems to me quite pious and compassion-   1
ate, for on it, as on Timon's famous tree, many have hanged
themselves to end life's afflictions. But here comes Lepidus,
whom I have expected for some time now.[10]

Lepidus. Greetings, Libripeta. Did the sacrifice detain me in the   2
temple longer than you would have wished?

Libripeta. Much longer. But tell me, what business did you have   3
with the gods that occasioned your lengthy discussions?

Lepidus. What, is it shameful to worship the gods devoutly and to   4
pray that they favor our wishes?

Libripeta. Doubtless under that roof, with its mob of bawling   5
priests, the gods hear you quite well!

Lepidus. Don't you know that everything is filled with gods?[11]   6

Libripeta. Then you could properly have done beneath this fig tree   7
exactly what, following the superstitious custom of the ignorant, you accomplished in the temple. But tell me, please, did   8
you pray only for yourself before those painted gods, or did you
act as an agent for others?

Lepidus. Why do you ask?   9

Libripeta. Because I would find you arrogant if you thought that
the gods hold you so dear that they are more moved by your
words than by those of people who truly need assistance. Be-   10
sides, in my view, whoever prays to the gods asks them above all
to bestow and protect blessings both present and future, and to
remove and avert misfortunes. What do you say to this?

Lepidus. I'm of the same opinion.

Libripeta. O foolish ones, do you want the gods to act as your   11
henchmen and brigands? For no goods can come to you but

13

12   accedere que non tum aliis possidentibus erepta sint. Quem
      mihi dabis vilissimum servum cui, ut istiusmodi scelus agat,
      honeste imperes? Quis usque adeo insolens suis perditis sicariis
      iubeat ut aliorum preda se locupletem reddant?

13   *Lep.* Scio quid hic dixeris. Non predones quidem, verum, ut ope-
      rarii essent, rogavi. Nam petii darent operam ut mihi in hortulo
      caules excrescerent aurei.

14   *Libr.* Quod si sapiunt, dii odere hanc vestram procacitatem.
      Lep. An tu, Libripeta, negabis deorum ope genus humanum in
      rebus adversis plurimum iuvari?

15   *Libr.* An tu negabis, Lepide, homines ipsos causam esse omnium
      malorum quibus vexentur? Conscende modo hanc ficum et te
      huic ramo suspende; dehinc deos ipsos ora ut auxilium prestent!
      Tu ni te ipsum multis vigiliis lectitans conficeres, Lepide, haud
16   palleres minimeque esses crudus. Mala que ferunt homines,
      eadem ipsi sponte subiere. Nullos, mihi crede, ad tempestatem
      levandam naute, nisi mari et fluctibus confiderent, uspiam deos
17   nossent. Sed ita consuevere: postquam sua ineptia et stultitia
      evenit ut gravissimis malis premantur, illico ad deos tendunt;
      qua quidem in re, dum velint deos prohibere que ipsi occepe-
      rint, mihi tum non rogare, sed certamen atque contentionem
18   inire videntur. Atque si tu causas malorum fugies, nunquam
      ullos ad malum abs te auferendum deos desiderabis; vel si ho-
      mines hominibus nocuos esse censeas, non deos defensores
      orare, sed vel magis homines ipsos placare opus est.

19   Quod si tandem ipsi dii causa malorum sunt, eos velim scias
      a sua vetere consuetudine tuis precibus minime degenerare.
20   Vetustum quidem est homines malis obrui. At vero aut fatum
      aut fors aut tempus efficit ut malis angamur, procul dubio non
      invitis diis eadem suo libere utentur officio vestrasque, o reli-
21   giosi, ieiunas precationes aspernabuntur. Preterea an tu deos

those snatched from others who own them. Can you show me   12
a servant so base that you could honorably bid him commit
such a crime? Is anyone arrogant enough to order corrupt as-
sassins to enrich him by plundering others?

Lepidus. I see your point. Yet I did not ask that they act as brig-   13
ands, but as laborers, for I asked them make golden cabbages
grow in my garden.

Libripeta. If they are wise, the gods will detest your impudence.   14

Lepidus. Will you deny, Libripeta, that the gods often aid mankind in adversity?

Libripeta. Will you deny, Lepidus, that men are themselves the   15
cause of all the ills that vex them? Just climb this fig tree and
hang yourself from this branch; then ask the gods to rescue
you. If you didn't ruin your health by reading in continual vigils, Lepidus, you would hardly be so pale or so dyspeptic. Men   16
willingly submit to the ills they suffer. Believe me, sailors would
recognize no gods who might calm the storm if they didn't
trust themselves to the surging sea. But such is their custom: 17
when their own senseless folly subjects them to the gravest dangers, they turn at once to the gods. Thus, by wishing the gods
to stop what they themselves have undertaken, they seem not
to pray, but to engage in conflict and contention. And you too,   18
if you avoid whatever causes your ills, will never require any
gods to remove them. Or if you judge that it is men who harm
other men, there is no need to invoke protecting gods, but to
reconcile men instead.

Now, if the gods themselves are responsible for our ills,   19
please consider that your prayers will scarcely cause them to
abandon their usual practice. For ages, men have been plagued
by adversity; and if something else—fate, or chance, or time—   20
causes our afflictions, without a doubt it exercises its office
freely and with the gods' assent, and will spurn your paltry sup-
plications, O men of religion! Besides, do you think the gods   21

nobis homunculis persimiles arbitraris, ut veluti imprudentes
atque incauti homines ex tempore consilium captent atque item
extemplo pristina consilia mutent? Profecto in tanta rerum ad-
ministratione nihil esset diis laboriosius. Audio ab his qui litteras profitentur, deos ordine pene eterno orbem agere. Que
quidem res dum ita sit, insani vos quidem longe deliratis, si
existimatis deos ab incepto et pristino cursu rerum vestris verbis aut persuasionibus ad novas alias res agendas animum aut
operam divertere. Adde quod esset genus quoddam servitutis
abiectissimum, si dii ipsi pro vestra expectatione atque voluntate sua instituta desererent.

Demum et meminisse oportet diis sat esse operis sole lu-
naque ac deinde ceteris omnibus stellis per magnum ethera
agendis. Tum et mari montes aquarum a diis volvi, ventos et
fulgura demitti infinitaque eiusmodi terribilia curari a diis vestri
religiosi palam affirmant, ut sane rebus tantis occupati dii ad
infinita inaniaque ac penitus inepta hominum vota auscultanda
minime vacent. Quod si minimis quoque rebus intenti sunt,
habent illi quidem cicadas et grillos quorum purissimas voces
audiant libentius quam hominum impurissimorum expostulationes atque ineptias. Tum sic habeto, deos non aliis quam improborum precibus obtundi. Nam bonis quidem que habent
probi plane contenti sunt malisque succumbunt nunquam, im-
probis vero neque bonis exposcendis neque malis ferendis ulla
ratio aut modus inest.

Lep. Que abs te dicta sunt, Libripeta, in disputationis locum
ita accipio, ut apud me tamen semper hec mens et opinio sit
de diis, ut censeam preces bonorum et vota superis esse non
ingrata. Tum ita semper apud me erit persuasum pleraque
emerita mala pietate deorum vitari eosque ipsos deos in bene
merentes esse quam beneficos. Vale.

resemble us small human beings? Do they make decisions on the spur of the moment, like imprudent and reckless people, and then abruptly change their former resolves? Indeed, men of learning tell me that the gods are incomparably industrious in their great task of administration, and that they rule the world according to a nearly eternal order. Consequently, you rave like madmen if you think your words or arguments will divert the gods' thoughts and actions from their age-old course toward new undertakings. Besides, the gods would be groveling slaves if they abandoned their own plans for the sake of your hopes and desires.

In fine, you must remember that the gods are quite busy moving the sun, the moon, and the other heavenly bodies through the vast heavens. Even your men of religion declare openly that the gods heap mountainous waves in the sea, hurl down winds and lightning bolts, and dispense countless such terrifying phenomena. Engaged in such great matters, the gods have little time to listen to the interminable, futile, and utterly ridiculous prayers of men. And if the gods pay attention to small things, they listen to the pure voices of cicadas and crickets more gladly than to the foolish entreaties of abominable men. Consider then that only the prayers of the wicked fall on the gods' deaf ears. For good men are content with the goods they have, and never succumb to adversity. But the wicked know no reason or restraint in demanding goods or bearing ills.

Lepidus. I accept your remarks, Libripeta, in the spirit of debate, but my view and opinion of the gods remain the same: I believe that they welcome the prayers and vows of good men. And I remained convinced that many of the misfortunes we deserve are averted by the mercy of the gods, who are most generous to meritorious men. Goodbye.

∶ 3 ∶

Virtus

1 *Mercur.* Virtus dea per epistolas oravit modo ad se huc ut exirem.
   Accedo ut percuncter quidnam me velit. Illico ad Iovem redibo.
2 *Virt.* Salve, Mercuri. Ago tibi gratias, quandoquidem tua pietas in
   me atque benignitas efficit ut non penitus despecta ab omni
   cetu deorum sim.
3 *Mercur.* Expecto quid narres. Tu modo perbreves narrationes facito: nam edixit ut confestim ad se redirem Iuppiter.
4 *Virt.* Etiamne tecum nobis non licebit nostras erumnas exponere?
   Quos igitur ultores in me iniuriarum habebo si non modo apud
   ipsum maximum Iovem verum et apud te, quem semper in fra-
5 tris amantissimi locum habui, condolendi facultas negatur? O
   me idcirco miseram! ad quos confugiam? unde auxilium petam?
   Me quidem, dum ita despiciar, malo truncum esse aliquod
   quam deam.
   Mercur. Tandem recita, dum prebeo operam.
6 *Virt.* Recito. Viden quam sim nuda et feda? Hoc ita ut sim, effecit
7 Fortune dee impietas atque iniuria. Aderam sane ornata apud
   Elisios campos inter veteres meos amicos media Platonem, So-
   cratem, Demosthenem, Ciceronem, Archimedem, Policlitem,
   Praxitelem et huiusmodi doctos, qui me, dum vitam agebant,
8 piissime atque religiosissime coluere. Interea loci, dum iam non
   pauci ad nos salutatum advolassent, e vestigio Fortuna dea insolens, audax, temulenta, procax, maxima armatorum turba con-
   septa atque stipata, properans ad nos iactabunda: 'Eu,' inquit,
   'plebea, tune maioribus diis adventantibus non ultro cedis?'
9   Doluit iniuriam nobis immeritis eo pacto fieri, ac nonnihil
   ira concita inquam: 'Neque tu, maxima dea, his verbis me

: 3 :

Virtue

Mercury. Just now, the goddess Virtue asked me in a letter to come 1
to her here. I'll approach and inquire what she wants of me.
Then I shall return at once to Jupiter.

Virtue. Greetings, Mercury. I thank you, for your kindness and 2
goodwill keep me from being utterly despised by every circle of
the gods.

Mercury. I await your story. But keep your account brief, for Jupi- 3
ter instructed me to return to him promptly.

Virtue. Even in your company am I forbidden to recount my afflic- 4
tions? Who shall I find to avenge my wrongs, if I am denied
compassion by mighty Jupiter, and even by you, whom I have
always considered a loving brother? Woe is me, then! To whom 5
shall I turn, or where shall I seek aid? If I am so despised, I
would rather be some dismembered torso than a goddess.

Mercury. Speak, then, while I am listening.

Virtue. I shall. Do you see how naked and dirty I am? This is the 6
work of the goddess Fortune's impiety and injustice. Nicely 7
dressed, I was walking in the Elysian fields with my friends
Plato, Socrates, Demosthenes, Cicero, Archimedes, Polycletus,
Praxiteles, and other wise and learned men who, while alive,
piously and devoutly worshiped me. At this point, as many of 8
them came forth to greet me, suddenly the goddess Fortune
came running up. Shameless, bold, drunken, forward, and es-
corted and encircled by a large gang of armed men, she rushed
toward me and crowed: "What, you common little woman,
don't you give way willingly when greater gods approach?"

I was grieved to be insulted for no cause, and as my anger 9
rose, I replied: "These words of yours, mighty goddess, cannot

plebeam efficies, neque, si maioribus cedendum est, tibi turpiter
10 cedendum censeo.' Illa vero illico in convitium sese effert advor-
sum. Pretereo hic quas contumelias in me primum, dum hec
11 inter nos geruntur, effuderit. Idcirco Plato philosophus contra
nonnulla de deorum officio cepit disputare. At illa excandes-
cens: 'Apage te hinc, verbose, inquit, non enim decet hic servos
12 deorum causam suscipere.' Ceperat et Cicero orator plura velle
suadere. At ex turba armatorum erupit Marcus Antonius prepotens, latera illa sua digladiatoria ostentans, gravissimumque
pugnum in os Ciceronis infregit.

13 Hinc ceteri amici mei perculsi metu, fuga sibi propere consu-
luere. Neque enim Polycletus peniculo, aut Phidias scalpro, aut
Archimedes horoscopo, aut reliqui inermes adversus audacissi-
mos armatos, eosdemque predis atque homicidiis suetos, belle
14 ad sese tuendos valebant. Ergo me infelicissimam, ab ipsis diis
omnibus qui aderant atque ab hominibus desertam, pugnis et
calcibus totam contrivere vestesque meas diripuere, in lutum
prostratam reliquere; demum abiere ovantes.

15 Ego vero ita confecta, cum primum licuit, conscendi huc ut
16 Iovem optimum maximum his de rebus facerem certiorem. Iam
quidem mihi, ut intromittar, expectanti mensis elapsus est;
dumque, ut id ipsum impetrem, omnes deos exeuntes ac re-
deuntes precor, novas tamen semper aliquas excusationes audio:
aut enim deos aiunt vacare ut in tempore cucurbite florescant,
17 aut curare ut papilionibus ale perpulchre picte adsint. Quid
igitur? Ne vero aliud sempiterne habebunt negotii, quo nos ex-
clusas teneant ac flocci pendant? Cucurbite admodo floruere,
papiliones lautissimi pervolant, tum et villicus dudum suscepit
curam ne cucurbite siti pereant: nos tamen neque diis neque
18 hominibus commendate aut cordi sumus. Has ob res te iterum
atque iterum precor obtestorque, Mercuri, quo semper apud
deos ipsos interpres omnium exstitisti, eo et causam hanc
19 meam iustissimam atque piissimam suscipias. Ad te confugio,

make me a commoner. And even if one should yield to one's betters, I do not deem that I should basely yield to you." She 10 instantly burst into reproaches against me, but I omit the insults she first heaped upon me in our exchange. To counter her, 11 the philosopher Plato began to discourse on duty among the gods. But she hotly rejoined: "Be off, wordy fellow! Slaves have no business pleading the gods' cause." The orator Cicero too 12 had tried to offer advice, but the powerful Mark Antony burst out of the armed mob, flaunting his gladiator's chest, and struck Cicero in the face with his mighty fist.[12]

At this, my other friends took flight in panic. No one—not 13 Polycletus with his brush, Phidias with his chisel, Archimedes with his astrolabe, or the others, who were unarmed—was able to defend himself against these armed bullies, who were used to plunder, murder, and war. How wretched I was! Deserted by all 14 the gods and men present, I was severely battered by blows and kicks. My clothes were torn to shreds, and I was left lying in the mud while the mob went off in triumph.

As soon as my weakened condition permitted it, I came up 15 here to inform best and greatest Jupiter of what had happened. Yet already a month has passed while I wait to be admitted. I 16 beseech all the gods who go in or out to help me, but I only hear new excuses. They say that the gods find time to see that gourds blossom in season, or that they take pains to see that butterflies have beautifully painted wings.[13] What then? Will 17 they always be so busy that they exclude and belittle me? The gourds are in full blossom, the butterflies fly about in splendor, and the farmer has long since made sure that the gourds do not die of drought. Yet I have neither gods nor men to love or protect me. So I beg and entreat you, Mercury, as you have always 18 been everyone's ambassador to the gods, take up my just and righteous cause. I take refuge in you; I beg you as a suppliant; 19

te supplex oro, in te omnis mea sita est spes atque expectatio. Da, queso, operam ne, dum a vobis excludor, ipsis quoque mortalibus sim ludibrio: non erit quidem decus deorum ordini, ubi homunculi me tametsi infimam dearum fortassis flocci pendant.

20 *Mercur.* Audivi, dolet. Verum pro vetere nostra amicitia unum admoneo: duram nimis atque difficilem causam te adversus

21 Fortunam suscepisse. Nam et Iuppiter ipse, ut ceteros deos omittam, cum se ob accepta beneficia nimium debere Fortune censeat, tum eius illius vires atque potentiam mirum in modum veretur. Fortuna enim ad celos diis ascensum prestitit atque, ubi velit, valens sua armatorum manu eosdem ipsos deos eiiciet.

22 Qua de re, si sapis, inter deos plebeos ignota, quoad Fortune in te odium extinctum sit, latitabis.

Virt. Eternum latitandum est. Ego et nuda et despecta excludor.

: 4 :

Fatum et Fortuna

1 ***. Isthanc sententiam tuam approbo, philosophe: mentes hominum plerumque inter dormiendum plane esse solutas atque liberas. Sed in primis abs te vehementer cupio illud de fato et fortuna pulcherrimum audire, quod te in somniis aiebas didi-

2 cisse. Age, queso, dum ambo sumus otiosi, recita, ut congratuler tibi quod, tam amplissima in re, plura dormiens quam nos alii vigilantes perspexeris.

3 *Philos.* Itane cupis, amicissime? Gero tibi morem. Audies quidem rem dignam memoratu. Narro.

in you lies my every hope and expectation. Please see that, if I am excluded from your divine company, I do not also become a laughing stock to men. The standing of the gods would be tarnished if feeble men were to belittle even me, the lowest of goddesses.

Mercury. I have heard your story, and am truly sorry. But as an old 20 friend, I must warn that you have brought too hard and difficult a suit against Fortune. For Jupiter himself—not to men- 21 tion the other gods—both owes a great debt to Fortune for the benefits she has granted him, and greatly fears her strength and powers. Fortune made possible the gods' ascent to heaven; and backed by her armed band, if she wishes, she can throw them out. Hence, if you are wise, you will hide yourself among the 22 class of common gods until Fortune's hatred of you is quenched.

Virtue. Then I must hide eternally. Naked and despised, I am excluded from heaven.

: 4 :

Fate and Fortune

[*Unnamed Interlocutor*]. I approve your view, O philosopher, that 1 during sleep men's minds are often released and set free. And I am especially eager to hear from you that excellent lesson about fate and fortune which you said you learned in a dream.[14] Come, then, since we are both at leisure, recount it, so that I 2 may congratulate you for having discerned more in your sleep than the rest of us do while awake.

Philosopher. Do you desire it, my dear friend? I shall comply, and 3 you shall hear something memorable. Let me tell you.

4   Advigilaram in multam noctem lectitans de fato quidquid esset a maioribus traditum litteris, ac mihi quidem cum multa apud eos auctores placerent dicta, perpauca tamen non admodum nobis satis facere videbantur; ita nescio quid ipse mecum

5 in ea re plus satis appetebam. Somnus interim defessum me vigilia vehementius occupat, ut nonnihil obdormiscere occeperim. Itaque sic inter dormiendum ipse mihi videbar supra cacumen excelsi cuiusdam montis inter innumerabiles veluti hominum umbras esse constitutus, quo ex loco omnis ea provincia bellissime poterat spectari: mons vero ipse omni ex parte ruinis, precipitiis atque abruptis ripis penitus inaccessibilis, uno tan-

6 tum sed angusto calle erat pervius. Hunc montem circum in se ipsum rediens ambibat fluvius omnium rapidissimus atque turbulentissimus inque fluvium innumere eiusmodi umbrarum legiones per angustum ipsum callem descendere minime desinebant.

7   Itaque et loca et infinitam multitudinem umbrarum demirans stupui, ac fui quidem usque adeo detentus admiratione, ut quid citra fluvium esset terrarum aut rerum neglexerim scrutari; quin et ille umbrarum copie unde in arduum montem manarent

8 non studui perpendere. Unica mihi tantum in primis aderat cura, ut que in fluvio miracula apparerent, ea quam diligentissime conspicarer; et erant quidem dignissima admiratione.

9 Nam ut primum in fluvium umbrarum queque descendisset, ita illico infantum membra et ora induisse videbatur. Ac deinceps, quo longius fluvio raperentur, eo illis quidem etatis et membro-

10 rum personam adcrevisse mihi apparebat. Cepi idcirco rogare: 'Et quid,' inquam, 'o umbre, siquid nostis humanitatis aut siquid uspiam estis ad humanitatem propense, quando humanitatis est homines rerum instructiores reddere, dicite, queso, quale sit huic fluvio nomen.'

11   Tum umbre in hunc modum referunt: 'Erras, homo, si quales tibi per oculos corporis videmur nos umbras putas. Sumus

I was awake late at night, reading everything the ancients   4
had written about fate, and although many of these authors'
observations pleased me, very few of them seemed entirely sat-
isfactory. For I still keenly desired to know something more on
the subject. Meanwhile, a heavy drowsiness overcame me, weary   5
as I was from sleeplessness, and I began to doze off. Now, in my
sleep I seemed to find myself on the peak of a high mountain in
the midst of countless shades that appeared to be human. From
this spot, I could easily survey the entire region in every direc-
tion. Its precipitous slopes and steep banks made the mountain
virtually inaccessible on all sides, except where a single narrow
path afforded a passage. The mountain was circled by the swift-   6
est and most turbulent river imaginable, which flowed back into
itself and into which the countless legions of these shades continually descended by the narrow path.

As I wondered at the place and the vast crowd of shades, I   7
was so dumbfounded and amazed that I failed to survey the
lands and objects which lay along the river. Indeed, I didn't try
to distinguish whence so many shades flowed onto the steep
mountain. My only care was to observe most carefully the mi-   8
raculous sights in the river, which were truly astonishing. As   9
soon as each shade had entered the river, it seemed at once to
assume the face and limbs of an infant. Then, as the river carried the shades farther, they appeared to age and grow larger.[15]
So I began to ask them: "If you partake of humanity, O shades,   10
or are at all inclined to human feeling, and it is humane to en-
lighten human beings, please tell me the name of this river."

The shades then replied as follows: "You err, O man, if you   11
think we are shades because we appear so to your corporeal

enim celestes, ut et ipse tu quidem es, igniculi qui humanitati debemur.'

12   Tum ipse: 'O me felicem, siquid unquam a superis meruero, ut vos apertius possim novisse! Nam intelligere quibus orte parentibus quove sitis loco sate ac procreate divinum quoddam esse munus deputem.'

13   Tum umbre 'Desine,' inquiunt, 'desine, homo, istiusmodi dei
14   deorum occulta investigare longius quam mortalibus liceat. Tibi enim ceterisque corpore occlusis animis non plus a superis velim esse concessum scias, quam ea tantum non penitus ignorare
15   que vos oculis intueamini. At fluvio quidem huic, ut expectationi tue, aliqua seu potius qua possum, omni ex parte satis faciam, *Vios* nomen est.'

16   His ego dictis commotus vehementius obstupui. Tum me ipsum exinde colligens, inquam: 'Vos, o celestes dii, oro, hec
17   nomina, quo apertius intelligam, dicite Latina. Nam, etsi Grecis omnia que ad laudem spectant, quantum velint, facile tribuam, nostra tamen lingua delectari me in primis non turpe duco.'

18   Tum umbre inquiunt: 'Is fluvius Latine Vita Etasque mortalium dicitur; eius ripa Mors, cui quidem, ut vides, ripe quisquis inheserit, illico iterum in umbram evanescit.'

19   'O rem admirandam!' inquam. 'Vel quid illos intueor nescio quos fronte tam elata utribus ab aquis superadstare, illos vero ex diverso alios tam egre per omnem fluvium rapi undis et contundi saxis, ut vix queant ore ipso emergere? Tanta, superi boni, unde disparitas est?'

20   Tum umbre 'Sunt illi quidem,' inquiunt, 'quos tu utribus fortassis tutiores esse arbitraris, maximo in periculo constituti: nam is fluvius totus sub undis preacutissimis confertissimisque
21   scopulis refertissimus est. En utres illos fastu et pompa tumidos! Ne tu perspicis ut ictibus undarum ad scopulos illisi perscindantur atque deficiant? Idcirco infelices qui utribus

vision. For like you we are celestial sparks destined for human life."[16]

Then I said: "How fortunate I am, if I deserve so well of the 12 gods that I may know you more clearly! For I would regard it a divine gift to understand from what parents you spring, and where you were begotten and born."

Then the shades said: "Cease, O man, cease to probe into the 13 secrets of the gods more deeply than mortals are allowed. To 14 you and to the other souls shut within a body, know that the gods grant but one thing—to understand some part of what your eyes see here. But to satisfy your curiosity as best I can, 15 the name of this river is Bios."[17]

Violently shaken by these words, I was struck dumb. Then I 16 came to myself and said: "O celestial gods, please say these names in Latin, so that I may understand more clearly. For 17 while I readily grant the Greeks all their praiseworthy achievements, I don't think it shameful to take special delight in our language."

Then the shades said: "In Latin, the river is called Life and 18 Mortal Age, and its bank is called Death. For, as you see, whoever clings to the bank at once fades again into a shade."

"Astounding!" I said. "But why do I see some rise above the 19 water, their faces raised above their floats, while others are so roughly tossed by the waves and beaten on the rocks that they can barely keep their heads above water? Dear gods, whence this great disparity?"

Then the shades said: "Those who seem to be protected by 20 their floats are actually in great danger, for beneath its surface the whole river is crammed full of jagged rocks. Do you see 21 how these floats, swollen with proud ostentation, are ripped apart and collapse when the waves dash them against the rocks?

22   confidebant. Viden ut passim medio in cursu omni presidio destituti trudantur ad scopulos? Miserandi, quam durissimum cursum agunt! Quod si utres laceros retinuerint, sibi ipsis impedimento sunt; si reliquerint, ita rapiuntur undis ut ferme toto

23   fluvio nusquam appareant. Meliori idcirco in sorte sunt hi, qui ab ipsis primordiis fisi propriis viribus nando hunc ipsum vite

24   cursum peragunt; namque cum illis preclare quidem agitur, qui natandi peritia freti atque adiuti, modo otiosi parumper commorari poneque sequentem naviculam aut tabulas fluvio devectas prestolari, modo item maximis viribus, ut scopulos evitent, contendere atque ad litus usque pro laude advolare didicere.

25   Atqui ut rem teneas, sumus quidem nos, natura imperante, in hos ipsos istiusmodi nimirum omnes affecti eorumque saluti et

26   glorie, quoad in nos sit, plurimum deservire cupidi. Vos quidem mortales eosdem ipsos honoris gratia industrios, gnavos, stu-

27   diosos, providos, agentes ac frugi consuevistis appellare. Qui autem utribus delectantur, illi quidem apud nos non eiusmodi sunt, ut eorum divitiis et amplitudini faveri oportere arbitremur; sed longe perfidiam, rapinas, impietatem improbitatemque atque eiusmodi flagitia, ex quibus ipsi utres contexti sunt, odiis dignissima putamus.'

28   Tum ipse inquam: 'Idcirco ex industriis nonnullos ad naviculas inherere, nonnullos insidere ad puppim, nonnullos naviculas ipsas restaurare vehementer gaudeo: namque qui multis prosint, qui manum laborantibus porrigunt, qui bonos recipiunt, sunt illi quidem cum laude et gratia hominum, tum etiam pietate deorum dignissimi.'

29   Tum umbre inquiunt: 'Recte, homo, sentis atque hoc te ignorare nolumus: eos omnes qui naviculis vehuntur quamdiu modesta velle, iusta exhibere, recta sapere, honesta agere, magnifica excogitare non desinent, tamdiu omnes illis superos pro-

30   pitios fore. Nulli enim hominum qui toto fluvio aguntur, quam

Unfortunate are those who rely on such floats! Do you see how 22
in midstream they are dashed against the rocks, once their support is taken from them? Poor wretches, what a harsh course
they run! If they cling to the punctured floats, they are ob-
structed. But if they abandon them, the waves carry them off
and they disappear into the river. Thus, the shades have a better 23
chance who from the outset rely on their own strength in
swimming to run the course of Life. Indeed, those shades fare 24
splendidly who, relying on their swimming skill and aided by it,
know when to pause briefly to wait for an approaching boat or
for planks borne by the river, and when to use their great
strength to avoid the rocks and to fly to shore in glory. You 25
should understand that we and the highest gods are, at nature's
behest, remarkably well-disposed toward such shades, and desire to do all we can to promote their welfare and glory. In their 26
honor, you mortals generally call them industrious, diligent,
studious, prudent, energetic, and temperate. But those who 27
cling to their floats seem to us unworthy of being favored with
wealth and status. Indeed, we detest their perfidy, thefts, impiety, and dishonesty, along with all the similar vices from which
their floats are woven."

Then I said: "I am very pleased that some of the industrious 28
shades latch onto the boats or ride in the stern, and others even
repair them. For those who aid many others, who lend a hand
to those who struggle and who succor the good most deserve
both the praise and glory of men and the favor of the gods."

The shades said: "You are right, O man, and we wish you to 29
know this, too. As long as those who ride in the boats practice
moderate desires, just behavior, upright wisdom, honorable
deeds, and splendid thoughts, all the gods will be propitious
toward them. For of the men carried down the whole river, 30

iidem ipsi qui intra naviculas fidem, simplicitatem atque virtutem spectant, apud superos immortales uspiam sunt gratiores.
31 Hec unica in primis deorum cura est: principibus navicularum
bene moribus et virtute merentibus obsecundare; id quidem
cum ceteras multas ob res, tum quod quietem multorum et
32 otium tueantur. Nam quas vides naviculas, apud mortales imperia nuncupantur; que quidem tametsi ad fluminis cursum
preclare peragendum vehementer iuvent, in illis tamen presidii
firmi et constantis ad asperrimos fluminis scopulos evitandos
33 nihil comperies. Nam cum aque pernicissimo cursu proruant,
tum fit ut navicule quo maiores sint, eo maiori in periculo
versentur interque scopulos impetu undarum illidantur; tum et
plerumque ita subvertantur, ut etiam periti atque experti minime inter fragmenta et globum periclitantium valeant nare.
34 Minores vero navicule ab his, qui eas consectantur, facile depre-
hense submerguntur; sed eo fortassis prestant, quod sunt ad
medium inter utrumque scopulum iter tenendum, longe quam
35 ample ille naves, accommodatiores. Verum maxima omnibus
navigiis ad evitandum naufragium facultas in his aderit, qui per
navim suis locis dispositi accinctique ita sunt, ut vigilantia, fide,
diligentia omnique officio casibus providere ac sese pro communi salute laboribus et periculis sponte subicere non recusant.
36 Cave tamen in omni genere mortalium esse ullos inter undas
tutiores arbitreris, quam eos quos admodum paucissimos toto
pectore inherere tabulis fluvioque huc atque illuc libere spectando tutissimos captare fluctus vides. Tabule quidem ille apud
mortales bone dicuntur artes.' Hec umbre.

37 Tum ego:'Quid ita? Non prestat virtute comite navigiis recte
assidere omniaque pericula subire, quam huius vite cursum
unica asserula conficere?'

38 Tum umbre inquiunt: 'Maximus quisque animus vel minimam naviculam potius quam privatam tabulam affectabit, sed
pacatum ac liberum ingenium non iniuria eos ingentes labores

none are dearer to the immortal gods than those who pursue
faith, candor, and virtue. The gods are particularly anxious to   31
foster those captains of boats who are distinguished by their
character and virtue.[18] They do this for many reasons, but especially in order to safeguard the peace and tranquility of others,
for the boats you see among mortals are called 'empires.' Al-   32
though they aid greatly in completing the river's course glori-
ously, you will find in them no sure or reliable assistance in
avoiding the sharpest rocks. For as the waters rush forward in   33
their ruinous course, it happens that the largest boats face the
greatest danger. They are dashed on the rocks by buffeting
waves, and often capsize, so that even the most skilled and sea-
soned can scarcely swim through the wreckage and the crowd of
the shipwrecked. The smaller boats in turn are easily overtaken   34
and sunk by their pursuers; but they may have this advantage:
they can steer a course midway between the rocks more easily
than the large boats can. Indeed, the greatest capacity for avert-   35
ing shipwreck is shown by those shades who stand at their assigned posts, ready to meet any emergency with vigilance, faith,
diligence, and a sense of duty, and who will not refuse to face
toils and dangers gladly for the common welfare. Do not think   36
that any in all the race of mortals are safer in the river than
those exceptional few who, as you see, cling wholeheartedly to
planks and by looking freely in all directions seek the safest
course. Among mortals, these planks are called liberal arts."
Thus the shades.

Then I said: "What then? Isn't it better, using virtue as a   37
guide, to devote oneself completely to the boats and to face all
dangers, rather than to complete this life's course with a single
plank?"

The shades replied: "Every great mind will aspire to even the   38
smallest boat, rather than to some private plank. But a tranquil
and free mind will rightly eschew such huge labors and the

eaque assidua et maxima navicularum pericula longe fugiet.
39   Adde quod his, qui sua domestica re contenti sunt, ineptia multitudinis et publici huiusmodi tumultus gravissimi sunt; tum
etiam inter ignavam plebem equum ordinem, decus quietemque
40   ac dulce otium servare durum sane ac difficile est. Que quidem
omnes res si ulla ex parte cessent, non facile dici potest quam
illico et reges et naute, denique et omne navigium periturum
41   sit. Quam ob rem ab his qui ad clavum sedent hec in primis
cura desideratur ut provideant, ne suam suorumve per ignaviam
aut luxum temere in scopulos aut in litus irruant, neve navis
ipsa inutili aliquo pondere supprimatur; eiusque levande gratia
non modo suos verum et se ipsum, dum ita deceat pro necessitate, in litus usque eiicere bene constituti principis officium est.
42   Hec dura quidem a plerisque putantur, quove minime ad tutam
et otiosam vitam apta, eo a modestis atque simplicibus animis
43   longe aspernantur. His accedit quod multo demum precaven-
dum est, ne maximus ille qui ad puppim subsequitur numerus
navim aut impellat in periculum aut pervertat. Et afferunt illi
quidem protervi non minus quam duri scopuli solicitudinem
nautis: nam clavum insolentes carpunt, transtra apprehendunt,
44   ordines remorum perturbant. Neque eos procaces atque audaces, nisi vi, abegeris, quos eosdem non mediocri cum iactura
et damno in navim receptos teneas: nam illic inepti, inutiles,
contumaces nullam in periculis porrigunt manum, in otio
supini, in agendis rebus graves et morosi, ut facile que eos re-
ceperit navicula iniquo hoc pondere pereat.'

45   Hec cum dixissent umbre, tunc ego mihi tacitus videbar
mecum non minus que audissem quam que oculis coram intue-
46   bar admirari. Dehinc ad fluvium ipsum oculos intendens, 'En!'
inquam, 'o dii, quosnam video in undis laborare inter paleas, ut
vix totis capitibus emergant? Facite, queso, me omnium istarum
quas video rerum certiorem.'

great and continuous perils of the boats. What's more, people 39
content with their private lives find intolerable the folly of the
masses and public disturbances. Indeed, among the indolent
commoners it is quite difficult to maintain just order, dignity,
tranquility, and sweet leisure.[19] For when these are in the least 40
wanting, it is hard to describe how suddenly commanders, sailors, and even the entire vessel will perish. Hence, special care is 41
required in the helmsmen to see that they do not heedlessly run
aground on the rocks or shore, either through their own indolence or laxity, or that of their crew. When a harmful cargo
causes a boat to sink, it is the duty of a sensible commander to
lighten the vessel and to cast ashore his own crew and, when
necessary, even himself. Many think such a policy harsh, and 42
modest and simple minds shun it as unconducive to a safe and
leisurely life. In addition, one must be very careful lest the large 43
crowds seated astern run the boat aground or capsize it. Indeed, such reckless men cause the crew no less solicitude than
do the rocks. In their insolence, they tear at the helm, seize the
rowers' seats, and disrupt the ranks of oars. Unless you use 44
force to drive off these bold and forward ones, they will cause
no little loss and harm if kept on board, for they are inept and
useless; in danger they defiantly lend no hand; in leisure, they
are idle; in activity, they are troublesome and peevish. Hence,
any small boat that takes them on board may perish by their
excessive burden."

When the shades had said this, I seemed to myself to be 45
wondering silently no less at what I had heard than at what my
eyes beheld. Then directing my eyes toward the river, I said: 46
"Look, O gods! In the waves, I see some struggling amid
straws, with their heads barely above the water. Please tell me
about what I see."

47 Tum umbre inquiunt: 'Id quidem genus mortalium pessi-
mum est: etenim suspitiosi, callidi invidique apud vos dicuntur.
48 Nam perversa natura et depravatis moribus prediti, cum nolint
nare, cum suis paleis gaudent nantibus esse impedimento.
49 Suntque his persimiles alii, quos vides, ut altera manu utrem
interdum aut tabulam ab aliis per vim et iniuriam rapiant, alteram enim manum musco et limo (qua quidem re inveniri in
fluvio molestius nihil potest) implicitam atque occupatam sub
undis habent; ac est quidem genus id impedimenti eiusmodi, ut
50 manibus semel inglutinatis perpetuo inhereat. Vos vero illos
ipsos estis avaros cupidosque nuncupare soliti. Tum deinceps
proximi, quos cernis super vitreas vesicas incumbere, assenta-
51 tores improbi atque audaces nominantur. Postremi vero, quorum vix ultimi pedes intuentur ac veluti inutile aliquod trun-
52 cum huc illucve undis propelluntur, nostin qui sint? Sunt hi
quidem quos philosophi verbis disputationibusque potius quam
moribus et vita ab se alienos esse predicant: sunt enim libidi-
53 nosi, edaces, submersi voluptatibus, perditi otio et luxu. Sed
iam, heus, exhibe summos honores illis quos ab omni turba se-
gregatos illuc vides.'

Tum ipse omnes in partes respectans, 'En,' inquam, 'at nullos
pene a multitudine dissidere intueor!'

54 'Ne vero,' inquiunt umbre, 'an non perspicis illos alatos cum
talaribus usque adeo agiles et aptos undis superlabier?'

'Mihi sane vel unum,' inquam, 'videre videor. Verum quid
ego illis deferam honoris? Quid meruere?'

55 Tum umbre: 'An parum meruisse videntur hi, qui simplices
et omni ex parte incorrupti a genere hominum dii habiti sunt?
Ale quas gestant veritas et simplicitas; talaria vero caduca-
56 rum rerum despicientiam interpretantur. Merito igitur vel
has ob res divinas divi habentur, vel quod primi quas per fluvium cernis tabulas, maximum nantibus adiumentum, con-
struxere titulosque bonarum artium singulis tabulis conscrip-

The shades replied: "Those are the worst kind of mortals,   47
men you call mistrustful, calculating, and envious. Of perverse   48
nature and depraved character, they choose not to swim, but
take pleasure in hindering other swimmers with their straws.
There are others like them whom you see, who with one hand   49
often violently and unjustly snatch a float or plank from others.
But they keep the other hand underwater buried in the muck
and slime, which is the most disgusting thing in the river; and
once their hands are caught in this glue, they can't escape it.
These people you generally call the greedy and avaricious. The   50
group next to them, whom you see lying on glass floats, are
called impudent and dishonest flatterers.[20] As for the last group,   51
whose feet are barely visible and who are driven here and there
by the waves like some worthless stump, do you know who they
are? These are the ones whom the philosophers — in their   52
wordy disputes rather than by their moral conduct — declare are
their opposites. They are the lustful and gluttonous, sunk in
pleasures and wallowing in sloth. But come, show great honor   53
to those whom you see set apart from the vast crowd."

I looked all around and said: "I hardly see any who keep
their distance from the masses."

"Indeed?" said the shades. "Don't you perceive those shades   54
with wings and winged sandals who glide nimbly and easily
over the waves?"[21]

"I think I may see one," I said. "But why should I honor
them? What are their merits?"

The shades replied: "Can the merits seem small of those   55
who, being perfectly candid and uncorrupt, are considered gods
by mankind? Their wings signify truth and candor, and their
winged sandals, contempt for transitory things. They are rightly   56
regarded as gods both for their divine traits, and because they
first fashioned the planks in the river as an invaluable aid to
swimmers, and inscribed on the various planks the names of

57   sere. Reliqui autem his diis persimiles, sed ex aquis tamen non
membris totis preminentes alasque et talaria non omnino integras gestantes, semidei sunt et proxime ad deos honore et vene-
58   ratione dignissimi. Id quidem ita eorum merito fit, tum quod
tabulas additamentis fragmentorum effecere ampliores, tum
etiam quod ex mediis scopulis atque ex ultima ripa pulcherrimum ducunt tabulas ipsas colligere novasque simili quadam
ratione ac modo struere suasque has omnes operas in medium
59   ceteris nantibus exhibere. Tribue idcirco illis honores, homo,
illisque meritas habeto gratias, quod ad tam laboriosum cursum
vite peragendum optimum hisce tabulis presidium prestitere.'

60   Itaque sic inter dormiendum videbar que dixi et cernere et
audire mirumque in modum affectare, ut quoquo pacto inter
61   eos alatos divos adnumerarer. Sed repente visus sum preceps
ruere in fluvium, quando neque tabule neque utres neque admi-
62   niculi quidpiam ad natandum suppeditabant. E vestigio exper-
giscor, ac mecum ipse hanc visam in somniis fabulam repetens
gratias habui somno, quod eius beneficio fatum atque fortunam
63   tam belle pictam viderim: siquidem, modo rem bene interpre-
ter, fatum didici esse aliud nihil quam cursum rerum in vita
hominum, qui quidem ordine suo et lapsu rapitur; fortunam
vero illis esse faciliorem animadverti, qui tum in fluvium cecidere, cum iuxta aut integre asserule aut navicula fortassis aliqua
64   aderat. Contra vero fortunam esse duram sensi nobis, qui eo
tempore in fluvium corruissemus, quo perpetuo innixu undas
nando superare opus sit. Plurimum tamen in rebus humanis
prudentiam et industriam valere non ignorabimus.

the liberal arts. The others, who are quite similar to these gods, 57
do not rise entirely above the water, and their wings and sandals are not perfect. They are semigods, worthy of honor and
veneration second only to the gods. And rightly so, for they 58
have enlarged the planks by adding bits and pieces to them, and
they delight in gathering planks from between the rocks and
from the furthest bank, in fashioning new planks of similar
shape and purpose, and in offering all their works to those who
swim. Pay them honors, O man, and give them due thanks, for 59
by these planks they have lent signal assistance for those completing the toilsome course of life."

Thus in my sleep I seemed to see and hear all that I have 60
related, and I felt a wondrous desire to be counted somehow
among the winged gods. But suddenly I seemed to be cast 61
headlong into the river, and had nothing to aid me in swimming—no planks, no floats, and no props. I awoke at once, 62
and, as I recalled the fable I had seen in my dream, I was grateful to my sleep for showing me Fate and Fortune so nicely depicted. For if I my interpretation is correct, I learned that Fate 63
is merely the course of human affairs, impelled by its own orderly current. I observed that Fortune is kinder to those who
fall into the river where there happen to be entire planks or a
small boat. By contrast, I found that Fortune is unkind to us 64
when we are plunged into the river just when we must sur-
mount the waves by swimming with unceasing effort. But we
shall not forget that prudence and diligence are of great value in
human affairs.

∴ 5 ∴

Patientia

1 ⟨*Pat.*⟩. Proh deum, quantis et quam variis vita hominum morbis refertissima est, ut plane cuivis facile posse videri arbitrer deos nullam aliam ob causam hoc omne mortalium genus fecisse, nisi ut essent quos irati infinitis modis seviendo excruciarent!

2 Nullum quidem usque adeo felicem comperies hominem, quin idem non multa ex parte infelicissimus sit. Quid quod eos quoque, quos primis fortune donis gaudere censeas, non tamen

3 omnino gravissimis erumnis vacuos invenio? At mihi quidem hominum sors et conditio nunc primum visa est pessima, quo multo quam antea eorum morbos curanti explorata esse occepit.

4 Profecto sub divo nihil homine quod vivat durius. Mitto ceteras

5 quas palam intueri licet egritudines mortalium. Hominem sane vel supremo quidem in imperio constitutum offendo neminem, qui non eque multos habeat quos vereri quibusve parere plerumque et obtemperare sibi invito opus sit; aliis, cum rerum copia adsit, desunt tamen non paucissima quibus et sibi et suis satis faciant; aliis inter iocos et festivitates luget et meret animus.

6 Itaque imperiis servitus, divitiis paupertas cumque risu et luctus et meror implicitus et commixtus est mortalibus. Adde his quod nullus est locus vacuus incommodis, nullum temporis

7 momentum non penitus momento dissimile succedit. Res item rebus contrarie et nocue ipsique homines quo aliis hominibus, eo et sibimet ipsis dissidendo graves atque multo infestissimi sunt. His rebus fit ut quem procul dubio perpulchre valere

8 existimes, is non sine gravi aliquo malo vitam trahat. Denique ita esse affirmo: omnes quos offenderis homines acerrimis curis

9 intimisque animi doloribus excruciari. Atque cum his quidem

38

: 5 :

Patience

Patience. By the gods, what great and diverse maladies completely 1
fill the lives of men! I think that anyone can easily see that the
gods have created this mortal race for only one reason—that in
their anger they may torment them savagely in countless ways.
You will find no man so happy that that he is not also most 2
unhappy in many respects. For don't I find that even those who
would seem blessed by the highest gifts of fortune are subject to
sore tribulations? And man's lot and condition seem to me 3
worse than ever, now that in treating his diseases I have begun
to know him more truly than before. Indeed, under the sun no 4
life is harsher than that of man. I say nothing of the sorrows of
mankind that all can see. I find no man, not even in positions 5
of the highest power, who is not constrained against his will
either to fear many others, or to obey and humor them. Some
men possess abundant goods, but still lack what would satisfy
themselves and their families. Others grieve and lament in-
wardly in the midst of games and festivities. For mortals, au- 6
thority and slavery, wealth and poverty, laughter and mournful
sorrow are inextricably intermingled. What's more, no place is
free of problems, and each moment of time is succeeded by a
completely different one; and human affairs contradict each
other and clash. By their disagreements, people are harmful and 7
even dangerous to themselves and others. In this way, someone
you suppose to be quite clearly in perfect health actually lives
with some grave complaint. In sum, I maintain that everyone 8
you meet is tormented by acute cares and mental anguish. In 9

meo iudicio bene agitur, quibus sua palam incommoda deplo-
rare liceat: nam miseris miserie commiseratores habere sola-
tium est.

10   Sed quid matrem meam huc trepidam proficiscentem intueor? Assurgo atque illi obviam pergo.

11 *Nec.* Quod ni isthic inter has ipsas abruptas rupes, ubi meridiare
solita est, meam reperio natam, quo ea abdita sit loco prorsus
ignoro. Huc ergo accedo. Sed eccam ipsam exeuntem ad me.

12   —Preter officium quidem agis, filia, ubi isthic diutius lati-
13 tans nostrorum egrotantium curas despicis. Te unam mirum in
modum languentes perplurimi exposcunt; ac medicum quidem
velim scias diligentem atque solertem in primis esse oportere:
nam morbi sane nonnunquam magis diligentia medici quam
14 arte ipsa et peritia levantur. Ceterum inscitia egrotum perdere
prope homicidium est; indiligentia vero in perniciem dare atque
deserere eos qui sese tue fidei commendarunt, et homicidium et
nefaria quidem proditio est.

15 *Pat.* Me ego ex isthoc rerum et tempestatum turbulentissimo estu,
quo omnia funditus exagitantur, mater, in tutam solitudinem et
16 otiosam hanc in umbram surripueram. Tum et parum intelligebam quid stulti mortales huc possent afferre, cur non eas diffi-
cillimas et laboriosissimas curas medendi longe fugiendas duce-
17 rem. Nobis egroti nulli admodum parent. At si qui nos audiunt,
hi tantum sunt qui aut fuste gravissimam aliquam plagam accepere, aut ita in profundam aliquam foveam cecidere, ut preter
defracti membri turpitudinem quam ostentant, obscenissimi
18 quoque luto et fedissimi omnibus fetori et stomacho sint. Neque hi quidem, ut ceteros longe contumaciores omittam, apud
me desinunt aut amarum poculum accusare aut de dietis per
convitium disputare aut denique omne pharmac⟨or⟩um genus
abhorrere: clamitant, excandescunt, execrantur, ut aut nove nobis medendi artes ex egroti ingenio et voluntate suscipiende aut
omnis eorum cura penitus deserenda sit.

my opinion, those who openly lament their misfortunes are well off, since it is a consolation when the miserable find commiseration for their misery.

But do I see my mother approach in great agitation? I rise 10 and go to meet her.

Necessity. If I don't find my child here among these steep cliffs 11 where she generally takes her siesta, I have no idea where she is hiding. Let me approach. But here she is, coming to meet me.

[*Necessity addresses Patience.*] You neglect your duty, my daughter, if 12 you hide here so long and disdain caring for our suffering mortals. Many of the infirm clamor for you alone. Remember that 13 a physician must above all be diligent and careful, for often maladies are relieved more by a doctor's diligence than by his science and expertise. Letting a patient die through ignorance is 14 practically murder; but if through negligence you desert and destroy patients in your care, it is not only murder, but also a horrible betrayal.

Patience. Fleeing the turbulence and tumults that so profoundly 15 agitate and vex the world, mother, I stole away to this safe solitude and leisurely shade. I could not see how foolish mortals 16 could persuade me not to avoid the difficult and laborious cares of treating them. Absolutely none of the sick obey us. The only 17 ones who listen to us are people who have been gravely wounded by a club, or who have fallen into a deep pit and now nauseate and disgust everyone by the deformity of their broken limbs and by their filth and stench. And to say nothing about even 18 more insolent patients, even these continually denounce my remedies as bitter, abusively contest their regimen, or even reject every sort of medication. They shout, flare up, and curse, so that I must either adopt new remedies according to the patient's whims and wishes, or abandon my treatment altogether.

19   *Nec.* Atqui eodum, filia! quasnam pultes apponis his qui ita ut
inquis iaceant?

    Pat. Nullas, mater; sed his tantum cantionibus interdum utor,
quas dudum edocuit Chronus. Nostin?

20   *Nec.* Multas novi cantiones; sed ubi rem res desiderat, frustra verbis opem afferes. Preterea hanc ipsam Chroni cantionem haud
satis memini esse approbatam. At enim recita.

21   *Pat.* Recito. 'Desine tandem, desine, infelix, queri; sic et ille bonus
atque item ille paria indigne admodum mala perpessi sunt. Teque nunc iam hominem ut natum sentis, omnem fortunam
eque ferendam disce.'

22   *Nec.* Mihi quidem isthec que sine sumptu fiat curatio, modo pro-
23   sit in tempore, non videbitur vituperanda. Sed illud non in
postremis ad istiusmodi morbos levandos laudo, quod apud veteres nostre artis scriptores litteris traditum est: 'emplastrum ex
floribus spei melioris atque ex frondibus expectationum confec-
24   tum.' Namque prisci omnes in hanc sententiam conveniunt:
ferme cunctas malas valitudines hoc unico procul dubio suavi
atque odorato emplastro in bonam valitudinem restaurari.

25   *Pat.* Ego, mater, ex his sum que non, queque litteris commendata
invenio, eadem certa et vera esse iudicem. Multos, cum dentes
dolent cumque hiberno algore torpent, isthec futilis medendi
26   ratio fefellit. Et, Superi boni, bonos quam multos hac tempestate malus male hic dentium morbus afficit!

    Nec. Proinde tu morbis his hominum et imbecillitatibus, filia, op-
27   timum quod prebeas presidium teneto.—Affer huc tu, Dromo,
cistellam isthanc aromatariam quam post me ad spatulas ap-
pensam defers.—Cape, filia, exque hoc iube manus inungi
languentibus.

28   *Pat.* At quisnam superinscriptus huic Samio pissidi est, mater, titulus?

    Nec. Lege.

Necessity. But wait, daughter, what poultices do you apply to those 19
 who lie ill as you say?

Patience. None, mother. But sometimes I use the incantations that
 Chronus once taught me. Do you know them?[22]

Necessity. I know many incantations, but when the case requires 20
 action, it is useless to offer mere words. Besides, I recall that
 few approved of Chronus' incantation. But recite it.

Patience. I shall. "Cease, then, cease to lament, wretch. Many a 21
 good man has wrongly suffered such ills. Recall that you were
 born human, and learn to bear every kind of fortune equally."

Necessity. A treatment that costs nothing, as long as it comes in 22
 time, is hardly to be spurned. Above all, I praise highly a rem- 23
 edy for such maladies which is recorded by the ancient authors
 of our art—a plaster made from blossoms of hope and from
 the leaves of expectations. All the ancients agree that nearly any 24
 kind of malady can be cured by this one sweet and aromatic
 plaster.

Patience. Mother, I am not one who regards as certain and true 25
 everything that has been written down. Many whose teeth ache
 or who are sluggish from the winter's cold have been disappointed by that futile method of treatment. Good gods! How 26
 many in our age are afflicted by this cruel malady of the teeth!

Necessity. Then take the best protection you can provide against
 men's maladies and infirmities. You there, Dromo, hand me 27
 that box of spices which you carry behind me slung over your
 shoulder.[23] Take this, daughter, and have the infirm rub their
 hands with its contents.

Patience. What is the label written on this bottle from Samos, 28
 mother?[24]

Necessity. Read it.

Pat. Lego: 'Unguentum ex succo industrie et laboris.' Hui, pretiosum! Dragmis trecentis unciam venire convenit.—Hem, hei, me miseram!

29 *Nec.* Dii te perdant, filia! Itane hoc fregisti vas?

Pat. Non meo hoc factum ex instituto, mater, putes oro, sed malo
30 casu; quod perunctus ac lubricus esset, effluxit e manibus. Tandem usque esse adeo irata, mater, desine. Reficiemus quidem illico unguentum hoc: nam grandes apud me eius herbe manipuli adsunt.

31 *Nec.* Desino sane, verum et unde industrie modo, que dudum exaruit, succum sumemus? Doleo, nam sine industria labor admodum inutilis est.

Pat. Quandoquidem isthuc deest, mater, alio quod suppeditet medicamento utemur.

32 *Nec.* Siquidem isthuc tua incuria iubet, filia, posthac ea vulgari medela utemur, ut his quibus nasus et digiti ad glaciem frigeant et his quibus fame dentes exasperascunt baccas assentationis sub lingua devolvendas demus.

33 *Pat.* Enim, mater, et quid, quod in *Amphorismis* scriptum extat, an illud improbas: 'abradendum supercilium, occiput capillo integendum manusque inspuendas esse,' que quidem medendi ratio paulo sumptu fiat?

34 *Nec.* Multa sine sumptu facta, posthac dispendium afferunt. Ac nescis quam illud supercilium setosum grande multis interdum es attulerit? Neque tamen curationem ipsam improbo quam
35 nonnullis profuisse palam est. Sed alius accommodatior de his rebus erit disserendi locus. Nunc opus est ad principes, qui te maiorem in modum expectant, properes.

Pat. At quos me ais expectare principes, mater?

36 *Nec.* Te quidem hi principes prestolantur, filia, qui in lubrico constituti contra perflantem austrum audaces reptant: nam impetu et appulsu turbinis prostrati obdurescent.

37 *Pat.* Ego eos, mater, non satis novi quonam terrarum loco sedeant.

Patience. I shall. "Ointment made from the essence of diligence and labor." How valuable! It must cost thirty drachmas an ounce. Oh no, wretched me!

Necessity. Damn you, daughter! Have you broken the jar?   29

Patience. Please don't think I did it on purpose, mother; it was bad luck. The canister was greasy and slippery, and slipped from my hands. Stop being so angry, mother. We'll soon replace this   30 ointment. At home I have large bundles of this herb of labor.

Necessity. I'll stop being angry, then. But where shall we find the   31 essence of diligence, which has already dried up? It grieves me, for without diligence, labor is completely useless.

Patience. Since that is lacking, we'll use another remedy that is available.

Necessity. Your carelessness forces us do so, daughter. We'll employ   32 a popular cure. To those whose noses and fingers are chilled by frost, and to those whose teeth ache from hunger, we shall give berries of flattery to dissolve under their tongues.

Patience. Tell me, mother, do you reject what is written in the   33 *Aphorisms?*[25] "The patient must shave his brow, grow his hair long in back, and spit on his hands." This remedy costs little.

Necessity. Many things that cost nothing eventually make us pay.   34 Aren't you aware that a bristling brow has often caused many great debts? But I won't reject a cure that has been shown to help some people. Still, there will be another time better suited   35 to discussing these things. At present you must hurry to the rulers, who anxiously await you.

Patience. Which rulers do you mean, mother?

Necessity. Those rulers await you, daughter, who in their danger-   36 ous situation crawl boldly against a continual south wind. Laid low by the onslaught and impact of the whirlwind, they will become hard and callous.

Patience. I don't really know where they live, mother.   37

Nec. Deducam.

38 *Pat.* Quid tum? Illis utrumne et supercilium abradi iubebimus?

Nec. De isthoc in tempore consulemus. Sed reges fortassis deceat pretiosius curari; itaque potius emplastro spei eos pulchre illiniemus. Posthac ad illam nostram catervam studiosorum, apud quos assidue diversor, applicabimus.

39 *Pat.* Vin fortassis et eos eodem ipso spei emplastro delibutos reddamus?

Nec. Minime.

40 *Pat.* Quid ita?

Nec. Quia pallidis et enervatis delitie tales non conveniunt.

Pat. Eos idcirco sola Chroni cantione curabo.

41 *Nec.* Laudo. Sed inter eundum de his fortassis quippiam providebimus. Sequere.

Pat. I pre. Sequor.

: 6 :

Felicitas

1 Itali mercatores patrum nostrorum etate ab Scytharum exercitu victore servos complures coemerant captos bello ex Asia, quam provinciam duce Themirio Scytharum rege decies centenis et
2 ducentis milibus armatorum ea tempestate vastarant. Emptos ergo servos in Italiam navi deportarunt, cumque Tarentum celebrem Italie portum incolumes salvisque rebus appulissent, placuit eo in loco festum diem agere ac superis congratulari, quod secundis ventis et percommoda navigatione exacta patriam repetissent.
3 Idcirco quos navi advexerant servos omnes in vetustum, quod in eo aderat litore, templum eduxerunt: quo loco, peracto sacrificio,

Necessity. I shall lead you there.

Patience. What then, shall we bid them shave their brows?   38

Necessity. We shall decide that at the proper moment. But perhaps
    it is fitting for kings to have a more expensive cure. We shall
    rub them liberally with a plaster of hope. Then we shall join the
    crowd of scholars, with whom I regularly stay.

Patience. Do you wish to apply to them the same plaster of hope?   39

Necessity. By no means.

Patience. Why not?   40

Necessity. Such luxuries are ill suited to the pale and languid.

Patience. Then I shall treat them with Chronus' incantation.

Necessity. I approve. Perhaps on our way we shall find something   41
    for them. Follow me.

Patience. Go ahead. I'll follow you.

: 6 :

Happiness

In our fathers' day, some Italian merchants bought a number of   1
slaves from the victorious Scythian army. The slaves had been
taken prisoner in the war when Tamerlane, king of the Scythians,
laid waste to Asia with his army of 1,200,000 soldiers.[26] The mer-   2
chants then transported the slaves they had bought to Italy by
ship. When they had safely arrived with all their goods at the busy
Italian port of Taranto, they decided to make holiday there to
thank the gods for the favorable winds and the prosperous voyage
which had brought them back to their homeland. All the slaves   3
they had brought on their ship they led to an ancient temple on
the shore. Having completed their sacrifice there, they stationed

quanta illic convenire arbitrabantur presidia armatorum pro valvis
templi disposuere, ne quis audax servus fugam aut arriperet aut

4 tumultum excitaret. Posthec eosdem omnes servos largissimis epu-
lis et vino donarunt bonamque ut haberent spem his admodo verbis hortati sunt:

5 'Adeste animis, homines. Vos quidem primum meminisse oportet non facinore nostro aliquo sed iniuria prepotentis Fortune in
istos adversos casus vos incidisse: a nobis enim nulla vobis impo-
sita servitus, sed nostro beneficio ab his qui libertatem vobis ra-

6 puere, ad mitiores patronos traducti estis. Ferte idcirco quam fata
sortem dedere animo forti et curis omnino libero, ac mementote
Italos cum ceteris virtutibus, tum pietate esse insignes: vetusta
apud nos religio est pietas vetusque disciplina per humanitatem et

7 facilitatem imperare. Sperate ergo atque expectate a nobis que a
piissimis hominibus sperari aut expectari uspiam possint. Interim
vino omnem merorem et acerbitatem lenite et mitigate, festoque
hoc die tristia desideria obliviscamini. Itaque tu, dispensator, prebe
merum; vos vero considentes bibite ac dehinc bene epoti cantate.'

8 Itaque, his dictis, cena procumbentibus apponitur, qua quidem
bene avide et neque non multis cum sermonibus absumpta, evenit
fortassis ut quibusque horum qui novam servitutem inierant in

9 mentem redierit patria, parentes, native atque item coniuges. Ex
quo mirum inter omnes silentium obortum est. Post interim in
huiusmodi querelas suspiriis et lachrimis irruperunt.

10 Qui enim servi seniores aderant: 'O nos infelices!' inquiunt, 'o
miseram nostram miseriam, qua nos etate in laribus et sedibus
maiorum defessos artus nostros per quietem sustentare oportuit,

11 ea nos apud externas gentes agitamur! O nos calamitosos, qui ab
omni domesticarum rerum copia in rerum omnium egestatem de-
cidimus! O cari nepotes, quorum ope et adminiculis iam nostre
senectutis onera levabantur! O desertam familiam, quam nos mo-

12 nitis et consilio nostro tuebamur atque regebamus! O idcirco

by the door an armed guard which they thought large enough to discourage any bold slaves from escaping or fomenting a riot. Then, lavishing plentiful food and wine on the slaves, they urged 4 them to hope for the best in roughly the following words.

"Take heart, people. First, recall that adversity has befallen you 5 not through some misdeed of ours, but through the injustice of all-powerful Fortune. For we have imposed no slavery on you. Rather, thanks to us, you have been transferred from those who robbed you of freedom to milder masters. So bear the lot which 6 the fates have given you with a stout spirit entirely free of cares. And remember that Italians are distinguished for many virtues, and particularly for their mercy. Our age-old religion is gentleness, and our ancient discipline is to rule with humanity and indulgence. Hope, therefore, and expect of us all that can be hoped and 7 expected of merciful men. For the moment, assuage and alleviate your bitter grief with feasting and drinking, and forget your sad longings on this holiday. You there, steward, pour them unmixed wine. And you, slaves, drink as you sit here, and having drunk your fill, sing."

When they had spoken, dinner was set before the recumbent 8 slaves. When they had devoured it eagerly amid much conversation, it chanced that some of the newly enslaved remembered their homeland, parents, children, and also their spouses. A strange si- 9 lence now fell over them all. Then with sighs and tears, they occasionally burst into laments and complaints like these.

The oldest slaves spoke first: "How unhappy we are! What 10 misery is ours, who were driven to a foreign land at an age when we ought to have been quietly resting our weary limbs in our ancestral homes! How unfortunate we are, fallen from the abun- 11 dance of our family goods to this dearth of all goods! How dear our grandchildren, whose aid and support used to lighten the burdens of our old age! How forsaken the family that we guarded and guided by our advice and counsel! How bitter our fortune 12

49

fortunam acerbissimam, qui nostris imperare consuevimus, aliis servire hac etate tantis honestissimis rebus perfuncti discemus! In hec igitur tempora a tantis bellis et vulneribus servati sumus!'

13   Hec senes. Quas res cum abunde conquesti essent, illico successere alii etate et ordine sedentes proximi. 'Quin immo vos, patres,
14 felicissimos putamus!' inquiunt. 'Servitus quidem communis nostra est omnium sors; verum in tanta miseria optime vobiscum agitur, quod propediem vos in libertatem non immatura mors
15 vindicatura est. Vos senes, vos honoribus functi, vobis liberi et nepotes crevere; vos cives et patria et ⟨pace⟩ et bello experta caros habuit, ut recordatione harum rerum dignissimarum afflictum so-
16 lari animum pulchre liceat. Nos vero quo potissimum tempore armis et consilio mereri, quo tempore gratiam et auctoritatem nancisci, quo tempore liberorum voluptate perfrui ceperamus, quo denique tempore nobis felicitatem partam arbitrabamur, o nos miseros! eo maxime tempore servi effecti sumus.

17   'Omnia et que adepti eramus et que sperare nos posse in posterum dabatur, eadem una fortune iniuria amisimus, ut nihil relictum nobis sit nisi ut mori admodum, cum velimus, liceat. Verum et quid tum? eo pacto morte intempestiva et acerbissima quid assequemur, nisi ut desperata libertate miseri in servitute moriamur?'

18   Cumque ita lugendo multas huiusmodi adiecissent comparationes, quibus seniores pro fato presenti felices, se autem etate minores infelices esse disceptarent, iuniores adolescentes servi his verbis fortunam incusantes suam successere:

19   'Quod si vos grandiores natu infelices estis, nos infelicissimi infelicissimorum sumus. Nos soli miseri a quibus amate sponse, nostre veneres cupidinesque, nostre delitie, ex ipso sinu decerpte sunt. Nobis hic erat annus futurus refertus voluptatibus: ducenda
20 uxoria pompa, spectandi ludi, recitanda poemata. O igitur miseriam nostram! pro coniuge salinarum sacculos et cistellas

that we, who used to command, must learn to serve others after a lifetime of honorable service. Have we, then, been spared through many wars and wounds only to see this day?"

Thus spoke the elders. When they had lamented at length, those next in age and rank followed them. "We consider you most fortunate, fathers," they said. "Slavery is the common lot of us all, but in such misery you fare well, since timely death will soon set you free. As elders, you have enjoyed honors, have seen your grandchildren grow, and have been valued as citizens by your country both in peace and war. You may easily console your afflicted spirits with the memory of such worthy deeds. As for us, just at the moment when we had begun to gain merit by arms and counsel, to acquire favor and authority, and to take pleasure in our children, at the very moment when we thought that we had achieved happiness — precisely at this moment, alas, we were made slaves!

"All that we had already accomplished, and all we could hope for the future, we have lost in one violent act of fortune. Nothing remains for us but to be permitted to die. And what then? What would we gain from such an untimely and bitter death, except to despair of our freedom and to die as wretches in slavery?"

After they had mournfully added many such comparisons, arguing that the elders were fortunate in their present fate, while they themselves, being younger, were unfortunate, the most junior of the slaves followed in lamenting their own misfortune in these words:

"If you who are older are unfortunate, we are the most unfortunate of the unfortunate, and we alone are wretched. Our beloved brides, our amours and passions, have been snatched from our embrace, and this coming year was to be filled with pleasures for us. We were to lead wedding processions, attend games, and recite poems.[27] What misery, then, is ours! Instead of our wives, we

13

14

15

16

17

18

19

20

metallorum amplectemur, pro pompa uxoria pecudes agende
erunt, pro ludis lutea porcorum duella, pro poemate has acerbissi-
21 mas querelas et lachrimas effundemus! Vale amata, valete arma
eque atque gratissimi ludi, valete cithare et dulcia amissa studia:
nos servimus et vivimus. O infelices amici, quos pari infortunio
coram affectos intuemur! O nos longe infelicissimos, quos tanta
22 calamitas a dulcissimorum sodalium cetu abripuit! Lugete, litora,
lugete; et una plangite nobiscum, maria; deplorate, venti, hunc
nostrum condolendum casum.'

Hec ubi iuvenes servi pene in infinitum deplorassent, consecute
sunt matres parvos natos multis cum lachrimis exosculantes.
23 Denique inquiunt: 'Quanta nostra hec miseria est! Quanti nos
dolores urgent, ut querelis ad incusandam Fortunam desit vox cui
24 meror pectoribus nostris viam precluserit! Tum hi parvuli nos penitus conficiunt cumulis miseriarum: hos enim immeritos pre omnibus infelicissimos esse intuemur. Quod si servitus dolori est, hi
25 ad perpetuum dolorem nati sunt. O filii calamitosissimi! Vobis
neque parentum pietas, neque piissimi alicuius affinis vestri officium ullum pro tanta rerum iactura poterit prodesse. Moriamur!'

26 Dumque sic inter lamentandum matres gravi dolore correpte
natos ad sinum et frontem dulce prementes repente obmutuissent,
iterum senes et omnis ferme reliqua etas una voce huiusmodi responsum dedere: 'Soli pueri infantesque in hac deterrima fortuna
felices estis, siquidem quod pati opus sit, id sine ulla animi contu-
27 macia perpeti discetis. Nulla vobis amissorum gaudiorum recorda-
tio merorem suscitabit, nulla fortune mutatio vobis sortem, nisi
plane meliorem, afferet.'

28 Has igitur lamentationes mercatores cum audissent, commise-
rati illico silentium lugentibus imposuere vinaque abunde misceri
iussere, ut eiusmodi turbulentas curas largo mero abluerent ac

shall embrace sacks of salt and crates of ore. Instead of wedding processions, we must lead herds of livestock. Instead of games, we shall wrestle with pigs in the mud. Instead of poems, we shall utter these bitter plaints and laments. Farewell, favorite things; farewell, arms, horses, and our dearest pastimes; farewell, lutes and the sweet studies we have lost! We serve and survive. Unfortunate are our friends, whom we behold before us stricken by equal misfortune! But most unfortunate by far are we, whom calamity has torn from the company of our sweetest companions! Mourn, O shores, mourn; weep with us, O seas; lament, O winds, our pitiful fate!"

After the young slaves had made their almost interminable laments, the mothers took their turn, fondly kissing their small children amid many tears. They said, "How great is our misery! What great sorrows oppress us! Yet we have no voice for complaints to accuse our fortune, for grief has choked our lungs. Our little ones completely overwhelm us as the culmination of our miseries. For we see that they are the most unfortunate of all, being innocent, since if slavery causes sorrow, they have been born to perpetual sorrow. O most ill-starred children, neither your parents' devotion nor a merciful relative's mercy can compensate your disastrous loss! Let us die!"

The mothers broke off their lamentations in sharp pain; and suddenly falling silent, they tenderly hugged and kissed their children. Then the elders, together with nearly all the slaves of other ages, in turn made this reply. "Only you infants and children are fortunate in this worst of fortunes, for you will learn to endure without defiance whatever must be borne. No recollection of lost joys will provoke your grief. No reversal of fortune can do anything but improve your lot."

When the merchants had heard these laments, they took pity and at once imposed silence on the grieving slaves. They ordered that wine be poured generously so that the slaves might wash away

29 denique tristitiam et langorem somno sepelirent. Qui vero inter mercatores prudentiores aderant: 'Vidistisne,' inquiunt, 'socii, ex variis istorum lamentis, ut omnis humana ratio, quidquid de felicitate atque infelicitate diiudicet, ea in re tantum opinione ducatur?'

their turbulent cares with bountiful drink and bury in slumber their sadness and weariness. The more sagacious merchants said: 29 "Have you seen, friends, from their diverse laments, how all human judgment concerning happiness and unhappiness is shaped solely by opinion?"

LIBER II

1 *Prohemium ad Leonardum Arretinum*

Pan, deus Arcadie, is qui Musas primus docuit dicere, ludi gratia
2 tres ad mercatum fistulas clauditibias attulerat. Une quidem erant
ex ebore, in quibus gemmarum ornamenta et omnis antiquitatis
memoria miri artificis manu insculpta pulcherrime aderant, quas
profecto ipse deum rex posset, dignitate servata, inflare; sed in illis
hoc aderat vitii, quod sonitum referebant penitus nullum. His erat
3 inscriptum pretium dragmarum centum. Altere ex citro percise,
bellissimis signis et omni gemmarum splendore illustres, quas ipse
Orpheus, reliquis omnibus spretis, cuperet; sed in his hoc aderat
vitii, quod inflate non sonitum, sed absurdum crepitum referebant.
4 Illisque inscriptum pretium ducente erant dragme. Tertie erant
puellares fistule ex arundine palustri, cera et iunco iuncte, rudes,
nulla manu expolite, sed que claram et festivissimam vocem ede-
rent. His pretium petebat dragmas nihilominus trecentas.

5 Quas tu me fistulas, si affuissem, earum trium censes appetisse?
Neque enim omnes tibi sumus similes, qui ad ingenii doctrine⟨que⟩
divitias summam quoque vim et copiam eloquentie adcumularas.
6 Et hi quidem sumus, qui antiquius ad laudem ducimus posse vel
ipsos rusticos in triviis ad saltum et festivitatem puerili hoc nostro
et inelimato dicendi genere movere, quam infinitis ornamentis
7 comparandis per silentium consenescere. Quod etsi fortassis fit his
nostris intercenalibus, ut aures multitudinis offendantur, non
tamen est cur nolim hoc pacto potius dicendo quam tacendo id
eniti, ut me docti, tuque in primis hac etate litterarum princeps,
Leonarde, studiosum esse intelligas atque idcirco vehementius

BOOK II

Preface to Leonardo Bruni of Arezzo

1

Pan, the Arcadian god who first taught the Muses to sing, as a jest took to market three shepherd's pipes. The first set of pipes were of ivory, and on them were most beautiful ornaments in gems and remembrances of all antiquity carved by a craftsman's wonderful artistry. Even the king of the gods could have played on them with no loss of dignity, but they had the defect of producing virtually no sound whatsoever. The price written on them was one hundred drachmas. The second set of pipes, carved of citron wood, were remarkable for their marvelous reliefs and the utter splendor of their gems. Orpheus himself would have spurned all others and desired them, but they had the defect, when blown, of producing no sound but a discordant creak. The price written on them was two hundred drachmas. The third set of pipes were a child's toy made of swamp reeds joined by wax and rushes, rough and not finished by any artisan, but they sent forth a clear and joyous sound. For these, Pan asked no less than three hundred drachmas.

Which of the three pipes do you think I would have wanted, if I had been there? Not all of us resemble you, who add the great power and abundance of your eloquence to your wealth of talent and learning. For my part, I think that I win greater praise if my puerile and unpolished style moves peasants in the streets to dancing and merriment, than if I grow old in silence devising countless ornaments. Now, if it happens that the ears of the masses are offended by these *Dinner Pieces*, I see no reason why I should not strive, by my speech rather than my silence, to be recognized as a scholar and deeply loved by men of learning, especially by you, Leonardo, who are the foremost man of letters in

57

8 diligas. Namque, ut Sostratum ad Arrium philosophum dixisse
ferunt, 'docti' quidem 'doctos servabunt, si docti erunt,' ita et studiosus studiosum diliget, si erit studiosus.

9 Que res cum ita sint, eo instituto iussi ad te hunc secundum
nostrum intercenalium libellum deferri, ut cum his artibus, quibus
tu omnium approbatione et consensu cunctos exsuperas, me
quoque aliquid adhibuisse opere et diligentie intelligas, tum me
10 proinde tibi cariorem habeas. Cui viro humanissimo si, ut cupio,
nostra scripta sensero non displicere, tuo iudicio et auctoritate
confirmatus pergam summis vigiliis et omnibus nervis id assequi,
ut et nobis non omnino omnia doctrine ornamenta defuisse videantur.

11 Tu interim hunc nostrum libellum perleges et emendabis. Is
quidem ostendit quam sint hominum cupiditates et animorum
motus penitus inter se varii quamque inepte a diis ea exposcantur
que in manibus nostris adsunt, mortalique cuique ferme semper
aliquid adesse quod eius animum excruciet: alios parsimonie ita
esse deditos, ut etiam aliorum liberalitatem oderint; alios avaritia
12 perire; denique plus interdum ex avaritia dispendii quam ex prodigalitate extare; incommodum quidem esse paupertatem atque
proinde fortassis prestare nos avaros haberi quam pauperes; sed
turpe esse nummum ut optimum deorum colere; divitiarumque
usu magis quam copia gaudere sapientem oportere.

::   I   ::

Oraculum

1 *Philar.* Demiror Apollinem isthunc marmoreum, quem circum
vulgus ille hominum adstat, a pristina primevaque sua benignitate atque liberalitate degenerasse: qui enim egenis pariter atque

our age. For as they say Sostratus told the philosopher Arrius, the 8
learned will save the learned if they are truly learned. And so a
scholar will love another scholar, if he is truly a scholar.[1]

For these reasons, I have had this second book of my *Dinner* 9
Pieces sent to you. In this way, when you see that I too have dedicated my diligent efforts to those arts in which everyone lauds and
concedes your supremacy, you will hold me all the more dear. And 10
if, as I hope, I sense that these works do not displease your generous spirit, I shall be encouraged by your judgment and authority,
and shall continue by my long vigils and strenuous efforts to show
that I did not entirely lack all the ornaments of learning.

For the moment, you will peruse and emend this little book of
mine.[2] It shows how utterly various are the desires and emotions 11
of mankind, how foolishly we ask the gods for things already in
our possession, and how every mortal nearly always has a problem
that torments him. Some are so devoted to frugality that they detest the generosity of others. Others perish through avarice. In 12
fact, avarice is sometimes more costly than prodigality. Poverty is
harmful, and thus it may be preferable to be considered a miser
rather than a pauper. It is base to worship money as the highest of
gods. And it is in the use of his wealth, rather than in its abundance, that the wise man should rejoice.

: I :

The Oracle

Philargirius. I am amazed that this marble statue of Apollo, sur- 1
rounded by that mob of bystanders, has abandoned its former
habitual generosity and liberality. It used to utter oracles free of

divitibus gratis responsa reddere consueverat, idem nunc nisi
2   premio accepto non loquitur. Utrumne idcirco et nobis hominibus erit turpe si movebimur donis? Sed accedo illuc propius, ut
responsum primus ab deo coemam.

    — Oro, Apollo, fave. Hoc plaustrum rusticanis instrumentis
onustum dono affero. Divitem me esse affecto.

3 *Ap.* Interdiu omne id ferramentorum genus defossum habeto; ves-
peri tanquam in speculo ipsum te in illis conspectato.

Philar. Hos ego labores semper fugiendos duxi.

Ap. Nullum ergo dedecus vereare.

4 *Proc.* Oro, Apollo, fave. Has gemmas atque nummos dono affero.
Invidiam metuo.

Ap. Eas tu pecunias inter bonos distribuito.

Proc. Non novi.

Ap. Plus quam duo te una oculi caveto spectent.

Proc. Haud quidem propter eam licet.

Ap. Operam ut plures tibi similes adsint dato.

Proc. Durum.

Ap. Ergo ne metue interimi.

5 *Philot.* Oro, Apollo, fave. Has tuas conscriptas laudes dono affero.
Laudari cupio.

Ap. Quam ob rem te laudent prebeto; id cum desit, multos ipse
collaudato.

6 *Scur.* Oro, Apollo, fave. Hanc ego tubam dono affero. Complures
opto iungere amicitias.

Ap. Isthac in tuba nomina illorum inscribito, frequens salutato, in
dies munus dato.

7 *Zel.* Oro, Apollo, fave. Hanc pateram lachrimis plenam dono affero. Desidero amores oblivisci.

Ap. Tuum his lachrimis tergus abluito.

Zel. Dolet perdere.

8 *Ap.* Mutus ac cecus esto, in primisque te minimum amari credito.

charge to both poor and rich alike, but now it speaks only upon payment.[3] Is it shameful for us men, then, if even we are 2 swayed by gifts and offerings? I shall approach and be the first to buy an oracle.

—Be gracious, Apollo, I pray. I bring this cart laden with rustic tools as an offering. I aspire to be rich.

Apollo. By day keep all such iron implements buried in the ground. 3 In the evening view yourself in them as in a mirror.

Philargirius. I have always thought such labors should be avoided.

Apollo. Then fear no disgrace.

Nobleman. Be gracious, Apollo, I pray. I bring these jewels and 4 coins as an offering. I fear envy.

Apollo. Distribute this wealth among good men.

Nobleman. I don't know any.

Apollo. Beware lest more than two eyes watch you.

Nobleman. Envy doesn't allow it.

Apollo. Seek the aid of people like you.

Nobleman. That's difficult.

Apollo. Then have no fear of being killed.

Philotimus. Be gracious, Apollo, I pray. I bring these eulogies of 5 you as an offering. I wish to be praised.

Apollo. Give others reason to praise you; if you can't, then praise many others.

Scurra. Be gracious, Apollo, I pray. I bring this trumpet as an of- 6 fering. I wish to form many friendships.

Apollo. Inscribe their names on the trumpet. Visit them often; perform daily favors.

Jealous. Be gracious, Apollo, I pray. I bring this bowl of tears as an 7 offering. I want to forget my love affairs.

Apollo. Wash your back with these tears.

Jealous. Loss is painful.

Apollo. Be mute and blind; and above all, don't believe that you're 8 loved.

Al. Oro, Apollo, fave. Hanc dono capram affero. Velim pudicam habere coniugem.

9   *Ap.* Eam tu capram nunquam solam aut solutam sinito; alienaque in domo quam in tua minime inspuito; tuisque in laribus nullas aranearum telas excrescere permittito.

10 *Libr.* Oro, Apollo fave. Hos libros dono affero. Aveo videri litteratus.

Ap. Sis, atque ut sis noctes diesque assidue lectitato.

Libr. Tedet; longeque malo videri quam esse.

Ap. Omnium ergo litteratorum obtrectator esto.

11 *Ypol.* Oro, Apollo, fave. Hec centum lintea dono affero. Uxorem meam esse in me facilem laboro.

Ap. Cum ipsum te apud illam receperis, his omnibus linteis caput tuum obnubito.

12 *Cert.* Oro, Apollo, fave. Hunc Pegaseum equum dono affero. Contendo meos inimicos superare.

Ap. Certans bene occluso hostio per fenestras aut salutato aut execrator; ac persequens fugiensve hunc ipsum equum fatigato.

13 *Meg.* Oro, Apollo, fave. Hos servos dono affero. Studeo me esse amplissimum.

Ap. Hos tu servos liberos totidemque liberos servos in dies facito.

14 *Meg.* Difficile.

Ap. Da operam multi te aut diligant aut metuant.

15 *Meg.* Quid si metui prestet?

Ap. Certamen aut vindictam in eternum prosequere.

Meg. Quid ubi amari iuvet?

Ap. Amato.

16 *Erast.* Oro, Apollo, fave. Has faces meis suspiriis incensas dono affero. Amata potiri ardeo.

Ap. His tu facibus amate pectus incalescat facito.

Erast. Spernor.

Ap. Obdura; plura quidem sedens quam currens capies.

Alochocratus. Be gracious, Apollo, I pray. I bring this goat as an offering. I wish to have a chaste wife.[4]

Apollo. Never leave this goat alone or at large. Spit in no one's 9 home but your own. Let no cobwebs grow in your house.

Libripeta. Be gracious, Apollo, I pray. I bring these books as an 10 offering. I wish to seem a man of letters.

Apollo. Become one by reading night and day. Earn the praise of others; if they don't praise you, praise others.

Libripeta. That bores me; I would rather seem than be.[5]

Apollo. Then be a detractor of all men of letters.

Ypolochus. Be gracious, Apollo, I pray. I bring these hundred linen 11 sheets as an offering. I strive to have a compliant wife.

Apollo. When you go to her, cover your head with all these sheets.

Certomopora. Be gracious, Apollo, I pray. I bring this Pegasean 12 horse as an offering. I strive to defeat my enemies.

Apollo. When you fight, firmly bar your door; then greet or curse them from your window. Tire this horse in pursuit or flight.

Megalophronus. Be gracious, Apollo, I pray. I bring these slaves as 13 an offering. I am eager to become great.

Apollo. Each day free some slaves, and enslave as many free men.

Megalophronus. That's difficult. 14

Apollo. See that many either love or fear you.[6]

Megalophronus. What if it is better to be feared? 15

Apollo. Always seek rivalry or revenge.

Megalophronus. What if it is good to be loved?

Apollo. Love.

Erastus. Be gracious, Apollo, I pray. I bring these torches lit by my 16 sighs as an offering. I am burning to possess my beloved.

Apollo. Warm her breast with these torches.

Erastus. I am spurned.

Apollo. Persist. You'll gain more by encamping than by running.

17 *Philod.* Oro, Apollo, fave. Hunc ensem iaspide ornatum dono affero. Famam concupisco.

Ap. Malos frutices eo ense cedito; iaspidem nitidissimam servato;
tum et in cacuminibus montium tecum ipse luctans sudato.

18 *Eth.* Oro, Apollo, fave. Hos soccos ex solido auro graves dono affero. Prudentem me esse studeo.

Ap. Eos tu soccos cursitans habeto, annosque integros decem lin-
guas tantum atque oculos comedito.

19 *Bard.* Oro, Apollo, fave. Hunc scipionem eburneum dono affero.
Cautum me atque astutum esse quero.

Ap. Eo tu scipione, quocumque agas, iter pretentato, omnique in
re quippiam subdubitato.

20 *Pen.* Oro, Apollo, fave. Quandoquidem nihil habeo preter verba
que dono dedam, Apollo, tue sunt partes efficere ut possim re

21 multo plura afferre quam ipse polliceor modo. Tu si me divitem
feceris, tripodes argentos, candelabra aurea, smaragdis onusta
dono afferam. Quid respondes, Apollo? (Obmutuit. Ipsi quoque
dii nos egenos adeo spernunt?). At unum hoc iterum atque
iterum precor obtestorque, Apollo, gratis dato: nequeo paupertatem ferre.

22 *Ap.* Eam tu arbori, infelicissime, suspendito.

Pen. Ipsum me suspendam iubet. Abeo.

∶ 2 ∶

Parsimonia

1 *Per.* Exeo ut revisam an istorum quispiam veniat: nam hi duo senes convivas morantur. Sed eccum Micrologum. — Salve, homo.
At ubinam Philocerdum nostrum dimisisti?

Philodoxus. Be gracious, Apollo, I pray.[7] I bring this sword studded   17
with jasper as an offering. I desire fame.

Apollo. Cut harmful plants with this sword. Keep the jasper radi-
ant. When you arrive at the summit, wrestle with yourself and
sweat.

Ethiconomus. Be gracious, Apollo, I pray. I bring these heavy slip-   18
pers of solid gold as an offering. I aspire to be prudent.

Apollo. Wear these slippers as you run; and for ten years feed only
on tongues and eyes.

Dullard. Be gracious, Apollo, I pray. I bring this ivory staff as an   19
offering. I seek to be cautious and astute.

Apollo. In whatever you do, test the way first with this staff. In
every affair, have doubts.

Penus. Be gracious, Apollo, I pray. Since I have nothing but words   20
to bring as an offering, it is up to you, Apollo, to see that I can
bring more than I just promised. If you make me rich, I will   21
bring as an offering silver tripods and golden candelabra laden
with emeralds. What is your answer? (Apollo is silent! Even
the gods scorn the needy.) Yet I beseech and implore you again
and again, Apollo; give me a gift. I cannot bear poverty.

Apollo. Hang it from a tree, wretch.   22

Penus. He bids me hang myself? I'm leaving.

: 2 :

Frugality

Periphronus. I'm going outside to see if any of my guests are arriv-   1
ing; these two old men keep them waiting. But here's Micrologus. Greetings, friend. Where have you left our Philocerdus?

65

2   *Micr.* Illico aderit; nam is iussit ut se prevenirem huc ad vos, quoad cum nonnullis mercatoribus Rhodiis paulum negotii conficeret. Sed tu, mi Periphrone, quidnam tibi vis? Sanusne es?

    Per. Quid ita?

3   *Micr.* Ne vero tu, uti ex puero tuo huc veniens modo intellexi, nobis familiaribus et domesticis tuis cenam tam lautam atque sumptuosam parasti?

    Per. Ut decuit.

4   *Micr.* Cave isthuc ita existimes: namque inter amicos parsimoniam, quam istiusmodi exa⟨u⟩ctam profusamque magnificentiam quisque non stultus et tui amans longe approbabit.

5   *Per.* Enecas iamdudum me, dum nunquam de parsimonia mecum cessas eloqui. Sic enim statuo, pusilli admodum atque penitus imbecilli animi esse non sibi, quamdiu iuvat, tamdiu victum affuturum polliceri.

6   *Micr.* Non isthuc inficior. Verum unum hoc te oro: dic, sodes, quid si apud te servi partim librarii, partim pictores, partim tignarii, partim aratores, partim argentarii, partim coqui fossoresve adessent, utrumne uno et eodem opere faciundo omnes illos aut colendo agro aut celandis vasculis exerceres?

7   *Per.* Nequaquam isthuc.

    Micr. Nimirum adeo, si saperes, singulos servos singulis, quibus aptiores et instructiores essent, rebus accommodares?

    Per. Sane cuique suum, ut foret ad ingenium, opus adigerem.

8   *Micr.* Id quidem ipsum censeo in pecunia esse faciundum: non quidem in hunc aut in illum usum pecuniam omnem erogandam, sed partem pecunie in libros, partem in victum, partem ad vestes et supellectilem reliquumve cultum domesticum ita distribuendam esse existimo, ut et ad amicos adiuvandos atque ad casus levandos, qui in vita solent evenire, in tempore non desint tibi.

Micrologus. He'll be here presently.[8] He told me to go ahead and 2
join you, while he finishes a bit of business with some merchants from Rhodes. But what is the matter, Periphronus? Are
you well?

Periphronus. Why do you ask?

Micrologus. Is it true, as I just learned from your servant on the 3
way here, that you've prepared a lavish and elegant dinner for
us, your friends and household?

Periphronus. As was proper.

Micrologus. You mustn't think so. Anyone who is not fool and who 4
cares for you would praise frugality between friends far more
than such sumptuous extravagance.

Periphronus. You've been killing me for a long time with your in- 5
cessant sermons on frugality. In my opinion, it is the sign of a
timorous or irresolute mind to doubt that one will have sustenance as long as one needs.

Micrologus. I don't deny that. But I ask you one thing. Tell me, 6
please: if some of your servants were secretaries, some painters,
some carpenters, some plowmen, some goldsmiths, some cooks,
and some ditchdiggers, would you put them all to work at the
same task, such as tilling the soil or carving bowls?

Periphronus. Of course not. 7

Micrologus. Then you would be wise to assign different servants to
do those tasks for which they were better suited and trained?

Periphronus. Yes, I'd set each his own task according to his abilities.

Micrologus. I think that you should do the same with money: not 8
all of it should be spent on only one thing or another. Rather, I
believe that you ought to apportion part of your money for
books, part for food, and part for clothing, furnishings, or
other maintenance. In this way, you will never lack funds for
aiding friends and for meeting the needs that often arise in life.

9 *Per.* Dixti pulchre. At tu contra, agedum, quid tu si peregre pro-
ficiscens complures haberes comites? utrumne semper is esses
qui vobis ignotas vias primus omnium scrutari atque obire hos-
pitemque, ut cenam sequentibus appararet, longe ante alios
petere ac excitare istiusmodique curis et sollicitudinibus ipsum
te velles afficere?

10 *Micr.* Minime, quin is qui id ageret meo iudicio ineptus et plane
desipiens habendus esset.

Per. Nimirum. Idcirco prudentis est que susceperit itinera, ea iocunde et festive conficere grateque apud eos hospites residere
quos ipsa divertendi hora et via obtulerit.

11 *Micr.* Recte sane.

Per. Id quidem ipsum in vita fieri oportere censeo. Non demum
perpetua et nimium timida vel potius odiosa suspitione cecos
atque ignotos fortune exitus longe indagare neque metu futuri
incommodi ipsum te presentibus bonis defraudare, sed quem
fortuna diem alacrem et, ut ita loquar, candidum attulerit, eum

12 grato et leto animo suscipere, sapientis, ni fallor, est. Mihi autem iocundos dies et festivos quos intercipio, quis hostis, quis
fur, quis casus poterit eripere? Fortune, ni fallor, bona, mi Mi-
crologe, non eorum modo sunt apud quos disposita, sed eorum

13 vel maxime sunt qui illis pulchre sciant perfrui. Denique, cum
ipsum me in dies mortalem memini, quid est quod vel unicum
in annum ipse mihi uspiam prospiciam? Si apud me non ade-
ri⟨n⟩t, non poscent amici; si poscent, fortasse que absint iuste

14 negabimus. Qui vero post nos laboribus nostris se fieri divites
cupiunt, iidem suam sibi industriam longe magis quam nostram
parsimoniam profuisse intelligent.

15 *Micr.* Incidit in mentem quod priscos philosophos dicere solitos
aiunt: aliquos ita abunde et profuse vivere ac si essent propediem morituri; alios autem ita parce et tenuiter victum agere ac

16 si eternam cum superis vitam depacti essent. Horum utrique
apud prudentes vituperatione digni sunt. Atque ex his ego sum

Periphronus. Well said. But tell me this. If you were journeying 9
abroad with several companions, would you always be the first
to explore unfamiliar roads, or to seek out an innkeeper and bid
him prepare dinner for those who follow? Would you choose to
subject yourself to such cares and worries?

Micrologus. By no means. Rather, anyone who did so should be 10
thought foolish and even mad.

Periphronus. Exactly. It is the part of a wise man to complete the
journey he has undertaken with pleasure and good cheer, and
to lodge gladly with the hosts that the time and place may offer.

Micrologus. Exactly.[9] 11

Periphronus. I think we must do the same in life. Constant fearful
and odious misgivings should not make us probe the blind and
unknowable ways of fortune. Nor should we forego present
goods through fear of future harm. Unless I am mistaken, a
wise man will face with cheerful pleasure whatever glad and
sunny day fortune brings him. What enemy, thief, or mishap 12
can snatch from me the joyful and festive days I enjoy? Unless
I err, my dear Micrologus, the goods of fortune belong less to
those who merely possess them than to those who wisely put
them to the best use. In short, if I bear in mind each day that I 13
am mortal, why should I plan even a year ahead? If I lack the
goods of fortune, my friends will not ask for them; or if they
perhaps do, I shall refuse to give them what I lack. If some 14
people want to grow rich by our labors after we are gone, they
will realize that their own industry is more profitable than our
frugality.

Micrologus. This reminds me of a saying attributed to the ancient 15
philosophers, namely, that some men live excessively and lavishly as if they would soon die; while others behave strictly and
thriftily as if the gods had granted them eternal life. Both types 16
deserve to be censured by wise men. For my part, I would

qui mallem in eam partem peccari abs te, qua tibi et tuis consu-
17   leres in posterum. Nolim sane tristem et plenam curis diem
atque frontem geras, sed moderatam et honestam vite totius abs
te cupio haberi rationem; eamque ob rem iterum atque iterum
admoneo, des operam ne ulla tibi dies minus amena et volup-
tuosa futura sit neve luxu aliquo in eum locum incidas, quo tibi
18   gravis aliqua aut incommoda fortuna ferenda sit. Nulla quidem
in prodigalitate emolumenta comperies preterquam quod ex
summis divitiis homines detrudat in paupertatem: in qua quidem destituti atque depressi illico parsimoniam laudare et am-
19   plecti discunt. Postremo illud non pretereo, quod te in primis
meminisse oportet: non tibi solum sed tuis quoque te natum
20   esse. Crescent et liberi, crescent et domi rerum perplurimarum
et minime negligendarum non modice neque interrare difficul-
tates: eo tibi prospiciendum est, illuc parare presidia opus est;
omnique cogitatione prudentem meditari convenit, quam nunquam prospera, equabilis perpetuaque cuiquam fortuna sit.

Per. His ego incommodis omnibus perpulchre evitandis accom-
21   modatissimum iampridem modum et rationem adhibui. Nam
cum ortam nobis filiam presensero, illico in marginibus agri
secundum fluvium trecentas ceduas arbores plantabo, que quidem ad annum quindecimum ad grandem virginis dotem, superis volentibus, excreverint (nolentibus enim, ut aiunt, superis,
22   nihil licet); proque maximo et prestantissimo dotali munere
pudicitiam secum a parentibus deferet filia, maribus autem omnium grandis, firma atque stabilis hereditas a me virtutis ar-
23   tiumque optimarum copia et peritia relinquetur. Me vero ita
contra fortune impetum atque iniurias armatum et communitum habeo, ut nullos adversos casus verear. Hoc velim scias, me
nullo posse pacto effici pauperem.

24   *Micr.* Rem miram atque incredibilem predicas.
Per. Tu quoque, dum me audias atque obtemperes, non ignorabis
perpetuo inter affluentes divitias gaudere.

prefer that you err by looking to your future and that of your family. I don't want sadness and worries to fill your day and your feelings; I prefer to follow a moderate and honorable plan of life. I therefore urge you repeatedly to take care that every day is pleasant and pleasurable, and let no extravagance drag you into misfortune or hardship. You will find that prodigality has but one benefit: it plunges men of immense wealth into poverty, so that, downcast and destitute, they learn to praise and embrace frugality. Let me add, finally, that you must remember that you were not born only for yourself, but also for your family.[10] As your children grow, so will the difficulties — neither minor nor infrequent — of the countless affairs that require your attention. You must plan for these needs and provide defenses against them. It befits a wise man to reflect in all his thoughts that fortune is never favorable, just, or constant to anyone.

Periphronus. I long ago devised a means of handily avoiding all such misfortunes. When I learn that we are expecting a daughter, I immediately plant three hundred timber trees along the river at the edge of my property. In fifteen years, these will have grown to supply a large dowry for the girl — if the gods are willing, for it is said that we can do nothing against their will. But as her greatest and noblest dowry, our daughter will learn chaste behavior from her parents. As for my sons, I shall leave them an abundant knowledge of virtue and liberal learning as their greatest and securest inheritance. As for myself, I am so armed and fortified against fortune's attacks and injustices that I fear no misfortunes. I would have you know that nothing can make me a poor man.

Micrologus. What you say is amazing and incredible.

Periphronus. If you hear me and heed me, you will know how to enjoy abundant wealth forever.

Micr. Nihil est quod eque ab te cupiam.

Per. Esto parcissimus.

25 *Micr.* Hen isthuc!

Per. Non rerum, inquam, sed voluntatum atque libidinum: pauca enim volenti, pauca nunquam deerunt.—Sed eccum Philocerdum. Itaque ingrediamur ad convivas.

⦂ 3 ⦂

Gallus

1 Inter gallos gallinaceos, qui aviaria reclusi observabantur, unus, quod omnes porrectas offas atque escas respueret, macie et tristitia 2 admodum confectus iacebat. Hunc conclusi consocii galli cum rogarent quid ita inter tantam rerum affluentiam sese inedia con- 3 ficeret, aiebat consulto id atque prudenter quidem fieri; qui vero voluptatibus indulgerent, eos cum ceteras ob res delirare, tum maxime quod pernitiem atque interitum eo pacto suum accelerari parum intelligerent, siquidem id palam esset non aliam ob causam tam exuberantes preberi escas, nisi ut quamprimum pinguefacti detruncarentur.

4 Cum igitur gallum istum pene macie et langore absumptum paterfamilias intueretur, veritus ne id contagioso aliquo morbo ceteris pullis noxio accidisset, valitudinarium ipsum gallum inter 5 carecta et vepres eiecit. Quem subinde cum exuriens lupus voraret, aiunt inter deplorandum sese eiectum gallum vehementer accu- sasse atque hanc unam rem sibi in primis ad supremum animi dolorem fuisse, quod adeo miseram usque atque egentem inter summas opes vitam duxisset, ut omni spreta voluptate sibi per- petua in miseria vivendum morteque ignobilissima e vita

Micrologus. There is nothing I desire more from you.

Periphronus. Then be extremely frugal.

Micrologus. What's this I hear?   25

Periphronus. I don't mean frugal with possessions, but frugal in your wants and desires. The man who desires few things will never lack them. But here's Philocerdus. Let's go in to join our guests.

: 3 :

The Cock

Among some poultry cocks who were kept shut up in a coop,   1
there was one who rejected all the feed and pellets offered him and
so lay utterly exhausted from emaciation and gloom. When his   2
companions in the cage asked him why he was killing himself by
fasting amid such abundance, he replied that he did so both delib-
erately and wisely. For those who indulged their pleasures were   3
especially mad, since they failed to see that by so doing they hastened their own death and destruction. It was obvious that such
abundant feed was provided solely in order to fatten them quickly
for slaughter.

Now, when the head of the household saw how this cock was   4
practically wasted away with starvation and faintness, he feared
that the reason was a contagious disease which might harm the
other fowls. So he threw the infirm cock into a thicket of brambles   5
and sedge, where a ravenous wolf instantly devoured him. They
say that amid his laments the cast-out cock bitterly reproached
himself; his greatest sorrow was having lived so wretchedly and
poorly amid such great abundance: rejecting any pleasure, he lived

6 discedendum fuerit. Atque preterea mirum in modum gallum eundem ferunt hominem quempiam potius quam truculentam et fe-
   dissimam beluam suo casu depasci optasse.

7   Hanc fabulam nostra in urbe plerique cives ad se pertinere fortassis non negabunt.

: 4 :

Vaticinium

1 *Xerx.* O mores, o civitatem honestam et modestissimam! Itane,
   importuni, ita per impudentiam didicistis cuncta exposcere?
   Iterum precor, sinite vel modicam isthic aream esse ante hos-

2 tium. Tu vero, decrepite astrologe, ne te vulgus opprimat, sedeto intus isthic. Ego vero in limine adero et quas tu ob ocu-
   lorum vitium et cecitatem parum discerneres signa et notas
   hominum referam.

3 *Astr.* Dixti pulchre. Consideo. Sed ea lege consultores admitte, ut
   boni malive quidquid predixero, non ex me id sed ab astris de-
   putent.

4 *Xerx.* Bene est. Clamo. Io cives! sua qui concupiscit fata discere
   huc accedat. Non enim divinum hunc nostrum astrologum pi-
   gebit consuluisse.

5 *Philar.* Adsum.
   Fact. Adsum et ego.

6 *Xerx.* Veniat post unum alter, post illum alius: nam eo pacto sine
   tumultu et turbatione satis fiet omnibus. Audite iterum, cives!

7 namque hoc ex memoria exciderat. Clamo. Io, cives! nummum
   aureum dato quisquis volet sortes explicari suas. — At quo abis
   tu qui tam festinus et properans ad nos ante omnes accursita-
   ras?

in perpetual misery, and died an ignoble death. They also say, sur- 6
prisingly, that the cock wished that his death had nourished a man
rather than a foul and savage beast.

Some citizens of our city will perhaps not deny that this fable 7
applies to them.[11]

: 4 :

Soothsaying

Xerxes. What manners![12] What an honorable and modest city! O 1
  rude churls, is this how in your impudence you demand everything? I ask you again: leave at least a little space before the
  door. And you, feeble old astrologer, sit down inside, where the 2
  mob can't trample you. I'll stand in the doorway and describe
  people's marks and features, since your blind eyes can barely see
  them.

Astrologer. Good idea. I'll sit here. But admit our customers on 3
  one condition. Whether good or bad, they must regard my
  predictions as coming from the stars, not from me.

Xerxes. Fine. I'll cry out. Hark, citizens! If you desire to learn 4
  your fate, come forth. You won't regret having consulted our
  divine astrologer.

Philargirius. Here I am. 5

Factiopora. And here I am.[13]

Xerxes. Get in line one after the other. In that way, we'll satisfy 6
  everyone without crowding and confusion. Hear me again, citizens! I forgot something. I'll cry out. Hark, citizens! Whoever 7
  wants his fortune told, must pay a gold coin. You there, where
  are you going, after you rushed in here in such a hurry before
  the others?

8 *Philar.* Haud quidem longius abero.

   Fact. Sine isthunc miserum, tene me, cape aurum.

9 *Xerx.* Adhibe animum, astrologe. Sunt homini huic, qui aurum prebuit, oculi milvini, capreum guttur, simus nasus, frons rugosa, cervix languida, angustum pectus, spatula hec sublata versus occiput, altera deorsum in pectus delapsa atque depressa, color cinereus. Tenesne qualem descripsi hominem?

10 *Astr.* Est quidem is nimis admodum callidus qui usque aliorum mentes teneat, nimium profecto astutus idem qui verbo aut vestigio unico tam illico voluntates hominum interpretetur!

11 *Fact.* At enim res sic se habet: homo nemo isthoc Philargirio miserior est.

   Astr. Preterea eris pertinax.

   Fact. Mene delitias facitis? Irridetis?

12 *Astr.* Nimis te item suspitiosum exhibes.

   Fact. Ergo restitue. Sat pronosticatum est. Satiastis!

13 *Astr.* Hunc nimis quoque fastidiosum esse oportet, quem tam subita satietas ceperit! Tu, homo, si potis es ipsum te continere, sedeto isthic; vicibus et ordine res ipsa agatur opus est. Cum locus aderit, fata omnia tibi decantabo tua, ut nihil desit.

14 *Fact.* Credin me in ludum incidisse? At sedeo. Sic enim convenit illis obtemperes a quibus quippiam cupias.

   Xerx. Cives, si libet, aperite huic advenienti callem quoad huc appulerit. — Officium nunc vestrum laudo.

15 *Ass.* Cape. Dicito.

   Xerx. O factum liberalissime! Astrologe, is qui nunc primum applicuit aureos mihi in gremium duos adiecit ex ipsa officina!

   Ass. Enimvero ex isthac liberalitate etiam a duris atque invidis

16 hominibus novi exorare obsequia. Tu demum, si rem malam vis effugere, omnia de me ad unguem vaticineris opus est.

   Xerx. Ha ha he, lepidissime!

Philargirius. I won't be gone long.   8

Factiopora. Let the wretch go. Take me next; here's my gold.

Xerxes. Pay attention, astrologer. This man who has offered us   9
gold has a kite's eyes, a goat's throat, and a monkey's nose, a
wrinkled brow, a drooping neck, and a narrow chest. His one
shoulder is raised toward the back of his head while the other
sinks toward his chest, and his complexion is ashen. Can you
picture the man I have described?

Astrologer. A man is overly clever if he reads men's minds, and   10
overly astute if he deduces their desires from a single word or
clue.

Factiopora. That's exactly right. No one is more wretched than   11
that fellow Philargirius.

Astrologer. What's more, you are stubborn.

Factiopora. Are you making fun of me? Are you mocking me?

Astrologer. You're acting too suspicious.   12

Factiopora. Return my money. Enough prophecy! I've had enough.

Astrologer. He must be very squeamish if he's already had enough.   13
You there, if you can calm down, sit over there. We must con-
duct our business in an orderly fashion. When it's your turn,
I'll unfold all your destiny and omit nothing.

Factiopora. Do you think I fell for your game? But I'll sit down.   14
It's best to humor those from whom you desire something.

Xerxes. Citizens, please make a path for this man to approach. I
thank you for your courtesy.

Assotus. Take this. Speak.   15

Xerxes. What generosity! Astrologer, the latest arrival has tossed
in my lap two gold coins fresh from the mint.

Assotus. In fact, by such generosity I know how to win favors even
from obstinate and envious men. Now then, if you want to   16
avoid trouble, you must predict everything about me in detail.

Xerxes. Ha! ha! ha! How charming!

Astr. Et quis est hic insolens usque adeo imperiosus? Describito effigiem istius ipsius.

17 *Xerx.* Huic quidem collum breve est humerique reiecti, frons turgida, gene fucose, porrectus venter.

Astr. At color?

Xerx. Sufflanti in focum persimilis.

18 *Astr.* Prebe huc istius manum.

Xerx. Eccam.

Astr. Hen, quid hoc rei est?

Xerx. Tali, tessere, tabelle.

Astr. Lege istas ipsas tabellas.

19 *Xerx.* Lego.

Astr. At clara voce, ut audiam.

Ass. Nempe ut et audiant omnes: meos enim amores studui nunquam esse occultos.

Xerx. Gero tibi morem, astrologe. Vos vero, cives, prebete operam
20 auscultando, dum has tabellas lego. 'Assotus Bacchidi s.p.d. — Tametsi tua erga me impietas efficit, ut me ceteris amatoribus tuis postponi intelligam et doleam, non eam ob rem tamen, meum mel, alieno in te animo, meum suavium, esse unquam potero. Nam cum menti ludos nostros, mea festivitas, repeto, mea spes, discrucior.'

21 *Astr.* Sat est. Hic igitur vacuus morbis erit nunquam: gutta, emicranea, cruditate atque huiusmodi doloribus et morbis sempiterne laborabit.

22 *Ass.* Missa hec facito, astrologe: si egroti erimus, conducentur medici. Heus! dicito de imperiis deque prestantissimis rebus mecum futurum quid sit!

23 *Astr.* O ineptissime! tu ergo spectas imperia qui vina et popinas oles? Mendicabis!

Ass. Superi te perdant! Mallem id aurum apud Bacchidem epotasse meam, quam igitur revisam. Abeo.

Xerx. Accedat alter.

Astrologer. Who is this insolent and overbearing man? Describe his appearance.

Xerxes. His neck is short, his shoulders thrown back, his forehead 17 swollen, his cheeks rouged, and his belly thrust forward.

Astrologer. His complexion?

Xerxes. Like someone blowing on a fire.

Astrologer. Give me his hand. 18

Xerxes. Here it is.

Astrologer. What's this?

Xerxes. Knucklebones, dice, and a notebook.

Astrologer. Read the notebook.

Xerxes. I shall. 19

Astrologer. Loudly, so that I can hear you.

Assotus. Indeed, let all hear it. I have never striven to conceal my love affairs.

Xerxes. I'll do as you say, astrologer. Citizens, listen carefully as I read this letter. "Assotus send greetings to Bacchis.[14] Although 20 your infidelity causes you to prefer other suitors, I cannot feel resentment, my darling, my sweet. For when I recall our pleasures together, my delight, my hope, I am tormented."

Astrologer. That's enough. This fellow will never be free of sick- 21 ness. He will forever suffer from gout, migraine, indigestion, and other such ills and diseases.

Assotus. Never mind, astrologer. When I get sick, I'll pay for doc- 22 tors. Come, tell me about high offices and splendid affairs: what is in store for me?

Astrologer. Fool, do you seek high offices, when you reek of taverns 23 and inns? You'll go begging!

Assotus. May the gods ruin you! I would rather have drunk up my gold with Bacchis. I'll go to see her.

Xerxes. Next!

24   *Philar.* Dudum affui. Cape aurum.

     Fact. Tentabo rursus. — Duos iterum aureos adicio: tu modo ne is mihi preferatur facito. Accipito. Sic institui perdere, ne se hic nobis anteferri glorietur.

25   *Xerx.* Enim, astrologe, aureos denuo duos porrexit idem ille quem commorari iusseras cuiusve tibi primum effigiem descripseram.

     Astr. An est quisquam isthoc invidentior? Verum tu quidem te-nesne aurum?

26   *Xerx.* Teneo.

     Astr. Serva.

     Fact. Insiste.

     Xerx. Abigenda hec nobis hinc molestia est.

27   *Astr.* Iam id faxo. — Tibi, inquam, improbe, hoc predico: semper acerbissimis curis excruciabere, nullos habebis fidos amicos, omnibus eris odio. Intellextin? Adde his quod tua isthec impro-bitas atque, ut rectius loquar, furia et rabies animi te conficiet atque perdet.

28   *Fact.* Hen, audacissimum ganeonem! Atque, furciferi, publice sic adeo furtum facitis? Redde tu mihi quos extorsisti aureos!

     Xerx. Egone invitus restituam quod ex compacto ac volens de-disti? Minime gentium.

     Fact. Ad iudicium vocabere!

29   *Astr.* Tu quidem prepotens, quo cives prepotentes iudiciis vexare ac iudicia omnia pervertere corrumpereque didicisti, eo nobis impotentibus et plane humilibus comminaris? Non succedet, audax, tuum isthoc inceptum.

30   *Fact.* Tamen conveniam iudices. Illic senties tibi rem esse cum homine gravi et frugi, non repetundarum tantum sed furti atque iniuriarum.

     Xerx. Abiit iratus.

31   *Astr.* In eiusmodi hominibus apud fortes viros nihil minus me-tuendum est quam quod propalam minitantur. Qui enim levi

Philargirius. I was here before. Take this gold.   24

Factiopora. I'll try again, and add two more gold coins. Here, take them, and see that I go first. I've decided to spend my money, so he can't boast being preferred to me.

Xerxes. Well, astrologer, here are two more gold pieces from the   25 man you told to wait, and whose appearance I described to you.

Astrologer. Is there anyone more envious? But you've got his gold?

Xerxes. I do.   26

Astrologer. Keep it.

Factiopora. Proceed.

Xerxes. We must drive away this nuisance.

Astrologer. I'll see to it. You there, reprobate! I predict that you   27 will always be tormented by bitter cares. You'll have no faithful friends; everyone will hate you. Understood? What's more, your shamelessness, or rather your fury and frenzy, will ruin and destroy you.

Factiopora. You shameless debauchee! You scoundrels, do you   28 cheat me thus in public? Give back the coins you extorted from me.

Xerxes. What, should I unwillingly return what you gave willingly agreed to give? Not on your life!

Factiopora. I'll take you to court.

Astrologer. Almighty one, is it your custom to harass mighty citi-   29 zens with your lawsuits, and to pervert and corrupt all court rulings? And do you now threaten us, who are humble and powerless? Your plan won't work, you brazen fellow.

Factiopora. I'll still go to see the judges. Then you'll find that   30 you're being sued by a serious and decent man, charged not only with extortion, but with theft and defamation as well.

Xerxes. He's gone off in anger.

Astrologer. With people like him, the last thing courageous men   31 have to fear is what they threaten in public. People whose anger

indignationis favilla ad iracundie flammas incenduntur, iidem
levi ratione extinguntur.

32   *Xerx.* Adeat igitur alter. — Verum, astrologe mi, quidnam hoc rei
est? Corona hec nostra consultantium rarescit, nullus admodum sese offert. Homo ille contentionibus atque convitiis rem
turbavit nostram.

33   *Philar.* Quin adsum, inquam, et prebeo aurum.

Xerx. Tris ceteri, tu unum atque eundem adulterinum offers?

Philar. Per ego sanctissima et religiosissima numina que vos ad
hec vestra mirifica vaticinia denuntianda colitis perque omnes
superos et inferos deos oro obtestorque, mi prudentissime, mi
sapientissime astrologe, ut quecumque sentias de me, audacter

34   proferas. Non sit tibi hoc tempore mecum ad nummum animus, namque alibi fecero ut intelligas me et memorem esse et
plane liberalem.

Xerx. Aurum prebeat, non verba quisquis divini istius hominis
operam concupiscit.

35   *Astr.* Ceterum et longe difficile atque arduum, tum etiam nonnihil
periculosum est ea que noris omnia explicare; quod nisi
imperium polliceraris, execrabere. Libere que sentias dixeris?
Ad iniuriam accipitur. Denique cum debentur munera, tunc
maxime contenditur precibus; ubi gratiam expectes, invidia et
odium rependitur.

36   *Philar.* Per eam quam in te habeo fidem atque integram spem, mi
homo, obsecro nihil istiusmodi in me vereare. Mihi enim mos,
victus et omnis vita mea pacata, innocens atque penitus modestissima semper fuit; eapropter nihil posse inter nos incidere
putato quod vel succensendi quidem minimum locum prestet.

37   *Xerx.* Quid tum astrologe? Utrumne ex hoc loco, siquidem hic
nisi verba dantur, discedimus?

38   *Philar.* Do tamen aurum uti edixeras. Ne vero in verbis fidem et
constantiam esse oportet? Num constitutam legem dedecet ipso
ex temporis momento immutarier? Sin lex indicta est, 'aurum

is ignited by the slightest spark of indignation find it cooled by the slightest reason.

Xerxes. Next! But what's this, astrologer? Our crowd of customers is dwindling, and virtually no one steps forward. That man hurt our business with his brawling and insults.   32

Philargirius. Here I am, I say, and offer you gold.   33

Xerxes. The others offer three coins, but you offer only one, and counterfeit at that?

Philargirius. By the holy and pious powers you worship for revealing your wonderful prophecies, and by all the gods in heaven and hell, I beg and beseech you, most wise and sagacious astrologer: confidently speak your opinion of me. For the moment, give no thought to money; I shall show you another time how grateful and generous I can be.   34

Xerxes. If you desire the services of this divine man, you must offer gold, not words.

Astrologer. It is very difficult, arduous, and even dangerous, to reveal all you know. If you don't offer high offices, you will be cursed. If you speak your mind freely, people take umbrage. And when gifts are being given, people compete with entreaties; and where you would expect thanks, you are repaid with envy and hatred.   35

Philargirius. By the faith and complete trust I place in you, my dear fellow, I beg you to fear nothing like that of me. My character and entire way of life have always been peaceable, innocent, and completely moderate. So don't think anything could come between us to arouse any anger.   36

Xerxes. What then, astrologer? Shall we go, since this fellow only offers us words?   37

Philargirius. All right, I'll give you gold as you said. Shouldn't our words be faithful and constant? Isn't it shameful to change our agreement at a moment's notice? If the law prescribes giving   38

dato,' quid tum? aurumne afferens aspernabitur? Itaque tu, heus! aurum sumito.

39 *Xerx.* Minime.

Philar. Non te laudo, si isthunc animum geris ut aurum flocci pendas: quam rem forte solent qui non satis didicere quantis laboribus es paretur. Questum qui negligit, meo iudicio, in omni re negligens et supinus est.

40 *Xerx.* Gratis apud nos philosophabere. Ac scin quid efficias his verbis?

Philar. Scio plane vos esse viros omnium prestantissimos.

Xerx. Prorsus ut inquis. Tamen nosti⟨n⟩ verbis apud nos quid assequare tuis?

41 *Philar.* At quidnam?

Xerx. Obtundis.

Philar. Utere potius humanitate et facilitate qua omnino profecto preditus videris.

42 *Xerx.* Enecas.

Philar. Non impetro quod si nosses qui sim? . . .

Xerx. Astrologe, surge. Ingrediar, dum aliud consilii captemus. Nam hic homo obruit me.

43 *Philar.* Mane, heus, inquam, mane!

Xerx. Extrahe, distrude ex isthac tua peruncta et putrida crumena, emunge, exprime puros et legitimos aureos.

Philar. Ha ha he! Sic iubes, lepidissime? Ac pareo. Eccum denique ceterum. Mihi oculum eruito, si preter duos istos apud me inveneris nummos.

44 *Xerx.* Iuraris?

Philar. Iuro sane.

Xerx. Au, periure! Atque isthic a latere in crumena quid turget?

45 *Philar.* Ha ha he, facetissime! Adesne? Quid tandem existimas? Namque hodie longe es quam velim fortunatus. Omnia enim evertens, nescio quo pacto alium quoque Philippeum nummum

gold, what then? Do you scorn one who offers gold? Here, take my money.

Xerxes. No. 39

Philargirius. I can't praise you for disparaging gold, as some may do who have not learned what great toils and cares are required to earn it. In my opinion, anyone who disdains making money is heedless and negligent in all his affairs.

Xerxes. You philosophize in vain. Do you know what you will 40 achieve by such words?

Philargirius. I know that you are most worthy men.

Xerxes. You're perfectly right. But do you know what effect your words have on us?

Philargirius. What is that? 41

Xerxes. You deafen us.

Philargirius. Then practice instead the humanity and affability that you so clearly possess.

Xerxes. You're killing me. 42

Philargirius. I'm getting nowhere. If only you knew who I am!

Xerxes. Get up, astrologer. I'll go in, and we can adopt another plan. This fellow is killing me.

Philargirius. Wait, please, wait! 43

Xerxes. Reach into and rummage that greasy and rotting purse of yours until you squeeze out and wring forth some pure and genuine pieces of gold.

Philargirius. Ha! ha! ha! Is that your command, you great wit? But I obey. Scratch out one of my eyes if you find I have any other coins.

Xerxes. You swear? 44

Philargirius. I swear.

Xerxes. Ha, liar! What's that bulging in the purse by your side?

Philargirius. Ha! ha! ha! Funny man, here you are! What do you 45 think it is? You're far luckier today than I would wish. Somehow, when I searched through everything, I was surprised to

aureum, preter spem, en fulgentissimum!, tandem comperi. Tu porro perquirito: nummorum quicquid reliqui est, peregrinum atque inutile quidem est.

46 *Xerx.* Dixti prorsus ut res est: siquidem omne quod apud istiusmodi et tibi similes astrictos et tenacissimos homines aurum est, inutile et incommodum est.

47 *Philar.* An tu quidem parum id ad virtutem conferre deputas, parumne illum prudentem statues qui in degenda vita rationem impensarum habuerit parsimoniamque servarit?

48 *Xerx.* Non est disputandi locus; neque si disputes, concedam ut avaritiam parsimoniam nuncupes.

49 *Philar.* Etenim quid hoc mali putas, cum animus cupiditate quadam et desiderio pendet tum iuvat ultro effundere, cumve quid institui tum preceps mihi ipse ut satisfaciam corruo? Tres perinde aureos habeto. Do lubens, do volens. Itaque dicito quid sentias.

50 *Xerx.* Dudum te spectans repeto memorie, nequedum comperio quemquam quem pre te insaniorem viderim unquam.

    Philar. Siccine delectat pro iure amicitie mecum iocari? Ergo te mihi amicum prebe. Do quidem aureos tris.

    Xerx. Minime.

51 *Philar.* Itane plures quam edixeras, pluresve quam ceteri afferens, aspernatur atque eiicitur?

    Xerx. Sic decet, quod nimium tenax atque pre ceteris periurus extitisti.

52 *Philar.* Licetne tandem hanc a vobis exorare gratiam ut beneficium? Alium quoque ex mediis ossibus meis nummum effodio. O me miserum! hoc mihi auri pondus semestrem victum prebuisset! Denique liceat, obsecro.

53 *Astr.* Liceat sane, ubi his nummis quadruplum adieceris.

    Xerx. Denique, astrologe, non recusemus, fruamur nostris moribus nostraque liberalitate. Mites nos quidem esse oportet in hunc qui oculum libentius quam nummum eroget. Tu si hunc

find another Macedonian gold piece, and a dazzling one at that. Take another look. The rest of the coins are foreign and worthless.

Xerxes. You've spoken the truth. Money in the hands of misers 46 and niggards like you is useless and bothersome.

Philargirius. Do you think it adds little to one's virtue? Do you 47 think there is little wisdom in a man who lives minding his expenses and practicing frugality?

Xerxes. This is no time for a debate. Even if you debate me, I shall 48 not let you call avarice "frugality."

Philargirius. Can you blame me? When my mind is set on some 49 yearning or desire, I feel an urge to spend; or when I have made a decision, I run or rush to satisfy myself. Here, take three gold coins. I give them gladly and willingly. Now tell me what you think.

Xerxes. Having observed you, I search my memory, but can't re- 50 member ever seeing anyone more insane than you.

Philargirius. Do you enjoy jesting with me as if in friendship? Then act as a friend. I give you three gold pieces.

Xerxes. Absolutely not.

Philargirius. So when I offer you more than the others, and more 51 than you asked, I am spurned and rejected?

Xerxes. It's only fair. You've been more miserly and mendacious than the others.

Philargirius. Won't you allow me to obtain this favor and kindness 52 from you? I'll dig another coin out of my very bones. O wretched me! This much gold would have paid for six months' food. Allow me at last, I beg you.

Astrologer. We'll allow you, if you'll add to these coins four times 53 their value.

Xerxes. Let's not refuse him, astrologer, but show our true nature and generosity. We must be kind to this fellow, who would more gladly give us an eye than a coin. If you could see him

aspexeris mussantem, pallentem, titubantem dum nummos enumerat, condolueris.

54 *Philar.* Enimvero . . .

Astr. Sileto, nam quidvis malo quam verba.

Xerx. Nempe aureos quatuor prebet, quos centies milies vigeties octies quater perfricavit manibus.

55 *Astr.* Quanta est hec summa?

Philar. At precor, quando aurum tenetis, ne diutius supersedeatis: amici me apud pretorem expectant.

Astr. Nequeo tantum numerum quadrare, quamquam non longe absum ab ipsis radicibus cubi. Prius tamen de diametro non-nulla discutienda sunt.

56 *Philar.* O me infelicem, quatuor extorsere a me aureos, nunc ludos faciunt!

Xerx. Ergo potes ad amicos proficisci interim, ne tuam operam desiderent. Cum autem redieris, astrologum mente ad rem
57 tuam expeditiorem habebis. Nam hominem vides ut iam ad calculum pendeat; ac solet ille quidem vehementius irasci, si quando ab huiusmodi investigationibus interpelletur. Consulo quidem amice, nam hoc ipse mea in re facerem: abirem.

Astr. Abiitne?

58 *Xerx.* Minime abiit: verum stat labiis pendulis, oculis reconditis, aspectu in ipsos istos nummos defixo, fronte tristi, superciliis porrectis, barba setosa, pectore incurvo. Iudica, queso, astro-loge, ut iam turbam hanc missam faciamus.

59 *Astr.* Peribit fame.

Xerx. Mallem siti. — Vos valete et hos mores irridete.

mutter, blanch, and falter as he counts his money, you'd take pity.

Philargirius. Indeed. 54

Astrologer. Be quiet. I prefer anything to words.

Xerxes. Now he offers four gold coins, which he has rubbed in his hands a hundred thousand times.

Astrologer. What's the total? 55

Philargirius. Please, now that you have my money, don't delay any longer. My friends expect me in court.

Astrologer. I can't square such a large number, but I've nearly got the root of the cube. Yet first we must discuss the diameter.

Philargirius. Wretched me! They extorted four gold coins from me, 56 and now they're making fun of me.

Xerxes. You may go join your friends now, so that they won't lack your help. When you return, you'll find the astrologer readier to deal with your case. You see how the fellow is intent on this 57 computation, and he often loses his temper when interrupted in the midst of such calculations. I'm advising you as a friend. If I were you, I'd go away.

Astrologer. Has he left?

Xerxes. No, he hasn't left. He stands with his lips drooping and 58 his eyes averted. His gaze is fixed on these coins, his forehead clouded, his eyebrows raised, his beard bristling, and his chest caved in. Give us your judgment, astrologer, so that we may dismiss this crowd.

Astrologer. He will die of hunger. 59

Xerxes. I'd rather he died of thirst. Farewell, spectators, and laugh at such behavior![15]

: 5 :

Paupertas

1 *Peni.* Itane mecum agis ac si mihi ab te, quocum diutissime et familiarissime vixi, quicquam ingratum aut iniucundum esse vereare? Omnis inter amicos circuitio verborum atque insinuatio,
2 meo iudicio, vituperanda est. Tum ego ex his sum qui frontem,
voluntates, consilia atque istiusmodi reliqua que ad fruendam
tuendamque aut colendam amicitiam valeant, apud me haberi
3 aperta et libera vehementer gaudeam. Quod siquid habes quo
me in colenda et ornanda amicitia meliorem tibique gratiorem
possis efficere, narra, obsecro, quid me velis.
4 *Pal.* Nempe aliud habeo nihil, quo mutuam erga nos benivolentiam firmiorem aut stabiliorem possim meis verbis reddere.
5 Unum tamen est quod te pro officio velim non latere. Tibi quidem affectissimi et plane probi viri plerique, cum norint qua
sim fide et benivolentia erga te preditus, iussere hanc provinciam, in qua mihi esset causa honoris tui commendata, suscipe-
6 rem; atque id quidem munus eo sum audentius aggressus, quo
te semper esse ingenio preditum modestissimo memini, ut que
a me pro tua laude augenda et amplificanda ineantur, ea te
7 non ingrato animo laturum existimem. Sed, mi Peniplusi, ut
rem totam quam succincte recitem, principio velim sic existimes, oculos omnium in te non secus atque in ceteros prima-
rios esse coniectos moresque vitamque tuam spectari diligentius, ut etiam que fortassis minima esse deputes, ea vulgus non
8 in postremis habenda et pensanda censeat. Atque arbitrari quidem oportet, quemadmodum de ceteris bonis civibus, ita et de
9 te non raros publice privateque sermones haberi. Sed in his
omnibus quibus ipse interfui sermonibus virtus quidem, que in
te eximia est, mirum in modum laudatur atque approbatur ab

∶ 5 ∶

Poverty

Peniplusius. Can you treat me as if I might find your behavior un- 1
pleasant or unwelcome, when I have been your close friend for
so long?[16] In my opinion, we should condemn any circumlocu-
tion and equivocation between friends. I for one take great de- 2
light in offering openly and freely the candor, goodwill, advice,
and everything that promotes, protects, and preserve friendship. So if you can suggest anything to help me maintain and 3
improve our friendship, and become your closer friend, please
tell me.

Paleterus. I can say nothing to strengthen or reinforce our mutual 4
affection, but there is one thing I feel duty bound not to conceal
from you. A number of worthy men who are well-disposed to- 5
ward you, having learned of my trust and affection for you, have
asked me to assume the mission of defending your honor.
Knowing your modest nature, I approached the task confi- 6
dently. For I am certain that you will not resent it if I do what
is necessary to increase and advance your reputation. Still, my 7
dear Peniplusius, to state the case as briefly as possible, remember that you are in the public eye no less than other prominent
men. Your character and behavior are closely scrutinized, and
even details you may think trivial are not considered unimport-
ant by the masses. You must reflect that, like other good citi- 8
zens, you are often the subject of both public and private discussions. Now, in every conversation I have heard, everyone 9
highly praises and admires your singular virtue. Yet one thing

omnibus, ni forte unum illud laudibus tuis propemodum ob-
stet, quod famam increbuisse aiunt, te nimis duriter atque
10 astricte esse parcum. Hac nota cum te amici teneri vulgo audiunt, quam id moleste pro officio ferant cogita. Eam ob rem
edixere ut commonerem, ne id committeres ut de te obloquendi
obtrectatoribus occasio vel minima prestaretur. Nosti quam
deceat sapientem pro laude et fama adipiscenda atque retinenda
11 omnia exponere. Quod si cuipiam sui cura nominis debetur,
tibi certe viro nobili, magnifice ingenueque a puero usque edu-
cato in primis advigilandum est, ut omne studium, opera et industria tua, omnis cogitatio, animus atque institutio ad laudem
virtutis propensa esse videatur.

12 *Peni.* Quod fame et nominis mei curam susceperis, habeo tibi
gratias, Paletere. Ceterum ipse operam, quoad in me erit, ut
13 laudem promeruisse videar, in dies dabo. Sed ubi neminem
ledo, is quidem sum qui obtrectatores omnes minime reformi-
dandos esse opinabar vulgique iudicium non contemnendum
quidem, sed ne tanti faciendum putabam, ut etiam domestice et
private rationes vivendi ad vulgi censuram essent instituende.
14 Siquidem id ita est: nam comperies usque adeo veram et soli-
dam hominis nullius famam, quin ea cum facile dicendo possit,
tum et soleat obtrectatione invidorum maxima ex parte labefac-
tari.

15 *Pal.* Dixti pulchre. Atque ego item unus ex illis sum qui semper
queque loquantur improbi et scelesti perminimi fecerim. Do
tamen operam, quoad in me est, ut flagitiosis quam minima de
16 me male loquendi facultas adsit. Nam id sapientis officium
duco, ita vitam degere ut, cum ledas nullos, tum te omnes merito et diligere et vereri assuescant, nemo reprehendat, cuncti
17 facta dictaque tua comprobent. Illud preterea in te pro amicitie
officio non negligo, quod aliquos plane video non obtrectantium
more hanc tuam vite agende rationem coarguere, sed permulta
sedulo eiusmodi in disceptationem adducere, que tu si dixeris

seems almost to detract from your praises. They say that common opinion regards you as too severely and strictly parsimonious. Consider how dismayed your true friends are, when they 10 hear that the masses brand you thus. Hence, they asked me to warn you not to give your detractors even the least reason to reproach you. You know how a wise man should do everything he can to earn and retain a praiseworthy reputation. And if 11 there is anyone who ought to care for his good name, surely you, who are noble and high-minded, and have been liberally educated since your youth, should take special care that all your efforts, actions, and endeavors, all your thoughts, inclinations, and resolves, seem to promote your reputation for virtue.

Peniplusius. I'm grateful to you for looking after my name and 12 reputation, Paleterus, and I shall every day do my best to seem worthy of praise. Yet as long as I harm no one, I believe that 13 detractors are scarcely to be feared, and that the judgment of the masses, while not to be despised, should not be valued so highly that their censures determine one's private and personal way of life. As a result, you'll find no man's reputation so certain 14 and secure that it can escape being destroyed by gossip, especially by envious detractors.

Paleterus. Well said. I too have never paid the least attention to 15 what vicious and wicked men say. Yet I do my best not to offer scoundrels the least opportunity of slandering me. For I think 16 that the wise man is obliged to avoid harming anyone, so that everyone will justly come to love and revere him, no one will reproach him, and all will praise his words and deeds. As your 17 dutiful friend, I must also tell you this: I am aware of people who do not openly censure your behavior, as detractors do, but who constantly hint at behavior which, if intentional on your

18 abs te consulto fieri, non profecto fugias suspitionem avaritie. Si
vero eadem te imprudente atque inscio fiunt, proderit, ni fallor,
iam nihil abs te ignorari posthac eius quod tibi vulgus possit ad
19 vituperationem adscribere. Quid censes iudicari apud cives, si
quando familiam egregii alicuius viri parum honeste vestitam
equosque neglectos, ipsum quoque dominum parum pro dignitate ornatum prodire ac domum denique omnem minus lautam
et urbanam esse quam vel maiorum largitate soleat vel pro more
20 atque expectatione civium deceat, intueantur? Hec tamen a me
pro amicitie officio dicta putes velim.

Peni. Quin immo tibi debeo gratias quod te geris amice. Tamen id
puta me, in rebus quas intelligo ad laudem et decus pertinere,
21 nunquam esse negligentem. Et novi quidem, ni fallor, quid deceat mihique hoc assumo, a nullo me vitio esse alienum quam
ab avaritia. Quas res ita esse intelliges, si memoria repetes
maiores meos quos vidisti fortunatissimos. Itaque me illis fami-
liamque meam ac denique omnem nostrum vivendi morem
22 compara. Mihi quidem quamquam tenuiores fortune suppeditent, nonne plures alo equos? nonne familiam ampliorem
pasco? Tum hospitum quotidianum longeque maiorem numerum apud me habeo quam illi omnes habere soliti sint.

23 Quid hoc? Deos testor, nisi tuo et reliquorum amicorum
suffragio levarer, interdum penitus de me esset actum. Quas tibi
24 debeo pecunias, hanc ipsam ob causam impensarum debeo. Iam
vero hec qui vultu et mente sustineat libentissima, quod ipse
facio, utrum eum avarum an prodigum iudicabis?

Pal. Ego magis eum laudarim, qui ex ipsis redditibus rationem
impensarum deduxerit.

25 *Peni.* Tota hac in causa sic velim putes: cum spectet ad gratiam et
dignitatem nos haberi divites, tum est ipsum paupertatis no-
26 men prorsus abhorrendum. Egenti enim fortune nescio quo
pacto comes et consocia est existimatio levitatis, impudentie,
audacie; scelerum turpitudinumque omnium suspitione et voce

part, would certainly arouse suspicions of avarice. Even if you   18
are unaware of such things, I think you must in future be alert
to any charges the masses may lay to your blame. Consider   19
what the public must think when they behold a prominent
man's family indecorously clothed, his horses neglected, and the
master himself unworthily attired — in short, the entire house
less sumptuous and elegant than it was in previous generations,
and than public customs and standards require. Please bear in   20
mind that I speak as a dutiful friend.

Peniplusius. In fact, I am grateful to you for acting as my friend.
But know that I am remiss in nothing which I regard as affect-
ing my honor and dignity. Unless I err, I believe I know my   21
duty, and I may claim that, of all the vices, avarice is the remot-
est from my character. You'll see that this is the case if you call
to mind my forebears, whose exceptional fortune you have witnessed. To them, please compare me, my household, and my
entire way of life. Although my fortune is less considerable,   22
don't I raise more horses and feed a larger household? Don't I
entertain each day a greater number of guests?

What then? I swear by the gods: if you and other friends   23
hadn't rescued me, I would have been completely ruined more
than once. If I owe you money, the reason is such expenses. But   24
if anyone acted as I do with a cheerful face and heart, would
you judge him a miser or a spendthrift?

Paleterus. I would praise more highly the man who met his expenses by drawing on his revenues.

Peniplusius. On this topic, I hope you'll agree with me: If we are   25
thought to be rich, our dignity and esteem benefit; we should at
all costs avoid even speaking of poverty. Indigence somehow   26
causes people to perceive unreliability, shamelessness, and effrontery — crimes and vices that everyone condemns privately

27 damnato. Si furtum factum est, nimirum necessitate ductus
pauper fecisse illud putatur. Siquid per imprudentiam admisit
28 pauper, adscribitur nequitie. Non auditur iurans, non adhibetur
iniurato fides, proscribitur ab amicitiis, repellitur a domestica
civium conversatione et familiaritate, postremo vitam degit sibi
atque omnibus notis gravem et refertam omni difficultatum ge-
29 nere. Atque ad miseriam accedit quod nulla in paupere unquam
tanta adest virtus que sibi vel minimam auctoritatem vel dignitatem afferat: progreditur tristis, iniocundus, suspectus, abiec-
30 tus, irrisus. Multa denique alia sunt in paupertate eiusmodi, ut
acerbitatem habeant in vita atque dedecus ignominiamque afferant. Iam quis est qui non audeat obiurgare, pessumdare ac
31 postremo iniuria afficere pauperem? At ille quidem remissus,
humilis, merens pauper omnes perpeti insolentes omnesque
divites in dominorum locum vereri, nihil ex voluntate agere, ad
aliorum arbitrium atque nutum ridere, loqui, tacere plorareve.
32 Quid plura? Deos denique omnes atque homines paupertati
infestos esse arbitror.

Contra vero dives qui putatur, hic tutius contendit, hones-
tius petit, valet auctoritate, potest gratia, habet frequentiam sa-
lutatorum, non desunt clientele, adsunt amici, favent, laudant,
33 oblectant. Ita profecto prestat viros magnos haberi avaros quam
pauperes. Avaritiam, non inficior, odere prodigi, sed magis paupertatem. Avaritiam qui frugi sunt vituperant, eandem tamen
34 nonnunquam in parsimonie locum fortassis laudant. Tum et
comperies bonos plerosque qui vel Platoni aut cuivis philosophorum paupertatem laudanti nunquam assentiantur. Avarum,
etsi inimici vituperent, parcissime tamen vituperant: mordax
35 enim maledicus armatum auro virum haud impune ledit. Tum
quis adeo erit insolens qui non divitem, etsi avarum, metuat
iratum magis quam avaritiam ipsam oderit? Siquidem facile
inveniri potest avarus quispiam qui in detractoris pernitiem

and publicly. When a theft is committed, we naturally think   27
that neediness drove a pauper to the deed. When a pauper errs
by mistake, we blame his baseness. When he swears an oath, we   28
ignore him; and when he swears no oath, we don't believe him.
We banish him from our friendships and exclude him from the
close friendship and intimacy of his fellow citizens. In short, he
leads a life burdensome both to himself and to his acquaintances, and filled with every sort of hardship. Besides this mis-   29
ery, no virtue can be so great in a pauper that it lends him even
the least prestige or dignity. He walks around in gloom, unwelcome, suspect, abject, and derided. Poverty entails many things   30
that make his life bitter and bring him disgrace and ignominy.
Is there anyone who dares not rebuke, ruin, or injure a pauper?
Yet the pauper must suffer all arrogant men mildly, humbly, and   31
sadly, and must revere all rich men as his masters. He can do
nothing as he wishes. He laughs, speaks, falls silent, or weeps at
the will and whim of others. Need I say more? In sum, I believe   32
that all the gods and men detest poverty.

By contrast, anyone considered wealthy may safely quarrel in
court or run for office. He prevails by his authority, and suc-
ceeds by his prestige. He is surrounded by well-wishers, and
lacks neither clients nor friends to applaud, praise, and amuse
him. Thus, it is better for great men to be considered avaricious   33
rather than paupers. Spendthrifts detest avarice, I know, but
they detest poverty more. Decent men disparage avarice, but
sometimes they praise it as a sort of frugality. You will find   34
many good men, moreover, who would never agree with Plato
or any other philosopher who praises poverty. A miser's enemies may censure him, but they do so sparingly, for a carping
slanderer cannot safely harm a man protected by gold. Is there   35
anyone so insolent that he would not fear a rich man's anger —
even a miser's — more than he would detest the vice of avarice?
We can easily find a miser who spends generously to ruin a

norit esse prodigus; metus quidem petulcum elinguem reddit.
36 Aut si avarum unus aut item alter qui aliena magis curet quam
propria maledictis prosequitur, pauperem ledendi cuique tuta
potestas est. Verba audiet avarus, pauper verbera perferet.

37 *Pal.* Haud quidem negandum puto paupertatem esse admodum
incommodam, sed quid tu, si quispiam apud te ageret? 'Rogo
possisne uberius tuam atque liberalius familiam alere. Si non
38 vis, ubi possis, facis preter officium. Si non potes, ubi velis, cur
non desinis nolle hoc luxu ac magnificentia servorum ac comi-
tum carere, quam tua res familiaris non capit, quasi dubites ne
parva familia bene culta et ornata populose, ut ita loquar, et
39 squalide sit non preferenda?' Quid hic ais? Dic, sodes: nam iu-
vabit iisdem ipsis rationibus te apud vulgus perpurgatum reddere.

Peni. Dicerem que tum pro re dicenda viderentur. Verum omnino
id in primis providerem, ne ulla divitiarum de me apud vulgus
40 opinio decresceret. Multi me observant, colunt amantque qui si
presenserint fortunas mihi esse angustas atque pusillas et ste-
riles, ut sic loquar, sive dubitarint meam sibi amicitiam minus
expectatione fructuosam futuram, ne vero quicquam erit me
41 apud illos abiectius? At tu quem nihil unquam volui latere mearum rerum omnium, si non vulgi opinione sed veritate atque
42 ratione duceris, ut me ad avaritiam propensum existimes, in
hoc erit, ni fallor, quo sententiam tuam atque iudicium tuearis,
non procul a turpitudine abesse eum qui non sponte ac leto
animo petentibus amicis atque indigentibus domesticis sua be-
43 neficentia opituletur; aut quidem me nimia lucri questusque
cupiditate occupari et detineri argues, quemadmodum qui de
his rebus disputant in his presertim constitutam esse avaritiam
volunt pariterque in vitio collocant pauca dare ac plura cupere
44 immodeste. Sed illud iampridem apud te exploratum est, omnes
a me turpes nummularias artes esse alienas; quin quod me,

detractor; then fear will silence an aggressive tongue. Now, 36
someone who minds others' affairs more than his own can heap
curses on a miser; whereas anyone is free to harm a pauper. The
miser will only bear words, but the pauper will bear blows.

Paleterus. You can't, I think, deny that poverty is quite unpleasant. 37
But what would you say if someone said the following: "I ask
whether you can support your family more lavishly or liberally?
If you can, but don't wish to, you neglect your duty. If you wish 38
to, but can't, why don't you forego the luxury and ostentation of
maintaining servants and attendants beyond your means? Can
you doubt that a small but well-furnished household is preferable to one that is 'populous' but shabby?" What do you say to 39
this? Tell me, please, for your reasons will aid me in clearing
your name among the masses.

Peniplusius. I would say to them whatever the occasion seemed to
require. Above all, I would be quite careful not to diminish the
popular belief in my wealth. There are many who esteem, re- 40
vere, and love me. But if they sensed that my fortunes were
cramped, meager, and unproductive, or if they suspected that
my friendship would prove less advantageous than they hoped,
could they find anything more despicable than me? I have never 41
sought to hide any of my private affairs from you. Now if you
are led by truth and reason, rather than by public opinion, to
regard me as inclined to avarice, then I suppose by your reason- 42
ing you would argue that a man is hardly free from this vice if
he fails to bestow his goods freely, gladly, and generously on
needy friends and relations. Or perhaps you will accuse me of 43
being completely dominated by an excessive desire for profit
and gain. For the men who discuss such matters assert that avarice consists principally in such faults as these, and they likewise consider it a vice to be immoderate by giving too little and
by wanting too much. But you have long known that I have 44
nothing to do with base arts of moneymaking. Indeed, when I

99

dum a te quippiam rogo, soles accusare neminem verecundius
timidiusve ab amico petere quam ipse faciam, neminem peten-
45 tibus tradere largius atque incautius. Que res cum ita sint,
quonam pacto illos audies qui me avaritie insimulent?

46 Reliquum fortassis erit, ut me de ambitione et levitate mea
tandem expurgem. Nam velle pompam domi recipere quam
nostre fortune vix substineant, immoderati quidem atque im-
prudentis esse fateor. Sed hac in causa te et patrono et iudice
47 utar accommodatissimo. Me quidem cum ceteris in rebus stul-
tum esse nunquam iudicasti, tum in hac ipsa, ni fallor, admodum prudentem esse non diffiteberis; tametsi is non sum qui,
fortasse ut velles, norim ab invidorum iudicio obtrectatorumque
48 sententia gesta mea omnia reddere purgatissima. Etenim sic
existimo: satis patremfamilias prudentem esse eum qui, honesta
imperando ac necessaria prebendo, suam sic tractat domum, ut
49 plane ab universa familia sua diligatur. Hic te appello: nosti
quo in me animo mei omnes affecti sint, quam diligant, quam
ament. Rem perinde meam familiarem satis meorum erga me
benivolentia comptam et ornatam esse puto; satisque, ni fallor,
lauta domus ea est, in qua domini humanitas, facilitas, gratia
50 omnibus pateat. Desinant igitur nos invidi durum et adstrictum
dicere, desinant ceteris laudibus nostris hac una falsa et ficta
insimulatione detrahere, ni fortassis ad laudem pluris faciunt
tapetes, bullas et phaleras quam virtutes.

51 *Pal.* Nihil est, ita me superi ament, quod eque cupiam quam
istiusmodi optimas et elegantes rationes mihi apud eos qui te
avaritie incriminantur in mentem incidisse: me enim quam
52 eloquentissimum exhibuissem! Nam amplificassem quidem eos
quos breviter strictimque tetigisti locos.

Peni. Nollem id quidem.

Pal. At qui id?

53 *Peni.* Namque id minime profuisset.

ask you a favor, you often reproach me for being too timid in making requests of friends, and too reckless and generous in granting requests. If this is so, how can you listen to those who 45 charge me with avarice?

Perhaps I should also finally clear myself of charges of ambition and inconsistency. For I admit that only an immoderate 46 and imprudent man chooses to introduce into his home ostentation which is beyond his means. In this matter, I may suitably employ you as both my advocate and my judge. For since in 47 other matters you have never thought me foolish, you will not hesitate, I think, to declare me quite prudent in this matter as well, even though I am not as capable as you might wish of defending my actions from envious detractors. In my opinion, a 48 householder is sufficiently prudent if, by ruling decorously and providing life's essentials, he manages his house so that he is clearly loved by his entire household. I appeal to you. You know 49 my family's feelings for me, and how they cherish and love me. I therefore believe that my family's affection brings sufficient honor and distinction to our house. And sufficiently splendid, I maintain, is a home in which everyone enjoys the master's humanity, affability, and favor. So let the envious cease to deride 50 me as harsh and tightfisted. And let them cease to disparage my reputation by their slanders, unless perhaps they think tapestries, studs, and bosses are more valuable than virtues in winning praise.[17]

Paleterus. By the gods, I could wish nothing more than that such 51 excellent and elegant reasons had occurred to me when I spoke with those who accuse you of avarice. I could have shown myself very eloquent by enlarging on those points which you have touched upon so briefly and summarily.

Peniplusius. I wouldn't wish you to.

Paleterus. Why not?

Peniplusius. It would do no good. 53

Pal. Ain vero? Quid ita?

Peni. Quia divitiarum opinionem minuere plus nocumenti et incommodi attulisset quam istiusmodi levem famam avaritie perferre.

54 *Pal.* Cogitemus iccirco, dum ita censeas, quibusnam argumentis
liceat, servata divitiarum opinione, te ab avaritie nota absolvere.

55 *Peni.* Adsis, adhibe animum. Bonos novi omnes rem suam agere
nostramque verbis facere deteriorem non curare; malos autem
et eos qui detrahendi voluptate omnia vituperent, minimi
pendo. Tum sat est ubi apud te virum optimum satis mea de-

56 fensa causa est. Quod si tandem hanc nequeo famam evitare
avaritie, isthic me obfirmo: infinite me, ut hoc instituti susci-
piam atque servem, hortantur et commonent rationes, quas

57 quidem omnes longum esset recensere. Hoc plane putes velim,
me non raro in hanc mecum disceptationem incidisse, utrumne

58 prestet avarum me an pauperem videri. Tandem, re bene atque
diligenter in omnes partes discussa, in hanc potissimum sententiam deductus hereo, ex qua me nemo distrahet, ut velim potius

59 censeri avarus quam fur, leno, proditor: que huiusmodi scelera
et flagitia omnia ita putantur paupertati annexa et complicita,
ut preter cetera que paupertas affert incommoda, quidvis potius
quam vel minimam paupertatis suspitionem prudenti ferendam

60 ducam. Tamen ut voluntati et desiderio tuo satis faciam, dabo
quidem operam, quoad in me erit, ut me omnes frugi esse intel-
ligant.

Paleterus. Why? What do you mean?

Peniplusius. Because diminishing my reputation for wealth would cause me more damage and detriment than would tolerating vague rumors of my avarice.

Paleterus. If that is your view, let us think of arguments by which 54 you may protect the belief in your wealth and absolve yourself of the stigma of avarice.

Peniplusius. Please listen to me. I know that all good men attend to 55 their own affairs, and give no thought to making mine worse by their gossip. As for wicked men and those who censure everything for the pleasure of detraction, I pay them no mind. It is enough that my cause is sufficiently justified before an honest man like you. And even if I cannot ultimately avoid a reputa- 56 tion for avarice, I shall not yield. Countless reasons, which it would be tedious to recount, urge and advise me to adopt this resolve and to persist in it. I would have you know clearly that 57 I have often debated this question with myself, namely, whether it is better to seem a miser or a pauper. Having thoroughly and 58 carefully examined every aspect of the question, I have been led to embrace one conclusion, from which no one can shake me. I would rather be thought a miser than a thief, pander, or traitor. For all such vices and crimes are inextricably associated with 59 poverty. Hence, leaving aside its other ill effects, I think a wise man should not tolerate even the least suspicion of poverty. But 60 to comply with your wishes and desires, I shall do my best to see that everyone perceives that I am frugal.

: 6 :

Nummus

1 Cum omnes pene, qui tum erant in toto orbe terrarum, litteratissimi prudentissimique sacerdotes prima Olympiade, qua etate et
doctiores et pauciores quam hac tempestate initiabantur, ad festum diem et solemnem celebritatem apud Delphos convenissent,
2 inter multas de diis et rebus divinis disputationes quas per eos dies
summa cum dignitate et audientium admiratione variasque atque
3 subtilissimas habuere, illud fuit omnium litteris et posteritati egregie commendandum quod in huiusmodi difficillimam et minime
vulgarem disceptationem inciderint: quisnam deorum in primis
4 esset sacerdotibus colendus. Longum esset recensere quibus argumentis alii Venerem, alii Hypocrisim, alii Bacchum primum deo-
5 rum esse suaderent. Qua in controversia suam quisque sententiam
non modo eloquentia et dicendi arte, verum etiam convicio tueri
atque defendere immoderatissime contendebat; iamque studiis
6 partium res ad gravem simultatem devenerat. Qua de re quo commodius controversia dirimeretur, placuit deum Apollinem consulere, hac prefixa et constituta lege, ut posthac nefas sit sacerdotibus
quemquam preter quem Apollo dixerit deum primarium colere.

7 Consultus deus unam obticuit diem. Id quidem in eam partem
sacerdotes accepere, ut deum hac ambigua re atque ancipiti tem-
8 pus ad consulendum suscepisse interpretarentur. Altera iterato
deus die rogatus quoque obmutuerat: quod ipsum item apud sacerdotes opinionem quandam confirmavit, Apollinem ad rem tantam tamque obscuram atque perplexam discutiendam secessisse
illinc atque apud concilium deorum ut de re ipsa consilium capiat
9 abesse. Postridie ingenti quadam cupiditate ducti discende in
causa tam gravi deorum sententie, quo surdum oraculum ipsum
facile et propitium suo beneficio redderent, sacrificium ei fecere

: 6 :

The Coin

During the first Olympiad, when fewer but more learned men 1
were ordained than in the present age, nearly all the most intelligent and erudite priests in the entire world convened at Delphi for
the celebration of a solemn festival.[18] At that time, they engaged in 2
many varied and subtle discussions concerning the gods and religious matters, which they conducted with the highest dignity and
which aroused the wonder of their audience. Of all these, by far 3
the worthiest of record for posterity arose when they engaged in
the difficult and recondite dispute: Which god should priests worship above all others? It would be tedious to recount the argu- 4
ments by which some advocated Venus, some Hypocrisy, and
some Bacchus as the foremost god. In the debate, each priest 5
strove to expound and defend his own view, not only with eloquence and rhetoric, but also with shameless insults. Soon, the
passion of the various factions turned the matter into a violent
quarrel. In order to resolve the controversy suitably, the priests 6
decided to consult the god Apollo. They agreed to do so on this
condition, that afterward it would be sacrilege if any priests worshiped as foremost any god but the one Apollo named.

When Apollo was consulted, he was silent for a day. The 7
priests interpreted his silence to mean that he had taken time to
ponder this ambiguous and problematic question. Asked again on 8
the second day, Apollo still remained silent. This confirmed the
priests' belief that he had withdrawn in order to examine this obscure and intricate matter, and had repaired to the council of the
gods to take counsel. On the following day, the priests were driven 9
by an intense desire to learn the gods' decision. So, to propitiate
the silent oracle with an offering, they made their greatest sacrifice,

10 maximum, quod a boum numero centibove nuncuparunt. Peracto
quidem quam religiosissime sacrificio, tale a deo responsum accepere:

Responsum Apollinis

Fronte senes, pueri votis animisque procaces,
Crastina lux numen quesitum ostendet in ara.

11 Itaque accepto responso, postridie mane multa cum expectatione et desiderio aditum dei petiere. At eo quidem in loco, quod
oraculi sententiam indicaret, inscriptum nihil reperere vocemque a
12 deo ipso nullam accepere. Ergo hanc rem se egre ferre tristitia
vultus et taciturnitate multa indicabant sacerdotes, in eamque sententiam admodum adducti erant ut existimarent oraculi iudicium
esse istiusmodi, ut nullum a sacerdotibus esse deum putandum
13 statueret. Dumque ita alter alterum spectans omnes proni et muti
hererent, Monopus natu grandior sacerdos, qui et ingenio pre aliis
esset acutissimo, ad tripodem intuens: 'Ne vero,' inquit, 'ignavi et
secordes, parum intelligitis quam pulchre et accommodate isthic
14 dei iudicium inscriptum extet?' Media enim in mensa fortassis
aderat nummus. Quem quidem non facile dici potest, cum a sacerdotibus esset cognitus, quam leti confestim omnes accursitarint
sponteque ad unum usque iurarint nummum apud se perpetuo
summum ac supremum deorum futurum.

15 Quod quidem iusiurandum, vel quod priscam et sanctissimam
maiorum suorum legem venerentur, vel quod dei iudicium et sententiam in ea re piissima maiorem in modum approbent, tanti a
sacerdotibus existimatum est, ut in hanc usque diem ne minima
quidem suspitione sacerdos quispiam in ea re periurus repertus sit.

which they called the hecatomb, according to the number of cattle. After the sacrifice had been most piously carried out, they received the god's oracle. 10

Apollo's Oracle

Old men in brow, yet boys importunate in prayers and spirit,
Tomorrow's light will show the god you seek upon the altar.[19]

Having received the oracle, the priests went to the god's shrine 11 the next morning, filled with keen anticipation. But in the place indicated by the oracle, they found no written word, and heard no utterance from the god. The priests' sad expressions and their si- 12 lence betrayed their disappointment. They were even inclined to believe that the oracle's pronouncement meant that priests should think there is no god. While they looked at each other, downcast 13 and silent in their bewilderment, Monopus, the oldest and shrewdest of the priests, looked at the tripod and said: "What, idle blockheads, don't you see how neatly and aptly the god's oracle has been recorded?"[20] For in the middle of the altar, there happened to be a 14 coin. When they saw this, it would be hard to describe how happily all the priests at once ran forward, and how eagerly each of them swore that money would forever be his supreme and sovereign god.

Whether they revere their forebears' ancient and sacred law, or 15 completely embrace the god's judgment in this pious matter, priests have valued this oath so highly that, even to the present day, none has incurred even the slightest suspicion of perjury in this regard.

: 7 :
Pluto

1 Aiunt Herculem deum, cum primum in celum defunctus conscendisset, singulos deos qui ab Iove ipso maximo sibi essent obviam emissi, preter Plutonem, quam familiariter consalutasse, hunc vero unicum ad congratulandum una cum reliquis accurrentem, vultu et verbis a se non secus atque obscenum aliquem et fedissimum 2 erronem abegisse; rogatumque Herculem quid ita ageret, respondisse: minime quidem se posse animo equo hunc esse in cetu deorum pati, quem nunquam toto orbe terrarum lustrato, nisi 3 ignavissimis desidiosissimisque hominibus familiarem vidisset. At Plutonem subrisisse ferunt Herculemque ipsum admonuisse ut meminerit sibi ceterisque diis templa et aureos honores a nullis maiores quam a Plutonis familiaribus deferri.

: 8 :
Divitie

1 Avus meus Benedictus Albertus, eques Florentinus, vir ob mores bonos obque virtutem clarus, cum a seditiosis civibus pulsus in exilium suum vite extremum diem apud Rhodum ageret, monitus ab his qui tunc illic aderant amicis velletne testamentum edere, 2 rogavit quasnam se vellent res testari. 'Tuas,' inquiunt amici, 'o Benedicte, quem inter Etruscos unum esse omnium ditissimum nemo dubitat.'

Tum ille: 'Nullius eque atque istius rei inscium ignarumque me esse affirmo. Iam enim eorum que vos dicere suspicor, meum quid

: 7 :

Pluto

They say that when Hercules died and first ascended into heaven 1
as a god, he greeted as friends all of the gods whom great Jupiter
sent to meet him, except Pluto. Pluto alone, hastening with the
others to congratulate Hercules, was driven away with scowls and
scorn like a foul and filthy vagabond. When Hercules was asked 2
why he did this, he replied that could not patiently tolerate in the
society of gods one whom, during his travels across the earth, he
had only seen as close friend of the most slothful and indolent
men.[21] Pluto, they say, smiled at this, and admonished Hercules to 3
recall that it was the close friends of Pluto who dedicated the
greatest temples and tributes of gold to him and the other gods.

: 8 :

Wealth

My grandfather, Benedetto Alberti, a Florentine knight famed for 1
his noble character and virtue, had been driven into exile by seditious citizens, and lay on his deathbed on the island of Rhodes.[22]
Urged by his friends to draw up a will, he asked them what things
they wished him to include in it. His friends replied: "Your own, 2
Benedetto, for no one doubts that you are the richest man in Tuscany."

He said: "I assure you that I am completely ignorant and unaware of 'my things.' As for what I suppose you mean, I scarcely

3 sit haud satis novi. Ac fui quidem in istiusmodi errore diutius ab adolescentia usque versatus, ut que vulgo esse hominis putent, ea

4 imprudens mea esse diiudicarim. Namque, uti aiunt, mea predia, mea bona, meas divitias ex communi reliquorum civium loquendi consuetudine appellabam.'

5 'An,' inquiunt amici, 'hec ipsa tua non fuere?'

Tum avus: 'Quin et quod magis mirere, corpus hoc ipsum, quo

6 inclusus iaceo, fuisse nunquam meum iampridem sentio. Nam cum memoria repeto quam membra hec, me invito, modo algore, modo estu, modo aliis doloribus capta atque occupata semper fuerint meisque optimis institutis et voluntatibus obstiterint atque

7 repugnarint; cumque repeto famem sitimque et eiusmodi duros agrestesque dominos quos corpus hoc perpetuo pertulerit; cumque animadverto ut divitias quidem opesque omnis patriamque fortuna rerum domina nobis die unica eripuerit in exiliumque pepulerit, quid est quod aut fuisse aut iam meum esse audeam dicere?

8 'Ut de divitiis ipsis ita sentiam, eiusmodi esse divitias in hominum vita veluti qui ludunt pila; non enim quod pilam diutius inter manus detineas, sed quod illam arte et ratione vicibus iactes atque

9 loco apte retorqueas ad victoriam confert; ita et divitiarum non possessionem quidem, sed usum ad consequendam felicitatem

10 conducere arbitror. Ceterum de me sic profiteor: nihil admodum apud me reliqui esse quod egregie meum censeam, preter conscientiam facinorum meorum atque recordationem quandam rerum

11 quas in vita perpessus sum. Itaque posteris meis hanc a me esse relictam hereditatem volo, ut possint profiteri me unum fuisse nostra in urbe civem amantissimum patrie, pacis, otii libertatisque cupidissimum, bonorum studiosum litterarumque et bonarum ar-

12 tium haudquaquam omnino rudem aut ignarum: qui quidem cum publica summa vigilantia et fide semper tutatus, tum privata mea re in primis nusquam fuerim non contentus. Mea igitur hec meorumque sunto.'

know what is mine. But in my youth, I labored many years under 3
such an error, and imprudently deemed mine those things which
are popularly thought to belong to a person. I followed the com- 4
mon usage of my fellow citizens, and called them *my* estates, *my*
property, and *my* wealth, as people do."

"But weren't they yours?" his friends asked. 5

"No," my grandfather replied. "Even more surprisingly, I realized long ago that even this body which confines me was never
really mine. For I recall how against my will these members were 6
always subject to cold, to heat, or to various pains, and how they
hindered and opposed my nobler intentions and wishes. I also re- 7
call how this body continually suffered hunger, thirst, and other
such harsh and savage masters. And I perceive how in a single day
fortune, mistress of our affairs, has snatched from me all my
wealth and goods and even my homeland, and has driven me into
exile. What, then, dare I call mine, either past or present?

"Here's what I think about wealth: wealth in human life is like 8
the players' ball in a game. You don't win by holding on to the ball
too long, but by throwing it skillfully and returning it accurately.
Just so, I judge that it is not the possession, but the use of wealth 9
that contributes to happiness. As for myself, I admit that I have 10
virtually nothing left that I may especially call mine, except the
knowledge of my deeds and the recollection of what I suffered in
life. I wish, therefore, to leave my heirs this sole inheritance. Let 11
them declare me, above all others in our city, the citizen most devoted to his country, and the most desirous of peace, tranquility,
and freedom; and a man versed in liberal studies, letters, and arts.
Just as I defended the public weal with great vigilance and faith, so 12
was I always content with my private estate. Let these deeds of
mine pass to my heirs."

LIBER III

∶ I ∶

Picture

1 Apud gymnosophistas populos vetustissimos, cultu virtutis et sapientie laudibus celeberrimos, templum fuisse ferunt Bone Male-
que Fortune, quod quidem omni ornamentorum copia opumque
2 varietate esset refertissimum. Nam illic intercolumnia, capitula,
epistilia, fastigia, lavacra et numero et amplitudine manuque artifi-
cum mirifica ex Pario marmore et ab ipsis ultimis Indorum Ara-
bumque montibus excisa, vasaque et candelabra et tripodes corti-
neque et eiusmodi reliqua omnia, que ad sacrificium exponerentur,
quam plurima illic et pulcherrima auro gemmisque ornatissima et
splendidissima spectabantur.

3 Sed hec missa faciamus. Illud rarius memoria cognitioneque
dignius, quod quidem hinc atque hinc parietibus templi mira ex
4 arte pictum fuisse referunt. Nam nos qui legerit cum delectabitur
picture varietate artificisque ingenio, tum se ad vitam cum ratione
degendam aliqua apud nos adinvenisse grata et amena, ni fallor,
congratulabitur.

5 Id quidem erat huiusmodi: nam in dextero templi pariete tabule
extabant picte decem, quibus pares itidem alie sinistro decem op-
6 posite in pariete tabule respondebant. At tabularum situs et sedes
ita erant dispositi, ut dextro in pariete quinque hinc et quinque
hinc tabule a medio ad extremas versus partes ordine succederent;
parique itidem ratione et descriptione quinque et quinque adverso
in pariete coequatis admodum spatiis distincte et locis composite
7 ad decus et ornamentum templi plurimum accederent. Medio in
pariete utrinque titulus inscriptus aderat huiusmodi: DUABUS
HIS EX MATRIBUS UTRINQUE PROGENIES EMANAVIT.

BOOK III

: I :

Paintings

In the land of the gymnosophists, a primeval community of per- 1
sons celebrated for their pursuit of virtue and praised for their
wisdom, they say there was a temple dedicated to Good and Ill
Fortune, which was replete with copious ornaments and diverse
riches.[1] Its intercolumniations, capitals, architraves, pediments, 2
and basins, carved in Parian marble and in stone from the remot-
est mountains of India and Arabia, were all wonderful in number,
size, and workmanship.[2] Its vases, candelabra, tripods, caldrons,
and other such articles displayed in sacrifices, were likewise numerous and beautiful, and splendidly adorned with gold and gems.

But enough of this. Even rarer and more worthy of record were 3
the wonderfully artistic paintings on the opposite walls of the
temple. The reader will not only delight in the paintings' variety 4
and the artist's invention, but will be grateful, I believe, when he
finds pleasing and enjoyable counsels for living wisely among ourselves.

The arrangement was the following. On the temple's right-hand 5
wall were ten paintings, to which corresponded another ten paintings on the left-hand wall. The paintings were arranged in this 6
way. On the right-hand wall, the paintings formed a symmetrical
line, five of them extending to each side from the middle. The
paintings on the opposite wall were arranged in the same manner,
so that the balanced spaces and intervals greatly enhanced the
grace and beauty of the temple. In the middle of each wall there 7
was this inscription: "FROM THESE TWO MOTHERS AROSE
THE PROGENY ON BOTH SIDES."

13

8   Itaque, ut a sinistro pariete incipiam, quo intercenalis hec nostra
letiore omine claudatur, matrum una ad medium parietem posita
9   loco primo in hanc erat formam expicta: mulier decrepita, toto
corpore incurva, facie pallens, oculis lippis, supercilio prelongo,
que quidem decempeda cruribus admota veluti puerulus obequi-
10   tat; altera vero manu perpendiculum exercet; at cervicibus simiam
sibi infestam, capillos, genas auresque unguibus lacerantem atque
dentibus gestat. Huic mulieri superinscriptum nomen est IN-
11   VIDIA MATER. Secundo loco mulier picta est facie vehementer
macra, aspectu vafra et, quemadmodum versutiloqua videatur, rete
contecta. Ea quidem flat ore flammas, manu altera flores osten-
ta⟨n⟩s, altera tribulos disseminans. Huic superinscriptus titulus
12   CALUMNIA INVIDIE FILIA. Tertio loco mulier picta est a cuius
stomacho atque occipitio indecenter tumido flamme une atque
item altere erumpunt, pugno astricto totam se in nervos compri-
mens. Huic superadscriptum nomen INDIGNATIO CALUMNIE
13   FILIA. Quarto loco mulier picta est vultu et oculis turbulentissimo, erecta in pedes, cervice sublata, manuum altera proiecta gla-
dium in nubes protendens, altera horoscopum fractum tenens,
pede vero saxum catena alligatum trahens. Huic superadscriptus
14   titulus INIMICITIA INDIGNATIONIS FILIA. Quinto loco mulier picta est nuda plorans, que quidem ambarum volis palmarum
lachrimas ex oculis manantes excipit. At lachrimarum tanta exube-
rat vis et copia, ut ex palmis superfluant et casu assiduo pedes
mulieris perforent. Huic superinscriptus titulus MISERIA INIMI-
CITIE FILIA.

15   Diverso deinceps parietis latere primo loco picta est mulier
fronte et pectore pertumido atque superbo, aspectu insolenti, ves-
16   titu regio adornata. Hec quidem tubam fractam et in suam faciem
retortam inflat, ex qua fumus turbulentus in eius conflantis oculos
effunditur. Altera vero manu, digito protenso, gemmas et aspera
signis aurea vasa solo proiecta ostentat. Huicque nomen ad-
17   scriptum AMBITIO MATER. Secundo proximo loco mulier picta

I shall begin with the left-hand wall, so that this dinner piece 8
may end more auspiciously. Of the two mothers placed in the
middle, the first was depicted as a decrepit and hunchbacked crone 9
with a pallid face, bleary eyes, and thick brows. She straddles a
ten-foot rule, which she holds with one hand, like a boy riding a
hobbyhorse, while in the other she holds a plumb line. On her 10
neck, she bears a savage ape who tears her hair, cheeks, and ears
with his nails and teeth. Above this woman is written the name:
ENVY, MOTHER. The second panel depicts a woman with an 11
emaciated face and a sly expression suggestive of deceitful speech.
She is covered by a net, and breathes flames from her mouth. She
holds out flowers in one hand, while she sows thistles with the
other. Above her is written: CALUMNY, DAUGHTER OF ENVY.[3]
The third panel depicts a woman who clenches her fists and con- 12
tracts all her muscles, while flames burst here and there from her
obscenely swollen belly and head. Above her is written: INDIGNA-
TION, DAUGHTER OF CALUMNY. The fourth panel depicts a 13
woman with turbulent face and eyes, who stands erect with her
neck raised high. With one of her hands, she points a sword toward the sky, while she holds a broken sundial in the other, and
drags a rock tied by a chain to her foot. Above her is written:
ENMITY, DAUGHTER OF INDIGNATION. The fifth panel de- 14
picts a weeping naked woman. She catches the falling tears in her
open palms, but they flow so abundantly that they spill from her
palms in a constant stream and drench her feet. Above her is written: MISERY, DAUGHTER OF ENMITY.

On the other side of the wall, the first panel depicts a woman 15
with a haughty brow, swelling breast, and insolent mien. Dressed 16
in regal garments, she blows into a broken trumpet, which curves
back toward her face and pours murky smoke in her eyes. With
her other hand, she points a finger at jewels and golden vases encrusted with reliefs, which have been cast on the ground. By her is
written: AMBITION, MOTHER. The next panel depicts a woman 17

est pregrandis, procera statura, libellis et singraphis vestita, que quidem manu altera uncos ligneos et urnarum refractas ansas

18 complures gestat. Altera manu, ac si quippiam maximo intervallo sepositum spectando recognitum sit, aciem visus a radi⟨i⟩s luminis distenta palma subintegit atque confovet. Huic titulus adscriptus

19 est CONTENTIO AMBITIONIS FILIA. Tertio loco mulier picta est que quidem a femore infra non homo sed capra sit dentesque atque os habet caninum. Hec manu altera agitat facem, altera vero coronam ex vespis atque crabronibus capiti suo admovet. Huic igitur superinscriptus titulus INIURIA CONTENTIONIS FILIA.

20 Quarto loco mulier picta est a genu usque insita infixaque saxo que quidem suo sibi ab humeris recepto exsectoque brachio pro clava utitur. Huic superadscriptus titulus est VINDICTA ⟨INIU-

21 RIE FILIA⟩. Quinto loco, veste pulla sordidissima induta, est picta mulier que quidem in medias undas posita scopulum insidet, ambabus manibus sibi occiput scalpuriens atque dilacerans. Huic

22 superadscriptum nomen CALAMITAS VINDICTE FILIA. Itaque quina superiora et quina proxima que recensui signa, sinistro in pariete picta conspectantur.

Dextro autem in pariete singulis quinis pari ordine quina re-

23 spondent picta simulachra mulierum. Nam primo loco ad medium parietem mulier formosissima picta est, vestita Coha, capillo arte annodato et mire composito, que quidem manu sibi altera os pres-sat, altera ad femur tenus vestem coadegit; locumque concinxit involucro vestis, sese ipsam pronis et meditabundis oculis ad si-num spectans. Huic titulus superadscriptus MODESTIA MATER.

24 Secundo proximo loco mulier picta est iocunda festivaque aspectu, oculis et fronte alacri, soluta veste et nullis nexibus incincta, aperto sinu floribus undequaque referta, que quidem aureis soleis preacu-tos surculos ex pavimento surgentes calcando urgendoque defrin-git; in eoque opere exequendo arridet. Huic nomen inscriptum

25 SECURITAS ANIMI ⟨MODESTIE FILIA⟩. Tertio loco mulier

of towering build, dressed in petitions and contracts. In one hand, she wields several wooden hooks and bent urn handles. With the palm of the other hand, she shades and protects her eyes from the rays of light, as if sighting something she recognizes at a great distance. By her is written: CONTENTION, DAUGHTER OF AMBITION. The third panel depicts a woman who, from the thigh down, is not human but goat-like, and who has the snout and teeth of a dog. In one hand, she brandishes a torch; with the other, she places on her head a crown made of wasps and hornets. Above her is written: INJURY, DAUGHTER OF CONTENTION. The fourth panel depicts a woman firmly rooted from the knees in a rock. Having severed one of her arms at the shoulder, she wields it as a club. Above her is written: VENGEANCE ⟨DAUGHTER OF INJURY⟩. The fifth panel depicts a woman dressed in sordid mourning weeds and seated on a rock in the midst of the waves of the sea. With both hands, she scratches and tears the back of her head. Above her is written: CALAMITY, DAUGHTER OF VENGEANCE. These two groups of five figures which I have described were painted on the left-hand wall.

On the right-hand wall, five painted images of women, grouped in the same pattern, correspond singly to the other five. Near the center of the wall, the first panel depicts a beautiful woman in a garment from Cos, her hair skillfully braided and wondrously arranged.[4] With one hand, she presses her mouth, while with the other, she clutches her robe to her thigh, wrapping her private parts in its folds, and gazes at her bosom with pensive and downcast eyes. Above her is written: MODESTY, MOTHER. The next panel depicts a woman with a cheerful and festive look and lively eyes, whose gown, being untied and bound by no clasps, is open at the bosom, and completely filled with flowers. Wearing golden sandals, she treads on sharp twigs that rise from the pavement, crushing them and smiling as she does so. Above her is written: PEACE OF MIND ⟨DAUGHTER OF MODESTY⟩. The third panel

18

19

20

21

22

23

24

25

picta est succincta veste et suffarcinata cum talaribus, que quidem,
cultro circum vepribus aureo cesis, aream pede putaminibus pur-
gat atque spatiosiorem reddit. Titulus huic superadscriptus CURA

26 VIRTUTIS SECURITATIS ANIMI FILIA. Quarto loco mulier
picta est procera et aspectu ipso prope virago, capillo soluto et in
aera inundanti, temporibus alatis, que quidem tubam signis et
gemmis asperam gestat et perflat, qua ex tuba innumere corolle
manant; mulierque ipsa corollis tota onusta et redimita est. Huic

27 nomen adscriptum est LAUS CURE VIRTUTIS FILIA. Quinto
loco aurea umbra hominis picta est in ara ⟨inter⟩ candelabra et divina ornamenta constituta. Huic titulus superadscriptus IMMOR-
TALITAS LAUDIS FILIA.

28   Diverso parietis ordine quina quoque altera expicta signa succe-
dunt. Namque loco primo mira imago adest picte mulieris, cui
plurimi variique unam in cervicem vultus conveniunt: seniles iuve-

29 niles, tristes iocosi, graves faceti, et eiusmodi. Complurimas item
manus ex iisdem habet humeris fluentes, ex quibus quidem alie
calamos, alie lyram, alie ⟨e⟩laboratam concinnamque gemmam, alie
pictum excul⟨p⟩tumve insigne, alie mathematicorum varia instru-
menta, alie libros tractant. Huic superadscriptum nomen HUMA-

30 NITAS MATER. Secundo vero loco mulieris effigies picta est formosissime, que quidem manu altera nummos enumerat in Samium
vas, altera solum rastro vertit in scrobes. Huic titulus adscriptus

31 est BENEFICENTIA HUMANITATIS FILIA. Tertio loco mulier
picta est nuda, cui quidem cordis loco ad pectus heret speculum et
in manu pro speculo cor substentat hominis, quo in corde speculi
expicta effigies est; in speculo vero ipso, quod pectori heret, tota
mulieris ipsius effigies insculpta est. Huic nomen superadscriptum

32 BENIVOLENTIA BENEFICENTIE FILIA. Quarto loco mulier
picta est que et colore et vigore vultus et omni facie corporis
mirum in modum bene valere appareat. Hec quidem templum

depicts a woman wearing a gown which is girt up and padded, and winged sandals. With a pruning hook, she cuts the golden thorn bushes around her, while with her foot, she clears the prunings from the threshing-floor, making it wider. Above her is written: CULTIVATION OF VIRTUE, DAUGHTER OF PEACE OF MIND. The fourth panel depicts a tall woman, practically an amazon, 26 with winged temples, and unbound hair that undulates in the breeze. Holding a trumpet encrusted with reliefs and gems, she blows into it, and innumerable garlands flow forth. Her whole body is laden and wreathed with garlands. Above her is written: PRAISE, DAUGHTER OF CULTIVATION OF VIRTUE. The fifth 27 panel depicts a gilded human shade, placed on an altar between candelabra and other sacred objects. Above the figure is written: IMMORTALITY, DAUGHTER OF PRAISE.

On the other side of the wall, another five painted figures fol- 28 low. The first panel there depicts an extraordinary image of a woman, around whose neck are gathered various faces, young, old, happy, sad, joyful, serious, and so forth. Numerous hands extend 29 from her shoulders, some holding pens, others lyres, some a polished gem, others a painted or carved ornament, some various mathematical instruments, and others books. Above her is written: HUMANITY, MOTHER. The second panel depicts the like- 30 ness of a beautiful woman. With one hand, she counts coins into a vase from Samos, while with the other she turns the soil with a hoe. Next to her is written: BENEFICENCE, DAUGHTER OF HUMANITY. The third panel depicts a naked woman. Instead of a 31 heart, there is a mirror on her breast; and she holds a human heart before her as a sort of mirror. In the heart appears the likeness of a mirror, and in the mirror on her breast appears the likeness of the entire woman. Above her is written: BENEVOLENCE, DAUGHTER OF BENEFICENCE. The fourth panel depicts a 32 woman whose splendid health is evident from the color and vigor of her face and in the entire appearance of her body. She is

atque aram pulcherrimam ex omni spicarum seminumque genere, ex omni baccharum pomorumque copia et varietate coedificat.

33 Huic titulus adscriptus PAX BENIVOLENTIE FILIA. Quinto loco simulachrum pictum est: mulier gravi et maturo aspectu que fasciculo coacto et belle edificato pro pulvinari utitur et florido in prato inter librorum multitudinem recumbit, solem superne levatis oculis adorans et manibus pronis venerans. Huic nomen superadscriptum FELICITAS PACIS FILIA.

34 His picturis, ni fallimur, aliquid voluptatis et ad bene beateque vivendum admonimenti attulimus. Id ⟨si⟩ pro instituto et sententia nostra assecuti sumus, maximum atque expectatissimum omniumque gratissimum lucubrationis nostre premium excepimus. O studiosi, favete!

: 2 :

Flores

1 Cum orbem terrarum deus optimus maximus principio constituisset, Phebo munus delegatum est ut pro arbitrio singulis rebus sua

2 in lucem prodeundi tempora distribueret. Idcirco Phebus rem totam in annos divisit annumque ipsum in ver, estatem, autumnum atque hiemem distinxit rebusque edixit, ne nisi attemperate pro-

3 dirent neque quid intempestivius conarentur. Itaque floribus et frondibus ver tempus deditum est; messibus placuit estas; musta auctumnum occupavere; nives et glacies ad hiemem reiecte sunt.

4 Hanc partitionem res omnes comprobarunt. Sed inter flores et frondes grandis admodum et que in hanc usque diem vix extincta

5 est contentio incidit. Quisque enim illorum ad pulcherrimum ver exornandum glorie et dignitatis causa primarium esse mirum in modum affectabat; sed erant flores ob sui generis prestantiam et

building a temple and beautiful altar from all kinds of seeds and ears of grain, and from an abundant variety of berries and fruits. By her is written: PEACE, DAUGHTER OF BENEVOLENCE. The 33 fifth panel depicts a woman with a solemn and mature face. Instead of a pillow, she lies on a tidy bouquet, and she reclines in a flowery meadow, in the midst of a multitude of books, worshipping the sun with uplifted eyes and downturned hands. Above her is written: HAPPINESS, DAUGHTER OF PEACE.

Unless I am mistaken, these paintings have offered my readers 34 some pleasure and some counsels for living well and happily. If I have attained my goal, I have reaped the most pleasant and desired reward of my nocturnal studies. Scholars, applaud!

: 2 :

Flowers

·

When God the Greatest and Best first created the world, Phoebus 1 was assigned the task of allotting to each created thing its season for coming forth. So Phoebus divided all time into years, and each 2 year into spring, summer, autumn, and winter. He bade all things come forth only in their season, and he warned them to attempt nothing unseasonably. Thus, flowers and foliage were assigned 3 spring, harvest chose summer, new wine claimed autumn, and snow and ice were postponed to winter. Everyone approved his 4 allotment. But between the flowers and the foliage there arose a great quarrel, which has hardly subsided even today. Both of them 5 vigorously contended for the glory and prestige of being the first to adorn the spring with beauty. The flowers were tremendously

6 nobilitatem vehementer tumido et elato ingenio. Quare non facile dici potest quanta ambitione hanc preveniendi a Phebo prerogativam exorarint. Id igitur Phebus cum assidue poscentibus floribus victus precibus concederet, 'Cavete,' inquit, 'ne hec vestra ingens
7 glorie cupiditas incommodi plus quam honoris afferat.' Illi studio glorie incensi Phebo aurem haud satis prebuere, sed e vestigio, ut ipsum ver approperare intellexerunt, certatim alacres ex tumidis ipsis gemmis obviam temere erupere. Neque id quidem impune.
8 Nam ut primum venti quibus ver advehebatur per hortos passim lasciviendo discursitare cepissent, tanta florum ruina consequuta est ut suorum stragem ex alto contuentes omnes suos ad gloriam conatus detestarentur et ad petulantiam ventorum ferendam frondibus firmioribus coisse optarint frondiumque societatem ad impetum ventorum sustinendum pene sero adoptarint.

: 3 :

Discordia

1 *Arg.* Adesne, Mercuri?
Mercur. Adsum. Salvus sis, mi Argos. Te ego ex summo Olympo in hoc supremo apud Fesulas monte considentem ut vidi, confestim huc advolavi. Quid tum igitur? deamne, quam Iovis verbis edixi ut compertam dares, Iustitiam adinvenisti?
2 *Arg.* Nulla a me uspiam gens, dum deam ipsam perquiro, indagando, pervestigando, sciscitando percunctandoque, pretermissa est. Postremo hanc sub his montibus quam vides pulcherrimam urbem adivi, quod eam arbitrabar lautissimis et ornatissimis
3 sedibus delectari. At deam nusquam minus. Quin vero ne mortalium quidem homo uspiam est, qui se illam vidisse audeat

haughty and overweening by virtue of the excellence and nobility of their race. It is hard to describe how they intrigued to win from Phoebus the privilege of appearing first. Overcome by the persistent urgings of the flowers, Phoebus acceded and said: "Beware lest your immense desire for glory cause you more harm than honor." The flowers, burning to win glory, paid him little heed. When they saw spring approaching, they raced at once to burst out of their swelling buds—but not unpunished. As soon as the spring breezes ran riot through the gardens, such widespread destruction ensued that the flowers viewed the devastation from above, and cursed all their strivings for glory. They wished they had yielded to the stronger boughs that could resist the winds' aggression, and, almost too late, they secured the alliance of the foliage in withstanding the onslaught of the winds.

6

7

8

: 3 :

Discord

Argos. Is that you, Mercury?

1

Mercury. Yes. Greetings, Argos. When I looked down from Olympus and saw you sitting on this high mountain near Fiesole, I flew down at once. Tell me, did you find the goddess Justice, whom at Jupiter's bidding I ordered you to find and bring to him?

Argos. In my search for the goddess, I neglected no people anywhere. I searched, tracked, questioned, and inquired everywhere. At last, I came to the beautiful city which you see at the foot of these mountains, for I believed that the goddess delighted in sumptuous and magnificent dwellings. But there is not the least trace of her. Indeed, there is no mortal anywhere who claims even to have seen her, apart from a few deranged

2

3

affirmare; preterquam quod, apud Evandri sedes, pauci admodum deliri senes ab avis suis dudum quantum a proavis audisse
4 fabulabantur: sua quadam sane ampla et pervetusta, sed admodum diruta atque deserta in urbe, Iustitiam ipsam diversari
solitam comminiscuntur.

5 *Mercur.* Quid igitur? an non ea apud inferos abdita est, siquidem
neque apud mortales neque apud superos latitat? Mihi iccirco
apud Stigias umbras demigrandum est. Nam deam ipsam summopere, ceteris omissis rebus, disquiri edixit Iuppiter. At tu?

6 *Arg.* Ego vero, toto terrarum orbe peragrato, cum hic paulum fessus consedissem, equum isthunc Pegaseum, unde tuo iussu
sumptus erat, ad fontem Eliconam reddere institueram.

7 *Mercur.* Laudo. Iamque bene vale; ipse quidem ad inferos deam
accitum proficiscar.

Arg. Quin prius oro, Mercuri, quenam superis tanta dee con-
veniende adsit cura dicito.

8 *Mercur.* Enimvero ipsam rem succincte audies. Acerrima inter
deos incidit disputatio, quemnam Discordie dee patrem de-
9 putent. Nam deorum nullus est qui non se vehementer studeat
illi esse in locum patris dee prepotenti, que quidem humana
divinaque iura omnia pro arbitrio queat pervertere queve sanguinis, affinitatis, cognationis amicitiarumque vincula omnia,
10 etiam diis invitis, valeat dirimere. Ea namque pietatem carita-
temque illam sanctissimam atque religiosissimam que inter
parentes ac natos extat, divellit e medio atque abiicit. Eaque
benivolentiam que inter fratres iocundissima atque iustissima
11 est, in odium atque acerbitatem convertit. Ea coniunctionem
atque convictum qui inter familiares, domesticos, affines atque
propinquos et amicos laudatur, discidiis atque simultatibus
12 rumpit et profligat. Summas eadem res publicas evertit, imperia
in servitutem subigit. Ipsos quoque supremos deos infimis
atque humillimis esse mortalibus demissiores, modo velit, efficere Discordia potest.

old men near Evander's dwelling who repeat a tale which their grandfathers had heard from their great-grandfathers. They allege that Justice used to lodge in their city, which, though large and ancient, is now quite ruined and deserted.[5] 4

Mercury. What then? Is she concealed in the underworld, since she is not hiding on earth or in heaven? If so, I must leave to visit the Stygian shades, for Jupiter has ordered me to abandon all else in my search for Justice. And you? 5

Argos. Having journeyed through the entire world, I sat down here to rest. I decided to take this Pegasean horse back to the fountain of Helicon, whence I had taken him at your behest. 6

Mercury. Good. Farewell, then. I'll proceed to the underworld to seek the goddess. 7

Argos. But first, Mercury, please tell me why the gods are so eager to find the goddess.

Mercury. I'll give you a brief account. A bitter debate has arisen between the gods: who is the father of the goddess Discord? 8
There is no god who does not strive to be thought the father of 9
this powerful goddess. She can subvert all human and divine laws as she chooses, and even against the gods' wishes can dissolve all bonds of kinship, marriage, and friendship. She utterly 10
undoes and destroys the sacrosanct piety and love between parents and children, and turns to bitter hatred the just and pleasant affection between brothers. By means of dissensions 11
and rivalries, she disrupts and ruins whatever familiarity and intimacy we praise between families, relatives, and friends. She 12
overthrows the greatest commonwealths, and reduces empires to slavery. If she chooses, Discord can render even the highest gods more abject than the lowliest and humblest men.[6]

13   Has ob res quisque deorum pro virili sese eius ipsius, que
penitus cuncta possit, dee patrem haberi student, idque ipsum
14   ceteris persuadere omni arte et ingenio elaborant. Imprimisque
clamitant nonnulli Plutonis hanc esse filiam multamque fenera-
15   torum catervam in testimonium adducunt. Adstat et Bacchus
deus magna voce deierans alium preter se nullum Discordie dee
parentem adiudicandum esse, neque sibi ad rem docendam
16   testes et graves et bonos defuturos pollicetur. Tum et Terminus
deus, sese dee progenitorem asserens, omnes legiones militum
omnesque iurisconsultorum scolas ad testimonium admitti
17   postulat. Neque preterea Priapus, ridiculus deus, a disserenda
causa eiicitur atque aspernatur, quod dicat omnes mortales pa-
18   lam profiteri Discordiam a se atque a Voluptate exortam. Sed
unus tantum ceteros omnes auctoritate et dignitate deus Honos
exsuperat, reges principesque omnes ac ipsos denique superos
testes compellans edocensque tum loca tum tempora, quibus
19   hanc ipsam ex Iustitia dea susceperit. Is unus pre ceteris oratione maxime rem persuasit. Iccirco edixit Iuppiter Iustitiam
acciri quo, re cognita, omnis controversia distrahatur. Itaque tu
iam rem tenes.

  Arg. Plane quidem.

20   *Mercur.* Adibo ergo inferos, ut institui. Tu vale. Sed muto sententiam. Prius quidem renuntiandum censeo superis hic inter mortales, apud quos putabant, minime adesse Iustitiam deam. Ea
dehinc que dixerit Iuppiter pro re exequar. Vale.

21   *Arg.* Iustitiam nusquam esse dicito, Mercuri; nosque abeamus.

As a result, every god does his utmost to be reckoned the 13
father of this virtually omnipotent goddess, and applies all his
craft and ingenuity to persuading the others. First, some cry 14
that she is Pluto's daughter, and cite the vast horde of usurers as
evidence.[7] Bacchus appears too, swearing in a loud voice that he 15
alone should be judged Discord's sire, and he promises that respected and worthy witnesses will soon appear to prove his
claim. The god Terminus also asserts that he is her progenitor, 16
and demands that all the legions of soldiers and all the schools
of jurists be admitted to testify.[8] Not even the ridiculous god 17
Priapus is excluded or rejected from pleading his case, when he
says that all mortals openly confess that Discord sprang from
him and Pleasure. But the one god who excels the others in 18
authority and dignity, Honor, summons as witnesses all kings
and rulers and even the gods, and divulges both the time and
the place in which he begat Discord by the goddess Justice.[9]
Since his arguments have been the most persuasive, Jupiter 19
summoned Justice to examine her and resolve the entire controversy. Now you know the story.

Argos. Clearly.

Mercury. I shall go to the underworld, as I intended. Farewell.— 20
No, I've changed my mind. First, I think I should report to the
gods that the goddess Justice is nowhere to be found on earth,
as they thought. Then I'll faithfully carry out whatever Jupiter
commands. Farewell.

Argos. Tell them that Justice is nowhere, Mercury. I too must go. 21

∴ 4 ∴

Hostis

1 Apud maiores nostros memoria proditum est bello quodam mari-
timo complures fuisse captos nobiles Pisanos a Genuensibus et,
parta victoria, ad senatum Genuensium relatum fuisse, quidnam
2 patres de ea captivorum multitudine fieri oportere censerent. Inter
patres fuere qui statuerent hostes captivos ad unum esse usque
necandos, illud Theodecti, quo Pompeium occidi persuasit, refe-
3 rentes: 'hominem mortuum non mordere.' Decere quidem id iure
belli, ut crudelissimum hostem gravi quadam vindicta proseque-
rentur, quo ab iniuria et immanitate posthac ceteri absterrerentur;
4 satisque ac super putandum, si eum semel quicum ⟨de⟩ vita et
sanguine decertaris manu armisque viceris, ni id quoque commit-
tas ut, post victoriam tantis laboribus ac periculis partam, tibi sit
5 denuo dimicandum; neque reclusos hostes, viros bellicosissimos et
ferocissimos, tempori occasionique servandos esse, quo duces inimicis et ministros Fortune ad calamitatem inferendam ab te us-
6 piam fuisse servatos peniteat; neque expedire quidem, tanti peri-
culi evitandi causa, eam velle gravem insuper observandis inimicis
intra urbem et omnium difficilem curam perferre, quam quidem
possis hora unica percommode atque non ⟨in⟩iuste deposuisse.

7 Alii captivos omnes incolumes ac liberos dimittendos suade-
bant. Seviendum quidem fore in eos qui armis odiisque sese infen-
sos prebeant, quoad infestos et lacessentes viceris; subditos autem
8 habendos ut imperes, non ut miseros perdas; neque decere quidem
eos, quibus aut fortuna aut victoria ipsa armatis et bellantibus pe-
percerit, fractos, inermes atque reclusos tanti facere, ut eorum
metu ipse crudelitatis ignominiam subeas, a qua quidem fortissimi
9 viri semper abhorruere; nec victoriam quidem tantum, sed pacem

∶ 4 ∶

The Enemy

Tradition relates that in our ancestors' day a number of Pisan no- 1
blemen were captured by the Genoese in a naval battle.[10] After the
victory, the question of what to do with the numerous prisoners
was brought before the members of the senate in Genoa. Some of 2
the senators thought that all the prisoners should be put to death,
and they cited the saying of Theodectus, who recommended that
Pompey be killed: "A dead man does not bite."[11] Thus, under the 3
code of war they should take harsh revenge on their cruel enemy,
so that others would be deterred from future violence and brutal-
ity. "We must by all means consider one fact," they said. "Now that 4
we have fought the enemy in deadly combat, defeated him by
strength of arms, and obtained this victory through great efforts
and dangers, we must do nothing which would force us to fight
again. We must not spare these warlike and savage captives for 5
another time or occasion when, as leaders of our enemies and ac-
complices of fortune, they may bring disaster down on us, and
cause us to regret having spared them. Nor is it expedient, to 6
avoid such great danger, to assume the onerous and difficult task
of keeping enemies under guard in our city, when in a single hour
we can eliminate the problem quite simply and justly."

Others argued that the captives should be released free and 7
unharmed. "We should only use violence," they said, "against those
who attack us with arms and hatred. But once you have vanquished your opponents, it is better to rule them as subjects than
to destroy them as wretches. Nor is it right that we, whom fortune 8
or victory spared in armed combat, should so fear vanquished,
unarmed, and imprisoned men that we disgrace ourselves by cruelty, which courageous men have always shunned. Rather than 9

potius eam fore appetendam que bellis sit finem impositura; pacem autem tum iustam et utilem et perennem futuram, cum non
10 metu sed benivolentia contineatur; eamque victoriam longe omnium censendam nobilissimam que inimicitiam, quam que inimi-
cum deleat; decereque viros fortes superato hoste id cavere, ne ipsi
11 iracundie aut furori succubuisse videantur; atque enitendum quidem ut, quos armis viceris, eos officio quoque et pietate devincias:
officii quidem esse ut, quos furor belli et irritatus miles non ab-
sumpserit, iustus et dignus imperio civis non perdat.

12   Aliorum longe diversa erat sententia, quam quidem ferunt Pisa-
num quemdam, imbecillum quidem hominem et admodum pauperem, sed quantum videre licet, ingenio non hebeti preditum, sua
13 proscriptum a patria vindicte gratia suasisse. Ea fuit huiusmodi:
neque occidendos captivos, neque esse incolumes dimittendos, sed
14 carcere asservandos. Meminisse quidem aiebat oportere. Pisanos
pervetusto et incredibili quodam erga Genuenses esse affectos
odio, neque tantarum cladium memoriam facile unico posse beneficio obliterari, quin immanes et irritati animi ad vindictam quam
15 ad beneficii gratiam sint propensiores. 'Quamdiu enim,' inquit,
'inter eos ulla elucebit spes vindicandi, nunquam arma et contentiones quieturas certo scio. Novi enim meorum animos et ingenium. Non tamen, si necentur, id e re publica arbitrandum est.
16 Sed expedire quidem arbitror primo eos apud vos quasi obsides
habeatis pacis, si pacem querendam uspiam statuetis; sin bellum
impendat, hos eque ad omnem bellorum eventum expectatote usui
17 futuros. Hac denique sententia et crudelem hostem severissime
puniri et pietatis rationem haberi: nam cum omnis civitatum amplitudo et robur in copia opum maxime atque in civium multitudine consistat, fore hoc pacto ut opes civium Pisanorum alendis
captivis exhauriantur, et nova futura soboles, matronis captivorum
18 non nubentibus neque parturientibus, interpelletur. Itaque pietatis
illud fore, cum vitam beneficio tuo is habeat, qui ferro tuam et

mere victory, we should seek a peace which will put an end to wars. And that peace will be just, expedient, and lasting, which is sustained by goodwill rather than fear. By far the noblest victory 10 of all is one which abolishes enmity rather than the enemy. After defeating their foe, valiant men must avoid appearing to yield to anger or rage. Instead, they should strive to subdue by kindness 11 and mercy those whom they have conquered by arms. It is our duty to see that these men, who were not destroyed by the fury of war and enraged soldiers, are not put to death by just and responsible civilians."

Still others were of a radically different opinion, which, they 12 say, was proposed by a certain Pisan, an infirm fellow and quite poor, but not, it would seem, of slow wit, who sought revenge for his exile. His proposal was this: neither to kill the prisoners, nor 13 free them unharmed, but to keep them in prison. We should re- 14 member, he said, that the Pisans bear an ancient and incredible hatred toward the Genoese. One generous deed could scarcely cancel the memory of such great defeats, for their savage and enraged spirits tended more to vengeance than to gratitude for favors. "As long," he said, "as they have even a glimmer of hope for 15 revenge, I am sure that armed strife will not cease. I know the hearts and minds of my countrymen. You must not think that 16 your state will profit by putting them to death. If you decide to seek peace, I deem it expedient to keep them as hostages. But if war should threaten, you may expect to find them equally useful in any wartime eventuality. By my proposal, the enemy is severely 17 punished, while mercy is observed. Since the greatness and strength of cities lie in the abundance of their wealth and in the number of their citizens, my plan will exhaust the Pisans' resources in supporting these prisoners, and cut off their future generations, since the prisoners' wives can neither bear children nor remarry. My plan is merciful: your generosity will spare those 18

vitam et sanguinem petiverit, et contra severitatis illud, quod adversarium infestissimum, quacunque possis ratione, imbecilliorem reddas.'

19   Placuit istius sententia, qua effectum est ut Pise prope delerentur. Ut iam non obscurum sit, unicum et eum quidem abiectum hominem posse in tempore universe rei publice pestem calamitatemque afferre.

: 5 :

Lapides

1   Quidam rotundi et admodum volubiles lapides sese alta ex ripa in eum qui subterfluebat torrentem studio nandi precipitarunt. Iamque leti atque nimium alacres, cum suo quo erant cadendo concitati motu, tum appulsu undarum, nonnihil erant secundo fluvio saltitando prolapsi, et congratulabantur rem ex sententia

2   succedere. Sed a nonnullis sui generis lapidibus, qui iampridem in hanc ipsam stultitiam natandi cupiditate ceciderant, interpellati adhesere.

3   'Et quidnam?,' inquiunt, 'ne vero nos quod pulchre deceat sero atque intempestive prospeximus? Que igitur nostra usque in hanc diem detestanda fuit ignavia, qui quidem ripam aquis proximam incolentes tam commodam, tam dignam, tam ad perdiscendum

4   facilem rem desidia nostra ignorarimus? Dispudet tanta in voluptate prope atque officio nos non iam antea fuisse versatos.'

5   Tum veterani lapides, cum hec audissent, 'O stultissimi,' inquiunt, 'et procul dubio male consulti! Vosne, quod undarum secundo impetu effectum est ut res pro temeritate vestra paulum

6   succederet, id vestra putatis posse fieri opera? Propediem quidem intelligetis, inepti, quantum intersit in antiquam posse ripam per

who have threatened your lives by the sword. And it is severe: you will weaken a dangerous foe in every possible way."

His proposal was adopted, and nearly destroyed Pisa. Thus it is 19 not difficult to see that on occasion a single person, even an abject one, may wreak injury and ruin on an entire nation.

: 5 :

Stones

Eager to swim, some round stones that were liable to roll around 1 threw themselves from a high river bank into the rushing stream below. Very joyful and happy, they skipped downstream, impelled by the momentum of their fall and by the impact of the waves; and they rejoiced in their success. But they were stopped by a 2 number of like stones, who had long ago lapsed into this same folly from a desire to swim, and were stuck fast.

"How is it," they said, "that we are so slow to see our best inter- 3 ests? What contemptible sloth possessed us until today? Living on this bank so near the water, in our idleness we neglected a thing so useful, noble, and easy to master as learning to swim. We are 4 ashamed that we did not engage sooner in this pleasure which is nearly our duty."

When the veteran stones heard this, they replied: "O fools, so 5 clearly ill-advised, do you think it is by your own effort, and not by the force of the waves, that your recklessness grants you this brief success? O silly ones, soon you will learn the difference 6

otium et quietem consenescere in libertate, an studio rerum novarum vobis ignotam et a vestris moribus et consuetudine penitus
7   alienam vite degende rationem inire. Tum quidem temeritatis
vestre penitebit, cum luto et limo obsiti, squalentes, in sordibus
immersi herebitis, aut per corruentem amnem provoluti, agitati
collisique, nullam iniquissimorum laborum et gravissimarum difficultatum molestiarumque requiem aut intercapedinem reperietis.'

: 6 :

Hedera

1   Pirus arbos, cum a sacerdotibus ornari templum herba hedera intueretur cumque illic inter aureos apparatus non mediocri haberi
2   in honore animadverteret, 'Quid hoc rei est?,' inquit, 'herbane hec
petulca, insolens, infecunda, nullos ad utiles usus nata, que quidem muros templi nonnunquam in ruinam traxit, que deorum
edificia non cessat multis in dies incommodis afficere, religioni et
3   piis ministeriis dedicabitur? Me vero innoxiam, que fructus dulcis-
simos prebeo, que pauperibus victum paro, que secundas divitum
mensas cenarumque delitias orno, puer quivis fustibus et saxis cedit?'
4   Itaque multa huiusmodi de rei iniquitate, de sua sorte, de sacerdotum improbitate deploranti piro respondit hedera his verbis:
'Etenim tu eras inscia,' inquit, 'quam hoc genus hominum nisi improbos, aut eos a quibus maiorem in modum possint ledi, neque
vereri consueverit neque diligere? Esto, heus tu! dura et acerba.'

between growing old on your former bank in tranquility, leisure, and freedom, and adopting, in your eagerness for revolution, a way of life which is foreign to your traditions. You'll regret your temer- 7 ity when you are stuck in squalor and covered with mud and slime, and when you are tumbled, tossed, and battered by the rushing stream, and find neither rest nor respite from oppressive vexations and overwhelming hardships."

: 6 :

Ivy

When a pear tree saw some priests adorn their temple with ivy, 1 thus giving this weed a place of considerable honor amid orna- ments of gold, she exclaimed: "How can this be? Will they dedi- 2 cate to religion and holy rites this aggressive, insolent, and infertile weed, which, born for no good purpose, has often dragged temple walls down to ruin and which never ceases daily to cause various damage to the buildings of the gods? I harm no one, yield sweet 3 fruit, feed the poor, and am the delight of rich men's desserts. Yet any boy can strike me with sticks and rocks."

As the pear tree complained of her unjust fate and of the 4 priests' wickedness, the ivy replied: "Weren't you aware that this breed of men has always revered and loved the wicked, and those who can harm them most? Come, then, be hard and bitter."

: 7 :

Suspitio

1 ⟨*Fama*⟩. Profecto quanto magis magisque cogito res hec haudquaquam eiusmodi est, ut a senatu bonisque civibus negligenda

2 esse videatur. Quod si lapidibus pluisse, si murum ⟨de⟩ celo
tactum, si natum quippiam informe renuntiarint, tametsi usi-
tata ea nec interraro visa sint, augures fatigantur, ad libros Sy-
billinos decurritur, animi civium passim solicitudine metuque et

3 pervestigandi quid sibi velint cura exagitantur. Nunc vero, cum
media in ara, medio ex igne sacro res istiusmodi perquam nefaria exorta sit, ·superi boni, quo esse civitatem in metu, qua
rerum novarum expectatione pendere animos civium oportet!

4 *Mnim.* Mirabar, quid garrula isthec sua pro consuetudine novi
aliquid circumferret. Sed iuvat quidem ex ea quicquid id ipsum
sit ediscere.

5 *Fama.* O salve, Mnimia. Audistin rem execrandam, ex ipso foco,
virginibus adstantibus et ignem foventibus, caulem exortum
esse herbe virentissime, que quidem, ipso temporis momento ut
apparuit, e vestigio (mirabile dictu!) ad cubiti altitudinem excreverit foliaque complura omnibus ignota, prelonga et admodum patula, miris omnium generum coloribus expicta, diversas
in partes explicuerit?

6 *Mnim.* Utrumne id monstrum illico extirpandum non curarunt?
Fama. Anceps et ambigua virginibus, que tum aderant, animi fuerat sententia. Nam alie evellendam herbam ipsam, alie non at-

7 tingendam iniussu augurum statuebant. Crebre varieque sententie dicte ardua in re fuere. Iccirco me atque Opinionem
virginem comitem, quam apud forum cetus hominum detinuit,
emisere ut collegio id renuntiaremus.

: 7 :

Suspicion

[*Rumor*]. The more I consider it, the more this matter seems to 1
demand the attention of our senate and leading citizens. For 2
when we hear reports that it has rained stones, that lightning
has struck a city wall, or that a monster has been born, such
portents are familiar and not unusual. But the augurs are harassed, people turn to the Sibylline Books, and our citizens'
minds are everywhere agitated by fear, disquiet, and anxiety to
fathom what such events mean.[12] And now that an utterly hor- 3
rible thing has sprung forth from the sacred fire in the middle
of the altar, great gods, what fear should seize our city, and
what foreboding of revolution perplex our citizens' minds!

Mnimia. I wonder what news this chatterbox is spreading about, 4
as is her custom.[13] It's best to learn it from her.

Rumor. Greetings, Mnimia. Have you heard this abomination? 5
While the virgins were tending the fire, the stalk of a hardy
plant sprang from the middle of the hearth.[14] At the very moment it appeared — wondrous to say! — it grew to the height of
a cubit, and sent forth foliage in all directions. Never seen before, its leaves were very long, quite broad, and speckled with
wondrous colors of every sort.

Mnimia. Didn't they try to uproot the monster at once? 6

Rumor. The virgins who were present were of two minds. Some
thought that the plant should be pulled out, while others
thought it should not be touched without an order from the
augurs. In this difficult matter, numerous diverse opinions were 7
voiced. So they sent me to report the matter to the sacred col-
lege, accompanied by the maiden Opinion, who was detained
by a crowd in the forum.

Mnim. Quid igitur sacerdotes ipsi, ecquid aiunt?

8 *Fama.* Obstupuere attonitique loco hesere. Gravis inter eos discre-
patio, multa ex libris sacris commemoratio. Sed, quantum ex
tota re potui intelligere, discidia ac discordias gravissimas capi-
9 taliaque odia non defutura autumant. Sed eccam Rationem
atque Veritatem, Vestales virgines e templo huc versus egre-
dientes. Ex his rem ut gesta est ex quo abfui disquiremus.

10 *Rat.* Nos, o Veritas, ad fontem expiatum a sudore hoc obsceno
manus frontemque expurgatum pergamus, quandoquidem tan-
11 tam pestem substulimus. Mox Opinionem virginem, que cum
Fama exierat, accersitum advolabimus ut ex Iani patris iussu
focum restauret mutatis vestibus. Quod, ni fiat, verendum asse-
verant ne monstrum ipsum reviviscat.

Fama. Obsecro, o Veritas, idne ex ara amovistis monstrum?

12 *Ver.* Et quanto, superi boni, cum labore tum periculo! Quod ni
Ianus pater, a diis ut arbitror missus, advenisset, quantum videre licuit, nos monstrum id formidolosissimum oppressisset ac
penitus confecisset.

13 *Mnim.* Ain vero? At qui id?

Ver. Nam immodicis suis foliis operire ignem atque flammas sub-
14 terfocare occeperat. Quod Ratio, manum cum appulisset ut
prohiberet, folia hinc atque hinc discerpere eniteretur, repente
monstrum, vi maxima foliorum emissa, in omnes partes sese
attollens virginis manum atque deinceps cubitum, mox pectus,
postremo os oculosque oppressit atque ita obinvolutam virginem arctissime compressam detinuit, ut pre metu et dolore
herere torpentem et prope deficientem propter aram coegerit.
15 Ego sorori totis viribus luctanti et renitenti opem allatura,
sumpto cultro quo ad sacrificium utimur, mei immemor conci-
16 dere monstrum frustra tentabam: nullas enim plagas accipiebat
quove infesta lacessendo instabam, eo monstrum superbius foliaque adversum quasi manus prehensitabundum protendebat
sororemque durius illaqueatam constringebat.

Mnimia. What about the priests? What do they say?

Rumor. They were struck dumb, and paralyzed with astonish- 8
ment. They held a solemn debate with many references to their
holy books. As far as I could gather, they assert that there will
be strife, grave discord, and deadly feuds. But here are the Ves- 9
tal Virgins Reason and Truth, coming toward us from the
temple. Let's ask them what has happened since I left.

Reason. O Truth, let us go to the fountain to purify our hands and 10
cleanse our brows of this foul sweat, now that we have eliminated this great plague. Soon we shall hasten to summon the 11
maiden Opinion, who left with Rumor. When she has changed
her robes, she will rekindle the hearth as father Janus commands.[15] Unless this is done, they say we must fear that the
monster may revive.

Rumor. Tell me, Truth, did you remove the monster from the altar?

Truth. Only, good gods, with great difficulty and danger! If father 12
Janus had not appeared — divinely sent, I think — the dreadful
monster would have overpowered and slain us.

Mnimia. Really? How? 13

Truth. It had begun to cover the fire, stifling the flames with its
enormous leaves. When Reason reached out to stop it and tried 14
to pluck its leaves, the monster suddenly sent forth a greater
mass of them and grew up on all sides. It overwhelmed the girl,
wrapping around her hand, then her elbow, next her breast, and
finally her face and eyes. It curled around her so tightly that she
was numb and nearly faint with fear and pain, and it pressed
her to the altar. While my sister resisted with all her strength, I 15
tried to rescue her. Not thinking of myself, I took up a sacrifi-
cial knife and strove in vain to cut the monster in pieces. It 16
could not be wounded. The more violently I strove to assail it,
the more boldly it extended its leaves like hands to grasp me,
and the more tightly it held my sister in its embrace.

17   Dum tanto in discrimine versaremur, Ianus pater insperato adventu opem nobis salutemque attulit. Edixit enim vi⟨n⟩ctam ipsam et nexus omnes enodarem truncumque ipsum igne tenus

18 carperem traheremque intrepide. Itaque parui. Ac monstrum, ut primum iuxta admovi manum, quasi sponte collapsum excidit omnemque cadens vim et atrocitatem amisit. Obstupuimus et, quod maiorem in modum admiraremur, trunco nulle aderant radices, nulle circum extabant fimbrie, nulla loco exierat

19 stirps. Tum Ianus pater 'Efferte id ocius,' inquit, 'sub divo.' At nobis iussa patris exequentibus, o rem incredibilem!, solem ut vidit, monstrum evanuit atque disparuit.

20 *Mnim.* Mira profecto narras. Verum et quamne illam esse herbam putarunt?

    Ver. Eam quidem Ianus pater vocari Suspitionem dixit.

While we were at this critical point, father Janus arrived un- 17
expectedly to bring us aid and salvation. He bid me extricate
my fettered sister from the monster's coils, and then to seize its
trunk near the flame and to pull without flinching. I obeyed.
As soon as I laid my hands on it, the monster collapsed, losing 18
all its strength and ferocity as it fell. We were struck dumb, and
marveled especially that the trunk had no roots, no tendrils,
and no runners. Then father Janus said: "Take it outside 19
quickly!" We obeyed his command; and, incredibly, as soon as
it saw the sunlight, the monster vanished from sight.

Mnimia. Your story is truly amazing. But tell me, what plant did 20
they think it was?

Truth. Father Janus said it is called Suspicion.

LIBER IV

Prohemium ad Poggium

⟨B⟩ubulas limoso in littore inter palustres herbas proiectas capram quandam, que ⟨in⟩ maceriem vetustissimi cuiusdam scrupeum supra saxum collapsi templi consederat, his verbis admonuisse

2 ferunt: 'Io! quenam te isthuc temeritas, o lasciva, rapuit, ut herboso spreto littore isthec ardua et penitus invia affectes? An non prestare intelligis dulci et succoso gramine exsaturari, quam aspera

3 continuo rudera et amarum alte caprificum sitiendo carpere? Velim tibi quidem consulas, ut quanto deinceps cum periculo ver⟨r⟩ucas istas ipsas ambias non peniteat.'

4 Bubulis aiunt capram huiusmodi verbis respondisse: 'He en! An quidem, gravissima et tristissima mollipes, tu ignara es, ut os ventri, ori pedes operam sedulo suppeditent? Mihi autem non

5 bubulus, sed capreus stomachus est. Tibi quidem si que ipsa carpo eo sunt ingrata, quo datum est eadem ut nequeas attingere, mihi tua isthec ulva eo non grata est, quo passim vel desidiosissimis

6 omnibus pecudibus pateat. Quod si supinam te aliorum pericula sollicitam reddunt, vultures quidem, que ab ipso sub stellis ethere exsangue aliquod pervestigant cadaver, admonuisse decuit. Namque illis quam nobis omnis est casus longe periculosior.'

7 Equidem, mi Poggi, hoc ipsum nobis, dum his conscribendis intercenalibus occupamur, evenire plane sentio: ut sint plerique qui nos cupiant uberioribus et commodioribus in campis eloquen-

8 tie ali et depasci; atque iidem, quod difficillimis istis et non illiusmodi inventionibus delectemur, que succo vulgatioris eloquentie et bonis fortune sint refertiores, vituperant. Qui quidem, si capram hanc nostram audierint, nihil erit quod nos, uti arbitror, repre-

9 hendendos ducant. Aut enim, si id vitio dabunt, quod nostram

BOOK IV

Preface to Poggio Bracciolini   1

While wallowing in the lowly swamp grass of a muddy riverbank,
some water buffalo, they say, saw a she-goat[1] perched on the ruins
of an ancient temple which had collapsed atop a rocky crag, and
admonished her in these words: "You there, wanton one, what te-   2
merity possesses you, that you spurn this verdant bank and attempt that arduous and virtually inaccessible height? Don't you
see that it is better to fill yourself with sweet and juicy grass than
to continually graze on rocky soil, thirstily picking at bitter wild
figs? Take care of yourself, lest you eventually regret your danger- 3
ous rambles on such steep heights."

The she-goat, they say, replied to the buffalo in these words: 4
"Ha! ponderous and gloomy tenderfooted beasts! Don't you know
that the mouth works for the stomach, and the feet for the mouth?
I have a goat's stomach, not a cow's. If you disdain so much what 5
I graze on because you can't reach it, I spurn your swamp grass as
accessible everywhere to even the idlest cattle. And if in your indo- 6
lence you worry about the danger of others, you should have re-
proved the vultures, who seek out carcasses from the highest
reaches of heaven. Their fall is far more dangerous than mine."

Now, the very same thing, dear Poggio, I find happens to me as   7
I engage in writing these *Dinner Pieces*. Many of my friends urge
me to seek food and sustenance in the more plentiful and pleasant
fields of eloquence. And the same people censure me for delight-   8
ing in difficult pursuits, rather than in those filled with the juice of
commonplace eloquence and material reward. But if these critics
will heed the goat in the fable, I think they will find no cause
to reproach me. If they blame me for choosing to spurn other   9

nos non inviti naturam, spretis reliquis nummulariis artibus,
sequamur, mathematicos quoque omnes illi, et eos qui astrorum
cognitioni, et eos qui rebus penitus sepositis dediti sunt, vitio
10 pariter adscribant necesse est: namque illi quidem, si ab ea spe qua
tam alte animos sublevarunt, ut celorum usque ultimos orbes
mente et cogitatione pervadant, ceciderint, quis non eosdem
11 quanto sint cum detrimento corruituri perspicit? Nemo tamen eos
liberale quippiam sectari inficiatur.

At nos rara hec delectant, que inter lautiores cenas ditiorum
quam me esse profitear scriptorum, veluti in pulmento subamare
12 interdum herbe, sint non reiicienda. Tum etiam in ea re, si nostre
iuvat industrie periculum facere, in qua quidem ingenio studium et
studio assiduitas subeat, quis ab huiusmodi varias et rarissimas
13 inventiones promendo sua nos invidia abducet? At enim qui nostra lectitarint et quibus in rebus quamque variis versari viderint,
⟨. . .⟩.

: I :

Somnium

1 *Lep.* Superi boni, ne vero tu es noster Libripeta? Quidnam hoc rei
est? Quid ita fedum atque luto delibutum te intueor? Unde
prodis? Quo pergis?
2 *Libr.* Egone? Isthinc exeo.
Lep. Obsecro, ex hacne fetenti cloaca, mi homo?
Libr. Ha ha he!
3 *Lep.* Insanis?
Libr. Minime. Quin—velim scias—me isthuc summa impulit
prudentia.

lucrative arts and for following my natural abilities, then they must also blame the mathematicians and all others who devote themselves to understanding the stars and profoundly recondite subjects. Can't everyone see how ruinously they fail when they fall 10 short of the hope that led them to contemplate the farthest realms of the heavens? Yet no one denies that they pursue a liberal goal. 11

For myself, I take pleasure in rare subjects which, like piquant herbs in an appetizer, should not be excluded from the lavish dinners of writers who, I confess, are richer than myself. Besides, if I 12 wish to test my diligence in this field — in which zeal furthers talent, and application zeal — whose envy can distract me from bringing forth diverse and rare inventions like these? For when they 13 read my works and see the variety of their subjects [. . .].[2]

: I :

The Dream

Lepidus. Good gods, is this my friend Libripeta? What is the mat- 1
    ter? Why do I see you so filthy and smeared with mud? Where
    are you coming from, and where are you going?
Libripeta. Me? I came from there. 2
Lepidus. What, from this stinking sewer, dear fellow?
Libripeta. Ha ha ha!
Lepidus. Are you mad? 3
Libripeta. Not at all. Rather, I was moved by great wisdom.

4   *Lep.* Rem teneo. Aliquos vetustissimos libros in cloaca esse audi-
     eras fortassis: idcirco tu, conducendis libris deditus, illuc te
     precipitaras.

5   *Libr.* Tua isthec lepiditas, Lepide, semper habuit minimum salis.

6   *Lep.* Nobis quidem ineruditis, quos tu in triviis appellas dementes
     atque insipidos, huiusmodi non insulsa placent. Tu tamen, age,
     recita tuam isthanc cloacariam prudentiam.

7   *Libr.* Cupis?
     Lep. Cupio.

8   *Libr.* Narro. Mihi quidem intuenti hoc diluvium stultorum homi-
     num, quo hec etas exuberat, admodum stomachato incidit in
     mentem moribus meis ad vitam degendam eum esse aptissi-
     mum locum, ubi sese qui somniant recipiunt. Nam illic tuto, ut
9   inter somniandum vides, licet pro arbitrio delirare. Eam ob rem
     conveni sacerdotem quemdam magicis artibus plane eruditum,
     a quo summis precibus tandem brevissimum illud iter didici ad
     eas ipsas provincias proficiscendi, ad quas pervolant somniantes.
     Illico me illuc properans contuli.

10   *Lep.* Ergo tu vigilans te inter somniantes habuisti? Miras profecto
     res narras!
     Libr. Miran tibi hec videntur?
     Lep. Ut nihil eque.

11   *Libr.* Multo magis miranda ea sunt que in illis provinciis conspexi:
     flumina, montes, prata, campos, monstra aspectu stupenda dic-
     tuque ac memoratu incredibilia, sed que tantum ad philoso-
     phantium litteras perpulchre spectent.

12   *Lep.* Ergo tu, qui te philosophum haberi optas, posteaquam
     mutam huc usque omnem etatem duxisti tuam, hanc laudis
     occasionem non deseres. Primum hoc quidem philosophandi
     munus recensendo somnio suscipies.

13   *Libr.* Utinam nostrum ad hanc rem exequendam satis valeret in-
     genium! nam esset voluptati describere tum cetera, tum eum

Lepidus. I see the reason. You had probably heard that there were 4
some ancient books in the sewer, and as an avid book collector,
you plunged right in.

Libripeta. Your wit, witty Lepidus, is never savory. 5

Lepidus. Unlearned men like me, whom you publicly call deranged 6
and insipid, enjoy slightly pungent remarks. But, come, tell me
about your sewer sagacity.

Libripeta. You wish it? 7

Lepidus. I do.

Libripeta. I'll tell my tale. As I was contemplating the flood of 8
fools in which this age is awash, it struck me in my indignation
that the place best suited to my character would be that to
which dreamers repair. For there, as we see when we dream,
one is safe to rave as one pleases. So I went to a priest who is 9
quite accomplished in the arts of magic; and after many entreaties, I finally learned from him the shortest way that leads
to the realms to which dreamers fly. I set forth at once in haste.

Lepidus. Then you consorted with dreamers while still awake? 10
Your tale astounds me.

Libripeta. It astounds you?

Lepidus. More than anything else.

Libripeta. Even more astounding were the sights I saw in those 11
realms: rivers, mountains, meadows, fields, and monsters — all
terrifying to behold, and incredible to relate and recall, but remarkably suited to the writings of philosophical men.

Lepidus. Wishing to be regarded as a philosopher, you previously 12
led a life of silence, and now you won't miss this chance to win
praise. By relating this dream, you'll perform your first act of
philosophizing.

Libripeta. I wish my intellect were equal to the task. It would be a 13
pleasure to describe what I saw, especially the river at the very

maxime fluvium qui in ipso provincie ingressu est, rerum omnium que dici aut excogitari possunt longe admiratione dignissimum.

14   *Lep.* Tetros fortassis, veluti Lethea flumina, liquores aut Stigiamne aquam fluit?

15   *Libr.* Minime. Verum — o rem incredibilem! — pro undis infiniti
16   hominum vultus volvuntur; at ex his videres alios vultus pallentes tristes valitudinarios, alios hilares venustos rubentes, alios oblongos macilentos rugosos, alios pingues tumidos turgidos, alios fronte aut oculis aut naso aut ore aut dentibus aut barba ⟨aut⟩ capillo aut mento prolixo prominenti ac deformi: horror,
17   stupor, monstra! At huius ipsius fluvii traiciiendi, scin que mira sit ratio et modus? Te ipsum in orbem coactum pervolutes oportet, non secus atque ipsa faciunt saxa que per proclive corruunt.

   Lep. Ridiculum.

18   *Libr.* Ne dixeris ridiculum. Est enim id profecto periculosum: nam sunt illi quidem vultus admodum mordaces, quod ni ipse, dudum meis dentibus lacessendo homines provocare et certare suetus, cutem multis acceptis morsibus callosam haberem, to-
19   tum me lacerum videres. Sed ago superis gratias postquam integro naso traieci fluvium.

20   *Lep.* Perdurissima tibi sit cutis oportet, quam nulli dentes ledant. Verum et quid tum, traiecto fluvio?

21   *Libr.* Res longe litteris dignissimas! Adsunt namque illic convalles montium, ubi res amisse servantur.

22   *Lep.* Utrumne et perditi hominum dies eo ipso in loco servantur? Vah! quantos tuos annos recognovisti? Quid ais?

23   *Libr.* Omnes. Sed quod mirere, primum illic partem non minimam mei cerebri offendi: eam quidem quam vetula quedam a
24   me amata emunxerat. Quod si licuisset — non enim fas est illinc aliquid auferre —, hanc dextram capitis partem vacuam modo atque inanem replessem.

entrance to this realm. For of all things that can be said or thought, that is by far the most worthy of admiration.

Lepidus. Does it flow with horrible liquids like the streams of Le- 14 the? Or with water like the Styx?

Libripeta. Not at all. Rather, incredibly, instead of waves, it flows 15 with countless human faces![3] Among them you would see some 16 pale, sad, and infirm; others ruddy, cheerful, and comely; some long, thin, and wrinkled; others with abundant, prominent, and misshapen foreheads, eyes, noses, mouths, teeth, beards, hair, or chins — all horrible, shocking, and monstrous! And do you 17 know by what strange means you cross this river? You curl yourself into a ball and roll across, like rocks tumbling downhill.[4]

Lepidus. Ridiculous.

Libripeta. Don't call it ridiculous. It's quite dangerous, for the faces 18 love to bite. If I hadn't been long accustomed to wounding men with my own teeth, and tough-skinned from the many bites I've received in continual insults and quarrels, you'd see me torn to shreds. But I thank the gods above, since I crossed the river 19 with my nose intact.

Lepidus. Your skin must be very tough to resist such teeth. After 20 crossing the river, what then?

Libripeta. Sights worthy of record! On the other side, there are 21 mountain valleys where lost things are preserved.

Lepidus. Are men's lost days kept there too? Ha, how many of 22 your own years did you recognize? Tell me.

Libripeta. All of them. But more astounding, I found there a large 23 part of my brain, which an aged mistress had swiped from me. If it had been permitted — but it is forbidden to carry anything 24 away — I would have filled the right side of my head, which is hollow and empty.

25 *Lep.* Cave existimes vacuum esse id quod repletum sit insania.
Quid tum? utrum et bone artes et prisce Latine littere illic
amisse iacent?

26 *Libr.* Isthic, inquam, prorsus que amiseris omnia reperies. Adsunt
quidem in mediis campis antiqua illa que leguntur imperia gentium, auctoritates, beneficia, amores, divitie et eiusmodi omnia,
que posteaquam amissa sunt, nunquam in hanc lucem redeunt.

27 *Lep.* Tu vero quonam pacto a ceteris rebus beneficia novisti, qui
ne minimum quidem tua omni in vita beneficium in quempiam
contulisti quive nihil unquam a quovis liberalissimo tibi deditum in beneficii locum putasti?

28 *Libr.* Ne novissem quidem quippiam, ita pleraque omnia illic alia
erant quam putassem, ni custodes qui aderant omnium fe-
cissent me rerum certiorem.

29 *Lep.* Quid ita?
Libr. Sunt namque in mediis campis imperia in unam congeriem
accumulata, que tu si videris, despexeris.
Lep. Ain vero?

30 *Libr.* Nam sunt ea quidem pregrandes vesice, plene licentia, men-
31 daciis atque sonitu tibiarum et tubarum. Proxime stant beneficia, atque ea quidem sunt hami argentei aureique; deinceps
adsunt plumbee quedam ale, quas dicunt esse auctoritates ho-
32 minum; tum prope adsunt manice atque compedes ignite, quas
dicunt esse amores; demum in ipsis pulveribus extant infinita
33 civium nomina insculpta stilo, ea dicunt esse divitias. Denique,
ne sim prolixior, isthic quevis omnia preter stultitiam reperies.

34 *Lep.* Sane, mi homo, iam nunc fateor hanc tuam peregrinationem
esse non indignam litteris philosophantium.

35 *Libr.* Quid, si cetera audias?
Lep. Recita, queso. Nam etsi totus fetes, non invitus tamen te
audio. Sequere, narra.

36 *Libr.* Narro. Illic iuxta eminet mons altissimus, in quo, ut ferunt,
veluti in lebete aliquo res omnes desiderate atque expectate

Lepidus. Don't think anything is empty that is filled with madness. 25
What then? Do the liberal arts and Latin writings of antiquity
lie lost there?

Libripeta. You'll find there everything that has been lost. In the 26
middle of those fields, there are the ancient empires of nations
we read about, as well as authorities, favors, loves, riches, and
all such things that never return, once they are lost.

Lepidus. How could you recognize favors, when you have never 27
done anyone a favor in your entire life, and when you have
never considered a favor even the most generous man's gift to
you?

Libripeta. I wouldn't have recognized them—so different was 28
nearly everything from what I thought—if there hadn't been
guardians present to explain everything to me.

Lepidus. What do you mean? 29

Libripeta. In the middle of the fields, there were empires gathered
in a heap that you would despise, if you saw them.

Lepidus. Really?

Libripeta. They consist of enormous bladders filled with license, 30
lies, and the sound of flutes and trumpets. Next to them lie 31
favors, which consist of silver and gold hooks; and next to these
are leaden wings, which they say are men's authorities. Nearby 32
are fiery manacles and fetters, which they say are love affairs.
Next, engraved in the dust with a stylus, there are countless
citizens' names, which they say are riches. In sum, to be brief, 33
you'll find everything there but folly.

Lepidus. Truly, my friend, I must grant that your journey is not 34
unworthy of the works of philosophers.

Libripeta. What will you say, if you hear the rest? 35

Lepidus. Recount it, please. Although you stink, I shall gladly listen. Proceed; tell your tale.

Libripeta. I shall. Nearby there is a very high mountain in which, 36
they say, all objects of desire and hope boil as in a caldron.

37 ebulliunt: hunc circa montem consident vota et preces hominum diis exposita. Mons vero ipse summo ex cacumine modo
has modo alias res evomit: ea casu partim hinc partim illinc a
monte corruunt. Sed his rebus visendis minime oblectabar.

38 Multa quidem huiusmodi seu negligentia seu satietate et fasti-
dio tantarum rerum, que hinc atque hinc sub oculis apparebant,

39 pretermisi. Tandem eo perveni, non longe ab his locis, ubi rapidissimus amnis percurrit, quem aiunt excrevisse lachrimis lu-
gentium atque calamitosorum hominum. Hunc ego quanto ca-

40 chinno fluvium tranarim, non facile dici potest. Namque adsunt
ad transportandos homines damnate quedam vetule, que dum
vitam agebant, iuvencule, superbe ac dure, vetule, superstitiose
atque malefice fuere. Ridebis, si tranandi modum dixero.

41 *Lep.* Porro et ridere et nihil abs te, quod ad peregrinationem hanc
pertineat, reticeri opto.

42 *Libr.* Gero tibi morem. Stant quidem illic ad litus vetule ille resu-
43 pine, nude. Tu genua in ipsis convallibus hilium infigis, manibus vero earum aures adprehendis atque quo velis traiicere
substrate vetule caput pro clavo dirigis. Illa calcibus et palmis
resupina remigat.

44 *Lep.* O te dignum tali naufragio! Verum an non persepius uterque
summergitur?

45 *Libr.* Minime vero. Nam, ut rem teneas, audies rem dignissimam
quam ex media philosophia illic didici. Pulmo quidem intesti-
46 nus efficit ut natantes superextent aquis. Strum⟨os⟩a vero mulier duos habet pulmones, unum in renibus, alium quem in
47 spatulis gerat. Tum accedit quod feminarum capita penitus
vacua optimum ad tranandum fluvium presidium prestant.—
Quid spectas?

48
49 *Lep.* Te, qui, si sapis, te in hanc iterum cloacam precipitabis. Nam
tu quidem plus hinc philosophie una isthac peregrinatione

Around the mountain lie all the vows and prayers offered by men to the gods. From its summit, the mountain spews forth 37 these and other things, and they spill down the mountain on this side and that. Yet I took little pleasure in this spectacle. I 38 have omitted many such sights, for their great number left me indifferent, sated, or disgusted. At length, I reached a place not 39 far off, where a swift river is said to swell with the tears of wretches and mourners.[5] You can't imagine how loudly I laughed as I swam across this river. Men are ferried across by 40 old women condemned to this task because as girls they acted haughty and cruel, and as hags practiced sorcery and witchcraft. You'll laugh when I describe how you cross it.

Lepidus. Continue. I want to laugh, so omit no details of your 41 journey.

Libripeta. I'll do as you wish. The old women lie naked on their 42 backs along the shore. Then you plant your knees in the folds 43 of a woman's belly, take her ears in your hands, and use her head as a rudder to steer your course. Lying on her back, she paddles with her heels and palms.

Lepidus. Just the shipwreck you deserve! But don't both ship and 44 cargo often sink?

Libripeta. By no means. You'll understand when I relate a notable 45 fact which I learned there from the heart of philosophy. Swimmers float above the waves by virtue of the lungs in their thorax. But a scrofulous woman has two lungs, one in her loins, 46 and the other in her shoulders. What's more, women's heads 47 are completely empty, and thus provide an excellent means of crossing a river. What are you staring at?

Lepidus. You, for if you're wise, you'll jump back into this sewer. 48 You've learned more philosophy in this one journey than in all 49

quam omni tua pristina etate tua omni ex maxima bibliotheca,
50   quam occlusam detines, adeptus es. Verum quid hic ais? Putastine tutum mulieris constantie et fidei te ita ridicule commendare?

51   *Libr.* Mihi quidem navigatio commoda et tutissima fuit. Nam mea a me amata vetula confestim sese mihi obtulit, ore illo suo dentibus vacuo ridens. Laudasses diligentiam eius, ita me fide
52   optima vectavit. Egi gratias atque ut primum in adversa ripa constiti, intueor prata quedam amplissima, ubi pro cespite atque foliis herbarum surgebant come barbeque hominum capillique mulierum atque crines iumentorum nec non et iube leonum, ut eiusmodi pilis nihil posset in prato non opertum
53   conspici. Enimvero, superi boni, quantum illic numerum somniantium perspexi nescio quas radiculas effodientes, quas qui edunt et vafri et docti, cum minime sint, videntur! Multam illic
54   consumpsi operam. Sed me ingens copia pediculorum, que ex prato convolabat, pene exedit, ut sola fuga salus mihi foret pe-
55   tenda. Idcirco conieci me in pedes, atque unde sese mihi exitus obtulit, inde me vesanum tanta ex peste eripuerim. Fata hanc nobis cloacam prebuere.

56   *Lep.* I ergo iam nunc atque te lotum redde. Ego ad meos, quos tu dictitas insanos et indoctos, redibo.

: 2 :

Corolle

1   *Rhet.* Contendi huc ut virginem hanc viderem, quam omnes esse formosissimam ferunt.
    Poet. Adesne, o rhetor?

the years you spent in your vast library. But tell me, did you 50
think it safe to entrust yourself so ridiculously to a woman's
constancy?

Libripeta. I had a safe and pleasant voyage, for my beloved crone 51
suddenly came to meet me, laughing with her toothless mouth.
You would have praised her care in ferrying me in such good
faith. I thanked her, and as soon as I got to the opposite shore, 52
I saw wide meadows where, instead of grass and leafy plants,
there grew men's hair and beards, women's tresses, beasts' tails,
and lions' manes, which covered the entire meadow from sight.
Good gods, what a vast number of dreamers I beheld there! 53
They were digging up roots which, when eaten, make people
seem clever and learned, even if they are not. I spent quite some
time there. But a vast swarm of lice flew up from the meadow 54
and nearly devoured me, so that I could only flee to save myself.
I took to my heels; and to escape that plague, I hurled myself 55
madly into a way out that I found. It was this sewer that the
fates offered me.

Lepidus. Go now and wash yourself. I'll return to my friends, 56
whom you constantly call insane and ignorant.

: 2 :

Garlands

Rhetorician. I'm here to see the maiden that everyone says is very 1
beautiful.

Poet. Is that you, rhetorician?

2 *Rhet.* O salve, poeta. Et (me superi!) forma est et indole virgo hec, quantum video, egregia et eleganti.

3 *Poet.* Mirum ni hec sit ex ipso dearum genere. Tanta enim dignitas tantumque specimen a diis extet opus est.

4 *Rhet.* Prorsus id quidem ut ais: huiusmodi enim venustas et decus oris oculorumque divinum quippiam et rarissimum sapiunt. Sed eccum divitem. — Tu quoque, o dives, virginem spectatum accessisti?

5 *Div.* Nempe isthuc. Sed quasnam habet ea corollas in gremium? Eodum, propius! ut percontemur. — Tu, virgo, hasne huc in forum corollas detulisti ut venundares?

6 *Laus.* Minime.
Rhet. Quid igitur his tibi corollis queris, virgo?

7 *Inv.* Ecquid tu cum hisce loqueris? Iamne te quidem fugit, o Laus, quod mater tua Virtus, cum e domo progrederemur, edixit tibi

8 caveres ne quempiam aspiceres procum, me inconsulta? Amatores nobis, non sollicitatores, inveniendi sunt; et istos quidem temerarios atque immodestos procaces irridere ludus est omnium pulcherrimus, quos tu me sinito more meo tractem. — Heus tu! homo, quid tibi vis?

9 *Div.* (Proh, o superi, quales oculos truces et nimium turbulentos vetula hec in me volvit!)

10 *Inv.* Quid tute tecum loqueris? Quid demum mussas?
Div. Corollam quidem empturus.

11 *Inv.* Tuas alibi divitias ostentato, fortunate. Nam est apud nos venale nihil.

12 *Div.* Dono dabis igitur.
Inv. Non tibi quidem, sed promerentibus et dignissimis.

13 *Poet.* Nobis idcirco dabis.
Inv. Tibin? At quasnam tu artes non ignoras?
Poet. Men rogas? Num tu poetas nosse omnia audisti?

14 *Inv.* Tu poeta?
Poet. Atque haud vulgaris.

Rhetorician. Greetings, poet. By the gods, this maiden seems to 2
possess elegant beauty and excellent qualities.

Poet. I'm sure she's a goddess, for such outstanding dignity and 3
appearance must come from the gods.

Rhetorician. You're quite right. The grace and nobility of her face 4
and eyes have a rare, divine quality. But here comes the rich
man. Have you too come to behold this maiden, rich man?

Rich Man. Clearly. But what garlands are these she holds in her 5
lap? Let's approach and ask. O maiden, have you brought these
garlands here to the forum to sell?

Praise. No. 6

Rhetorician. Then what are they for, maiden?

Envy. What, are you speaking with these fellows? Have you al- 7
ready forgotten, Praise, that as we left home your mother Virtue warned you to look at no suitors without my permission?[6]
We must find you lovers, not seducers. But we shall have some 8
fine sport if we mock these brash and impudent scoundrels. Let
me deal with them in my way. You there, fellow, what do you
want?

Rich Man. Ye gods, how fiercely and furiously this hag stares at 9
me!

Envy. Why are you talking to yourself? What are you muttering? 10

Rich Man. I'm here to buy a garland.

Envy. Flaunt your wealth somewhere else, rich man. There's noth- 11
ing for sale here.

Rich Man. Then you'll give me one as a gift. 12

Envy. Not to you, but to deserving and worthy men.

Poet. Then you'll give one to *me*. 13

Envy. To you? Are there arts you don't know?

Poet. How can you ask? Haven't you heard that poets know everything?

Envy. You're a poet, then? 14

Poet. Yes, but not a common one.

15 *Laus.* Dignus eris corona. Sed disticum edito. Nam nos quidem maxime delectat versus.

16 *Poet.* Isthuc quidem erit perfacile. Nam quicquid studeo dicere, versus est.

17 *Inv.* Denique tu quidem id, quicquid est, quod dudum protracto supercilio et protenso ore irruminas, expuito.

18 *Poet.* O carmen luculuntum atque acclive!

arma virum galeeque, sed non moriemur inulte.

Quid? hoc ne vero Maronem ipsum nihil sapit?

19 *Laus.* Ut nihil magis!

Poet. Coronam ergo promeritus.

20 *Inv.* Alterum huic si adegeris, coronabere.

21 *Poet.* Ergo abeo hinc ad bibliothecam, ex qua versiculos plus centum una lucubratione depromam.

22 *Inv.* Isthuc tibi esse censeo faciendum, ut eo pacto in litterarum cultu et opere te exerceas quoad fervescat animus, qui ad dicen-

23 dum sit futurus paratior et promptior. Nam desidia quidem ac lectitandi scriptitandique intervallis obtorpere ingenium et om-

24 nino cessator fieri consuevit. Neque a vobis poetis quippiam est, nisi omni ex parte absolutum et perpolitum, quod probari nobis possit.

Sed poeta abiit.—Tuque, pallidule, an non cum illo incompto et impexo quicum adveneras abvolas?

25 *Rhet.* Non esse meum reor huc accessisse ut spretus abeam, neque videbor munera isthec vestra, etsi maxima atque amplissima,

26 demeruisse, siquid satis me fortasse noritis. Sum enim et virtute aliquantisper ornatus et doctrina excultus, ut me ingenuum et libere educatum audeam dicere.

27 *Inv.* Quid igitur? Qua demum fretus industria apud nos, petulce, instas?

28 *Rhet.* Vestra fisus humanitate, o formosissime, magis quam industria mea. Omnium me fere unum profiteri audeo qui ab ipsa

Praise. You deserve a garland. But first recite a distich. I really love 15
poetry.

Poet. That will be very easy. Everything I say is in verse. 16

Envy. Well then, spit out whatever you have been ruminating 17
there with knit brows and pursed lips.

Poet. Here's a splendid and lofty poem: 18

> Arms and the man and the helmets; we shall not die
>   unavenged.

Well, doesn't that smack of Vergil?[7]

Praise. Absolutely. 19

Poet. Then I've earned a garland.

Envy. If you'll add another verse to this one, we'll crown you. 20

Poet. I'm off to the library, where in a night's study I shall produce 21
more than a hundred verses.

Envy. That's what you must do: apply yourself to literary studies 22
until your mind boils over with ready and rapid invention. Your 23
wits will generally become dull and sluggish through inactivity
and long breaks from reading and writing. We can only fully 24
approve perfect and polished works by you poets.

The poet has gone. And you, pale little man, why don't you
run off with your untidy and unkempt companion?

Rhetorician. I didn't intend to come here only to be dismissed in 25
scorn. Nor do I think myself undeserving of your great and
glorious rewards, if you know me sufficiently. For I am some- 26
what distinguished by virtue and scholarly refinement, so that I
dare profess myself a gentleman of liberal education.

Envy. Indeed? What merits make you bold to harass us, you ob- 27
noxious fellow?

Rhetorician. Confiding more in your generosity than in my own 28
merits, fairest ladies, I dare to assert that, more than anyone

ineunte etate, a teneris, uti aiunt, unguiculis, omnem operam, diligentiam, assiduitatem, solertiam, in studii⟨s⟩ humanitatis, in cognitione litterarum, in peritia bonarum artium, in ratione et modo bene beateque degende vite, ac postremo in dicendi gloria consumpserim.

29
30 *Inv.* Hui, lingulacem! Verum si te exhibueris quem fronte isto confidenti predicas, corona ornatus decedes. Et hoc velim non ignores: nostris donis utimur nunquam temere. Quare, ea in re quam nosse te profiteare, fieri a te periculum expectamus.

31 *Rhet.* Geram tibi morem ut voles. De nostris mihi maximis et prestantissimis laudibus disserendum est: quo in munere ob-
32 eundo res a me miras et inauditas audietis. Grande quoddam amplumque atque canorum orationis genus afferam; sed ero pro rei magnitudine dicendo brevis, et quoad potero, succinctus. Vos prebete operam auscultando.

33 *Laus.* Aurem prebemus.

Inv. Isthuc potissimum exposcimus teque orantem grate ac perbenigne audiemus.

34 *Rhet.* Quamquam mihi omnes insigni prestantique ingenio prediti, qui quidem priscos gravissimos et sanctissimos viros pro ingenii viribus imitati, in ea sibi presertim re ex qua precipuam et mirificam bonorum gratiam divine cuidam laudi complicitam
35 et connexam assequerentur, a diis immortalibus porrectam et propositam sibi spem posteritatis atque immortalitatis, non morum quidem et doctrine tantum, sed vel in primis egregia
36 elegantique virtutis et fortitudinis opera; famam et nominis claritatem summis lucubrationibus optime de re publica bonisque civibus merendo summa diligentia, vigilantia et assidui-
37 tate; auctoritatem cum dignitate et recta ac provisa quadam cum officii ratione et via, ope suffragioque superum piissimo-
38 rum, non abiecta et posthabita veteris discipline norma; necessitudines et coniunctiones beneficiorum cumulis mutuoque

else, from my earliest years and tenderest childhood, as the phrase has it, I have dedicated all my efforts, diligence, assiduity, and talent to the humanities, to the study of literature, to the mastery of the liberal arts, to the pursuit of the good and happy life, and finally to the glory of eloquence.[8]

Envy. Oof, what a prattler! If you prove to be as good as you so confidently boast, you'll take home a garland. But bear in mind that we don't grant our gifts lightly. We expect you to give proof of the mastery you claim.   29 30

Rhetorician. I'll do as you say. I must discuss my greatest and most excellent achievements. As I do so, you shall learn astonishing and unheard-of things. I shall employ a lofty, copious, and sonorous style. Yet I shall be brief, considering the greatness of my topic, and as succinct as I can. Please give me your attention.   31 32

Praise. We shall.   33

Envy. It is our fervent wish. We shall listen gladly and most generously to your speech.

Rhetorician. Although all remarkable and exceptional geniuses who, by strenuous imitation of antiquity's most venerable and learned men — particularly in those endeavors which merit that signal and singular gratitude of good men which brings them divine praise — although, I say, they have attained the hope of immortality and posterity which the immortal gods offered and placed before them, not so much by their character and learning as by the excellent and elegant example of their virtue and fortitude; although they have attained glorious fame and renown by their arduous studies and by their worthy services to the state and all good citizens; although they have obtained authority through their great diligence, vigilance, and perseverance, coupled with dignity and the strict observance of duty, and have, with the aid and support of the most merciful gods, formed bonds of friendship in consonance with the dictates of   34 35 36 37 38

39   officio nacti sunt: tum ad maximorum facinorum gloriam plerumque omnes celeberrimi viri ita animo et cogitatione pendere interdum mihi videri solent, ita in ea re fructuum acervos

40   expectare, ut, cum unanimes et concordes natura quasi duce id concupiscant quod fragiles caduceque hominum spes, inanes futilesque expectationes ieiunaque ac levia consilia depro-

41   munt—tamen a depravata corruptaque imperitorum ratione indecora et improbatissima ea ratio emanat, ut ea vis mentis, quam apud Grecos Stoici philosophi 'proneam' vocant, virtute

42   haudquaquam previa et ductrice negligatur, qua in celum nobis aditus patefacimus et ad cetum deorum viam expeditissimam commodissimamque communimus, non artibus ocii et desidie, sed perseverantia, integritate, dictorum factorumque constantia

43   et firmitudine: hec igitur cum ita sint, hi profecto qui non penitus soluta et libere fluenti constrepentique, sed numeris quibusdam adstricta huiusmodi et composita dicendi arte exculti sunt, hasce profecto coronas apud bonos et graves demeruisse

44   minime videbuntur. Itaque, ut brevibus, quod institui, rem totam diffiniam—nam, ut vidisti⟨s⟩, nulla exornatione, nulla commoratione, nulla amplificatione dicendo usus sum—peto a vobis mihi promerenti coronam dedatis.

45   *Laus.* O mi homo, traderem quidem volens ac lubens, sed non corolle nostre tuum hoc pregrande et tumidum caput belle incingerent!

46   *Rhet.* Mihi idcirco coronas pulcherrimis meo ingenio conquisitis et selectis floribus contexam.

47   *Obtr.* Superi boni, quot modis homines delirant! Is rhetor, homo insulsissimus, quod putas, an didicit aliud preterquam audere

48   proloqui? Quam sua multa verborum copia rem nullam dicere gloriatur! Quod si sapis, virgo, has mihi omnes coronas dabis.

49   *Laus.* Hui petulcum hominem hunc, o Invidia, et impudentem! quin et manum protervus intulit ut raperet! Nostin hunc, Invidia, qui sit?

tradition by conferring favors and exchanging courtesies; yet   39
often the most celebrated men seem to me, by devoting their
hearts and minds to the glory of great deeds and by expecting
occasionally the greatest rewards for their labors, to desire, un-   40
der nature's guidance, the objects of mankind's frail and short-
lived hopes, the objects of vain and futile aspirations, and of
trivial and lightheaded counsels; and a shameful and blamewor-   41
thy opinion arises from the depraved and corrupt judgment of
the ignorant, so that the mental power which the Greek Stoics
call Pronoia[9] is neglected and abandoned by that guiding virtue
which opens our way to heaven and which constructs the clear-   42
est and safest road to the company of the gods, not by sloth and
idleness, but by perseverance, integrity, constancy, and stability
in both word and deed; and consequently, it is those who are   43
most skilled not merely in flowing and high-sounding prose,
but also in a style governed and regulated by rhythm, who seem
to good and worthy citizens most deserving of these garlands.
Therefore, to state the case briefly, as I intended — for you have   44
seen that I have employed no embellishments, no elaborations,
and no amplifications — I ask you to grant me the garland I
deserve.

Praise. Dear fellow, I would gladly give you one, but our garlands   45
would not fit your swelled head.

Rhetorician. Then I shall fashion my own garlands from the exqui-   46
sitely beautiful flowers that my genius invents.

Detractor. Good gods, in how many ways men rave! Has this in-   47
sipid rhetorician learned anything except how to speak auda-
ciously? How pompously he employs his vast store of words to   48
say nothing! If you're wise, maiden, you'll give all the garlands
to me.

Praise. Oof, what an obnoxious and impudent scoundrel! Like a   49
thief he even boldly laid a hand on me. Do you know who he
is, Envy?

50 *Inv.* Ain vero? Mihin isthunc parum cognitum reris, qui quidem
ex me genitus sit et apud me educatus, ut omnes quas ipsa novi
51 artes egregie didicerit atque ad unguem teneat: detrahere omnibus, facta dictaque improbare omnium inque triviis bonis atque
pravis, doctis atque indoctis succensere, vera falsaque promis-
52 cue ad ignominiam decantare? Hec enim omnia egregie et perquam belle novit, me magistra et instructrice. Verum, age sis,
Obtrectator, nate mi, hac una corona, quod tuo belle officio
utaris, contentus abi.

53 *Obtr.* Ex urticane et vepribus? grata tamen est, cum ob meriti
signum, tum ob id quod me primum omnium donastis. Itaque
54 capiti eam incingo meo. Ei mihi, ut affigit stimulos! Neque
tamen deponam, quo spectatores istos invidia afficiam. — O,
heus vos, pulcherrimum insigne!

55 *Laus.* Appage te hinc cum isthac insolentia! tuam quidem dicaci-
tatem veremur.

56 *Inv.* Aufugit. Nunc igitur, virgo, cum iam nulli amatores adsunt,
hinc abimus.

Laus. Ut lubet.

Inv. Quid igitur cessas?

57 *Laus.* Adolescentem isthunc, qui dudum tacitus in os respectat,
intuebar. Ac mihi quidem fortassis non indignus videbatur, ut
eius modestiam non aspernarer.

58 *Inv.* Elingues ego odi; petat, qui dari sibi volet quippiam. — Tu
ecquid spectas, adolescens?

59 *Lep.* Non sum quidem ut rhetor ille eloquens: idcirco tacitus
vestras has pulcherrimas coronas demirabar, et qui possem a
vobis unam impetrare ipse mecum excogitabam.

60 *Inv.* Quid igitur erat in te vecordie et pusillitatis, ut ab ea que ut
61 daret prodiit non ultro posceres? Audendum quidem est aman-
tibus atque efflagitandum idque iterum atque iterum actitan-
dum, quo et ipse ex animo velle videare, et que datura sit
volentem se fore nactam non dubitet.

164

Envy. You ask me? Do you think I don't know someone whom I 50
bore and brought up? He has thoroughly mastered all my arts.
He disparages everyone, condemning their words and deeds. In 51
the streets, he burns with indignation at all men, both good
and bad, both learned and unlearned, and denigrates people by
mixing truth and falsehood. He understands perfectly every- 52
thing I taught him as his tutor and teacher. Here, my son, take
this one garland for your fine performance, and go away satisfied.

Detractor. What, one made of nettles and thorns? Still, I am 53
pleased because it is a token of my merits, and because you gave
the first gift to me. I'll circle my head with it. How it stings me!
But I won't take it off, for I must arouse the envy of onlookers. 54
Look at my splendid insignia, everyone!

Praise. Begone with your insolence! We fear your sarcasm. 55

Envy. He's run off. Now then, maiden, since we have no more 56
suitors, let's go.

Praise. As you wish.

Envy. Why do you hesitate?

Praise. I noticed a young man gazing at me in silence. He some- 57
how seemed to deserve my consideration for his modesty.

Envy. I hate reticent people. If he wants something, let him ask. 58
What are you looking at, young man?

Lepidus. Unlike that verbose rhetorician, I was silently admiring 59
your beautiful garlands, and contemplating how I might win
one.

Envy. What cowardice or faint spirit kept you from asking her 60
openly for what she came to give away? Suitors must be bold, 61
and should plead repeatedly, so that we see how truly they desire, and how eager they are to receive what is offered.

62   *Lep.* Ego te austeram ac nimis rigidam verebar, ne repudium con-
tumacius dares.

      Inv. Hen!

63   *Laus.* Non recte de nobis sentis, adolescens, si eos qui sese non
omnino imperitos neque immodestos afferant, parum esse apud
nos acceptos arbitraris.

64   *Lep.* Ex his ego sum qui cum litteris delecter, tum semper studuerim, servata dignitate, ut esse⟨m⟩ ipse mecum et apud familiares
meos festivitate et risu non vacuus.

65   *Inv.* Ergo, id age, rideto!

      Lep. Hei mihi, hei!

      Laus. Ecquid agis, adolescens, ploras?

66   *Lep.* Hen, quidnam hoc mali est? Sed leviter hoc mihi ferendum
statuo, quoniam preter consuetudinem meam non excidit. Ne-

67   que te, virgo, ulla rei huius admiratio velim capiat. Nam ita fato
quodam meo evenit, ut ex eo die quo in lucem veni, nulla ne
minima quidem res mihi ex animi mei sententia successerit.

68   Mirum ut omnia preter spem nobis, atque contra quam insti-

69   tuerim, cadunt: si amicos officiis et beneficiis paro, inimicos
excipio; si studiis bonarum artium gratiam sector, invidia rependitur; si neminem ledendo rem meam pacate et modeste
agere enitor, obtrectatores, delatores, occultos inimicos nequis-
simosque proditores offendo, qui instituta consiliaque mea om-

70   nia perturbent. Denique quicquid aggredior, quicquid enitor,
omne secus accidit quam studuerim.

71   *Laus.* Nimirum tu ridiculus es! Tibi ergo hanc coronam desumito.

72   *Lep.* Habeo tibi gratias, virgo, quod me duplici dono affecisti.
Nam et coronam dedisti, qua meum caput exorner, et ex herba
coronam eiusmodi condonasti, ut et cum exaruerit, non medio-

73   criter ad patinas tergendas valeat. — Atat, et quid agis, vetula?
Itane repente, itane coronam ipsam a me diripuisti, etiam usque
irritata eam dilaceras dentibus, tum et pessundas?

74   *Inv.* Quid tibi nominis?

Lepidus. I feared your unbending severity, and thought you might   62
    insolently rebuff me.

Envy. Ha!

Praise. You misunderstand me, young man, if you think I reject   63
    the learned and modest.

Lepidus. I take delight in letters, and I always strive to afford mer-   64
    riment and laughter to myself and my friends, without sacrific-
    ing my dignity.

Envy. Then go ahead and laugh.   65

Lepidus. Woe is me!

Praise. What, are you weeping, young man?

Lepidus. Alas, what misfortune! Still, I must bear it lightly, since   66
    such an event is not unusual for me. Please do not be surprised
    at this, maiden. For by some fate, ever since my birth, not the   67
    least affair has turned out as I wished. It is strange how every-   68
    thing happens contrary to my hopes and expectations. If I seek   69
    to win friends through courtesies and favors, I make enemies. If
    I seek to win favor by liberal studies, I am repaid by envy. If I
    attend to my affairs in tranquility and modesty, offending no
    one, I meet with detractors, denouncers, secret foes, and villain-
    ous betrayers who confound my plans and projects. In short, no   70
    matter what I undertake or pursue, nothing turns out as I wish
    it.

Praise. You are truly ridiculous. Take this garland for yourself.   71

Lepidus. I am grateful to you, maiden, for you have given me a   72
    double gift. You have given me a garland to grace my head; and
    you have bestowed on me verdant leaves which, when dried,
    will serve to scour my pans. But stop, what are you doing, old   73
    woman? Why have you snatched the garland from me? Why
    do you tear it so furiously with your teeth?

Envy. What is your name?   74

Lep. Mihin? Lepido.

75 *Inv.* Tu Lepidus? Quin immo mordax et asper atque irrisor! Abeamus, virgo. Nam hoc toto in foro reperies neminem corona dignum.

76 *Laus.* Eccum iurisconsultos et physicos et sacrarum litterarum studiosos.

77 *Inv.* Nihil est quod illi minus quam tuas coronas pensitent. Aurum est, virgo, atque ambitio, quod appetant.

Laus. Tum astronomi et mathematici.

78 *Inv.* Insomnia isthec. Abeamus.

: 3 :

Cynicus

1 ⟨*Mercur.*⟩. Omnes eos qui proximis diebus superioribus e vita de-
2 cessere, o Phebe, huc ad te adduxi, ut iusseras. Itaque vos, o anime, que quidem iterato novissimis susceptis corporibus in vitam estis mortalium rediture, considete isthic, ut queque Phebus imperarit confestim possitis nullo cum tumultu exequi.
3 Tu vero, Phebe, id si tibi ita videbitur, quam primum hos ipsos
4 qui huc appulere transmittes ad mortales. Nam confertissime in horam caterve convolant eorum qui e vita cecidere, ut iam infestus futurus tibi sit immanis animarum numerus.

5 *Pheb.* Id quidem ipsum uti admones, Mercuri, mihi esse faciendum censeo. Sed commodius rem ex instituto expediemus, si hanc que adest legionem defunctorum quasi in centurias et manipulos descripserimus, quo expeditius singulis, que facto
6 esse opus arbitrabimur, edicamus. Ea de re, o anime, pro studiis ac geste vite ratione gregatim congruite. Tu, Mercuri, id sedulo

Lepidus. Mine? Lepidus?

Envy. Lepidus? The witty one? You should rather be called snap- 75
pish or bitter or mocker. Let's go, maiden. You'll find no one
worthy of a garland in this forum.

Praise. See, there are jurists, physicians, and theologians. 76

Envy. They have not the least interest in your garlands. Gold and 77
ambition are what they strive for, maiden.

Praise. There are astronomers and mathematicians, too.

Envy. Mere dreamers. Let's go. 78

: 3 :

The Cynic

[*Mercury*]. I have brought you the souls of those who died in the 1
past few days, O Phoebus, as you bid me. You there, O souls, 2
will receive new bodies, and then will return anew to the life of
mortals. Sit down there, so that you can promptly obey Phoebus' commands without confusion. And you, Phoebus, will 3
send the new arrivals back to earth as soon as possible, if you
choose. For dense crowds of souls flock here each hour after 4
they have died, and their enormous number will soon prove
troublesome.

Phoebus. I believe I must do as you say, Mercury. But we'll finish 5
our business more easily if we form the present legions of dead
souls into some sort of centuries and maniples.[10] In that way,
we can quickly command each one what we think needs to be
done. Assemble, O souls, according to your pursuits and your 6
way of life. And you, Mercury, make sure that they don't lie

7   provideto, nequid isti, cum rogantur, mentiantur. Namque
     ferunt etate hac didicisse mortales in omni re fingendo et fal-
     lendo videri velle astutiores.

8   *Cyn.* Id ego curabo, o Phebe, qui et omnibus hisce notus et hosce
     ferme omnes ad unguem novi. Tum vos, o Mercuri, quoniam
     dii sitis, esse maledicos dedecet.

9   *Pheb.* Et quisnam hic est tam comiter arrogans?
     Mercur. Non quidem novi.
     Cyn. Num me nosti, qui te deorum primarium semper colui?
     Mercur. Et quis tu?

10   *Cyn.* Num tu Etruscum illum philosophum meministi, cuius
     opera iam deperdite littere reviviscunt?

11   *Pheb.* Quisquis sis, profecto non te exhibes infacetum, ut hanc
     non indecenter tibi delegem provinciam istorum vitam et mores
     recensendi. Sed iam anime ordinibus disposite consident; itaque
     huc propius accedamus.

12   *Cyn.* Ha ha he, o gentem ineptissimam et immodestissimam! Non
     possum facere quin rideam, o Phebe, morositatem et scenicos
     istorum gestus, qui tanta ambitione et fastu completi sunt,

13   ut toto pectore atque ipsis etiam oculis tûmeant. En gentem
     superbam et arrogantem! etiamne inter defunctos sese primis

14   locis assidendo collocarunt? Ne vero, o inverecundi, diis appro-
     pinquantibus non assurgetis? (*Tandem nutabundi assurrexere*).

15   Huc vos! qui mitra gemmis onusta et ornamentis deorum redi-
     miti extatis, dicite qualem degistis vitam, ut hinc ad mortalium
     cetus regredientes simillima vestris moribus corpora subeatis.

16   *Sac.* Fuimus interpretes deorum, curavimus rem sacram, coluimus
     pietatem, ut nos vulgus hominum merito patres et sanctissimos
     presides nuncuparint.

17   *Cyn.* Non committam ut susceptum officium deseruisse videar:
     decantabo vestram improbitatem, neque diis presentibus a vobis

18   erit quod verear. O Phebe, isti more quidem suo mentiuntur,
     docti omni vita id eniti, ut sibi ipsis multo dissimiles videantur.

when questioned. For they say that today's mortals always dis- 7
semble and deceive as proof of their cunning.

Cynic. I'll see to it, O Phoebus. All these souls know me, and I 8
know nearly all of them perfectly. And since you're both gods,
O Mercury, it ill befits you to be speak abusively.

Phoebus. Who is this affable upstart? 9

Mercury. I don't know him.

Cynic. Don't you recognize me? I have always worshipped you as
the foremost of the gods.

Mercury. Who are you?

Cynic. Don't you remember the Tuscan philosopher by whose ef- 10
forts letters once lost are now revived?

Phoebus. Whoever you are, you certainly display some wit. So I 11
may properly assign you the task of reviewing the lives and
character of these souls. But they are already seated and arranged in ranks. Let us approach them.

Cynic. Ha ha ha! What an impudent and impertinent race! I can't 12
help laughing, Phoebus, at their peevishness and histrionic gestures. They are so full of haughty ambition that their breasts
and even their eyes puff and swell. Here's a proud and arrogant 13
race! Have they occupied the front seats even among the dead?
What, shameless ones, won't you rise when gods approach? 14
(*The souls finally rise hesitantly.*) Come here, you who flaunt your 15
miters laden with gems and images of the gods, and tell us what
kind of life you led.[11] When you return to mortal society, you
are to assume the bodies that best suit your character.

Priests. We interpreted the will of the gods, celebrated their rites, 16
and practiced piety. The masses rightly called us fathers and
most holy guardians.

Cynic. I cannot act as if neglecting my duty. I shall denounce your 17
depravity; since gods are present, I need not fear. O Phoebus, 18
they are lying, as they often do, for in their entire lives they

Nam improbi impientissimique cum sint et omni turpidinis nota fedissimi, id simulando agunt, ut viri esse boni videantur.

19 Tantaque sunt impudentia, ut sese celitibus noctes integras loqui et maxima cum superis atque inferis diis habere commercia suadeant: qua fallacia modum invenere, ut ociosi et supini per

20 inertiam ex alieno crapulentur. Sacram rem quam sancte et pie fecerint, isthuc, dii, apud vos exploratum reor.

Sed num subaudis, o Phebe, armorum strepitus et cadentium gemitus fragoremque ruentium tectorum et urbium, quo

21 maria montesque reboant? Id malum isti conscelerati conscivere suis fraudibus et perfidia, hos ad iniuriam inferendam, hos contra ad vindictam irritando. Gens pestifera! de quibus omni-

22 bus ut succincte proloquar. Sunt quidem ignavi et desidiosi, luxu et somno perditi, gula immensa, lingua procacissima,

23 fronte inverecundissima, cupiditate et avaritia inexplebili. Et huiusmodi cum sint, alia ex parte iidem odiis inter se concertant, discordias inter pacatos conflant, bella et cedes concitant: scelerum denique flagitiorumque omnium insignes mirificique auctores et artifices sunt.

24 *Mercur.* Religione isthec? Sed me reprimo: ab deorum enim pietate foret impietatis odio etiam adversus impios non esse piissi-

25 mos. Nam qui bonis bene fecerit merito id fecerit, siquidem

26 merenti ni bona tribuerint dii, boni ipsi non sint. Malis quoque hominibus queque condonarint superi, isthuc pertinet, ut pro his que sponte et ultro erogata sint maiorem in modum obligati, quoad in se sit, par esse a se meritis relatum cupiant.

27 *Cyn.* Equidem isthic, Mercuri, operam perdis. Optimas, sed non usquequaque intellectas eiusmodi sententias recensebis, his presertim apud quos sanctissime huiuscemodi admonitiones assi-

28 duo decantantur? Atqui agunt id quidem, non quo sese dictis et exhortationibus ad virtutem excitent, sed ut multitudinem fallant verbis et vultu quoad de se opinionem bonam

cleverly strove to dissemble their real natures. Dishonest, shameless, and fouled with every vice, they made a pretense of seeming virtuous men. Their impudence is such that they claim 19 to spend entire nights communing with celestial powers and conversing with the gods of heaven and hell. By this deception, they have managed to live in lazy indolence, getting drunk at the expense of others. How pious and holy their worship has 20 been, I expect that you gods know full well.

But don't you hear the sound of arms, O Phoebus, the groans of wounded men, and the din of collapsing buildings and cities with which the seas and mountains resound? These 21 depraved men have wrought this woe through their fraud and treachery, inciting one faction to violence and another to revenge. Baneful race! Let me briefly describe them. They are idle 22 and indolent, and sunk in debauchery and drowsiness. Their gullets are immense, their tongues impudent, their brows brazen, and their greed and avarice implacable. By their nature, 23 they contend among themselves in hatred, foment discord between men at peace, and stir up war and destruction. In short, they are the principal instigators and architects of all crimes and sins.

Mercury. Are these acts of religion? But I restrain myself. Divine 24 piety cannot allow its hatred of impiety to deny piety even to the impious. Whoever does good to good men acts justly, for, if 25 the gods were to deny good to just men, they would not themselves be good. But if the gods also bestow favors on wicked 26 men, they hope that such freely given gifts will greatly oblige the wicked to seek to repay the gods with equal good.

Cynic. You're wasting your breath, Mercury. Will you review their 27 noble maxims, which are so imperfectly understood by the very people who constantly rehearse such pious admonitions? They 28 seek not to encourage their own virtue through precepts and exhortations, but to trick the masses by words and looks into

proseminent; nequissimique et omnium sordidissimi, aures adeo habent obtusas, ut cum de religione propalam declamitent ipsos sese nequaquam audiant.

29 *Mercur.* Enimvero, o Phebe. Et quidnam est quod tute tecum suspensus animo tacitusque despectas, ac si gentem hanc odisse videare?

30 *Pheb.* Equidem meditabar quenam huic generi forme animantium debeantur: namque quod voraces quidem fuerint, anseres, quod ocio et somno marcescere didicerint, tassos, quod sordidissimum vite genus delegerint, porcos fortassis condicere opinabar.

31 Verum quod tantas calamitates sua perfidia et impulsu mortalibus accumularint, pro eorum avaritia et scelerum feditate quodnam illis adiudicarem monstrum non suppeditabat, ni fortassis arpias decressem.

32 *Cyn.* Non id approbem, o Phebe, ni fortasse pestem hanc sacerdo-
33 tum parum fuisse generi hominum gravem statuas. Quod si, humano cum clausi fuerint corpore, inhumanissimi omnium atque immitissimi erant, quid censes futuros, ubi effigiem bellue teterrime nacti suis moribus sevisse et crassari efferatius
34 licuerit? Meum nimirum id commodius in hac re aderat consilium, ut eos in asinos reiiceres, quo imbelles ad nocendum assiduo et turpi labore atque tedio abiectissima in servitute vitam crebro sub fuste degant.

35 *Pheb.* Dixti pulchre. Vos este asini.
Mercur. O factum belle! At vos deinceps proximi adeste.

36 *Mag.* Adsumus.
Pheb. Quale vobis fuit vite genus?

37 *Mag.* Urbes iustitia reximus, libertatem tutati sumus, imperium in populos consilio et diligentia gessimus, rem publicam ornatissimam victoriis et virtute reddidimus.

38 *Pheb.* Hec qui fecerint in deorum numerum recipiendi!

spreading their good reputation. But the ears of these corrupt and sordid men are blocked, so that they can't even hear their own public harangues on religion.

Mercury. Tell me, O Phoebus, why do you look down, silent and   29
undecided, as if you loathed this race?

Phoebus. I was pondering what form of animal would suit them. I   30
thought perhaps it was fitting to make them geese because they were voracious, or badgers because they languished in drowsy sloth, or pigs because they chose a filthy way of life. But since   31
their treacherous instigations have heaped such great disasters on mankind, I could find no monstrous form commensurate with their hideous avarice and vices, unless perhaps I chose harpies.

Cynic. I wouldn't approve, Phoebus, unless perhaps you think this   32
priestly plague has done too little harm to mankind. For if in   33
their human bodies they were utterly brutal and violent, what do you think will happen when they assume the likeness of noisome monsters, and may indulge their savagery and prey more ferociously on others? My own suggestion is more appropriate: 34
you should change them to asses. Then ignoble labors and constant weariness will render them powerless to harm, and they will spend their lives in abject slavery amid frequent thrashings.

Phoebus. A fine suggestion. Become asses!   35

Mercury. Well done! You in the next group, come forth.

Magistrates. Here we are.   36

Phoebus. What kind of life was yours?

Magistrates. We ruled cities with justice, and protected freedom.   37
We exercised authority over our peoples with prudence and diligence. Our victories and virtue did honor to the state.

Phoebus. Men who have done such deeds should be counted   38
among the gods!

Mercur. Profecto ut inquis, Phebe. At tu, Cynice, quid hic ais? Itane obmutuisti? Quid hesitas? Accede huc propius. Dicito in aurem nobis libere queque de hisce noris.

39 *Cyn.* Gero vobis morem. At secedamus item paululum, non enim in istos armatos . . .

Mercur. Diisne presentibus est quod vereare?

40 *Cyn.* Nempe, ac metuo quidem. Nam sunt isti contemptores deorum audacissimi, qui res sacras rumpere, templa incendere nul-

41 losque deos superos aut inferos vereri consueverint. Et didicere in inferenda iniuria id agere, ut legibus ipsi tutissimi sint. Moribus et vita fuere huiusmodi: temulenti et contumaces, crudeles,

42 inexorabiles. Domestico in magistratu considendo dicendoque iure, pupillos, viduas imbecillioresque quosque cives expilarunt.

43 In offitio gerendo, non libertatem tutati, sed pro intoleranda libi⟨di⟩ne omnia suo arbitrio gessere: cives cunctos, qui libertatis cupidi videbantur, odere; pueros impuberes virginesque inge-

44 nuas constuprarunt; eos qui sese tantis sceleribus aut vetando aut oppugnando obiecerant, mulctaverunt, in exilium, in carcerem pepulerunt; contumeliis, cruciatu, tormentis, peccandi

45 impunitate et licentia quos visum est affecerunt, necarunt. In rebus agendis sola temeritate et contumacia usi sunt. Arma sepius in suos cives, adversus commoda et dignitatem publicam,

46 quam contra hostes sumpsere. Denique patriam colluvione scelestissimorum ex omni fece a suis urbibus eiectorum excepta,

47 bonis et honestis civibus exterminatis, replevere: qua manu teterrimorum et sordidissimorum, quibus ipsi omni laude virtutis erant inferiores, ad exequenda scelera uterentur, ad leges patrias evertendas, ad sacra et profana, publica et privata omnia pro libidine pervertenda, ad durissimas et criminosissimas insontibus et bene meritis civibus conditiones imponendas, nullo metu deorum, nulla verecundia, nulla fide, nulla in dictis aut factis

Mercury. You're right, Phoebus. But you, Cynic, what do you say? Why are you silent? Why do you hesitate? Come closer, and tell me freely in private what you know about them.

Cynic. I do as you say. Let us withdraw a little, lest those armed   39
men . . .[12]

Mercury. When gods are present, can you be afraid?

Cynic. Yes, I fear them. They are bold despisers of the gods, ac-   40
customed to destroy sacred objects, to burn temples, and to revere no gods in heaven or hell. They know how to wrong others   41
under the law's protection. In their character and behavior, they
were drunken, insolent, cruel, and inexorable. In the sessions   42
and sentences of their civil courts, they despoiled orphans, wid-
ows, and other defenseless citizens. In carrying out their offices,   43
they did not protect liberty; but obeyed their intolerable lust in
conducting all their affairs. They hated all citizens who seemed
desirous of liberty, and raped young boys and girls of good family. They fined, jailed, or exiled any who opposed their crimes   44
by protest or resistance. In their impunity and license to commit wrongs, they slandered and tortured and murdered anyone
they pleased. In all their actions, they practiced audacity and   45
arrogance. They took up arms more often against their fellow
citizens, and against the welfare and authority of the state, than
against foreign armies. And finally, they flooded their country   46
with the dregs of exiled miscreants, and banished upright and
honest citizens. This gang of loathsome and filthy men, to   47
whom they were themselves inferior in merit of virtue, they
employed in order to commit their crimes — to subvert state
laws, to pervert at will all things sacred and secular, public and
private, and to impose harsh and shameful conditions on innocent and virtuous citizens. They had no fear of the gods, no
shame, no trustworthiness, and no constancy in either word or

48   constantia prediti. Summam et quasi capita, o Phebe, flagitiorum, quibus anime istiusmodi consceleratissime referte sunt, exposui.

49   *Pheb.* Huc igitur vos, o magistratus! este accipitres atque e vestigio e conspectu evolate.

50   *Mercur.* Expectabam quidem parem his vitam atque superioribus pontificibus futuram, quod essent moribus non dissimiles, ut eque fuste et lassitudine penas luerent.

51   *Pheb.* Etsi satis penarum dedere, quandoquidem ad inferos ferme illorum descendit nemo sine obsceno gravique vulnere et cede,

52   tamen rei huic a me percommode provisum est. Nam cum vita fuerint rapaces, id illis vitium pro pena fore relictum statui, quo assidue excrucientur; quod autem libertatem odere aliorum, provisum a nobis est ut aut in servitute et compedibus marcescant, aut difficili in libertate sibi victum in horam non aliunde

53   quam ex preda capiant. Itaque ad reliquos istos expediendos pergamus. Verum et quenam hec succedit pallentium et abesorum turba, ut cum morbo et fame eternum luctasse videantur? Accedite huc vos!

54   *Philos.* Adsumus.

       Mercur. Et quinam estis?

55   *Philos.* Vestre, o Mercuri, sumus delitie, tuque, Phebe, favete: nam celitum dignitatem et numen apud ignavos mortales omnibus nostris in litteris tutati sumus in omnique nostro instituto degende vite ab omni corpori⟨s⟩ et humanarum rerum commertio, supera et divina spectantes, alieni fuimus, ut vestre iam sint partes id providere, ne denuo ad ullam carnis molem nobis invisam retrudamur.

56   *Cyn.* O gentem petulcam, improbam, insolentem! Num dispudet etiam diis legem indicere? Idne ita vobis licere arbitramini, quod tanta fueritis tamque insigni imbuti arrogantia, dum vitam inter homines agebatis, ut non modo privatis civibus populisque regibusque, sed vel orbi terrarum et ipsis astris et universe

deed. I have given only a summary and outline, Phoebus, of the   48
crimes with which these wicked souls are filled.

Phoebus. Come here, magistrates, and become hawks! Now fly at   49
once from my sight!

Mercury. I expected the same life for these as for the priests who   50
preceded them. For their character was similar, and they could
rightly have been punished by blows and exhaustion.

Phoebus. They were sufficiently punished, for nearly every one of   51
them descended to the underworld with foul and bloody
wounds. But I dealt with them quite aptly. Since in life they   52
were rapacious, I decided to leave them this vice to torment
them continually. Since they hated the freedom of others, I
have made sure that they will either languish in the chains of
slavery, or live in perilous freedom, rarely finding food as preda-
tors. Now let's proceed to dealing with the others. What is this   53
crowd of pale and wasted souls which approaches? They seem
to have struggled against perpetual sickness and hunger. Come
here!

Philosophers. Here we are.   54

Mercury. Who are you?[13]

Philosophers. We are your darlings, Mercury and Phoebus, so show   55
us your favor. In all our writings, we defended the dignity and
sanctity of the heavenly gods against base mortals. In every aspect of our way of life, we shunned contact with the body and
with human affairs, and looked only to heavenly and divine
things. It is your duty to see that we are not thrust again into
bodies of loathsome flesh.

Cynic. What an obnoxious, immodest, and insolent race! Aren't   56
you ashamed to lay down laws to the very gods? Do you think
that you are permitted to act this way, since during your human
life you were imbued with such signal arrogance that you foolishly dared to hand down laws not only to private citizens,
nations, and kings, but even to the earth, the stars, and all of

nature legem sitis ausi inconsultissime inscribere? Unum admoneo, o Phebe, si hos auscultes sophistas, in eam procacitatem proruent ut coram non te esse deum contendant.

57 *Philos.* Tu quidem, o Cynice, more hoc agis tuo, qui obtrectando
et maledicendo frustra philosophum te dici obliterasti.

58 *Cyn.* Quid putes hosce, o Phebe? De contemnenda gloria scripti-
tarunt, cum preter gloriam nihil in eo opere affectarint; paupertatem non esse malam affirmarunt, cum suas ⟨et litteras⟩ et
studia ad questum nundinarias habuerint.

59 *Pheb.* Heus, Mercuri, ne convitiis tempus teramus! Evoca gar-
rientes istos tibi (ut ostentarunt) familiares quibuscum statue
60 quasnam sibi dari formas velint. Vos Mercurium sequimini.
Animis enim, ne in otio cessent, dari volo corpora quibus sempiterne in officio vigeant. At vos proximi, ne eos non consequi-
mini?

61 *Scrip.* Non eadem nobis atque his fuit in studiis litterarum opera
et cura. Vestra enim, o dii, gesta tradidimus litteris et tempo-
rum ⟨con⟩versiones et volubilitatem fortune descripsimus, ut
qui nos legerint et doctiores et prudentiores fiant.

62 *Cyn.* Hi quidem omnium sunt qui pre se ferant, si eorum scripta
perlegas, nihil scisse vacuum mendacio dicere. Finxere principes
invictissimos, contiones habitas, superatos montes et maria,
63 denique debellatas gentes que hostem nullum viderunt. Alia ex
parte reclusi bibliothecis, bene meritorum famam rodendo voluere putari vulgo litteratissimi, et tanta flagrant invidia, ut
64 preter se alios litteratos haberi nullos cupiant. Et in hac levitate
gloriantur posteris immortalitatem sui nominis reliquisse!

65 *Pheb.* Hos ego, etsi leves fuerint, qui tamen id egere ut in vita
fuisse videantur, laudandos censeo. Estote idcirco mures. Vos
vero proximi?

nature? I warn you, Phoebus: if you heed these sophists, they will have the effrontery to argue to your face that you are not a god.

Philosophers. You speak in character, Cynic. For by detracting and disparaging, you made men forget how little you deserved to be called a philosopher. 57

Cynic. What do you think of them, O Phoebus? They wrote about disdaining glory in works that sought nothing but glory. They declared that poverty is not evil, but brought their works and efforts to market for a profit. 58

Phoebus. Come, Mercury, let's not waste time in insults. Summon these blatherers who claim to be your friends, and determine with them what form they wish to take. All of you, follow Mercury. Lest these souls lie idle, I want to give them bodies that will perpetually be at work. But you souls in the next group, won't you follow them? 59 60

Writers. Our writings and studies were different from theirs.[14] We recorded your deeds, O gods, and described the vicissitudes of history and the mutability of fortune, so that our readers would gain learning and wisdom. 61

Cynic. If you read their works, you will see that, more than anyone else, they could write nothing but lies. They invented invincible rulers, public orations, expeditions over mountains and oceans, and even nations conquered by nonexistent foes. Or they locked themselves in libraries and gnawed at the fame of meritorious men, hoping that the masses would think them great men of letters; and they burn with such great envy that they want nobody other than themselves to be considered men of letters. In their shallowness, they boast of having left to posterity the immortality of their name! 62 63 64

Phoebus. For all their shallow wits, I think they should be praised, for they acted as if they had truly lived. Become mice! And you, the next! 65

66 *Poet.* Sumus poete.

   Pheb. Odi quidem vos, quod generi deorum tantas notas vestris fabulis inurere non sitis veriti; quod ni lyra et plectro delectassetis, persolveretis penas.

67 *Cyn.* Cave, Phebe, hos qui adsunt deputes tanto fuisse ingenio, ut veteres illos imitari potuerint qui de vobis diis ludicra finxere, sed a veteribus auctoribus versiculos unos itemque alteros deflorarint, quos tanto in honore haberi volunt ut Museum Orpheumque longe sibi postponendum asseverent.

68 *Pheb.* Estote papiliones. Num et vos una cum istis?

69 *Rhetor.* Tametsi, o deorum optime, pro tua iustitia et pietate . . .

70 *Cyn.* Quasnam verborum ambages inceptatis? Negabitisne eius-
71 modi ferme vobis atque illis fuisse artes? tametsi ipsi nequiores estis, qui vestras primas laudes in eo posuistis, quod applaudendo et assentando gratiam inire, obtrectando vero atque maledictis quemvis trahere in odium atque invidiam sitis docti.

72 *Pheb.* Sitis apes.

   Cyn. En, ut frontem obduxere! O factum probe! Nihil apud hos natura loquacissimos fuit hac in re molestius, quam exordiri et exquisite proloqui non licuerit.

73 *Rhetor.* Tantamne vim habere delatores putes, ut etiam optimos deos suis calumniis moveant?

   Cyn. Ha ha he! Garriendo evolant.

74 *Pheb.* At vos deinceps proximi adeste ocius. Et quid hesitatis? Hui! quid hoc mali est, quod tantis cicatricibus adeo inscripti estis? — Tu vero, Cynice, quid rides?

75 *Cyn.* Istos quidem qui sese montes, maria, terras, ethera ac denique orbem ipsum a centro ad supremum celum metiri, qui futurorum eventum, qui te, o Phebe, qui Martem, qui Iovem et reliquos celicolas qua lege dispatiari soliti sitis nosse affirmant, dum ita sunt ingenio hebeti, ut tractandis acutis illis quibus utuntur triangulis pene membratim se ipsos conciderint.

Poets. We are poets.　　　　　　　　　　　　　　　　　　　66

Phoebus. I detest you, for in your fables you never scrupled to
　　brand the gods with marks of disgrace. If you hadn't pleased me
　　by playing the lyre, you would pay the penalty.

Cynic. Don't think, Phoebus, that these poets were gifted enough　67
　　to imitate those ancients who invented ludicrous tales about
　　you gods. Instead, they culled verses from the classics and then
　　sought to win praise for them, so that they could declare them-
　　selves far superior to Musaeus and Orpheus.

Phoebus. Become butterflies! Is this next group with them?　　68

Rhetoricians. Although, O best of the gods, in your justice and　69
　　mercy . . .[15]

Cynic. What circuitous speech are you starting? Can you deny　70
　　that your arts were like those of the poets? No, you are even　71
　　greater scoundrels, for your greatest glory was your ability to
　　win favor through fawning flattery and to arouse hatred and
　　envy through disparaging abuse.

Phoebus. Become bees!　　　　　　　　　　　　　　　　　　72

Cynic. See how they frown! Nicely done! Nothing could vex these
　　chatterers more than to deny them their finely-wrought pre-
　　ambles and exordia.

Rhetoricians. Do you think informers are so powerful that their　73
　　slander can sway even the almighty gods?

Cynic. Ha ha ha! They fly away jabbering.

Phoebus. You in the next group, approach quickly. Why do you　74
　　hesitate? My word, what's wrong, what left you so badly
　　scarred? But you, Cynic, why are you laughing?

Cynic. I see those who claim to measure mountains, oceans, conti-　75
　　nents, the sky, and the entire world, from its center to the far-
　　thest heaven, and who claim to foresee the future and to know
　　by what law you, O Phoebus, Mars, Jupiter, and the other ce-
　　lestial powers traverse the skies. Yet they are so dull-witted that
　　they nearly cut themselves to pieces in handling their sharp

76 Sed ineptiarum suarum multa ex parte penam persolverunt. Nam siquid predicendo, sive artes aut error, ⟨eos⟩ fefellit, insani habiti sunt; siquid vero ex eorum dicto successit, non ipsi laudati, sed veluti a pueris et stultis casu id excidisse vaticinium interpretati sunt. Tu contra et quid rides, Phebe?

77 *Pheb.* Cum te in primis, qui ridiculus sis, tum et mortalium ineptias. Effecisti memoria ut repeterem atque irriderem qui non modo mathematicis, sed vel nostris quidem vatibus, cum quid monemus, fidem adhibent nullam, nisi cum ad id ventum est,

78 ut emendari vitarique calamitas nequeat: quo demum in statu rerum perturbatissimarum constituti, ⟨cum⟩ cuiusvis vesani et stolidi meminerint dicta, eadem pro dei oraculo reputant. Sed quidnam istos esse statuimus?

79 *Cyn.* Testudines.
Pheb. Este testudines. Sed eccum Mercurium et philosophos qui secesserant. Depactine estis quippiam?

80 *Mercur.* O gentem insolentem et inter se discordem!

81 *Cyn.* Innatum id quidem illis et perdomesticum vitium est, Mercuri. Nulla unquam in sententia convenere, neque cum de bono et malo, neque cum de vero et falso, neque cum de causis et

82 progressibus rerum loquerentur. Semper enim inter eos fuere diverse et pugnantes opiniones. Et illud didicere, ut cum disceptando et argumentando quod instituerant satis nequeunt persuasisse, ad convitium et contumeliam decurrant.

83 *Pheb.* Et quidnam nunc, quid aiunt?

84 *Mercur.* Insaniunt. Mereri enim se de diis grandia autumant: multum attulisse mortalibus luminis ad bene beateque vivendum,

85 deos fecisse ut vereantur. Quid multa? Alii leonem, alii elephantum, alii aquilam, alii cete et grandia nobiliaque huiusmodi suis animis condicere corpora protestantur.

86 *Cyn.* O arrogantissimi!

triangles.[16] But they have paid dearly for of their absurdities. 76
When their science or some error misled them in their predictions, they were thought mad. And when one of their predictions came true, they were not praised, but the prophecy was interpreted as if accidentally uttered by children or dolts. But why do your too laugh, Phoebus?

Phoebus. I laugh at you, who are ridiculous, and at the follies of 77
mankind which you cause me to recall and deride. For mortal men believe neither astrologers nor even our own prophets when we warn them, unless it is already too late to avert catastrophe. But when they find themselves overwhelmed by utter 78
chaos, they remember the words of some madman or dunce, and think them a divine oracle. What shall we make them?

Cynic. Tortoises. 79

Phoebus. Become tortoises! But here come Mercury and the philosophers who withdrew. Have you reached an agreement?

Mercury. What an insolent and quarreling race! 80

Cynic. That is their native and peculiar vice, Mercury. They never 81
agree about anything, not about good and evil, nor about truth and falsehood, nor about the origin and development of the world.[17] Their opinions are always divergent and contradictory. 82
Yet they have learned one thing. When they can't win a debate or an argument, they have recourse to insults and abuse.

Phoebus. What are they saying now? 83

Mercury. They are raving. They think they've won great merit 84
with the gods for bearing light to mortals about the good and happy life, and for teaching them to fear the gods. In short, 85
some propose lions, some elephants, some eagles, and some whales or other great and noble creatures as the bodies suited to these souls.

Cynic. How arrogant! 86

87 *Mercur.* Sunt tamen inter eos nonnulli modestiores qui se cuniculos optent, quo visceribus terre perscrutandis et herbarum radicibus indagandis delectentur.

88 *Pheb.* Inveni quidem quo pacto eorum superbiam retundam. Adeste vos, sophiste! Minutissimum decerno corpus et in officio perseveretis iubeo: deferte lumina et este noctiluce. Demum nos, o Mercuri, ad Iovem redeamus.

    Mercur. Ut lubet.

89 *Mercat.* At nos, o Mercuri, ne despectos deseres?

90 *Cyn.* Tu istos ad superos redire, si sapis, prohibebis, Phebe, qui quidem, ac si eternum essent victuri, in parandis opibus nunquam fuere satietate affecti.

91 *Mercat.* Nullosne cessabis lacessere, o mordax Cynice? Num te perspicis ut odio sis omnibus, calumniator? Inter mortales homo nemo diis dedit munera, nemo superis fecit vota quam
92 nos maiora et frequentiora. Tum et sepe rem publicam libertatemque civium et salutem ab impendentibus incommodis nostro ere et opibus tutati sumus.

93 *Cyn.* O perfidissimum genus! Vos quidem diis vota, non nego, mare periclitantes, inter latrones collapsi, fecistis; maxima vero
94 ea, sedato periculo, exequi penitus neglexistis. Siquid diis condonastis, pompe id, non religionis gratia condonastis. Postremo, cum satis et veste et argento et ostentatione divitiarum intumuistis, ere alieno onusti, fide obpignerata decoxistis.

95 *Pheb.* Erunt isti scataveones. Nos demum abeamus, o Mercuri.

96 *Mercur.* I pre, sequor. Sed nostrum Cynicum?

    Pheb. Ohe! Tu musca eris auripellis.

Mercury. Yet some of them are more modest, and wish to be rab- 87
bits, so that they may delight in examining the bowels of the
earth and investigating the roots of plants.

Phoebus. I've found a means of curbing their pride. Come here, 88
sophists! I assign you a tiny body, and command you to continue your duties. Bear lights, and become fireflies! Now then,
Mercury, let us return to Jupiter.

Mercury. As you wish.

Merchants. O Mercury, do you despise and desert us? 89

Cynic. If you're wise, Phoebus, you won't let these souls return to 90
the upper world. For as if they were to live forever, they never
had their fill of amassing wealth.

Merchants. When will you cease to harass everyone, snappish 91
Cynic? Don't you perceive that everyone detests you, slanderer?
Among mortals, no one made greater offerings or more frequent vows to the gods than we did. With our money and 92
wealth, we often defended our country's well-being and our
citizens' freedom from pressing dangers.

Cynic. Treacherous breed! I don't deny that you made vows to the 93
gods when you were threatened at sea or captured by bandits.
But when the danger was past, you completely neglected to
fulfill your great promises. If you gave gifts to the gods, it was 94
for show, not religion. Swollen with garments, silver, and the
ostentation of your wealth, you found yourselves burdened with
debt, so you pawned your credit and went bankrupt.

Phoebus. They will be dung beetles! Let us go, Mercury. 95

Mercury. Go; I follow. But what about our Cynic? 96

Phoebus. Ah! You'll be a gold-winged fly.

: 4 :

Fama

1 *Lep.* Quidnam hoc rei est, Libripeta, quod te semper fedum atque obscenum intueor?

2 *Libr.* Ne vero et tu, Lepide, non affuisti dum bellum gessimus?

3 *Lep.* Si quidem procacitate et maledictis pugnandum fuit, te illic, puto, perstrenuum habuisti.

4 *Libr.* Iam tandem, oro, desine mecum usque adeo esse mordax.

5 *Lep.* Iuvat his quas a te didici rebus me apud te non ignarum videri. Verum desino. At enim quale gessistis bellum, queso? Armisne?

6 *Libr.* Et, dii immortales, quam illis quidem inusitatis! Nunquam tali armorum genere pugnatum esse memorie proditum est. Sed quid agimus? Te ego aliud facturum, me vero tu hic frustra detines. Vale.

7 *Lep.* Heus, ne absis! Cupio quidem isthuc de bello abs te discere.
Libr. Ridebis.
Lep. Tanto eris gratior.

8 *Libr.* Rem ergo enarrabo, ut potero, breviter. Apud forum, non longe a templo Fortune, perpaucis cognitum sacellum pervetustum ac religio⟨sis⟩simum dee Fame dedicatum, quod quidem qui sint ingressi eternum vivent; idcirco a sacerdotibus, nequis

9 temere ingrediatur, summa custodia observatur. Cui muneri sacerdotes assidue quatuor, Divitie, Potentia, Facinus et Occasio, advigilant, mores et vitam adventantium perscrutantes. In valvis sacelli tituli huiusmodi inscripti sunt: ODI IGNAVOS. ANIMAM DEDITO.

10 Idcirco plerique studiosi litterarum, sane inepti atque inopes, eo bovem unum macie ac senecta ita extenuatum deferebant sacrificii gratia, ut eum ex his qui, igne cornibus ab Hannibale

: 4 :

Fame

Lepidus. Why is it, Libripeta, that I always see you foul and filthy? 1

Libripeta. Weren't you present at the battle we fought, Lepidus? 2

Lepidus. If it was a battle of shameless curses, I'm sure you showed 3
your valor.

Libripeta. Enough, please. Stop being so snappish with me. 4

Lepidus. I enjoy showing you how much I have learned from you. 5
But I'll stop. Tell me, what battle did you fight? Was it fought
with weapons?

Libripeta. Yes, by the immortal gods, and what unusual ones! His- 6
tory records no battle fought with such weapons. But what are
we doing? You have other things to do, and are wasting my time
too. Goodbye.

Lepidus. Wait, don't go. I want to learn about the battle from you. 7

Libripeta. You'll laugh.

Lepidus. All the better.

Libripeta. I'll tell the story as briefly as I can. In the forum, not far 8
from the temple of Fortune, there stands an ancient and holy
chapel, known only to a few, and dedicated to the goddess
Fame. Whoever enters it will live forever, so its priests keep
close watch to let no one enter it without good cause. There are 9
four priests who continually stand guard, examining the life and
character of passersby. They are Wealth, Power, Achievement,
and Opportunity. On the chapel doors are the inscriptions: I
HATE THE IDLE and OFFER YOUR LIFE.

A number of literary scholars with no talent or money led 10
an ox there to sacrifice. The beast was so emaciated and weak
with age that I thought it had wandered in the woods since

11   immisso, in hunc usque diem sylva aberrasse⟨nt⟩ putem. Hos ego studiosos a longe segregatus, otiosus, ludi gratia consectabar. Ecce illico Occasio sacerdos, pro more nobis factus obviam,

12   nostram et vitam et mores discit. Potentia vero sacerdos et Divitie, qui tum nonnullis mercatoribus eo asinum ad sacrificium protrudentibus hinc atque hinc quam poterant apertas valvas tenuerant, nobis, cum eo appulimus — inique factum! — easdem illas quas mercatoribus aperuerant, nobis succludunt valvas atque in eum locum firmissimis vectibus ita confirmant, ut vix homo unus nudus sese, in latus quasi per rimam inserpens, in sacellum queat emergere.

13   Tum Occasio sacerdos, nobis ut paulo apertior ingressus prestaretur orantibus, inquit: 'Siquidem isthuc agitis, agite pro viribus dum adsum. Nam, si abero, nullus vobis patebit aditus.'

14   Hisque dictis verbis in templum sese recipit. Nos illico quisque accingi manumque adigere, ut cornipetam bovem et recalcitronem cauda, quantum queat, in sacellum viribus traheremus,

15   annitebamur. At dum huic ridiculo operi frustra insudaretur, bovi cauda evulsa est. Eam ob rem placuit bovem eo ipso in templi vestibulo mactare frustrisque percisum distribuere, ut

16   singulas singuli partes in sacellum deportarent. Pauci integrum aliquod membrum, quisque tamen honestam sibi partem sumpsit; ego ventrem, qui humi relictus esset, in gremium recipio.

17   *Lep.* Ha ha he! dignum te tali onere!

      Libr. Pulchre.

      Lep. Sequere.

18   *Libr.* At sacerdotes 'indignum facinus! profanari templum' acclamarunt. Confestim plebs tumultuans undique in nos irrupit; ereptisque ab his qui conferebant cornibus, iisdem pro armis

19   utuntur. Ego, ut vi agi rem intellexi, illico, ventre deiecto, una cum plebe studiosos convicio prosequor. Quidni? hominis pro-

20   vidi est in tempore sibi aliqua fraude consulere. Sed quod aiunt sepius fraudem quam fidem eos in quibus vigeat decipere, nobis

Hannibal set its horns on fire.[18] Being at leisure, I followed 11
these scholars at some distance, just for fun. At that moment,
the priest Opportunity appeared before us and, as is his wont,
asked about our life and character. The priests Power and 12
Wealth had been holding both doors open to some merchants
who were pushing forward an ass to sacrifice. But when we
tried to follow them, they partly closed the doors which they
had opened to the merchants—a nasty trick!—and bolted
them so firmly with strong bars that an unarmed man, turned
sideways as if slipping through a crack, could barely get into the
chapel.

When we asked them to open the doors wider, the priest 13
Opportunity said: "If that is your aim, do your best while I'm
here; for if I leave, you'll gain no entry." Having said this, he
went into the temple. Each of us made ready and laid hold of 14
the ox, which butted and kicked as we tried to pull it into the
chapel by its tail.[19] While we were vainly sweating in this ridic- 15
ulous effort, the ox's tail was pulled off. So we decided to
slaughter the ox in the forecourt of the temple, and to carve it
up so that each of us could take one of the pieces into the chapel. A few of us got an entire limb, and others a decent portion. 16
I took the stomach, which had been left on the ground, and
clutched it to my bosom.

Lepidus. Ha ha ha! A fitting burden for you! 17

Libripeta. Exactly.

Lepidus. Proceed.

Libripeta. The priests cried out "A foul crime! Our temple is des- 18
ecrated!" Suddenly, a roaring mob set on us from all sides, seiz-
ing the ox's horns from those who bore them, and using them
as weapons. When I saw the matter turning violent, I tossed 19
the stomach away and joined the crowd in heaping abuse on the
scholars. After all, won't a prudent man use fraud in a pinch to
save himself? But as they say, we're deceived more by fraud than 20

21   profecto res ipsa preter institutum successit. Nam mihi quidem
ore quam apertissimo vociferanti nescio quis ventrem in caput
meum confregit.

22 *Lep.* Ergo tu hoc pacto eternum vives, Libripeta.

Libr. Sane quidem eternum, ubi ex eo diluvio evasi.

Lep. I te lotum.

Libr. Eo.

∴ 5 ∴

Erumna

1 ***. Salve, ac tibi dii quidem faciles ac propitii sint tuumque hoc
quicquid est gaudii secundent, ut esse te animo isthoc alacri
curisque vacuo letor. Et quidnam est, quod tute isthic solus
rideas?

2 *Philop.* O me miserum!

3 ***. Tamne repente ad merorem, in quo te esse audieram, Philo-
poni, recidis? Etenim ea de re huc advolaram, ut amici officio

4 uterer consolando, iuvando. Nunc autem qui ut erumnam abs
te levarem accesseram, si ab animi letitia te adventu meo in
luctum revocari⟨m⟩, doleo.

5 *Philop.* An est ut hominem mihi quempiam dari te iocundiorem
aut gratiorem posse existimes? Neque tu mihi non vehementer
acceptus, neque ad has conceptas miserias tolerandas eris non

6 accommodatissimus. Sed hac fortune plaga et durissimo tempestatis impetu perculsus et prostratus, cum te ceterosque nostre familie cupidissimos intueor commiseratione calamitatis
nostre esse subtristes, nequeo non facere quin ipsum me
quoque, in quem omnis hec quassate et funditus everse domus

7 ruina concidit, animo et cogitatione respectem: quo fit ut tantis

by fidelity, and my plan backfired. As I was shouting at the top   21
of my lungs, someone smashed the stomach on my head.

Lepidus. So you'll live forever like this, Libripeta.   22

Libripeta. Forever and ever, after escaping that flood.

Lepidus. Go and wash yourself.

Libripeta. I'm going.

∶ 5 ∶

Affliction

[*Friend*]. Greetings! May the gods be favorable and propitious to   1
you, and may they foster your joys! I am glad to find you so
cheerful and carefree. Why are you laughing to yourself?

Philoponius. O wretched me!   2

[*Friend*]. Can you relapse so suddenly, Philoponius, into this de-   3
pression of which I heard? It moved me to hasten here to console you, as a friend should. But having come to relieve your   4
affliction, I am grieved if my arrival has turned your happiness
into grief.

Philoponius. Do you think anyone's presence could delight or please   5
me more than yours? You are entirely welcome, and will be of
no little help to me in bearing my misery. But I have been   6
struck down and laid low by this blow of fortune and by the
fierce onslaught of this tempest. When I see you and other
friends of my family saddened in sympathy for our calamity, I
can't help reflecting on myself, on whom the entire weight of
our battered and ruined house has fallen; and I grieve even   7

ac tam insperatis esse me obrutum malis vehementius indoleam.
8 Namque mihi quidem infelicissimo, in ultimas miserias constituto, relictum esse nihil intelligo, quo ulla vel minima expecta-
9 tione melioris fortune coheream. Et siqua fueram iocunda spe
solitus perfrui, ea erepta atque abducta est. Et res quibus fidere
licuit, omnes uno funesto ac penitus misero casu cecidere: fama,
auctoritas dignitasque familie nostre, que mihi ornamento fu-
10 tura et sperabam et expectabam. Nec, ne possum quidem hoc
ferre animo equo: celebrem in hanc usque diem et claram familiam nostram privatis simultatibus, indignissimis discidiis im-
moderatisque contentionibus consanguineorum meorum, qui
eam tueri et in dies honestiorem reddere debuissent, iam tum
11 esse dehonestatam et perditam. Quam nostram duram, acer-
bam sortem tu et amici, pro insigni humanitate vestra erga nos
12 et misericordia, deploratis. Et incommodorum nostrorum alienos a nostra familia maiorem animo suscepisse molestiam,
quam hi quorum fidei splendor decusque familie esse cordi de-
buerat, demiror.
13 ***. Malo te animi tui gratia ad risum deducere, quam ista que
commemoras acerba prosequi. Aliud enim erit tempus ista
14 commemorandi. Etenim, agedum, mitte ex animo istas tristes
curas mihique hanc operam presta, qua fiet ut cum ipse quoque
15 rideam, tum et tu interim molestia vaces. Recita quid mente et
cogitatione versabas, cum tacitus et perfamiliariter ipse modo
pro meo more et consuetudine superveniens, te hic in bibliotheca ridentem repperi.
16 *Philop.* Equidem recte admones ac morem tibi geram. ⟨***⟩ philosophum—hominem, ut nosti, sordidum et agrestem—suaque
omnia disputandi prodigia et commenta, quibus tam audacter
17 et impudenter abutitur, irridebam. Nam is, ut nuper ad me
consalutatum accessit, lacernam pertritam et putridam usu et
vetustate, multa immurmurans multaque secum ipse garriens,
18 solvit ex humeris. Tandem, aliquo quasi ab insomnio excitatus,

more deeply that such great and unexpected ills have overwhelmed me. I am most unhappy in my utter misery, and not   8
even the slightest hope of better fortune is left to me. Every   9
pleasant hope that I once enjoyed has been snatched and stolen
from me. This one fatal and quite pitiful disaster has destroyed
everything on which I once relied — my family's reputation, its
authority, and its prestige — all the things that I hoped and expected would lend me distinction. Nor can I calmly bear to see   10
our once renowned and celebrated family disgraced and destroyed by the private rivalries, base factions, and unrestrained
feuding of my kinsmen, who should have protected it and daily
added to its good repute.[20] Your remarkable humanity and sym-   11
pathy for us lead you and other friends to deplore our harsh
fate. Indeed, I marvel that persons outside our family have suf-   12
fered greater distress at our misfortunes than those who should
by rights have cared for their family's splendor and distinction.

[*Friend*]. For your happiness, I would rather see you laugh than   13
dwell on those bitter memories, which you may recall another
time. So come now, put those sad cares out of your mind, and   14
help me too to laugh, and you to forget your distress for a
while. Tell me what you were thinking about when I arrived   15
quietly, as is customary for a friend, and found you laughing
here in the library.

Philoponius. Your advice is sound, and I shall comply. I was laugh-   16
ing at the philosopher X, a filthy and rustic fellow, as you know,
and at the monstrous fabrications he so boldly and shamelessly
uses and abuses in debate.[21] When he came to see me recently,   17
he mumbled and chattered to himself as he took off his cloak,
which is tattered and putrid from years of wear. At length, as if   18
roused from a dream, he looked at me with his muddled gaze.

me spectans oculis turbulentis, 'Et quid? o, heus tu, inepte!'
grandi voce inclamitat, 'Quidnam turpe non ducis, homini forti
presertim atque litterato tibi simili, cadere in merorem et curis
19   tristibus succumbere? Ubi animus a te expectatus, fortis et
contra omnes impetus fortune ratione et caducarum rerum de-
20   spicientia armatus atque munitissimus? Et quid metuis paupertatem? Dives est, cui nihil deest. Quid optas amplitudinem?
21   Cum illo agitur preclare, cui adimere possit fortuna nihil. Quid
est, quod indigne ferendum ducas? illudne quod tui fortassis
partam a maioribus tuis laudem et claritatem temere disper-
22   dant? Ornatissimus omnium est is qui vitio et turpitudine
vacat. Gaude idcirco, vir animi generosi, te virtute ac peritia
bonarum artium esse neque inexpertum neque incultum.'

23   At ipse, cum hominem omni facie corporis contemptum
atque abiectum satis inspexissem, vix continui risum. Tum ille
exhilaratus: 'Et quidnam, proh superi, potest ratio?' inquit.
24   'Unico vel minimo disputationis congressu, duce ratione, animos errore et falsis opinionibus imbutos ad rectam et veram
virtutem et sapientiam philosophi revocamus atque restitui-
mus.' Cum hec dixisset, lacerna correpta, abiit.

25   ***. Tu vero, etsi illius vitam atque mores agrestes et rudes non
vehementer probabas—neque enim mihi illius hominis Cynica
26   superstitio unquam probari potuit—, sed rationi fortassis et
suasionibus istiusmodi acquiescebas atque in eam sententiam,
ni fallor, adducebaris ut existimares neque metuendum quod
nullam te malis afficiendi vim haberet, neque maximopere op-
tandum quod facile deperdi atque amitti posse arbitrere, neque
non facili et equo animo ferendum quicquid vacuum turpitu-
27   dine sit, atque postremo propriis animi viribus in primis fiden-
dum suisque, non admodum alienis, bonis letandum esse.

28   *Philop.* Mihi quidem ista que recitas haudquaquam levia possunt
aut ieiuna videri, quandoquidem a gravissimis et doctissimis
29   viris, uti tu es, coram disputantur. Sed quo auctoritati vestre,

"Ho, what's this, you fool?" he shouted in a loud voice. "Don't you think it base, especially for a brave man and scholar like yourself, to succumb to such grief and sad cares? Where is the 19 courage expected of you, who are strong, fortified against all fortune's blows, and armed with disdain for transitory things? Why do you fear poverty? Rich is the man who wants nothing. 20 Why do you wish for opulence? Prosperous is the man whom fortune cannot rob. What is it that stirs your indignation? Is it 21 perhaps that your own kinsmen recklessly destroy the praise and renown which your ancestors won? Most illustrious is the 22 man free of vice and turpitude. Rejoice then, noble-spirited man, that you are neither unacquainted with virtue nor uninstructed in liberal learning."

After examining the fellow's completely despicable and abject 23 appearance, I could hardly restrain my laughter. Then his face brightened, "Ye gods above, what can reason achieve?" he said. "In this one brief exchange of debate, guided only by reason, we 24 have restored to the true virtue and wisdom of philosophy a mind which was imbued with error and false opinions." So saying, he picked up his cloak and departed.

[*Friend*]. You hardly approved his rude and rustic manner, and I 25 could never approve his Cynic credulity.[22] And yet you may 26 have taken comfort in such arguments and exhortations. Unless I err, you were persuaded that you should neither fear what could not harm you, nor desire what you could easily lose; that you should bear with equanimity whatever is not dishonorable; and finally that you should rely above all on your own spiritual 27 strength, and rejoice in your own good qualities rather than in those of others.

Philoponius. Your remarks can hardly strike me as trivial or insub- 28 stantial, when they are openly advanced by grave and learned men like you. Still, while I greatly esteem your authority, which 29

que apud me semper valuit, tribuo plurimum, eo esse queque
asseveretis non neganda censeo, magis quam ut isdem me ab
egritudine et molestia levatum sentiam.

30   ***. Quid, si quispiam roget easne ipsas philosophorum sententias futiles penitus et leves esse existimes, an veras easdem
potius et graves deputes?

31   *Philop.* Veras quidem.

    ***. Quid tum, si roget rursus ratio te ipsa et veritas an non mo-
veat?

    Philop. Dixero: me ipsa res et accepta calamitas arctius detinet
quam ut vestra commoveant verba.

32   ***. An ea sunt fortassis in te illata incommoda maiora quam ut
ab eo qui rationi pareat perferri possint?

33   *Philop.* Me quidem vis calamitatis et adversus impetus in eam egri-
tudinem et animi imbecillitatem coniecit, ut lucem veritatis
contui et gravissimam rationis vocem auribus sine molestia non
possim capere.

34   ***. Et quid, si huius tue egritudinis quispiam abs te causam que-
rat, partim disputandi gratia, quod libenter soles, partim ut
cognitis atque perceptis morbi rationibus, quod fieri posse non
diffido, ad ponendam erumnam et secludendam omnem molestiam opem auxiliumque afferat?

35   *Philop.* Hanc ego te auctore susceptam disputandi consuetudinem
perlibenter sequar, qua ne ipse quidem diffido fore, tua iuncta
prudentia et sapientia, ut animum collapsum et fractum ex-

36   citem atque restituam. Idque quo efficias commodius, tibi
operam sine ulla contumacia prestabo causasque tristitie huius

37   mee planius explicabo. Nam sepe iam antea una tecum, vetere
parentum nostrorum amico, quem ipse patris amantissimi loco

38   habeo, de iniquitate meorum querebamur, quod in eis tanta
esset insolentia et temeritas ut, dum illorum quisque sese impudenter principem familie haberi ac dici vellet, non id virtute ac
diligentia communi(s)que rei cura promereri elaborabant, sed

has always carried much weight with me, I am more inclined to accept your assertions than to feel that they relieve my anguish and distress.

[*Friend*]. What would you say, if someone asked you whether you 30 consider the philosophers' opinions completely worthless and trivial, or regard them as true and weighty?

Philoponius. As true, clearly. 31

[*Friend*]. What then, if asked whether reason and truth fail to move you?

Philoponius. I would say that the reality of my disaster prevents me from being moved by your words.

[*Friend*]. Then are your misfortunes too great to be borne by a 32 man guided by reason?

Philoponius. .The violence of my calamity has plunged me into such 33 anguish and moral weakness that I am unable to behold the light of truth or hear the weighty voice of reason without distress.

[*Friend*]. Suppose someone asked the cause of your anguish, ei- 34 ther for the sake of discussion, which you often enjoy, or in or- der to discover and diagnose the causes of your malady — as I am sure is possible — and to aid you in dismissing your afflic- tion and putting away your distress.

Philoponius. At your suggestion, I shall gladly continue this mode 35 of debate. For I too am sure that your prudence and wisdom will aid me in reviving and restoring my fallen spirits. To make 36 your task easier, I shall give you my full cooperation by explain- ing more clearly the causes of my sadness. Since you are an old 37 friend of my parents, and someone whom I regard as a dear father, I have often complained to you about the injustice of my kinsmen. Their insolence and recklessness were so great that 38 each of them brazenly wanted to be considered and called the family's leader. Yet they did not seek to merit this by virtue and diligence in caring for our estate. Instead, crazed with

per intolerabilem quandam animi elationem et fastidium in-
saniebant inque eos qui fortunis essent in familia inferiores, non
patrium imperium sed tyrannorum pene dominium sibi arro-
gabant his legibus, quibus sibi erga minores iracundia et im-
39 portunitate omnia licere arbitrarentur, neque parem quidem
sibi fore ulla in re quempiam sine indignatione et contumeliis
paterentur, in omnique sua, quecumque illa esset dura et per-
vicax sententia aut opinio, ut persisterent, non rationibus illi
quidem suadendi et ingenio, sed convitiis, iurgiis et altercationi-
40 bus eniterentur. Hinc fiebat, certandi studio vincendique cupiditate, ut suo etiam maximo cum discrimine quisque eorum
ceteros omnes in calamitatem cadere elaboraret quo, exhaustis
divitiis quibus elati ipsi et supra quam par esset confidentes ef-
ferrentur, nulli per egestatem sibi pares admodum essent futuri.
41 Qua ex re que acerbissime inter eos iniuriarum et vindicte
contentiones, que gravissime discordie, que pernities et interitus
facile subsecutus sit, non recenseo: res ante oculos versatur mi-
seranda et collugenda.

Sed omnis hec calamitas, me miserum!, in me penitus co-
42 heret. Nam ipse qui modo, dum darem operam virtuti dumque
litterarum et bonarum artium cognitione atque peritia me in
dies ornatiorem et comptiorem facere studuissem, multa pol-
43 licebar in eaque eram spe optima constitutus, ut non diffiderem
me affinium meorum opera assecuturum aliquid earum rerum
que fame, auctoritati dignitatique familie nostre deberentur
queve non sine fraude quadam et iniustitia esse ab his, qui ea
44 conferre possent, denegata omnes diiudicabant; qui item, cum
non pauci homines potentissimi adessent qui, celebritate et ve-
teri beneficentia familie nostre commoti, sponte omnia pollice-
rentur, in eum me propediem locum venturum expectabam, ut
illorum suffragiis et intercessione mihi gratiam multorum et
benivolentiam possem obsequiis et omni officiorum genere accumulare.

intolerable haughtiness, they exercised not a father's authority, but a tyrant's dominion over their less wealthy relations. And on their own terms they felt justified in committing any act of anger or oppression against their younger kinsmen. They suf- 39 fered no rivals without indignation or insults, and they strove to defend all their harsh and headstrong views, not by arguing with reason and intelligence, but by reproaches and altercations. Hence, in their love of strife and desire to conquer, each of 40 them strove to ruin the others, even at his own great peril. For each hoped that poverty would eliminate his rivals if they exhausted the very wealth which inspired their own elation and excessive presumption. I won't recount their bitter contentions 41 in insults and reprisals, or the destruction and dissolution that naturally ensued. This pitiful and deplorable situation is clear to all.

This entire catastrophe has landed squarely on me, wretch that I am! By devoting myself to virtue and by striving to attain 42 ever greater perfection and distinction in mastering letters and liberal studies, I expected to do great things and nourished fine hopes. I had no doubt that with my kinsmen's aid I would 43 achieve things which our family's renown and prestige required and which, everyone agreed, would be denied me only through the fraud or injustice of those who may confer them. Not a few 44 powerful men, moreover, were of themselves moved by our family's renown and past kindnesses to promise me their aid. With their support and mediation, I expected that soon my services and friendly offices would win the considerable favor and goodwill of many.

45   Ea tamen cum ita essent, in hanc calamitatem incidi, ut neque fortunis meis, neque affinium opera, neque pollicitatorum
opibus habeam unde meis queam necessitatibus satis facere.
46   Nam et ipsi affines mei, accepto vulnere quod illorum propria
temeritas concitavit, fortuna inflixit, ad sese ab ultima pernitie
47   tuéndos vix valent; et ceteri quidem omnes qui iam nostras esse
res perturbatas et perditas sensere, ne graves sibi nostris incom-
48   modis simus, ⟨nos⟩ refugere atque excludere consuescunt. Ego
autem, et a fortuna abiectus, et a meis despectus, et a ceteris
49   desertus iaceo. Quare, cum a tanta spe ceciderim, cum tantum
infortunium et durissimam sortem subierim, quanto me idcirco
in dolore animi versari censes, maxime dum id animo repeto,
me prope a summa felicitate uno hoc tempestatis momento in
infimam esse miseriam deiectum, a firmaque et grandi melio-
rum rerum expectatione in desperationem rerum omnium, a
copia et frequentia eorum qui se amicos profitebantur in solitu-
dine atque egestate relictum?

50   Et qui animo summam capere voluptatem consueverim,
quod in familia copiam heredum et iuventutis speciem crescere
atque florescere intuerer, nunc idem dolore permaximo afficior
quod eos, non ad gloriam maiorum equandam, quam cura et
diligentia eorum quibus familia commendata esset facile assequi
potuissent, sed ad fortune ictus perferendos, ad incommoda
51   perpetienda natos video; qui preterea splendore veteris familie
nostre et claritate gloriabar — quas res a maioribus nostris com-
paratas patres nostri in exilio per alienas provincias errantes
pulchre servassent — idem, indignissima et detestabili conten-
tione eorum quibus in patriam restitutis regende tuendeque familie cura et officium commissum esset, omnem pristinam exis-
timationem et amplitudinem domus nostre extinctam non sine
52   lachrimis reminiscor; denique et qui prius tibi atque ceteris
amicis et bonis omnibus qui in meis affinibus caritatem et
pietatem erga me desiderabant, illud esse ferendum egre

It was at this point that disaster befell me. Neither my per- 45
sonal fortune, nor my kinsmen's assistance, nor the wealth of
those who promised their aid permit me to meet my needs.
Even my kinsmen, having suffered the blow provoked by their 46
own temerity and inflicted by Fortune, are scarcely able to keep
themselves from utter destitution. And everyone else, learning 47
of our confused and ruined affairs and not wishing to be burdened by our misfortune, begins to avoid and exclude us. Thus 48
I lie prostrate, cast down by Fortune, disdained by my family,
and deserted by all others. I have lost my great hopes and suf- 49
fered the harsh fate of this great misfortune. Can you imagine
the pain I feel, especially when I reflect that, in a single moment, I plunged from the heights of bliss to the depths of misery, from great hope for success to despair of everything, and
from the wealth and companionship of my professed friends to
this loneliness and poverty?

I used to take the greatest pleasure in watching our numer- 50
ous heirs and splendid youths grow and flourish in our family.
But now the utmost pain afflicts me. For I see that those youths
who, under the diligent care of the men responsible for our
family's welfare, would easily have attained the glory of their
forebears, now are born to bear Fortune's blows and to suffer
misfortunes. I used to glory in the splendor and renown of our 51
ancient family, which our fathers inherited from their forebears
and maintained intact even while wandering in exile through
foreign lands. But now I recall with tears how our former reputation and magnificence have been completely wiped out by the
shameful and odious strife of men who, on returning to their
homeland, were entrusted with the task of governing and pre-
serving our family. I once agreed with you and other virtuous 52
friends who found my kinsmen lacking in love and affection for
me. You said it was intolerable that some of my kinsmen, whom

assentiebar, quod eorum me nonnulli, quibus in hanc usque
diem, parente meo mortuo, non secus atque genitoribus obtem-
perassem, preter pietatem ac preter quam quod homini virtuti
dedito debebatur, parvi facerent, idem iam nunc doleo meos
omnes ita esse affines a fortuna adductos ut, ne illis quidem
volentibus, ullam in me pietatis aut officii satis accommodatam
rationem experiri possint.

53   Et quod nunc a fortuna prohiberi doleo, id tum a fortunatis
54   denegari minus quidem ferebam moleste. Nam cum bona illorum fortuna letabar, tum fortassis aliquando fore futurum ipse
mihi persuadebam ut, cum me illi ob probitatem diligerent,
tum ob meam in eos observantiam ipsi commodis meis ali-
55   quando studerent. At vide quam mecum pessime agatur! Qui
enim ceptis studiis meis, dum per fortunam licuit, multam
operam et assiduitatem animo liberiore impertiebar, nunc, tantis curis exagitato animo et necessitatibus undique urgentibus
concussus, interpellor et distrahor, ut profecto esse miserum me
nequeam non profiteri.

56   Neque non possum non facere, o Fortuna, quin te accusem,
que quidem impudentes, improbos ac flagitiosos plerosque
omnes divitiis auges, gratiis confirmas, auctoritate exornas.
57   Quid tantis odiis bonos sectaris? Quid eorum commodis ad-
versaris? Quid tantis iniuriis honesta queque eorum pervertis
58   atque omnem degende vite rationem perturbas? Tu efficis ut
litterarum et laudatissimarum rerum cupidissimus per egestatem a cultu sapientie et a pervestigatione doctrine distrahatur;
59   tu imperitissimos et omnium bonarum artium et ingeniorum
inimicissimos atque hostes ad summas opes et delitias evehis;
60   tu industrium, agentem, assiduum et optimis studiis deditum,
in omni rerum inopia prostratum, iacentem, opprimis, suffragia
61   et adminicula omnia opum et amicitiarum eripis; tu inertibus,
vecordibus, desidiosis, supinis, rerum affluentiam, clientelas,

I had obeyed as parents since my father's death, slighted me in violation of their familial duty and the respect due a virtuous man. But now I too must grieve to see them so reduced by Fortune that, even if they wished to, they could not show me any affection or kindness.

In fact, my indignation when they denied me aid was less 53 than my pain now that Fortune prevents my aiding them. For I 54 once rejoiced in their good fortune, perhaps because I was convinced that they would someday love me for my integrity and would aid me as one who revered them. But now, see how ill I 55 fare! While Fortune permitted, I devoted my untroubled and undivided attention to my studies. But now that my mind is vexed by great cares and urgent needs, I am hindered and distracted, and can only declare myself completely wretched.

I have no choice but to accuse you, Fortune. You lavish 56 wealth on scoundrels, show favor to reprobates, and lend dignity to miscreants. Why do you persecute just men with such 57 great hatred? Why do you thwart their well-being? Why do you subvert their virtuous actions by your injustices and ruin their way of life? You allow destitution to tear the student of 58 letters from his pursuit of wisdom and erudition. You elevate to 59 the highest wealth and luxury the men who are most ignorant of liberal learning and most hostile to talent. You oppress with 60 abject poverty the man who pursues noble studies industriously, actively, and assiduously, and you snatch from him the aid and support of friends and funds. You shower prosperity, clients, 61

hospitia ac incredibilem etiam principum gratiam et benivolentiam subministras, quo ad luxum et omnem prodigalitatem
62   atque libidinem intemperantissime abuta⟨n⟩tur; tu eum qui non
mediocri virtutum ornamento et admirandis rebus suo studio et
ingenio inventis iam prope celeberrimus sit, qui fortuna optima
ab omnibus dignus iudicetur, de honesto suorum statu, de iusta
spe, de emerita expectatione deturbas atque ad miseriam pro-
63   pellis; tu, Fortuna iniquissima, sordidos, impuros, immeritissi-
mos, in amplissimam dignitatem protrahis, eorum spes stultas
atque immanes longe maximis propositis expectationibus et
fructibus vincis, eorum expectationes et libidines efferatas, de-
testabiles, copia et affluentia bonorum omnium exples.

64   Sed malo hec omnia preterire atque, si queam, oblivisci.

65   ***. Essent qui tua ista omnia prolixiori quam instituerim oratione ducerent confutanda et in hac causa, que multam ad
dicendum copiam subministrat, omne suum ingenium et elo-
66   quentiam consumerent. Mihi autem brevi et concisa tecum esse
argumentatione utendum statuo; atque id quidem, cum ceteras
ob res, tum ut apertius intelligas non dicendi vi aut arte, sed
simplici veritate confisum, me tibi utilem et amico condignam
67   animi tui a morbo levandi curam suscepisse. Ac fingo quidem
me esse Fortunam, in quam tu tanta perorasti.

    —'Te quidem,' inquam, 'et prelongam expostulationem tuam
audivi, quem, si per humanitatem tuam et eas litteras quas tenes liceret, esse cuperem in me non isthoc animo irritato et
68   concito. De⟨de⟩cet enim litteratum et ingenue educatum in
convitium, nisi cum res postulet, et id quidem perquam modice,
69   irrumpere. Etenim, mi ⟨Philoponi⟩, vide qualem me tibi pres-
tem. Sino illud, pleraque abs te dici bona que bona esse possim
70   negare, et incommoda que sapienti incommoda non sint. Nam
quod affinium tuorum casum condoleas, non id redarguo:

hospitality, and even the enormous favor of rulers on idlers, fools, and sluggards, who squander them without restraint in luxury, prodigality, and lust. If a man is illustrious for his superior virtue or marvelous studies, or if he is universally declared worthy of the highest fortune, you remove him from his family's position of honor, cheat him of his rightful hopes, and reduce him to misery. Unjust Fortune, you advance to the greatest dignity men who are vile, tainted, and undeserving. You encourage their foolish and monstrous hopes by offering them immense hopes and rewards. You satisfy their savage hopes and lusts and their abominable longings with an abundance of riches. 62 63

But I prefer not to dwell on such things, and would forget them if I could. 64

[*Friend*]. There may be some who would think your remarks require a lengthier confutation than I intend to make, and who would expend all their wit and eloquence on this topic, which provides so much matter for discussion. But I think I need only use a brief line of argument. In this way, you will clearly see that I rely not on the power of rhetoric, but on the simple truth, as I undertake the task — so beneficial to you and worthy of me as your friend — of relieving your depression. I shall pretend that I am Fortune, against whom you directed your long peroration.[23] 65 66 67

"I have listened to you and your lengthy complaint. If it were possible by virtue of your humanity and learning, I would not wish you to bear me such vehement anger. A man of letters who is liberally educated should resort to reproaches only when the situation demands it, and then quite moderately at that. My dear Philoponius, you see how I treat you. I allow you to call 'goods' things which I might deny are good, and 'harmful' things which do not harm a wise man. Nor do I contest your grief at your kinsmen's misfortune, for I attribute to affection your wish 68 69 70

pietati enim tue concedo ut, quos honestissimos et modestissi-
mos cupias, eosdem locupletes atque amplissimos optes, tametsi
permaximi interest ut hi, quos tu duros erga te et immites ex-
periebare, ad statum hunc devenerint quo minus ob divitias in-
71   solescant. Neque id abs te non honeste et sancte desiderari dico,
ut tua in familia adolescentes cura maiorum probatissimi et ab
omni vitiorum labe intacti et nullis sordibus contaminati excres-
72   cant; tametsi ea te preditum fore prudentia arbitrabar, ut recte
intelligeres quam hi qui ab aliis partum sibi decus et lumen
servasse non didicerint, non per eos facile reliquam iuventutem
73   ad glorie splendorem posse adduci. Sed non te audiam, si hac
tua in expostulatione aliorum incommoda congeris, ut miseria-
74   rum tuarum cumulum exaggeres. An ego in mearum rerum
possessione insanire et iactabundos vagari permittam eos qui
suis uti bonis nesciant? An illi apud se firmum aliquid et diu-
turnum putent consistere, quod contentionibus susceptis atque
discidiis, omni studio et opere moliri atque funditus evertere
75   diu elaborarint? Egone illi isthec servabo que is, cui ea servanda
sint, perdere maximopere enitatur? Qua de re illos affines tuos
missos faciamus a tuaque illos causa disiungamus.

76   'Ceterum, tu demum, age, quid tibi vis? Omnia tibi que sine
iniuria liceant, perlubens petenti dabo. Hanc tu conditionem, si
nos querelis tuis moveri vis, non recuses oportet.'

77   ⟨*Philop.* Non recuso.⟩

78   ***. 'Utar tecum omni, ut voles, liberalitate, modo ea ab officio et
iustitia seiuncta non sit. Namque id a me petere, ut tibi com-
modem quod cum aliorum iactura fiat, impudentis esse⟨t⟩, et ea
in te munificentia si utar qua immeritus quispiam ledatur, non
me, uti arbitror, frugi et satis consultam deputes.'

to see them not only honorable and moderate, but also wealthy
and eminent. (And yet it is to your great advantage that those
who were so unkind to you should be reduced to a condition
which curbs the insolence their wealth inspired.) I also regard   71
as honorable and blameless your desire to see your family's
youths grow up, under their elders' care, virtuous and free from
any stain of vice or turpitude; even though I thought that in   72
your mature wisdom you would understand that kinsmen unable to maintain the honor and renown won by others could
scarcely lead their younger relatives to glory and splendor. But I   73
shall not heed you, if in protesting you pile up the misfortunes
of others in order to exaggerate the heap of your own miseries.
What, shall I allow people to run mad aimlessly and to glory in   74
possessing what is mine, when they are incapable of using what
is theirs? Do they think any of their goods will remain stable or
lasting, when by their feuds and factions they continually strive
to undermine and undo them completely? Should I preserve   75
those possessions which their very owner seeks to destroy? So
let us dismiss your kinsmen, and keep them separate from your
case.

   "Tell me, then, what do you seek for yourself? I shall quite   76
gladly grant your request for anything I may grant without injustice. If you want your laments to move me, you may not refuse this one condition."

Philoponius. I accept.   77

[*Friend*]. "I shall treat you with complete generosity, as you wish,   78
   provided it is consonant with duty and justice. For only a
   shameless man would ask me for something that entails another's loss. And if I were to show you munificence which would
   harm an innocent person, I don't think you would regard me as
   decent or prudent."

79 ⟨*Philop*. Aliorum divitias nec posco nec, si mihi commodes, volo.
Peto ut mihi a cultu et studiis bonarum artium, quibus semper
fui deditus, feliciora rependantur⟩.

80 ***. 'Visne te divitem et locupletem reddam, dum ipse non ques-
tui faciendo, sed litteris ediscendis dies ac noctes assideas? dum
tu omnem lucri faciendi rationem et occasionem longe spernas
atque pre disciplina posthabeas? cum a re nulla tuus animus

81 eque atque a questus cura atque opere abhorreat? Heus tu! pecunias accumulare et accumulatas servare qui negligit, quod

82 ipse facis, insanit, si se divitem eo pacto futurum expectat. Vis
te principum gratia et benivolentia communitum reddam, cum
a re nulla animi tui generositas sit magis quam a servitute
aliena, qua una re maxime principum animi, ut nos diligant,

83 flectuntur? Obsequii enim et beneficii voluptate et fructu principes, non officii specie moventur; et quam tu in principe gratiam et benivolentiam appellas, ea meram servitutem sapit.

84 Nam eum animi motum in principe, quo in nos esse affectus
videatur, percepti commodi ratio, non cogniti officii meritum

85 efficit. Tune idcirco is eris qui opere prestatione magis quam

86 virtutibus placere expetis? Non tu, litteris et doctrina excultus,
vel speciem ipsam servitutis iudicio et omni sensu detestaturus
es?

87 'Te a dignitate et amplitudine in miseriam detrusisse dicor.
Quid ita? quod fortassis tuorum improbitatem excitavi ut, sua
pervicacia amissis rebus, te de maxima et firmissima spe depel-

88 lerent? Cave posthac huiusmodi criminationibus utaris, adolescens minime male sed ignare.'

89 ⟨*Philop*.⟩. Quasi non illi ipsi infames et abiectissime pestes morum, te freti, Fortuna, nos omnes sui dissimiles omnibus qui-

90 bus queant iniuriis prosequantur; quasi non tuo exemplo ducti
immanes, crudeles naturaque maleficos atque impiissimos et
sibi paribus vitiis et flagitiis coinquinatissimos exquirant atque

Philoponius. I do not desire the wealth of others, nor want them if 79
you offer me. Rather, I ask that you repay me for my long devotion to the liberal arts.

[*Friend*]. "Do you wish me to make you wealthy, when you are 80
engaged night and day, not in gainful pursuits, but in literary studies, when you spurn every chance to make money as being less important than your learning, and when a concern for profit is the furthest thing from your mind? Really! Anyone 81
who, like you, does nothing to accumulate and protect his wealth is mad if he expects to become rich. Do you want me to 82
fortify you with the favor and goodwill of rulers, when there is nothing more foreign to your noble spirit than servility, the one quality which most sways rulers' minds to love us? Rulers are 83
moved by the pleasure and profit they take in our fawning and favors, not by our displays of duty. What you call a ruler's favor and goodwill smacks of pure servility. Those emotions which 84
make a ruler appear fond of us are stirred when he perceives his own advantage, not when he recognizes our meritorious service. Will you seek, then, to please by some office more excellent 85
than your own virtues? Won't you rather, as a student of letters 86
and learning, despise wholeheartedly even the appearance of servility?

"You claim that I cast you down from dignity and affluence 87
to misery! How can that be? Did I perhaps excite your kinsmen's audacity so that, when their obstinacy destroyed their estate, they would make you relinquish your greatest and firmest hopes? See that you don't repeat such accusations, O inno- 88
cent but ignorant youth."

Philoponius. As if those vile and abject plagues of all good conduct 89
did not rely on your aid, Fortune, in heaping every possible injury on everyone unlike them! As if they did not follow your 90
example when they seek out cruel and impious criminals, men tainted by vices and crimes equal to theirs, and thrust them

appetant quos, spretis bonis, ad dignitates atque amplitudinem
convocent atque intrudant.

91   ***. 'Maxima et dignissima dona igitur a me illis deferuntur, qui
alios ex arbitrio magnos atque amplos reddunt.'

92   *Philop.* Profecto immensa, sed indignissima.

     ***. 'Que tu fortassis appetas atque exposcas.'

     Philop. Ea si dentur, novi quo pacto pulchre teneantur.

93   ***. 'Te quidem non mediocriter esse animo commotum video,
94   sed quo dudum volebam, ut opinio mea fert, appulisti. Qui
quidem si, uti pollicitus es, hanc sine contumacia mihi operam
huius morbi tui curandi prestas, profecto efficiam ut erumnam
hanc ponas et omnem erga me conceptam acerbitatem mitiges.
Huc, precor, animum adhibe!

95   'Pridie apud me Triscatarus his verbis utebatur: "Fortuna,
quid tibi vis? cur me in hanc inanem et futilem amplitudinem
ac levem fastum substulisti, in quo me penitus miserum esse
96   sentiam? Mihi enim semper aliquis timor impendit, ut ne minimum quidem temporis momentum tum ad animi quietem
97   ⟨tum⟩ ad ipsum me recipiendum detur. Nam hinc varie, multi-
plices et gravissime rerum agendarum cure solicitant, hinc
concursus imminentium periculorum et ipsi⟨s⟩ pene oculis pre-
vise tempestates, invidie odiique, iacture et incommodorum fi-
nitimorum suspitiones perterrefactum me agitare et iactare non
98   desinunt. Quid non me vitam placidam et tranquillam agere
permittis, ut ingenuis quibus ille artibus dat operam, ut studiis
bonarum rerum animo pacato et tranquillo, et ab his quibus
premor vexationibus mente soluta et libera liceat insistere?
99   O me felicem, ⟨si⟩ apud studiosos eiusmodi amicos iocunde
festiveque versari liceat, apud quos ad pervestigandam rerum
occultarum rationem et modum studii concitatione et solertia
artibus delecter, quoad ingenii laudibus famam et celebritatem
nancisci queam!"

into positions of dignity and prominence, while good men are
scorned!

[*Friend*]. "I give the greatest and worthiest gifts to those who will-   91
ingly make others great and eminent."

Philoponius. Greatest, yes, but least worthy.   92

[*Friend*]. "They are gifts you yourself may desire and demand."

Philoponius. Were they given to me, I would know well how to
keep them.

[*Friend*]. "I see that you are quite agitated, and have come to the   93
point, I believe, where I have long wanted you. If, as you prom-   94
ised, you help me relieve your malady without resisting me, I
shall see that you put aside your affliction and soften your bit-
terness toward me. Please give me your attention.

"Yesterday Triscatharus spoke to me.[24] 'Fortune,' he said,   95
'what is your intent? Why have you raised me to this position
of vain grandeur and empty ostentation, in which I feel utterly
miserable? Some fear always hangs over me, and I haven't the   96
briefest moment to relax or recover. On one side, I am harassed   97
and oppressed by the multifarious and burdensome cares of my
affairs. On the other, I am incessantly terrified and tormented
by a host of imminent dangers and disturbances which loom
before my eyes, by the havoc wrought by envy and hatred, and
by my fears of similar misfortunes. Why don't you permit me   98
to lead a placid and tranquil life, so that I may pursue liberal
studies and fine learning, as that man does, with a peaceful
spirit and a mind freed from the troubles that oppress me
now?[25] How happy I would be, if I could join the cheerful and   99
festive company of scholarly friends! Investigating difficult subjects in their company, I would delight in exciting studies and
ingenious contrivances, and would finally win fame and renown
for my talents.'

100   'Hec Triscatarus cum apud me prolixius et, quod homines
dolore acti solent, immodica orationis copia disputasset seque
101   omnino infelicissimum diceret, que eram animi tui ignara et
⟨cum⟩ neminem a suo, in quo esse velit, statu dimovere instituissem, ⟨negavi mutari posse sortem quam ei dedissem⟩, eadem idcirco nunc, quod ex animi tui sententia fieri arbitror,
tuas cum Triscataro fortunas permutes volo; eo pacto tuis atque
illius desideriis et expectationibus percommode satis factum iri
arbitror.'

102 *Philop.* Etenim quid est quod cum illo commutem? Namque non
mihi quidem divitie, non opum affluentia, non clientele, non
hospitia, non qui afferant dona, non qui sese ultro subigant,
non qui summisse precentur suumque in gratificando studium
103   consumant, adsunt; nulla denique amplitudo apud me est. Quibus rebus omnibus ille maiorem in modum abundat.

104 ***. 'Recte admones; atqui que apud te sint, pleraque optima
105   atque in primis expetenda, succincte recensebimus. Ac, ni fallor,
apud te sunt littere studiaque optima, firmitas animi, turpitudinis verecundia, exercitationis consuetudo, industrie laus, modestie fructus, gravitas, fides, equitas, morum decus, officii ratio
religioni et rerum optimarum cognitioni et inventorum glorie
106   cum fama et claritate coniuncta. Hec igitur et eiusmodi, quibus
ab ineunte etate egregie fuisti deditus, qualiacumque apud te
107   sint, cum illius bonis, me interprete, ut voles, commutabis. Tibi
ille divitiarum vim maximam, tu contra illi rerum rarissimarum
cumulum; ille statum et dignitatem et principis gratiam, tu bonorum amicitias et splendidum nomen atque preclaram de te
opinionem et iudicium expones in medium; denique tu bona
et mala omnia illius, ille tua queque ad se recipiet. Hecque ut
facias, iterum atque iterum suadeo.'

"Thus Triscatharus argued, at too great length and with too   100
little restraint in his oratorical outpourings, as suffering people
often do, and declared himself the most wretched of men. I was   101
as yet unaware of your state of mind, and had resolved not to
remove anyone from circumstances which were to his liking. So
I said I could not change the lot I had assigned him. But now I
think you will give your complete assent when I ask you to
change places with Triscatharus. I believe that this will quite
easily gratify your desires and hopes, and his too."

Philoponius. What could I possibly exchange with him? I have no   102
wealth, no abundance of goods, no network of patronage, and
no bonds of hospitality. No one brings me gifts, no one gladly
prostrates himself before me, no one humbly begs my aid, or
spends his time currying my favor. In short, I have no prestige,   103
while he has all these things in greatest abundance.

[*Friend*]. "You are correct. But let us briefly review your posses-   104
sions, many of which are excellent and desirable. What is yours,   105
unless I err, are letters and fine learning; moral steadfastness
and an abhorrence of vice; the habitual exercise of your abilities; renown for your industry and rewards for your moderation; sobriety, loyalty, and fairness; a splendid character, and a
sense of duty coupled with conscience, profound learning, and
the fame and glory of your inventions. By my mediation, these   106
and other such qualities, which you have singularly cultivated
from your youth, you shall now exchange for his goods, if you
wish. He will give you the great power of his wealth, and you   107
will give him your abundance of excellent qualities. He will offer you status, dignity, and the ruler's favor; and you will offer
him the friendship of good men, your illustrious name, and
your splendid reputation. In short, you will receive all that is
his, both good and bad, and he will receive all that is yours. I
strongly urge you to do this."

108   *Philop.* Tanti ego divitias faciam, ut illius monstri iniustitiam, socordiam, impudentiam, desidiam, ignaviam, temeritatem, levitatem, perfidiam, inconstantiam, turpitudinem impietatemque

109   non oderim? Ego sine doctrina, sine studio bonarum rerum, sine cultu virtutis, me esse in vita velim? Vel quid ego cum illo, elato omni levitate et consecutarum rerum stulta letitia exultante ac principis benivolentia temere gestiente, exitioso prodi-

110   gio et peste iuventu⟨ti⟩s commutem? Dignusne est ullis in vita hominum bonis, qui quidem ob immanitatem, crudelitatem, ob stupra et veneficia sua superis atque inferis invisus est? qui ocio, langore desidiaque inter voluptates confectus ne hominum qui-

111   dem aspectu aut luce dignus est? Itane firma, fixa et omnino permanentia, que ipse meo studio, industria et labore, que meis lucubrationibus et maximis vigiliis adeptus sum bona, cum istis fragilibus, caducis et inconstantissimis bonis, que tu, Fortuna, illius ignavie et desidie condonasti, ut commutem suades?

112   ***. 'Enimvero non tu iam illum esse iniquum, sed te quidem, qui iracundius in illum inveheris, subimportunum ostendis. Et quid

113   inter vos intersit, queso, prospicito. Te et frugi et gravem et plane bonum Triscatarus deputat. Non ingenium istud tuum acre et versatile, quo non minus quam labore et vigiliis plurima consecutus extitisti, tibi esse dicit a Fortuna indigne elargitum.

114   Non accusat sortem suam, quod indoctus et nullis ingenuis moribus a puero educatus excreverit, sed dicit preter modesti viri officium isthuc fieri abs te, dum hanc quam sua industria adeptus sit amplitudinem principi miris modis obsequendo, tu

115   aliorum esse beneficio condonatam asseris. Et in qua re ille maximos labores, multas vig⟨i⟩lias, omne tempus consumpserit suaque opera et industria effecerit ⟨ut in ea re ex sententia succederet quicquid optaverit⟩, id tu ad eius ignaviam esse delatum

116   predices. Illud etiam addit: splendorem vite, lautitiem celebritatemque suam domesticam et omnem signati argenti et operum apparatum, pro quibus rebus habendis sudore et sanguine

Philoponius. Could I value wealth so much that I would not abhor   108
this monster's injustice, indolence, impudence, sloth, audacity,
levity, perfidy, inconstancy, turpitude, and impiety? Could I   109
choose to live without learning, without liberal studies, and
without the pursuit of virtue? How could I change places with
this deadly monster and plague on our youth, who revels in inconstancy, exults with foolish joy in his acquisitions, and vainly
glories in our ruler's goodwill? Can any man deserve prosperity,   110
when his cruelties, debaucheries, and poisonings have earned
him the hatred of all the gods in heaven and hell? A voluptuary
exhausted by idle and languorous leisure is unworthy of men's
sight and the light of day. How can you urge me, Fortune, to   111
exchange the lasting and eternal goods I have won by diligent
study and long vigils, for the fragile, transitory, and imperma-
nent goods which you have bestowed on the idle sloth of this
man?

[*Friend*]. "By inveighing angrily against him, you don't prove his   112
wickedness, but your own perversity. Please consider the differ-
ences between you. Triscatharus regards you as decent, serious,   113
and thoroughly good. He doesn't say that Fortune has unfairly
given you that keen and versatile genius, by which, no less than
by your laborious vigils, you have accomplished so much. He   114
doesn't accuse his fate because he grew up without learning or
gentlemanly manners. But he says that you forget propriety
when you attribute to others' generosity that distinction which
he has won by his own industry and by his marvelous services
to our ruler. And everything he achieved through great labors   115
and many vigils — industriously laboring to obtain what he
truly desired — you call the rewards of his idleness. He also   116
notes that the splendor of his life, the luxury and celebrity of
his house, and all his furnishings, silver coins, and artworks —
things for which men toil with their sweat and blood — are not

117 mortales elaborant, tuis ieiuniis et vacuis virtutis et probitatis
titulis esse non multo postponenda; seque facile in media lauti-
tie in mediaque affluentia bonorum, ubi opus sit, modestum,
parcum et continentem futurum fore, tibi autem, rerum notitia
glorioso, non licere ex animi sententia et arbitrio splendide ele-
ganterque convivere, ubi ea que opus ad eam rem sint non sup-
118 peditent; et prestare quidem imperitum esse, dum te peritissimi
observent atque vereantur, quam disertum, dum etiam ignavi et
abiecti, quorum in numero eum esse asseveras, contemnant ac
119 despiciant. Quod si fortassis apud se cura rerum agendarum et
periculorum moles aut metus ullus impendet, dignitas tamen,
amplitudo, licentia ac rerum affluentia sibi non deest.

120 'Tibi quidem voluptas omnis deest, necessitas et solicitudo
121 inest, cura et tristitia perferende paupertatis non deest. Ac
plerumque fortasse tuum invidia irrepit in animum atque omnis tuas compositas et ad virtutis fructum directas rationes dis-
122 turbat et pervertit. Quis enim, ⟨modo⟩ ab omni sensu hominum alienus omnino non sit, uspiam reperietur, qui in miseria
123 constitutus felicibus non invideat? Est hominum hec mens, ut
prospera et secunda in aliis animadvertamus diligentius cum
ipsi adversis urgemur, et aliis passim res quibus careamus sup-
124 peditari indoleamus. Itaque, spe optima et letis successibus
confirmatus, Triscatarus non se superis, quantum res ipsa do-
cet, invisum arbitratur, cui profluenter, prospere ac beate tante
fortune opes omnisque copia desideratissimarum rerum ad
125 quamvis magnificentiam et prodigalitatem subigantur; iratos
sibi quidem videri deos ait illis quos egestas urgeat, solicitudo
conficiat, incommoda oppresserint.

126 'Quod si forte dispudeat Triscatari locum et vite conditionem
subire, fortassis ob eam quam de te opinionem suscepisti, do
127 tibi hoc ⟨. . .⟩. Concedo quidem ut quemvis hominum omnium
seligas, cuius tu commoda et incommoda omnia malis tibi esse

much less to be esteemed than your meager and empty titles of
virtue and integrity. In the midst of his luxury and sumptuous   117
goods, he may easily choose to live moderately, frugally, and
chastely, if need be. But you, who vaunt your erudition, cannot
live as splendidly and elegantly as you truly desire, for you lack
the necessary means. It is better to be unlearned, if learned men   118
respect and revere you, than to be eloquent, if you are con-
temned and despised by idle and abject men, among whom you
reckon him. Although many duties, dangers, and fears may   119
weigh upon him, his dignity, distinction, privilege, and affluence
never desert him.

"You lack every pleasure, suffer need and anxiety, and must   120
bear the sad cares of poverty. Often envy may creep into your   121
mind, disturbing and destroying the thoughts you direct toward
virtuous pursuits. Can you find anyone so lacking in human   122
feeling that in his misery he does not envy the fortunate? Hu-   123
man nature is such that we are most aware of others' prosperity
and success when we ourselves are pressed by misfortunes, and
that we grieve to see others possess the things we lack. Encour-   124
aged by his great hopes and happy successes, Triscatharus cannot think the gods oppose him, and the facts bear him out. For
his immense fortunes and the abundance of valuables which
permit his magnificence and extravagance are ministered to him
effortlessly, prosperously, and lavishly. He says that the gods   125
seem angered with those who are burdened by need, consumed
by anxiety, and crushed by adversity.

"Still, if you are utterly ashamed to accept Triscatharus' posi-   126
tion in life, perhaps because of the opinion you have formed of
him, I grant you this . . .[26] I allow you to choose any other   127
person whose advantages and disadvantages you prefer to your

quam tua. Hunc aliquem ut primum compereris mihi renuntiato: faciam e vestigio ut eius statum assequare.

— Quid iam conticuisti tandem? An nondum quempiam
comperisti?'

128   *Philop.* O mi suavissime, specimen humanitatis, quam apud me
129   maximi momenti et ponderis tua hec fuere verba! Tu homo salis, suavitatis leporisque refertissimus, ita ab iracundia ad equanimitatis modum deflexisti animum meum, ita meam omnem
ad me totum considerandum cogitationem et mentem vertisti,
ut quanto magis magisque cogito, tanto pervestiganti et cogitanti mihi homo sese nemo offert, quem cum diligentius pensi
130   tem pre me esse fortunatum dicam. Nam si est in dignitate, in
amplitudine constitutus, solicite et inquiete vivit; siquid eruditione prestat, sordidissimam et infamem vitam agit; alius, si
probus et optimis rationibus constitutus est, sibi cum Fortuna
sempiternum esse paratum duellum sciat; denique siquis deinceps est, qui in rerum copia studiis et doctrina delectetur, multis et animi et corporis vitiis excrucietur.

131   Itaque sic statuo prudentis esse, se velle eum esse qui sit.
Quam ad sententiam, superi boni, quos et memoria et mente
celeres et mirificos ipse mecum discursus nunc primum feci!

132   Longum esset enumerare omnes qui, male contenti vestigiis ⟨in⟩
quibus domestica instituta eos constituissent, rerum novarum
cupiditate periere. Sed aliud erit ea pulcherrima, que ingenio et
mente perspicio, enumerandi tempus.

133   ***. 'Novi perspicaciam ingenii tui et acre studium, ut, cuivis rei
intendas, facile assequaris. Ea de re, opinor, dignam aliquam et
134   insignem ad scribendum materiam hinc eris nactus. Sed interea, ut me omnino esse tecum facillimum intelligas, cedo sane
triduum desumas ad consulendum, quo per templa, theatra et
fora omnia commodius possis disquirere et pervestigare. Nam

own. As soon as you find this person, tell me, and I shall instantly see that you take his place.

"What, are you finally silent? Haven't you found anyone
yet?"

Philoponius. My sweetest friend, paragon of humanity, what great 128
force and weight your words have had for me! Your abundant 129
wit and sweet charm have turned my mind from anger to equanimity. You have completely changed the way I view myself.
Indeed, the more I think about it, the less I am able to find
anyone whom, on careful consideration, I would regard as more
fortunate than myself. If a man lives in dignity and prominence, 130
his life is troubled and restless. If he excels in learning, he leads
a squalid and maligned existence. If he is honest and holds high
principles, he must expect perpetual strife with Fortune. And if
he delights in learned studies amid abundant wealth, his mind
and body are plagued by many disorders.

Hence, in my opinion, a wise man will choose to be himself. 131
Gracious gods, how many swift and wondrous reflections I
have just made to arrive at this conclusion! It would be tedious 132
to enumerate all those men who, discontented with the path
which their family's tradition had determined for them, perished in their desire for revolutionary change.[27] But on another
occasion I shall recount the wonderful insights I now perceive.

[*Friend*]. "I know how your natural acumen and your keen enthu- 133
siasm help you achieve easily whatever you undertake, and I
think you will find here worthy and notable material for writing. For the moment, I shall indulge you by granting you three 134
days in which to conduct your search in temples, theaters, and

fortassis quempiam offendes, quem esse te, quam qui sis, malis . . . !'

135 *Philop.* Taceo admodum et maximam per te egritudinis levationem
accepisse fateor, et congratulor et gaudeo.

: 6 :

Servus

1 *Parm.* Ha ha he! Et quanti est philosophis obtemperare!

2 ***. Salve, Parmeno. Et quid est quod tute isthic tecum rides?
Parm. Adesne? Birriam nostin, Clinie servum, supinum illum
atque inter ambulandum qui stertit?
***. Quidni? homo est, semel qui illum viderit, facile perpetuo
oderit.

3 *Parm.* Recte sane.
***. At quid tum, obsecro?
Parm. Rem lepidam, si audias.

4 ***. Equidem ociosus isthuc ipsum vehementer cupio.
Parm. Mihi quidem haudquaquam ocii satis est, tibi ut satis, quod
cupio, faciam. Vale.
***. Non abis, recita.

5 *Parm.* Rure hoc vespere me recipiam oportet.
***. Sine.
Parm. Tum quidem curarum sum plenus.

6 ***. Ergo tu adeo festinans considerabas et pre cura gestiebas.
Parm. Quid, si scires quam sim fractus fessitudine?
***. Novi quidem incredibilem tuam in omni re diligentiam, ut in
rebus agendis nihil velis tua, quantum possis, opera defuisse.

7 *Parm.* Hoc totum diei nulla me miserum habuit quies.

other public places. Perhaps you will encounter someone whose life you prefer to your own?"

Philoponius. I remain silent. But I confess with gratitude and joy   135
that you have relieved my anxiety.

: 6 :

The Slave

Parmeno. Ha ha ha! What value there is in heeding the philoso-   1
phers!

[Speaker]. Greetings, Parmeno. Why are you laughing to yourself?   2

Parmeno. Is that you? Do you know Birria, Clinia's languid slave
who snores as he walks?

[Speaker]. Of course. One look at him, and you'll despise him
forever.

Parmeno. That's right.   3

[Speaker]. What about him, pray?

Parmeno. A charming tale, if you'll hear me.

[Speaker]. I'm at leisure, and greatly desire it.   4

Parmeno. But I scarcely have time to satisfy you. Goodbye.

[Speaker]. Don't go! Tell me.

Parmeno. I'm due back in the country this evening.   5

[Speaker]. Never mind that.

Parmeno. Besides, I'm full of worries.

[Speaker]. Then even in your haste, you were pensive and impa-   6
tient with worry.

Parmeno. If only you knew how exhausted I am with fatigue!

[Speaker]. I am well aware of your incredible diligence in everything. You spare no labor in getting things done.

Parmeno. I haven't had a moment's rest all day long.   7

***. Parum tibi indulgere mihi visus es, Parmeno, persepius, dum aliis queque placeant sedulo studeas et tibi duriter imperes ad laborem.

Parm. Parmenone qui utitur, iam tum sero noscet defunctum.

8 ***. Ergo morere!

Parm. Dictu facile! Non est tanti ut moriar, cum non pigeat vite.

***. Vah, quam ad omnem disceptandi rationem calles! Sed quenam diutina tam te exercuit cura?

9 *Parm.* Haud preter consuetudinem meam quippiam: senex noster Laches. Nostin hominem morosum, tenacem, illepidum?

***. Pulchre, qui rus in parsimoniam secessit.

10 *Parm.* Ipsus. Neque enim est homo ex hominum opinione frugi. Verum aliunde exorditur pulchrius. Domi socrus cum nura discidium gerunt. Intellextin hoc?

11 ***. Antiquum id et peculiare.

Parm. Aiunt. Tametsi de adolescentula est quippiam quod suspicer. Sed ad rem redeo. Superstitiosa est anus.

12 ***. (Eccam servorum linguam!)

Parm. Quid tu tecum loqueris?

***. Te admiror.

13 *Parm.* Dignus quidem. Nam queque ruri et queque domi facto opus sunt, Parmeno tuus perago.

***. Dignus qui imperes.

Parm. Ne vero sum ex raro hominum genere?

***. Ut egregio tibi par sit bonorum nemo.

14 *Parm.* Missa hec faciamus. Rure igitur durus me senex, hic vero domi fatua isthec nostra mulierum caterva inique ex ⟨s⟩tudio defatigant, dii boni, quibus et quam ineptis imperiis! Centipe-

15 dem tricentimanumque esse me oportuit. Undique obstrepit

[*Speaker*]. You have often seemed to me, Parmeno, to indulge yourself too little. By continually striving to please others, you are a harsh taskmaster to yourself.

Parmeno. When Parmeno's boss learns of his death, it will already be too late.

[*Speaker*]. Then die! 8

Parmeno. That's easy to say! But there's no point in dying when I don't regret living.

[*Speaker*]. Ha, how versed you are in every kind of argument! But what worry has been bothering you so long?

Parmeno. Nothing unusual—just old Laches.[28] Do you know the 9 fellow? He's peevish, stubborn, and rude.

[*Speaker*]. Quite well. He's the one who retired to the country in his frugality.

Parmeno. The same, although the fellow isn't as frugal as people 10 think. But I'd better begin in another way. At home, the in-laws, mother and daughter, are feuding. Do you understand?

[*Speaker*]. An old tale, and classic. 11

Parmeno. So they say. I don't quite trust the girl. But to the point. The old woman is superstitious.

[*Speaker*]. (How slaves gossip!) 12

Parmeno. What are you muttering?

[*Speaker*]. That I admire you.

Parmeno. I deserve it. If there's a job to do at home or in the coun- 13 try, Parmeno is your man to get it done.

[*Speaker*]. You deserve to give the orders.

Parmeno. Am I not a rare breed of man?

[*Speaker*]. None of our best citizens rivals your excellence.

Parmeno. Well, enough of this. As I was saying, in their zeal both 14 the stubborn old man in the country and the foolish flock of women here at home are unfairly wearing me out. Good gods, what ridiculous orders! I should have been born with a hundred feet and three hundred hands. The whole house resounds 15

domus imperiis in Parmenonem, ut pre illarum odio memet
interdum surripere et inter dolia latitare assueverim, unde
potare atque una dicta factaque singulorum observare ex in-
sidiis possim.

16 ***. Vigilantem!

Parm. Volo a reliquis metui, dum Pamphilo unico, qui meis con-
silii⟨s⟩ hereat, facillimo utar. Ac fit quidem domi nihil quod ille
17 non ex me resciscat. Enim adeo domi opere exacto, ad portum
Pamphili mei adventum percunctatum mane accesseram, quo
illi primus, si appulisset, gratificarer atque congratularer. Non
possum esse ociosus.

18 ***. Preclare tu quidem vitam instituisti, dum per negocium vivis.

19 *Parm.* Pamphilum ex sententia inventum adduxi domum maxi-
misque de rebus suis feci ut esset certior. Quid multa? Beavi
hominem. Retulit gratias palamque professus est se mea sapientia in lucem esse ab Orco effectum reducem.

20 ***. Ne vero ab Orco? At quid ita?

21 *Parm.* Haud opus est prolatu. Itaque iterum domo, ne ineptias
muliercularum spectarem applaudentium Pamphilo, discessi ad
portum; pueris pondera adiuvi; nequid nostri illic reliqui esset,
diligenter perspexi; postremus de portu movi, sed cursitando id
egi, ut longe ante alios Pamphilus redisse me salvis rebus intue-
22 retur. E vestigio in arcem fessus et mehercle sitiens, quod trans-
curso fore opus intelligebam, advolavi.

23 ***. Tantumne id a sapientia esse tua facinus alienum voluisti, ut
quam extinguere, priusquam insurgeret, malam sitim potuisti,
24 non tum primum provideris? Longe enim providisse in
posterum sapientem decet, nequid sua sibi negligentia eveniat
demum quod peniteat.

25 *Parm.* Culpam non casum prestabit sapiens, ac mihi quidem nihil
preter opinionem, sed preter institutum sitienti evenit; neque
mortalibus contra casum undique prospexisse relictum est,

with orders for Parmeno. To spite them, I occasionally steal off
and hide among the storage jars. There I can have a drink and
observe from my hiding place what each says and does.

[Speaker]. What vigilance!   16

Parmeno. I want the others to fear me. Only Pamphilus is kind to
me and heeds my advice.[29] Nothing happens in the house that
he doesn't learn from me. This morning, when I had finished   17
my work at home, I went to the port to see whether Pamphilus
had arrived so that I could be the first to congratulate him. I
can't keep still.

[Speaker]. You've arranged a fine life, if you live to be busy.   18

Parmeno. As I hoped, I found Pamphilus and brought him home   19
while I informed him of his important affairs. In short, I
cheered him up. He thanked me, and declared openly that my
wisdom had brought him back from the dead.

[Speaker]. From the dead? How?   20

Parmeno. There's no need for a long account. I didn't want to wit- 21
ness the folly of the women doting on Pamphilus, so I left the
house again and went back to the port. I helped the slaves with
their loads, and checked carefully to see that none of our goods
were left behind. I was the last to leave the dock, but by running, I was by far the first one whom Pamphilus saw returning
with our goods intact. Suddenly I was tired and very thirsty, so   22
I fairly flew through the town, knowing how fast I had to move.

[Speaker]. Were you so lacking in your usual wisdom that you   23
didn't make sure you quenched your thirst before it troubled
you? A wise man ought to plan far in advance, so that he won't   24
regret any oversights.

Parmeno. A wise man will answer for mistakes, but not mishaps.   25
Although I was thirsty, nothing happened contrary to my expectations, only contrary to my plan. It is not left to mortal
men to provide against every accident; rather, they must yield

quominus tempori parendum non sit; iuvatque, dum in officio
perstes, ea ferre animo non ingrato que vitasse nequeas.

26 ***. Beata familia, que philosophum te habeat domi! Sed quenam
isthec fuit necessitas, que te in arcem compelleret?

27 *Parm.* Ut Caridemum ignotum quemdam, quem mihi descripse-
28 rat cadaverosum hospitem Pamphilus, convenirem. Nemo quisquam illorum fuit, apud quem non diligentissime de monstro
isthoc sciscitarer; quem dii male perdant, et una Pamphilum,
qui obscenis huiusmodi amicitiis delectatur! Multa brevitatis
29 causa me preterisse existimes velim. Longum esset referre quot
ineptos et protervos, ut est civitas hec stultissimorum hominum
refertissima, offenderim, qui quidem me verbis lacessire inni-
terentur. At ego, proh superi optimi, quam bellissime eorum
petulantiam retunsam reddidi!

30 ***. Novi quidem te, ut soleas inter arridendum ambiguis dictis
aculeos proloqui.

31 *Parm.* Mea est illa in primis gloria. Sed multo illud gloriosius,
quod multo⟨s⟩ consilio monitisque meis meliores beatioresque
32 reddidi. Sed missa hec faciamus. Utinam sic mihi auscultaret
33 Pamphilus, ut esset mea sapientia felicior! Itaque necdum, primum me, ex illa legatione me domum receperam, cum me
iterum contuli in pedes, Pamphilum ut letissimum redderem.
34 Sed nolo mea omnia gesta recensere: non enim suppeteret dies,
ita sum multis et maximis in rebus fide optima et singulari dili-
35 gentia versatus. Preterea sum, antequam rus pergam, pleraque
acturus negocia, que nonnisi Parmenoni tuto commendantur.
Vale, ne me detine.

36 ***. Tantumne erat quod tute iam tum hoc ridebas modo?

37 *Parm.* Hem! At isthuc exciderat ex mente admodum.

38 ***. Sic solent qui variis istiusmodi rebus animo occupentur: nam
cura alia, ut aiunt, aliam obliterat.

Parm. Plane ut ais.

***. Atqui iterum rides!

to circumstances. As long as you do your duty, it is best to accept gladly what cannot be avoided.

[*Speaker*]. Blessed the family for whom you are the household 26 philosopher! But what urgent matter made you run through town?

Parmeno. I had to meet a certain Caridemus.[30] I didn't know him, 27 but Pamphilus had described him as his zombie friend. I dili- 28 gently asked everyone I met about this monster. Damn him, and Pamphilus too, who enjoys such foul friendships! Please bear in mind that I'm omitting many details for the sake of brevity. It would be tedious to recount how many silly and im- 29 pudent people I met who tried to provoke me with their words: the city is full of them. But, O gracious gods, how cleverly I curbed their rudeness!

[*Speaker*]. I know your way of smiling when you make ambiguous 30 and barbed remarks.

Parmeno. That is my principal glory. It is even more glorious that 31 my advice has made many people more virtuous and more pros- perous. But enough of this. If only Pamphilus would listen to 32 me and let my wisdom make him happier! I had no sooner re- 33 turned from my errand than I took to my feet again to cheer up Pamphilus. I don't want to relate everything I did. The day 34 would not suffice to tell you: that's how loyally and diligently I attend to so many important affairs. Besides, before I return to 35 the country, I have a number of errands to do, which can be safely entrusted only to Parmeno. Goodbye. Don't detain me.

[*Speaker*]. Is that all you were laughing about just now? 36

Parmeno. Oh! That completely slipped my mind. 37

[*Speaker*]. Such is the way of people with too many things on 38 their minds. One worry, they say, cancels another.

Parmeno. It's just as you say.

[*Speaker*]. And now you're laughing again!

39 *Parm.* Maxime. Ha ha he! Neque enim potest mea a memoria illud de Birria, quem vidi, servo aboleri.

40 ***. Potisne es rem ipsam olim enarrare, ut et me, tuo pro more, tuarum voluptatum participem reddas?

41 *Parm.* Hanc vis operam ceteris a negociis meis maximis surripiam, tibi ut accomodem?

42 ***. Percupio.

43 *Parm.* Et profecto solus ipse dignus es, cui ob lepiditatem voluptas adsit sempiterna: has enim urbanas delitias rusticane plurimo-

44 rum aures non capiunt. Narro. Tantis rebus confectis eram, ut dixi, fessus; tamen, quod pulchre postremo una cum Pamphilo potaram, ante edes nostras meam ipse mecum vivendi rationem commentabar, aliud in animo ex alio ducens ac reputans qui

45 homo prestet homini. Nam et aliquos ita fore ad beneficentiam natos, ut vel inscii ac imprudentes multo prosint: quo quidem in numero optimorum esse me et gratulabar et glorior. Sed de

46 me alias. Dum hec mecum pensito, eccam odium convicinie, Sostratam, Pamphili matrem, succurvam, tremulam, manibus propendulis . . .

47 ***. Dii te perdant cum scenica isthac gesti⟨culati⟩one!

48 *Parm.* 'At enim, Parmeno,' inquit, 'mi, cum quid recte factum cupi- mus, tibi mandemus necesse est. Abi rus, obsecro, ac pueris

49 edicito nequid preparent, namque rus institui non accedere.' At ego illam intuens: 'Et quenam,' inquam, 'libido derepente isthec in te incesserat modo, ut preter consuetudinem in rus usque

50 peregrinationem susciperes, anus, imbecilla, sola? Institueram quidem, quantum in me fuerat, stultitie ab eo te consilio abster- rere.'

51 Itaque me in pedes contuli. Demum inter eundum stomacha- bar hanc unam esse diem qua omnes coniurarint meme ambu-

52 lando rumpere. Interea quemdam offendo barbatum hominem tristem, quem dudum audieram posse animis levare egritudi- nem. Eum ipsum hominem vulgo philosophum appellant.

Parmeno. Yes indeed. Ha ha ha! I just can't forget what I saw hap-   39
pen to Birria the slave.

[Speaker]. Can you tell me the story some time? It's your custom   40
to let me share your amusements.

Parmeno. Do you want me to take time from my important affairs   41
for your benefit?

[Speaker]. I greatly desire it.   42

Parmeno. You're the only one I know whose wit is a source of con-   43
stant delight. Most people are too boorish to grasp such urbane
delights. Here's my story. As I said, all these errands had worn   44
me out. But finally, after several drinks with Pamphilus, I was
standing in front of the house, reflecting on my way of life, and
following a chain of thought about why one man is better than
another. Some are born to acts of kindness, and even unwit-   45
tingly do a lot of good. I was congratulating myself and taking
pride in being one of their number. But about me, another
time. As I was rapt in thought, there appeared the terror of the   46
neighborhood, Pamphilus' mother Sostrata, bent over and
shaking with her hands dangling at her side . . .

[Speaker]. Damn you, a pantomime for the stage!   47

Parmeno. "My dear Parmeno," she said, "when we want a job done   48
well, we have to entrust it to you. Go to the country, please, and
tell the servants not to make any preparations. I've decided not
to go." I stared at her and said: "Whatever possessed you to   49
make this unusual trip to the country alone, when you are so
old and feeble? I was resolved to do all I could to dissuade you   50
from such folly."

So I set out. On my way, I resented how everyone had   51
conspired today to wear me out with running. Meanwhile   52
I came across a sad, bearded fellow who, I once heard, could
free your mind of anxiety. People call him a philosopher.

53 Accedo ad hominem; saluto; operam auscultando ut prebeat
impetro. Rem, mores vitamque meam ordine aperio, ut me ad
54 miseriam omnino esse natum videat. At philosophus ipse habere mecum disputationem occepit, ita suavem, ita amenam, ut
oblivisci, dum vivam, nequeam.

55 ⟨***⟩. Et manus et os hominis teneo.

56 ⟨Parm.⟩. 'Enimvero,' inquit, 'quid, si fecero ut hero te esse tuo bea-
57 tiorem ex re ipsa sentias?' Hic ego subindignatus: 'Ain tu?' in-
58 quam, 'ut quisquam me non stultus beatum dicat? Servio.' Tum
philosophus subridens: 'Agedum,' inquit, 'an isthuc evenit unquam ante lucem noctu ut esset iter ineundum tibi, quo domini
59 iussa exsequerere?' 'Evenit,' inquam. 'Num et pre cura, ut frugi
et fidelis servi officium est, horam ad iter capessendum obser-
vans, parum commode,' inquit, 'requiesti dormiens?' 'Ecquidem
60 isthuc,' inquam, 'mihi omnium maxime.' 'Timueras fortassis,'
inquit ille, 'ne te iurgio herus aut verberibus excitaret?' 'Minime
isthuc,' inquam, 'sed amari cupidus, solertem me maxime videri
61 affectabam.' 'Nullus ergo durus te,' inquit ille, 'id ita ut ageres
62 dominus compellebat.' 'Homo nemo prorsus,' inquam. 'Qui si
affuisset,' inquit philosophus, 'neque te somnos capere infestus
permisisset, durior tuane adeo fuisset conditio?' 'Plane,' inquam,
63 'et gravior.' 'Quid igitur,' inquit, 'tuus si aliquem herus istiusmodi perferat dominum, cuius importunitate nocte⟨s⟩ in-
somnes, dies curarum, laborum plenos agat?' 'Liberum me,'
64 inquam, 'deputem pre illo atque illum penitus servum.' 'Quid,'
inquit, 'herus tuus istiusmodi si plures perferat infestos dominos?' 'Infelicissimum illum,' inquam, 'iudicem.'

65 Tum ille 'Rursus adsis, precor,' inquit; 'audistin uspiam fore
aliquid quod etiam ipsis regibus imperet?' Tum ipse: 'Non me-
66 mini.' Tum ille: 'Audistin unquam assiduam inter mortales
vagari deam, quam Necessitatem nuncupant?' 'Non,' inquam,
67 'memini.' 'Ut sitias,' inquit, 'exurias frigeasve, ne non id fieri
tuam preter voluntatem interdum sentis?' 'Maxime,' inquam.

I went up to the fellow, greeted him, and asked him to hear my 53
story. I gave him a detailed account of my life and character, so
that he would understand how I was born to misery. The phi- 54
losopher began a discussion with me so sweet and pleasant that
I shall never forget it as long as I live.

[*Speaker*]. I can see his gestures and expression exactly. 55

Parmeno. "What would you say," he asked, "if I showed you that 56
you are more fortunate than your master?" I was slightly an- 57
gered, and replied: "Do you mean that a reasonable man would
call me fortunate? I am a slave." The philosopher smiled and 58
said: "Come now, has it ever happened that, in order to do your
master's bidding, you had to start a journey at night?" "Yes," I
said. "And in your concern as a loyal and honest slave," he 59
asked, "did you sleep poorly awaiting the hour to set forth?"
"Yes," I said, "more than anyone." "Were you perhaps afraid," he 60
asked, "that your master would awaken you with reproaches
and blows?" "No," I said, "but I wished to be loved, and strove
to seem a diligent servant." "Then no harsh master forced you 61
to act," he said. "No one," I said. "And if there had been a savage 62
master to prevent your sleeping," the philosopher said, "would
your condition have been harder to bear?" "Clearly," I said, "and
more painful." "What would you say," he asked, "if your owner 63
obeyed so relentless a master that he spent sleepless nights, and
days full of cares and toils?" "I would think myself free," I said,
"in comparison to one so completely a slave." "And what," he 64
asked, "if your owner should obey several troublesome masters?" "I should think him very wretched," I said.

   Then he said: "Please pay attention. Have you ever heard 65
that there is something that rules even over kings?" "I don't recall," I said. "Have you heard," he asked, "that a goddess called 66
Necessity wanders among mortals?" "I don't recall," I said.
"When you are thirsty, hungry, or cold," he asked, "don't you 67
sometimes find that it happens against your will?" "Yes, truly," I

68 'Id te ita que cogit, Necessitas est,' inquit, 'enim.' Tunc ipse: 'O
69 duram deam, philosophe!' inquam. At philosophus: 'Huic dee,
     vel inviti, supremi etiam parent reges. Credin?' 'Et quidni?' in-
     quam, 'si homines sunt.'

70   'Ne vero,' inquit ille, 'pabulum iumento cum prebet herus,
     rem agere hominem haud satis necessariam dices?' 'Pernecessa-
71 riam!' inquam. 'Quid ita?' 'Quia ni det,' inquam, 'faciat dam-
     num, siquidem inedia enervatum et exangue, ad rem domini fiat
72 inutile atque incommodum.' 'Tum preterea,' inquit ille, 'vestem
     cum tibi et victum herus prebet, eiusmodine agit rem in qua
73 cessasse oportuit aut iuste potuerit?' 'Minime.' 'Necessitati igi-
     tur,' inquit, 'morem in ea re gerit.' 'Prorsus ut ais,' inquam.
74 'Quid, ni opportune pro cuiusque necessitate prospexerit? an
     illum,' inquit, 'amabis?' 'Non quidem illum, ut facio maxime.'
75 'Quid, si negligat?' inquit, 'num sedulo et sine contumacia illi
     obsequere?' 'Non quidem,' inquam, 'ut iam nunc facio maxime.'
76 'Num,' inquit ille, 'si quando eo vos pacto tractet inhumaniter,
77 vulgo famam de sese sentiet malam?' 'Maxime.' 'Num despectui
78 erit bonis?' 'Maxime.' 'Num idcirco et apud rem publicam mi-
79 nus fiet acceptus?' 'Ut decet.' 'Etenim,' inquit, 'utrumne huic
     apud cives infamie quam apud domesticos gratie curam esse
80 minus animo acrem putas?' 'Acrem,' inquam. 'Utrum famam
     ipsam et bonorum gratiam negligenti odium a civibus nullum
81 rependetur?' 'Stat ratio,' inquam, 'ut oderint.' 'Penamne id an
82 non futuram putas?' 'Pena⟨m⟩,' inquam. 'At molesta?' 'Nempe
83 et molesta.' 'Hunc igitur,' inquit, 'qui et suorum commodis et
     fame serviat, Necessitati subservire intelligis? Ac si peccet, si-
     quid minus diligenter curet, penam ut luat fore non inficiaris?'
     Annui.

84   'Itaque,' inquit ille, 'quales hominem agere somnos reris, cum
     quid dea pertinax imperarit? Similesne his quos tu minime in-
85 terruptos transigis?' 'Minime,' inquam. 'Hoc ergo,' inquit philo-
     sophus, 'esse illum pre te longe inferiorem an nondum perspicis,

said. "It is Necessity that compels you," he said. "What a harsh 68
goddess, O philosopher!" I cried. And the philosopher said: 69
"Even the greatest kings obey her, albeit unwillingly. Do you
believe this?" "Of course," I said, "if they are human."

"Now," he said, "when the owner feeds his mule, do you 70
think his action necessary?" "Absolutely necessary," I said.
"Why?" he asked. "Because if he doesn't feed the mule," I said, 71
"he will suffer loss, for a starving beast is useless and even
harmful to his master." "Well then," he said, "your master fur- 72
nishes your food and clothing. Should he, or could he, justly
fail to do so?" "By no means." "Then he is obeying Necessity," 73
he said. "Exactly as you say," I said. "If he didn't satisfy every- 74
one's needs," he asked, "would you love him?" "Not as much as
I do." "If he were negligent," he asked, "would you obey him 75
eagerly and willingly?" "Not as much as I do." "If he treated you 76
so inhumanely," he said, "wouldn't his reputation suffer?" "A
great deal." "Wouldn't good men despise him?" "A great deal." 77
"Wouldn't he seem less suited for public life?" "As is proper." 78
"And don't you think public disgrace would trouble him as 79
keenly as his household's opinion?" "Certainly," I said. "If he 80
neglected his reputation and the favor of good men, wouldn't
he pay in public hatred?" "They would have reason to hate
him," I said. "Don't you think that would punish him?" "Yes," I 81
said. "Severely?" "Very severely." "You see, then," he said, "that in 82
serving his reputation and the good of his house, he is subject 83
to Necessity? And if he errs by being negligent, you won't deny
that he must pay the penalty?" I nodded my assent.

"Well then," he said, "how well do you think he sleeps when 84
this obstinate goddess orders him about? As well as you, in
your untroubled slumbers?" "By no means," I said. "Don't you 85
see, then," said the philosopher, "that he is greatly inferior to

quod animo pervigili excubat, quod opera assidua exquirendis
rebus exercetur, quod in se unum curas suorum omnium tam
multa ex parte susceperit, dum singulis prospicit, ne qua urgeat
86   fames, ne qua vis frigoris, ne calorum molestia afficiatur?' Tum
ipse hec omnia mecum repetens et quam sim ad omne lucrum
ineptus et quam nulla re egeam, cum seni nostro a me non mi-
nimas fore gratias reddendas, tum non pessime agi mecum ad
felicitates assentiebar.

87   Igitur philosophus: 'Itane,' inquit, 'asseverabimus isthun⟨c⟩
hominem eos omnes dominorum habere loco, quos domi alen-
88   dos acceperit?' 'Atqui id,' inquam, 'haud satis intelligo.' 'Nempe,'
inquit ille, 'quod singulorum necessitati pa⟨bu⟩lum imperitanti
89   et gravia illa minitanti obtemperet.' 'Profecto isthuc,' inquam, 'ut
ratio ipsa edocet. Nam familiam suam et rem domesticam ne-
90   gligenti odia atque infamiam non defuturam edocuisti.' Tum
ille: 'Unum,' inquit, 'igitur aut alterum, Parmeno, habes dominum. Et tuus quos diximus eque plures atque eosdem assiduos
sibi herus adesse non sentit dominos?' 'Sentit,' inquam, 'ut
91   opinor.' 'Itaque humanum tu,' inquit, 'habes, indulgentem, exo-
rabilem, sub quo interdum peccasse impune possis; ille contra
inhumanos durosque complures, a quibus etiam erroris veniam
92   non impetret. Quid ais?' 'Isthuc scilicet,' inquam. 'Tu,' inquit,
'interdiu ad quietem, omnibus solutus curis, bene potus te pros-
93   ternis noctemque deinceps ociosam ociosus dormitas. Ille assidue in horam insurgentis Necessitatis importunum imperium
94   perfert. Tu, quantulum ab te exigit opere, prestas; reliquum tibi
totum vivis. Ille operam, i⟨n⟩genium, curas, studium, diligentiam vestra singulorum gratia exercet suam. Et quid hic ais?'
95   'In hanc me,' inquam, 'sententiam adduxisti, philosophe, ut
iam sim animi dubius servumne qui sim prestet esse me quam
96   dominum. Nam, si recte interpretor, quis bene consultus ·non
isthuc fugiat, habere domi tam multos, quorum gratia multi-
plices istiusmodi curas solicitudinesque gerat? Ni illud me

you? He lies awake in bed, troubled by the constant needs he must face. He alone is responsible for all of his household, and must see that none of them goes hungry or suffers from heat or cold." When I reflected how little I could earn and yet how lit- 86 tle I lacked, I agreed that I should warmly thank my master and that I did not fare poorly in terms of happiness.

Then the philosopher asked: "Shall we say that your owner 87 serves as his master all those he supports in his household?" "I don't understand," I said. "I mean to say," he replied, "that he 88 obeys the necessity that demands food for everyone and threatens him with grave consequences." "Yes," I said, "reason shows 89 this. And you have shown that he will face hatred and disgrace if he neglects his family and property." "Parmeno," he said, "you 90 have only one master. But doesn't your owner endure several unrelenting masters, as we have said?" "Yes, I believe so," I said. "Then you have a humane, lenient, and flexible master," he said, 91 "under whom you may occasionally err with impunity. But he has several inhuman and harsh masters who will not pardon his mistakes. What do you think?" "Exactly that," I said. "By day," 92 he said, "you can drink and stretch out for a nap, completely carefree, and undisturbed you may sleep undisturbed nights. But he submits to each relentless command of necessities that 93 arise at every hour. You furnish the small effort that he de- 94 mands of you, and the rest of the time live for yourself. But he employs all his energy, talent, care, zeal, and diligence for the sake of each one of you. What do you think?"

"You've convinced me, philosopher," I said. "I begin to doubt 95 whether it is not better for me to be the slave that I am rather than a master.[31] For, if I understand correctly, no wise man 96 would want so many dependents who bring him such varied

97
98   moveat, quod ipsum libertatis nomen aureum est.' 'De isthoc
        lente,' inquit ille, 'ut voles ipse tecum diiudicato. Sed illud ad-
        moneo, huc animum adhibeas tecumque iterum atque iterum
        ipse consideres, hunc qui suas omnes fortunas summo labore et
        periculis partas tibi communicet, ut non sibi plus sumat ex opi-
        bus voluptatis, quam impertiat vobis quantum pro siti, fame
        frigoreve abspellendo conveniat, forene dominum magis quam
99   amicum deputes?' 'Quin,' inquam, 'illum procuratorem affirmo.'
100   Preterea multa inter nos istiusmodi tum fuere disceptata,
        quoad constituimus fortunatissimum quidem me hominum di-
        iudicandum, qui talem sim patronum nactus frugi et liberalem:
101   qua letitia adductus non potui non facere quin philosophum
        ipsum amplecterer, qui meme mihi in libertatem suis dictis
        vendicasset.

102   At servus ille Birria—etiamdum hominem rideo—una me-
        cum aderat nutuque omnia philosophi dicta, aperto ore exque
103   narrantis oculis pendens, comprobabat. Tandem, quasi a somno
        resipisceret: 'Ecquid, o philosophe,' inquit, 'mihi tum consilii
        futurum erit, qui hero serviam illepidissimo, cui queque fecerim
        sunt ingrata?'

104   Tum philosophus: 'In hunc modum,' inquit, 'carus eris tu
        quidem hero, si in te plus esse fidei senserit quam ostentationis,
        plus operis quam verborum ad res domesticas tuendas atque
105   peragendas; si neque laboribus peperceris, neque voluptatibus
        indulseris; si illum plus te sapere et te meliori subesse equum
        fore existimaveris; si id omni diligentia studueris, ut diligere te
106   et vereri suos intellexerit.' His rebus auditis Birria ceperat
107   animo iam secum esse suspenso. Quem philosophus intuens,
        'Animadvertistine unquam,' inquit, 'quercum, ut multa maxi-
108   maque commoda de se prestet? Agri litem dirimit, glandem
        umbramque pecori prebet et eiusmodi multa affert beneficia,
109   nullam tamen a villico satis dignam mercedem excipit. Non
        stercoratur, non putatur et, quod commisereare, cum etatem in

and troublesome cares." "Take time to decide this question as 97
you will," he said. "But I urge you to consider this again and 98
again: if someone shares with you the entire fortune he has won
through great toils and perils, and yet himself derives no more
pleasure from his wealth than what he allots to you for your
natural comforts, wouldn't you call him a friend rather than a
master?" "I'd even call him my steward," I said. 99

Our discussion touched on many other topics like these. We 100
concluded that I was very fortunate to have found such a decent
and generous patron. In my joy, I couldn't help embracing the 101
philosopher for liberating me by his arguments.

Now, all this while, Birria the slave was present. I'm already 102
laughing at the fellow. He approved the philosopher's words by
nodding and gaping as he listened with rapt attention. At 103
length, as if awakening from slumber, he asked: "Can you give
me some advice, philosopher? I serve a boorish master who
finds fault with everything I do."

The philosopher replied: "Your owner will value you if he 104
finds in you more loyalty than ostentation, and more work than
words in caring for his estate; if you don't spare any efforts or 105
indulge in any pleasures; if you think it just to serve a wiser and
better man than yourself; and if you diligently strive to show
that you love and respect his family." When Birria heard this, 106
he seemed perplexed. The philosopher looked at him and said: 107
"Have you ever noticed how many great benefits an oak tree
provides? It settles land disputes, furnishes acorns and shade to 108
cattle, and offers many such benefits. Yet it receives no worthy
reward from the farm steward. It is not manured or pruned, 109
and, most pitiful of all, after it has spent the summer in

officio beneficentiaque contriverit, formicarum populis intimum
110 exeditur. Perspextin,' inquit, 'hoc?' Tunc Birria: 'Isthuc,' inquit,
111 'ac sepius.' 'Num tibi id facinus indignum videtur?' Tum 'vide-
112 tur,' inquit Birria, 'atqui perquam indignum.' 'Quercum tu igitur
esse herum tuum putato,' inquit philosophus. 'Nam cum vos,
turbam suam familiarem ociosissimam, pascit atque confovet,
113 quid est quod illi par pro tanto beneficio referatis? Curarum ille
plenus est causa vestra, quibus quidem curis non minus quam
ipsum truncum formicis exeditur. Vos vero ut pecudes illius
114 beneficia abutimini.' 'Perpulchre,' inquit Birria, 'illum esse quercum sentio, cum ipsum me fuste cedit!' Risimus.

115   'Tum preterea,' inquit philosophus, 'et quid tu, cum noctu
116 ante catervam funale fortassis accensum defers? fitne ut, cum
illis luceat, tum interdum tibi inter umbram perambulanti digi-
117 tus saxo illidatur pedis?' 'Sepius isthuc,' inquit Birria. 'Sic igitur,'
inquit ille, 'in hominum genere evenire velim cogites, Birria, ut
sint qui in vitam ea conditione veniant, ut aliis quam sibi longe
118 accumulatius bona conferant. Quo in numero hominum quem
maxime collocabimus, herumne tuum potius an ipsum te, qui
aliorum munificentia vestem et calceos habeas integros alie-
noque ex sudore victum excipias, ut congratulandum fortune
tue magis quam non equissimo animo sortem ferendam tuam
119 existimem? Ni tu forte hac in re aliter sentias.' Obmutuerat
120 Birria. Tum philosophus: 'Audin tu homo?' inquit, 'cuique adeo
suam novisse sortem eo plane ad sapientiam conducit, quo sese
quisque tempori accommodet atque eam in partem queque
eveniant accipiat, ut gravia fieri ferendo leviora statuat et, siqua
penitus non difficillima inciderint, cessura ea ad voluptatem as-
suescendo non diffidat.'

121   Cum pleraque istiusmodi disseruisset philosophus, tum Birria
subirritatus: 'Dic,' inquit, 'meliora! Namque hunc tu Parmenonem effecisti, ut esset suorum patronorum dominus; me quidem
122 perpetuo iam cupis fore servum.' 'At enim idcirco tu,' inquit

benefiting others, its inner core is eaten by hordes of ants. Have 110
you observed this?" Birria replied: "Yes, quite often." "Doesn't it 111
seem unjust to you?" "Yes, it seems very unjust," Birria then
replied. "Now, think of your owner as an oak tree," said the 112
philosopher. "Although he feeds and cares for all of you, his lazy
bunch of servants, how do you repay his great generosity? For 113
your sake, he is filled with cares which gnaw him no less than
ants a tree trunk. But, like cattle, you abuse his generosity."
"Well said," replied Birria. "I feel his oaken nature when he 114
cudgels me." We laughed.

"What's more," said the philosopher, "when at night you bear 115
a torch before a crowd, does it ever happen that, in lighting 116
their way, you yourself walk in darkness and stub your toe
against a rock?" "Quite often," said Birria. "You must consider 117
that this is what happens in human life, Birria," said the philosopher. "Some are born to bestow more blessings on others
than on themselves. Whom shall we place in this category, your 118
owner or you yourself, who are clothed and shod by others'
generosity and fed by others' sweat? I think you should rejoice
in your good fortune, rather than bear your lot impatiently. Or 119
do you think differently?" Birria was speechless. The philoso- 120
pher continued: "You may have heard it said, my friend, that
understanding one's lot leads to wisdom. By doing so, one can
adapt to circumstances, and accept whatever happens by reflecting that patience lightens our burdens and turns to pleasure all
but the gravest mishaps."

After the philosopher had made many such observa- 121
tions, Birria lost his temper and said: "God forbid! You've
made Parmeno lord over his master, but you want me to remain a slave forever." "Then be idle," said the philosopher 122

philosophus subridens, 'esto igitur iners.' Hanc equidem sententiam noster Birria facto ipso probabat longosque sermones apud
123   quosque ex studio protrahere admodum inibat. Quem cum
herus, cuius mandata neglexerat, garrientem repperisset, plus
viginti in eum infregit pugnos. Risi ac mearum memor rerum
abii. Sed iam advesperascit. Vale.

124   ***. Vale.—Abiit homo. Audistin hec? Quidni igitur prestat nullos habere servos quam domi istiusmodi bipedes pascere, ut
plerique omnes sunt, aut supini, stolidi, futiles, aut garruli
125   maliloquentissimique servuli? Etenim in rebus agendis rudem
atque ignarum si habueris servum, quid erit quod ad eam mo-
126   lestiam addi possit? Condocefacias imperitum, instruas ignavum oportet et queque iusseris ferme omnia ipse exequare opus
127   est. Contra subcallidum et vafrum si habueris servum, fit ut
128   pestem in familia versari sepe indoleas. Non enim recte sapit
hero servus qui nimis sapit. Et in servorum genere frugi cum
rarus extet, tum est idem in servitio percontumax.

with a smile. Birria put these words into action, and eagerly struck up long conversations with everyone he met. When his 123 owner found him prattling and neglecting his chores, he struck him more than twenty blows with his fist. I laughed and, remembering my own affairs, departed. But evening falls. Goodbye.

[*Speaker*]. Goodbye. 124

The fellow's gone. Did you hear this? Isn't it better to have no slaves, rather than nourish these two-legged rogues, most of whom are lazy, stupid, unreliable, loquacious, and foulmouthed? Is there any greater nuisance than having your affairs 125 managed by a boorish and ignorant slave? You must train an 126 unskilled slave and teach an ignorant one, and still you have to do nearly everything yourself. By contrast, if you have a sly and 127 clever slave, you'll often regret keeping such a pest in your household. A dull slave is no help to his owner, but an honest 128 slave, while rare, is defiant in serving you.

LIBER VII

Prohemium

1 Fauni et Satyri plerique, leves dii, lunam perdite adamare et sectari occeperant. Ea re ut paulum consisteret suique adeundi viden-dique copiam liberalius prestaret, obtestari non intermittebant.

2 Luna vero vaga et lasciva miris modis amantes ludificasse ad volup-tatem ducebat: ⟨modo obscuris in nubibus latitabat⟩, modo quasi

3 ex rimula ut se interea spectarent exhibebat. Amantes idcirco cum spretos ac despectos se intelligerent, quod per gratiam et beni-volentiam singuli nequissent, communi coacto in unum consilio, vi

4 et dolo consequi instituerunt. Perspecta igitur procul sylva unde luna emergere inque auras sese consuesse attollere videbatur, illuc omnes convolarunt locumque ardenti opera maxima vi omnium retium infinitaque laqueorum copia circumseptum et obvallatum

5 reddiderunt; compositisque rebus suas ad pristinas sedes ea spe rediere, ut arbitrarentur non defuturum longius quin postridie il-

6 lam irretitam invenirent. Itaque diurno pro opere et labore fessi, noctem ipsam obdormiere.

7 Cum autem mane crepusculo illuc omnes leti redissent et se falsos ac frustratos intellexissent, tamen quod machinas illas cas-sium insidiasque omnes integras et intactas reperirent, in futuram

8 noctem supersedendum censuerunt. At nocte insequenti, ut lunam ipsam alacri vultu et veluti ludibundam e sylva atque, ut ex inter-vallo spectantibus videbatur, mediis ex plagis sublatam ethere spa-tiari animadvertissent, multo maiori retium copia adacta, in se-quentem noctem stationibus positis, fuse ac late a prima vigilia sese regionibus disposuerunt atque edixerunt, ut suo quisque excubiarum loco omnia curiosissime circumspectans et lustrans

BOOK VII

Preface

Some fauns, satyrs, and other lesser gods once conceived a pas- 1
sionate love for the moon and began to court her. They incessantly
implored her to pause briefly and offer them a more generous opportunity to approach and contemplate her. But the capricious and 2
wanton moon took remarkable pleasure in making fun of her
suitors, sometimes hiding in darks clouds and sometimes revealing
herself as if through a small crack. Seeing themselves spurned and 3
despised, her suitors decided to take counsel together, in order to
obtain through force or fraud what none of them singly had been
able to win through favor and affection. Now, having seen in the 4
distance a forest from which the moon generally appeared to
emerge and rise into the air, they all hastened to it. Laboring zeal-
ously, they encircled the place and walled it in with a great quan-
tity of nets and countless snares. Then, having set their traps, they 5
returned to their ancient dwellings, expecting that by the next day
they would find the moon ensnared. Weary from the day's labori- 6
ous efforts, they slept through the night.

At dawn the next day, they all merrily returned to the forest, 7
but felt deceived and disappointed. Still, finding that all their snar-
ing devices and traps were untouched and unharmed, they resolved to wait until the next night. Yet on the following night, as 8
they watched at a distance, the moon seemed to rise out of the
middle of their nets with a cheerful and almost gleeful expression,
and to walk through the upper air. So they assembled a far greater
number of nets for the following night, and having set up guard
posts, they stationed themselves far and wide, beginning at the
first watch. They ordered each guard to keep his position under

9   pervigilaret. Eo enim pacto futurum opinabantur, ut posset nus-
10 quam luna effugere quin a multitudine interciperetur. Dumque se
ita solertes haberent, evenit cuique, ut per sylvam dissipati ac dis-
persi erant, ut luna certo aliunde ex loco quam fuerant suspicati
11 delabi videretur. Protinus alter alterum ut vel ferro, si aliter nequeat, fugientem remorentur summis clamoribus admonendo, passim defatigabantur raucique omnes clamitando effecti sunt. Risere
Naiades.

12   Et quid igitur, mi ⟨. . .⟩, id ipsum an non in studiis litterarum
evenire perspicuum est, siquidem ut nunc id ita est, ut videre
videor, neminem tantisper tinctum litteris qui, etsi intervallo
maximo, speciem sit aliquam eloquentie conspicatus, quin idem
illico eam de sese spem suscipiat ociosus, ut propediem summum
13 in oratorem evasurum se confidat? Cum autem sibi ad rem tenen-
dam plus quam oscitans opinabatur adesse negocii intellexit, tum
omni librorum copia contendit, ac si ipsis libris, non acerrimo
14 nostro studio dicendi simus rationem adepturi. Cumque sese
eloquentie locos satis preter ceteros quisque tenuisse opinetur, fit
inter nos ut non consequenda ipsi laude, sed in aliis carpendis et
15 redarguendis fatigemur. Denique rauci omnes sumus hac etate
oratores, ut perpaucos in eorum numero qui sese eruditos haberi
velint offendas, quem sine risu et stomacho possis contionantem
16 audire: ita omnes qui suggesta conscenderint, non orare, sed
quasvis ineptias, que dicendo assequi possint, verbis, vultu, voce et
omni gestu conari exprimere videntur.

17   In aliorumque scriptis pensitandis ita sumus plerique ad unum
omnes fastidiosi, ut ea Ciceronis velimus eloquentie respondere, ac
si superiori etate omnes qui approbati fuere scriptores eosdem
18 fuisse Cicerones statuant. Inepti! unum habuit rerum natura Ciceronem, in quo quicquid posset ad eloquentie gloriam et palmam
coniecerit; qui tamen etate isthac nostra tantam inter invidorum
copiam tantamque inter doctorum et librorum inopiam si versetur,

careful and vigilant surveillance. For in this way they thought that the moon could not escape being intercepted by one of their large number. Yet while they were thus carefully placed, it happened that each of the guards, being scattered and dispersed throughout the forest, seemed to see the moon slip away in a place different from where he expected. All at once, they began to shout loudly, urging each other to stop the fugitive, even by the sword, if necessary. In every part of the forest, they grew tired and hoarse from shouting. The Naiads laughed.

Well, my dear X, isn't it obvious that the same thing happens in literary studies?[1] For if my impression is correct, there is no one even slightly imbued with letters who does not in his leisure conceive the hope that he will soon become a great orator, even if he has only seen the face of eloquence at a distance. But, when he realizes that mastery of this art involves more difficulty than he idly thought, he strives toward this goal by reading every available book, as if we could acquire our style from books alone, rather than by our own intense efforts. And since each thinks he has achieved greater eloquence than anyone else, we inevitably weary ourselves in criticizing and confuting others, rather than in attaining distinction. In sum, all of us in this age are so hoarse as orators that, among those who wish to be thought learned, you will find only a few whom you can bear to hear without laughter or irritation. For all who mount the speaker's platform seem not to orate, but to express every absurdity of style through their words, faces, voices, and gestures.

In judging others' writings, we are nearly all so fastidious that we expect them to match Cicero's eloquence, as if all the excellent writers of an earlier age thought themselves Ciceros. Fools! Nature produced only one Cicero, in whom she united every possible element of eloquence and excellence. But if he were living in our age and faced such an abundance of envious men and such a dearth of scholars and books, he would undoubtedly forget how to speak.

19 profecto dediscat loqui. Et utinam recto aliquo constantique iudicio, dum alios vituperant, uterentur! si nemo ferme est a quo
doctior discedas, ex suoque quisque sensu non ex re ipsa, ut par
esset, aliorum scripta reprobat, studiosorumque nemo est cui certa

20 et non reliquorum iudiciis repugnans sententia adsit. Alios enim
nihil nisi coturnatum ampul⟨l⟩osumque delectat; alii quicquid
⟨non exquisitius atque⟩ accuratius editum promitur, durum id

21 et asperum deputant; alii flosculos et lautitiem tantum verborum
rotundosque periodos lectitando libant et olfaciunt: pauci vim
ingenii artisque modum et rationem in scriptore animadvertunt.

22 At enim varia res est eloquentia, ut ipse interdum sibi Cicero

23 perdissimilis sit. Magna itidem res est dicere apte et luculenter,
maiorque atque excelsior quam ut possis, nisi divino pre aliis per-
voles ingenio, non dico apprehendere, sed ne propius ad eam quidem accedere: quod ipsum veterum quoque perpauci potuere;

24 tamen omnes lectitantur et in delitiis habentur. Ea de re illos ego
hac etate haudquaquam esse aspernandos reor, qui aliquid in medium, qualecumque illud sit, afferant, quod quota ex parte nos
delectet.

25 Itaque, mi ⟨. . .⟩, cum tu me esse ridiculum scriptorem semper
affirmaris rebusque nostris nonnihil delectari consueveris, ut es
fama auctoritateque inter litteratos princeps, hunc nostrum Inter-

26 cenalium libellum perlegens, ni fallor, Naiades imitaberis: ridebis,
tum quod in eo multa me esse frustra fortassis conatum intelliges,
tum quod apud me ea comperies quibus facile possis iudicare,
non me elaborasse ut studiosos instruct⟨i⟩ores, sed alacriores redderem.

If only these critics would use some correct and constant standard   19
of judgment when they censure others! Since there is practically
no one who can teach you, everyone condemns others' writings
according to his own views, rather than by their real quality, as
would be just. And there isn't a single scholar whose judgment is
definitive or even compatible with the opinions of others. Some   20
are delighted only by elevated bombast, while others regard all
meticulous compositions as harsh and severe. Still others cull and   21
savor flowery ornaments, elegant turns of phrase, and rounded
periods as they read. Yet few pay attention to the power of a
writer's genius or the method in his art.

Now, eloquence is so varied that even Cicero is sometimes very   22
un-Ciceronian. It is a great thing to write aptly and excellently—   23
too great and elevated to approach, much less attain, unless you
have a divine talent that soars above the others. Very few of the
ancients achieved it, and yet today they are all read and praised to
the skies. Hence, I think that our contemporary writers are not to   24
be scorned, as long as they produce something that affords some
small pleasure.

My dear X, you have always declared me a comical author, and   25
have usually taken pleasure in my works. You are the foremost
man of letters in fame and authority, and when you read this small
book of *Dinner Pieces*, I believe you will imitate the naiads. You will   26
laugh, both because you will see that I have perhaps attempted
much in vain, and because you will find elements in my works
which make it clear that I have striven not to instruct scholars, but
to amuse them.

: I :

Maritus

1 Cum de re uxoria deque mulierum ingenio versuto et volubili inter
familiares meos apud me sermones haberentur multisque modis
vulgatum illud Catonis approbaretur 'maritum qui se bonum gerat
laude esse dignum,' quesitum est quenam leges maritum bonum
constituerent, desiderandane in coniuge sit facilitas potius an seve-
2 ritas. Multa quidem, que longum esset referre hoc loco, ab his qui
3 aderant in partem utramque fuere disceptata. Tandem illud consti-
tuisse videbantur, ut neque facilitatem habendam que contemp-
4 tum pareret, neque severitatem que odium excitaret. Ad hancque
rem Valerii veteris poete sententiam comprobarunt, qui 'nolo nimis
facilem,' inquit, 'difficilemque nimis'; 'nec volo quod cruciat, nec
volo quod satiat'; 'illud' igitur 'quod medium est atque inter utrumque probamus.'

5   Dum hec agerentur, ⟨. . .⟩, senex cui etas, littere rerumque memoria multam auctoritatem, cui etiam iocandi consuetudo, festivitas leposque orationis plurimum attentionis dicenti adaugebat,
alacri fronte: 'Enim,' inquit, 'viri optimi, siquid iuvat de re uxoria
6 discere, audite me, qui iam tertium victor uxorem extuli. Fateor
quidem connubia esse altercationis plena et rixe, ab uxoreque
eadem omnia proficisci mala que modo recensuisti⟨s⟩: familie
perturbationes, continue simultates, odia inter domesticos, rei
familiaris iactura, amicorum discordia denique atque infamia.
7 Sed audite qualem sese maritum gesserit quidam convicinus meus,
mihi ab ineunte etate amicissimus, quem profecto, ni fallor, istis
ipsis philosophis, quos tanti facimus, minime postponendum

: I :

The Husband

At my house, a number of friends were discussing marriage and 1
the cunning and versatile character of women. We all variously
lauded Cato's famous remark that "a man is worthy of praise if he
shows himself a good husband."[2] The question arose: what principles would make a good husband, and whether tolerance or severity is more desirable in a spouse? Many arguments were ad- 2
vanced on both sides of the question, which it would be tedious to
recount here. Eventually, everyone seemed to agree that a husband 3
should practice neither tolerance which breeds contempt, nor severity which arouses hatred. On this topic, all approved the epi- 4
gram of the ancient poet Martial, who says: "I don't want someone
too indulgent or too strict; nor do I want anything that torments,
or anything that cloys; I commend that mean which lies between
both."[3]

At this point, X spoke up. He is an elderly man, whose age 5
and knowledge of history and letters enhance his great authority, and whose habitual jesting and charming wit heightened our
attention as he spoke. With a cheerful mien, he said: "Gentlemen, if you wish to learn about marriage, listen to me, for I have
just buried my third wife in triumph.[4] Now, I admit that mar- 6
riages are full of squabbles and quarreling, and that wives cause
all the ills you have just enumerated: disruption of the family,
continual feuding, hatred between members of the household,
the ruin of the family estate, and discord and disgrace among
one's friends. But hear how a certain neighbor of mine, who 7
has been a close friend since childhood, comported himself as a
husband. Unless I am mistaken, we shall judge him by no means
inferior to the famous philosophers whom we regard so highly.

8 iudicabimus. Audietis quidem exemplum, quo ad rem uxoriam pulchre agendam vos per me esse eruditiores factos congratulemini.

9 'Sic se res habuit. Vicinus quidam meus olim per meridiem, qua hora apud ⟨. . .⟩ spatiari consueveramus, videre sibi visus est

10 uxorem suam iuvenem quempiam ad se domo recepisse; qua quidem suspitione plurimum perturbatus, diligentius omnia que ad rem perscrutandam pertinerent, solus, nullo adhibito interprete, observavit, quoad uxorem amantemque aula reclusos animadvertit.

11 Quid, o amici, frontem contraxistis? Rem quidem inauditam atque inusitatam amoribus operam dare mulierem, ac iuvenem

12 cum amante ludere voluptatemque capere! Quid igitur facit homo hic noster, me superi!, bonus et frugi? Num clamat? Num iratus irrumpit? Minime. Num patitur alienum esse apud suam coniugem? Patitur quidem interim, ac facit profecto quod fieri oportuit.

13 Principio namque et servos et familiares omnes domesticos ita in varias agendas res emittit domo, ut cum edes omni interprete vacuas reddidisset, tum eius rei quam esset acturus suspitio eos nulla aut admiratio caperet; obclusoque dehinc vestibuli hostio uxorem

14 petiit. Mulier, etsi insperato sibique nimium incommodo viri adventu esset perculsa et animis prostrata, tamen, quoad tempus sese

15 obtulit, illico confugit. Adolescenti quidem recluso nullus ad

16 evadendum locus tutus patebat. Itaque "animos," ut aiunt, "a crimine desumpsit": amantem quo potuit in abdito collocat subindeque sese letam e studio et ludibundam marito profert; multa rogi-

17 tat inherendo, sectatur, blanditur, applaudet, in os arridet. At maritus gravis, subtristis, alias res simulans, latentem quasi ex im-

18 proviso offendere queritabat. Tandem delitescentem obscuro in angulo et formidantem repperit. O animi fortitudinem insignem

19 et mirificam! O consilium optimum! Quid putatis, hunc me-

20 chumne concidisse, iugulasse? Minime. Prudens enim maritus quieti et tranquillitati perquam pulchre providit: noluit enim ini-

Indeed, you will hear an example which will cause you to con- 8
gratulate yourselves for having learned from me the best way to
conduct a marriage.

"Here's the story. One day at noon, when we used to walk to Y's 9
house, my neighbor thought he saw his young wife let someone
into his house. Troubled by suspicion, he carefully took every step 10
necessary to examine the situation alone and with no witnesses,
and found that his wife and her lover had shut themselves in a
room. Why do you scowl, my friends? Is it so strange or unusual 11
for a woman, especially a young one, to engage in love affairs, to
sport with a lover, and to take her pleasure? What then, by the 12
gods, does our good and honorable friend do? Does he cry out?
Does he burst in on them enraged? Not at all. Does he suffer another man to enjoy his wife? Yes, for the moment, and in fact he
does what he should have done. First of all, he sent away the ser- 13
vants and other domestics on various tasks, so that he emptied the
house of any witnesses, thus precluding any suspicion or surprise
at his next actions. Then, having locked the main door, he went to
find his wife. Although she was both stunned and overwhelmed by 14
her husband's unexpected and awkward return, his wife at once
took refuge while she had time. But the young lover, shut inside, 15
found no safe place to escape. So the wife took courage from her 16
crime, as they say, and placed the youth in hiding as best she
could.[5] Then she came out to meet her husband, acting happy and
playful. She clung to him and asked him many questions, following him closely with flattery, fawning, and smiles. But her grave 17
and melancholy husband, while acting preoccupied, sought to
discover the hidden lover as if by chance. At last, he came across 18
him hiding and cowering in a dark corner. What singular and remarkable fortitude! What excellent · judgment! What do you 19
think? Did he beat the adulterer or kill him? Not at all. This 20
prudent husband nicely ensured his own peace and tranquility. He
didn't want the enmity that would be aroused by taking revenge,

micitias subire vindicando, quo erumnosiorem sibi conditionem imponeret, sed indulgendo amicitiam parare commodius et antiquius duxit, quo eius salus et fama a gravioribus adversis casibus foret tutior.

21 'Quid igitur? Perterrefacti quidem ac admodum trementis adolescentis dexteram manum prehendit leva leniterque ac benigne in mediam aulam deduxit suaque altera dextra contra manu protensa constitit ac "Bono," inquit, "adolescens, esse te animo iubeo: nihil

22 est a me tibi quod sit verendum. Neque enim mihi viribus aut armis tecum esse certamen paratum volui, quo quidem perfacile, dum ita instituissem, manu meorum, quos omnes abesse iussi, superassem; sed amicitia inter nos fore contendendum statui, quam quidem, fateor, letioribus fundamentis iactam cuperem.

23 Sed quanti refert, modo illam, utcumque exorta sit, honestissimis

24 officiis inter nos coluerimus? Persuade tibi me constantissimi amici animum erga te suscepisse et fretum amicitia quid sentiam liberius allocuturum.

25 '"Ego vero, si dixero nullam esse abs te nobis illatam iniuriam,

26 neque quod sentio neque quod ipse affirmes dixero. Potuissem quidem iniurias prosequi, sed duxi esse prestantius beneficio inter

27 nos et benevolentia constituta certare quam iniuriis vincere. Vides idcirco quam mihi, cum ob remissam iniuriam, tum ob novam

28 porrectam gratiam, debeas. Eam quidem in dies tibi esse accommodatiorem, quoad in me sit, profecto senties, ut tuas iam hinc esse partes arbitrere, ita te accinctum et paratum exhibere ad hanc nostram coniunctionem inter nos tuendam fovendamque, ut abs te nihil desit quominus nostram tibi beneficentiam fore gratissimam

29 intelligam; idque ut facias iterum atque iterum precor. Quod si quippiam abs te pro accepto beneficio deberi nobis non negas, fili mi, age, da operam ut, dum tue et vite et fame hodierna die plurimum concessi, tu ne honori quidem nostro per te uspiam detractum iri velis.

which would have made his situation more distressing. Instead, he thought it preferable to win the youth's friendship by forgiving him, thus protecting his own good name and well-being against graver misfortune.

"What did he do, then? With his left hand, he grasped the 21 right hand of the terrified and trembling youth, and led him gently and kindly into the middle of the room. Then, extending his right hand, he said: 'Cheer up, young man. You have nothing to fear from me. I have not chosen to fight with you either armed or un- 22 armed. Had I decided to do so, I could easily have prevailed with the help of my household. Instead, I sent them away, resolved that any rivalry between us should be in friendship, although I admit that I would have desired to build on a happier foundation. But 23 what does that matter, as long as we maintain our friendship—no matter what its origins—by honorable acts of kindness? Rest as- 24 sured that my feelings toward you are those of a friend, and of that I shall speak freely, trusting in your friendship.

"'If I were to say that you have done me no wrong, I would not 25 say what I feel or what you yourself would admit. I could have 26 taken my revenge, but I thought it better to rival you in good deeds and goodwill, rather than to triumph by hurting you. You 27 see, then, that you are in my debt, both for the wrong I have for- given and for the goodwill I extend. You will find that, if it is in 28 my power, my goodwill will serve your interests more and more each day. So I believe it is your duty to promote and protect this bond between us. By doing this promptly and readily, you will show me how welcome my generosity is; and I ask you repeatedly to do this. For if you don't deny that you are in my debt for this 29 favor, my son, see to it that you do nothing to damage my honor, since I have today spared your life and reputation.

30 '"Multa in hanc partem dicerem, et esse huiusmodi de uxore quam abs te accepi contumeliam, ut eam nemo sit quin gravissi-
31 mam et acerbissimam deputet. Tuque pro tuo alioquin bene mo-rato et bene constituto ingenio is eris in primis qui, ut arbitror, nusquam negabis frugi et temperantem esse neminem, qui se velit
32 hoc in facinore certe turpi et detestabili fore deprehensum. Ac de-decet profecto ingenuum et libere educatum hos vetitos et insanos amores turpesque istiusmodi reliquas omnes voluptates non longe
33 odisse. Nefasque est pusille ac sordide voluptatis gratia erumnas et pericula indecenter ita subisse, ut sordido abiectove in loco aliquo latitandum et in discrimine vite expavescendum deque capite et salute, nullo proposito laudis aut emolumenti premio, parata igno-minia, sit dimicandum.

34 '"Quare tute hoc meum consilium si sequere, ut spero, operas ingeniumque tuum ab amore traduces ad rerum honestissimarum curam, ad laudem, ad decus bonis artibus nanciscendum, ad op-
35 time de tuis civibus, de patria promerendum. Quam ad rem pre-clare assequendam me tibi opera, studio, caritate comitem, coadiu-torem, auctorem promptissimum, paratissimum cupidissimumque
36 futurum polliceor. Ac volo quidem tuis et publicis et privatis in rebus omnibus me tibi eum deputes, quem pro etate et pietate parentem, pro fide et benivolentia fratrem, pro omni reliquo officio
37 amicissimum libere possis adire. Nusquam te mea opera, cura, dili-gentia fallet; vincam sedulitate et re ipsa tuas de me expectationes."

38 'Huiusmodi igitur vir ille prudentissimus apud adolescentem sermones habuerat graves et dignos memoratu, quibus id provide-rat ut, siquid sibi ex uxoris impudicitia esset ignominie, ad futu-rum percommode sublata videretur, et ⟨in⟩ tollenda ignominia si-quid fortasse inimicitiarum foret subeundum vitarit, inque vitanda
39 inimicitia dignitatem auctoritatemque suam multo servarit. Sed nolo hic esse in ornando homine prolixior, cuius prudentia et consilium quale sua reliqua in vita omni fuerit unico hoc exemplo facile intelligitis.

"'I could say more on this topic, for the indignity I have suffered 30
on account of my wife is such that everyone must consider it grave
and bitter. But as your character is gentlemanly and reasonable, 31
you will be the first to concede that no honorable and temperate
man would wish to be caught in such a base and detestable act. A 32
noble and enlightened mind is bound to detest utterly these illicit
and insane passions and any similar pleasures. And it is sinful to 33
subject oneself, merely for the sake of petty and sordid pleasure, to
the distress and danger of hiding in a filthy and squalid place, of
fearing for one's life, and of fighting to the death with no hope of
praise or reward, but only of inevitable disgrace.

"'If, as I hope, you take my advice, you will turn your thoughts 34
and energies from love to more honorable pursuits, to attaining
praise and distinction in liberal learning, and to the meritorious
service of your fellow citizens and your country. For you to attain 35
this goal with glory, I promise that, by my work, zeal, and affection, I shall be your ready companion, your prompt assistant, and
your eager spokesman. In all your affairs, both public and private, 36
I wish you to approach me freely as your parent in years and love,
as your brother in trust and goodwill, and as your close friend in
every other office. My aid, care, and diligence will never disappoint 37
you, and my zeal and my deeds will exceed your expectations.'

"Such were the grave and memorable words of this wise hus- 38
band to the youth, by which he avoided the disgrace which his
wife's immorality might have caused. By bearing this disgrace, he
avoided any enmity that might have arisen; while, by avoiding enmity, he preserved his dignity and authority. But let me not be 39
prolix in praising the man. From this one instance, you may easily
understand what prudence and wisdom he demonstrated in all his
conduct.

40 'Redeo ad rem. Adolescentem idcirco multis verbis confirma-
tum comiter ac perdomestice domo eduxit in trivium, ut si qui
spectatores affuissent, quidvis aliud inter hosce negotii fuisse sus-
41 picarentur quam rem ipsam. Cum in publico constitissent, inquit:
"Superis faventibus spero hodierna die ea esse amicitie funda-
menta inter nos iacta, in qua tu nihil dubitare a me, ego nihil de
42 nobis posthac dolere debeamus. Uterque enim queque ad commo-
dum et emolumenta, queque ad famam, ad laudem, ad gloriam
accommodentur, ab altero petere, expectare, exposcere pro amicitie
iure, pro mutua reciprocaque benivolentia et possumus et debe-
mus. Tu me amabis."

43 'Denique adolescentem, ridens familiarissime et iocum fronte ac
44 vultu suggestiens, a se missum fecit. Iuvenis autem superiori metu,
novissimo preter spem eventu exagitatus, abiens non usquequaque
sui compos, verbis partim interruptis partim depressis, demisso
vultu, amate a se mulieris salutem marito commendatam facere
45 conatus est. Cuius dictis omnibus aurem frontemque maritus per-
humanissime prebuit. Posthec, animi sedandi causa, suam se in
suburbanam villam transtulit.

46 'Diebus aliquot elapsis domum ad uxorem rediit supercilio, ver-
47 bis, gestu nihil preter solitum tristiori. Vidisses interim perterri-
tam mulierem ex intervallo maritum suspicientem atque e vestigio
48 in lachrimas subirrumpentem. Et eis quidem hoc acerbius lachrimis, quod percunctantibus suis quidnam esset quod ita in luctu et
squalore vitam traheret, tanti concepti meroris causas aperire nefas
49 ducebat. Adde quod per hanc mariti erga se facilitatem incredibilem non poterat non vehementius, in tam atroci suo delicto perpe-
trato, aliquid insidiarum pertimescere.

50 'Verum vos animadvertite, queso, equanimitatem, constantiam,
insignem inauditamque prudentiam viri huius, qui quidem talem
se gessit, ut in eo concepto animi dolore prorsus nihil uxori de
pristina dignitate domi aut foris esse detractum voluerit, in omnique reliqua vita eum se prebuit, ut omnibus in rebus comem,

"I return to my story. Having reassured the youth by these   40
words, he led him from the house into the street in a courteous
and friendly manner, so that, if any witnesses were present, they
would suspect that the business between the two men was anything but what it actually was. When they had stopped in public,   41
the husband said: 'With the gods' favor, I hope that today we have
laid the foundation of a friendship which will neither cause you to
doubt me, nor me to regret our bond. By virtue of the laws of   42
friendship and our mutual affection, we may both expect and demand of each other whatever serves our interest and advantage,
and our reputation, praise, and glory. You will be grateful to me.'

"Then, with friendly laughter and a jesting countenance, he   43
dismissed the youth. Shaken by his recent fright and by the bewil-   44
dering outcome of the affair, the youth uttered some incoherent
and choked words, and tried with downcast eyes to bid the husband take good care of the woman he loved. The husband listened   45
and reacted most humanely to his words. Then, to calm himself,
he repaired to his villa outside the city.

"After several days had elapsed, he returned home to his wife,   46
his expression, speech, and actions no sadder than usual. Yet oc-   47
casionally you would have seen his terrified wife glance at her
husband from a distance and suddenly burst into tears. Her tears   48
were all the more poignant when the servants asked why she
seemed so mournful and desolate, for she considered it sinful to
reveal the causes of her great sorrow. What's more, her husband's   49
incredible tolerance made her fear that he was planning some trap
to punish her awful crime.

"Please note what equanimity and resolution, what remarkable   50
prudence the man displayed. Despite his inner grief, he chose not
to diminish his wife's previous reputation either at home or in
public. In all his behavior, he acted in such a way that all believed

51 dulcem optimumque maritum putarint et affirmarint. Rem a me
    prope incredibilem audietis. Homo hic uxori, ut apud se genitalis
    lecti assueta sponda pro casta atque innoxia accumberet, vetuit
    nunquam, passusque est impudicam deprehensam adolescentulam
    integras noctes iacere propter se laterique inherere, nulla a se re-
    pulsa, nullis contumeliis, nullis morsibus verborum iniectis.

52 'At dicet quispiam: "Quid tum? graviterne compertum uxoris
53 facinus an non tulit?" Non sum is qui audeam isthuc dicere, mari-
    tum, etsi sapientissimum, inveniri quempiam, qui ob uxoris adul-
54 terium animo non idem sit vehementer perturbato. "Num igitur
55 iniurias prosecutus non est?" Profecto, ac severissime! "Quid ita?
    Hoc enim non fit verisimile, hunc, qui ne verbis quidem lacessi-
    verit, in proxima sponda receperit, severum fuisse, ni forte, captato
56 tempore, noctu strangularit aut veneno eam sustulerit." Minime.
    Id enim scelus si admisisset, in eam nefandam crudelitatem si ir-
    rupisset, quis unquam sane mentis aut satis composita ratione
57 preditus non vituperasset? Quis hunc non redarguisset, qui cras-
    sando assequeretur, non ut amissa posset recuperasse, sed ut fame
    iacturam gravioremque fortunam reddidisse postea indolendum
58 sibi foret? Et profecto convitiis esset idem prosequendus, si et levi-
    tatem coniugis et propriam crudelitatem, male fortunam suam fe-
    rendo, vulgo futuram fabulam non effugisset.

59 'Non igitur in illam erumnarum quippiam attulit, atqui, quo
    magis mirere, nulla adhibita vi et nulla crudelitate maximas a mu-
    liere penas desumpserit ea ulciscendi arte et ratione ut, quo plus
60 quove acrius puniret, eo minus in se odii excitaret. Nam cum in
    rebus ceteris esset istiusmodi, ut ad facilitatem erga uxorem addi
    nihil posset, una tantum in re vindicis partes servavit, ut ex ea die
    posteaquam corruptam esse uxorem cognovit, tametsi omnibus
    illecebris a formosissima, amatoriis in artibus callidissima exercita-
    tissimaque coniuge impeteretur, in illam tamen incaluisse ad libe-
61 ris operam dandam visus est nunquam. Cave dubites castigande et
    conficiende mulieris quamquam audacissime et contumacissime,

and declared him a courteous, kind, and devoted husband. I may   51
add what seems almost unbelievable. The man never forbade his
wife to sleep next to him in their marriage bed, as if she were
chaste and innocent. He suffered this young woman, whose un-
chastity he had discovered, to lie beside him all night and to cling
to his side, without rebuffing or rebuking her with sharp words.

"Someone will say: 'What then? Didn't he take badly the dis-   52
covery of his wife's misdeed?' I daresay that any husband, no mat-   53
ter how wise, would be greatly disturbed by his wife's adultery.
'Didn't he avenge the wrong?' Yes, most severely. 'How then? If he   54
                                                                        55
did not reproach her and even admitted her to his bed, it seems
unlikely that he acted with severity, unless he was waiting for the
right moment to strangle her in her sleep or to poison her.' Not at   56
all. If he had committed such a crime or erupted in such impious
cruelty, what sane or reasonable man would not have condemned
him? Who would not have censured a man who resorted to vio-   57
lence which, instead of recovering what was lost, would later cause
him to regret having brought greater disgrace and disaster on
himself? He would have merited our reproaches if, by bearing his   58
misfortune badly, he had caused his wife's inconstancy and his
own cruelty to become the talk of the town.

"He therefore inflicted no suffering on her. Even more astonish-   59
ing, without using any force or cruelty, he inflicted the utmost
punishment on his wife. His means of taking revenge was calcu-
lated to punish her all the more severely because it did not arouse
her hatred. This he did by showing his wife the greatest tolerance   60
in all respects but the one he chose as his revenge. From the day
he discovered his wife's infidelity, he never warmed up to having
intercourse with her, even though he was tempted by the many
allurements of his beautiful wife, who was highly skilled in the arts
of love. Do not doubt that any safer or severer method can be   61

62 posse rationem aliam severiorem ac tutiorem reperiri: ardentem ira
    et flagrantem furore feminam frigens vir ridendo et dormitando
63 frangit dicacemque silentio mutam atque elinguem reddit. Et quid
    putas sentire hanc de se mulierem, quam atrox animi certamen
64 metus adversus fiduciam excruciabat, que in luctu, in squalore, in
    solitudine, sui ipsius conscientia damnata, vitam ducebat, que in
    tantis suis occultis doloribus, cetera familiarium turba inscia pro
    consuetudine circum arridente et applaudente, palam lugere et
    queri ignominie metu prohibebatur?

65   'Vidi ego illam tantum in furorem odio tedioque sui nonnun-
    quam incidisse, ut sese emori cupere acclamaret multisque in
    virum dehinc convitiis insultaret, quo illum ad iram et ferrum
66 fortassis excitaret. Hec vobis incredibilia videri non admiror. Nam
    etsi pro mulierum natura id fieri diiudicem, que cum desint qui-
    buscum irate concertent, iracundie et furoris sui vim in se ipsas
    exercent, vix tamen persuadebatur ut, que coram hisce oculis in-
67 tuebar, facta satis crederem. O rem incredibilem, mulierem te-
    mulentam, excandescentem in virum, tacendo et ferendo posse
68 devinci! Misera mulier! que his gravissimis et molestissimis curis
    confecta in eam est valitudinem collapsa, ut consumptis in dies
    viribus, abesa et penitus extenuata, defecerit, ita in virum suum
    affecta ut preter se culpamque suam moriens alium neminem incu-
69 sarit. Etenim cum spiritum extremum duceret, "Iuvat, inquit, ex
    his miseriis decedere, tum alias ob res, tum vel maxime ne tibi sim,
    vir optime, diutius gravis."

70   'En facinus dignum memoria: unum hunc fuisse, qui uxorem
    impudicam et corruptam ita perpeti, ita occidere didicerit, ut sibi
    illius ex morte nulla impietatis nota, ex vita vero nulla adscribi
71 potuerit ignominia; ex utrisque rebus nulla animi penitudo! Docu-
    mentum quidem ad rem uxoriam probe et prudenter gerendam
    egregium et singulare, quod ferendo iniurias punire, puniendo
72 amari condocefaciat! Patientiam hominis virilem, quam cum omni

found for punishing even the most shameless and insolent wife: a cold husband's laughter or slumber can break a woman's ardent   62
wrath and burning fury, and his silence can make a chattering woman mute and speechless. How do you think his wife felt?   63
What terrible discord between apprehension and assurance tormented her mind? Living in squalid grief and solitude, she was   64
damned by her own guilt. While the rest of the household, ignorant of her crime, surrounded her with their usual smiles and approval, fear of disgrace prohibited her from suffering openly, despite her hidden pain.

"I myself saw her occasionally lapse into fits caused by her self-   65
hatred and revulsion. She cried out that she wished to die, and she insulted her husband with reproaches, hoping to arouse him to anger and armed violence against her. If this strikes you as incred-   66
ible, I am not surprised. I ascribed her behavior to the nature of women, who often turn their anger against themselves if they cannot vent it on others. But I could hardly bring myself to believe what I witnessed with my own eyes. How incredible that this   67
drunken woman's raging against her husband could be subdued by silence and patience! Wretched woman! Exhausted by her grave   68
and troublesome cares, she fell into such poor health that her strength faded each day, and she wasted away, consumed and utterly emaciated. Yet in her affection for her husband, she accused no one but her guilty self as she lay dying. When she breathed her   69
last, she said: 'I am glad to leave my misery, especially because I no longer wish to burden you, my good husband.'

"Here was a memorable case! This one man knew how to toler-   70
ate a shameless and adulterous wife, and managed to kill her without her death causing a scandal, her life causing a disgrace, or either of these causing him any regret. This exceptional lesson in   71
conducting one's marriage wisely and well teaches us how, while bearing wrongs, we may punish them, and how, while punishing them, we may still be loved. You will admit that a man's mature   72

in vita laudes, tum inter coniuges permaxime necessariam profitea-
73 ris! Patientia lites et iurgia secluduntur, improborum petulantia
frangitur, audacia plerumque retunditur, stultitia persepius coher-
74 cetur. Patientia demum ea est, que paratos ad lacessendum atque
ledendi cupidos retrahit atque retardat. Illudque postremo maximum et primarium habet in se bonum patientia, ut ad acerbissi-
mas iniurias severissime vindicandas bellissime accommodetur.

75   'Sum hac etate qua me videtis prope decrepitum; sum in rebus
agendis usu et experientia non ignarus; vidi, memini multa; illud
animadverti, neminem, qui tolerare suosque animi impetus ferre
76 nequiret, scisse vincere: ut admonere adolescentes iuste et vere solitus sim, ne quid dicant neve quid agant animo exagitato, sed iram
77 patientia temperent consiliaque maturent. Nam cum hec semper
fuerit omnibus utilis virtus, tum maxime his qui connubii vinculo
78 adiuncti sunt admodum semper erit necessaria. Discite, coniugati,
ferre uxores vestras patientia! Leve animal femina et ad voluptates
79 prona. Quod si hec una amoris vis in prestantissimis et maturissi-
mis viris tantum valet, quantum passim in dies tota urbe discerni-
mus, quis tantopere muliercule, natura ipsa lascivissime, succen-
seat, ut non multa ex parte sexui, imbecillitati et conceptis flammis
indulgendum censeat?

80   'Sed vos quamnam "legem," quam "mediocritatem" querebatis?
Illamne fortassis quam in solo fuisse Platone—philosophorum, ut
quidam fatentur, principe—asserunt, ut difficillimam illam gravi-
81 tatis societatem cum humanitate coniunctam tenuerit? Conferte
hu⟨i⟩c veteres illos magnos et laudatissimos viros. Quid? eum qui
a Scipionis matre divertens eam rem inculpantibus ostendit cal-
82 ceum—nota historia—, num huic nostro non postponemus? Non
dico illud, nescisse fortasse ignominiam malamque familie sue famam evitare. Sed esto, scivit ille quidem "tollere uxoris vitium,"
fateor, at id non usquequaque scivit, prout oportuit, "tolerare."
83 Quid? Socrates ille ipse deorum approbatione sapientissimus, qui
contumacia immodeste uxoris didicit apud ceteros cives et peregri-

patience, while laudable in every aspect of life, is especially necessary for husbands. Patience silences arguments and strife, over- 73
comes the insolence of the wicked, checks audacity, and often re-
presses folly. Patience restrains and inhibits those who are eager to
offend or harm. And finally, patience has this great and important 74
virtue: it avenges the bitterest wrongs most severely.

"At my age, I am very feeble, as you see. My years of experience 75
have given me some knowledge of human affairs. I have seen many
things, and remember them. I have noticed one fact. No one is
able to conquer who does not know how to brook and withstand
his mind's urgings. I generally give young people this just and 76
sound advice: never act or speak in excitement, but temper your
anger with patience, and let your decisions ripen. Patience has al- 77
ways been a useful virtue, and is especially necessary to those who
are bound by the bond of matrimony. Husbands, learn to treat 78
your wives with patience! Woman is a fickle creature and given to
pleasure. Hence, if the singular force of love has as much power 79
over mature and worthy men as we daily witness throughout our
city, could anyone be so angry with a woman who is naturally lustful that he would not in large part indulge the sex's weakness and
burning passion?

"Now, what principle, what moderation were you seeking? Were 80
they those found in Plato, who is said by many to have been the
greatest philosopher, and the only man to combine rigid severity
with humanity?[6] Compare the famous men of antiquity to my 81
example. What, shall we find this husband inferior to the man
who divorced Scipio's mother (you know the story) and responded
to his critics by showing them his shoe?[7] I won't claim that he 82
failed to avoid disgrace to himself and his family. Granted, he
knew how to *remove* his wife's vices, I admit, but knew not how to
reprove them, as he should have. Or consider Socrates, who was 83
called the wisest of men by the very gods' approval.[8] His wife's
obstreperous abuse taught him the tolerance and humanity that he

265

nos facilitatem atque humanitatem servare quemve uxorem admirari solitam referunt vultu quo exisset eodem semper illum redisse domum, scivit ille quidem uxoris vitium ⟨tolerare, at non scivit⟩ tol⟨l⟩ere.

84   'Quid igitur, an non vestris sententiis maritus hic noster multo
85 erat omnibus preferendus? Is enim unus est, qui non iurgia modo, quibus sunt matrimonia omnia refertissima, verum et maximas et immodicas impudice uxoris iniurias scivit quam mitissime, modes-
86 tissime occultissimeque perpeti. Ipsus quidem est, qui non eodem continuo vultu solum, ut Grecus ille, verum et amplius eadem stabili et constanti perseverantia in suscepto animi instituto laudatissimo perstitit, summaque et mirifica cum indulgentia et facilitate coniunctam severitatem vindicando servavit.'

∴ 2 ∴

Uxoria

1   Lacenas fama est omnium inter vetustos Grecos urbem fuisse unam claram armis et artibus pacis admodum insignem, quam fi-
2 nitimi externique populi merito amarint et veriti sint. Ac monimentis litterarum aliqua eius urbis preclarissimorum civium nomina celebrantur, qui quidem egregia virtute sua nomen sibi atque gloriam patrieque dignitatem atque auctoritatem plurimum accu-
3 mularint. Hos inter ferunt Cleiodramum unum fuisse civem qui et foris armorum expeditionibus et domi consilio atque prudentia primariis laude et benivolentia dignis civibus minime unquam
4 postponeretur. Is cum etate esset grandi et morbo ad extremum gravi laboraret, suscepta pretexta toga regia et aurea gemmis gravi insignique corona reliquisque ornamentis triumphalibus, que sibi dono bene merenti a patria forent elargita, sese strato lecto medius

showed both to his fellow citizens and to foreigners. His wife often marveled that he left home and returned without changing his
expression. He knew how to *reprove*, but not *remove*, his wife's
vices.

"What then? Do you not judge our modern husband superior   84
to the others? He alone knew how to suffer in mild and modest   85
silence both marital strife and a flagrantly wanton wife. Not only   86
did he continually present an unchanged expression, like the famous Greek, but he also persevered in his fixed and firm resolve.
In taking revenge, he combined severity with supreme indulgence
and remarkable tolerance."

: 2 :

Debate on Marriage

Tradition records that among the ancient Greeks, the city of   1
Sparta was so famous in war and so distinguished in the arts of
peace, that nations nearby and abroad rightly loved and feared her.
Extolled in written records are the names of her most outstanding   2
citizens, whose remarkable virtue won fame and glory for them
and great distinction and prestige for their homeland. Among   3
them, they say, was a certain Cleiodramus, whose military exploits
abroad and prudent counsel at home proved him in no wise inferior to the most lauded and loved citizens. When in his old age he   4
was suffering from a fatal illness, he took up his royal purple-
bordered toga, his crown of gold encrusted with jewels, and the
other triumphal insignia which his country had awarded him for
his meritorious service. Donning them, he sat in the middle of his

considens adornavit, accitisque tribus carissimis sibique omni
laude persimilibus quos habebat filiis (maiori Mitio⟨ni⟩, minori
Trissopho, medio erat Acrinno nomen), frontem sibi et barbam
plenam maiestatis alterutra manu demulcens, quid sibi ad testamentum ultimamque voluntatem conscribendam animi esset his
verbis edocuit:

5   'Etenim, o filii,' — inquit — 'que nobis a vestro avo, patre meo,
viro non indigno, quem unum omni memoria et benivolentia
etiam demortuum prosequamur, bona relicta sunt, eadem in hanc
usque diem fide et diligentia mea sedulo servata vobis restituo,
quantum videre licet, culta adeo et reddita meliora, ut hinc cum in
re familiari diligentie tum et omni in reliqua vita modestie mee
6   signa et manifesta indicia esse apud vos futura expectem. Id ipsum
instituti et vos prosequamini hortor, filii, quantum facturos qui-
7   dem spero. Huiusmodi enim ut essetis curavi ac probe ex animi
mei sententia vos esse intelligo permodestos et perquam diligentes.
8   Itaque dabitis operam (tuaque imprimis hec siet, Mitio, cura: nam
ut etate prestas, tibi ita apud fratres locus patrius debetur; ergo id
age pro viribus, fili) ut nostri nepotes eque parsimoniam vestram
et victus modestiam vestram, atque ipsi vos meam — ni fallor —
9   facitis, et probent et imitentur. Etenim quod in me fuit ingenii
industrieque, id omne pro viribus et virili summo studio exposui,
ut eum me vobis preberem in dies patrem, cui esse vos filios non
10   iniuria et congratulari et, si ita liceat, gloriari possetis. Vestrum id
esse officium duco, id acrius eniti, ut siquid vita defunctis animi
sensus nobis relictus erit, unus ego pater cum hinc excessero
voluptatem hanc mecum ad inferos deferam, meis vos institutis
et monitis vere laudis cupidissimos et inter vos coniunctissimos
11   amantissimosque reliquisse. Ac vos quidem laudo quod vestra observantia et pietate in me nunquam non id maxime elaborastis, ut
per vos mihi vita esset, quoad fortuna sineret, iocundissima atque
12   felicissima. Que cum ita sint, filii, siquidem mee fuere partis ut
precipuam in erudiendis vobis curam ipse gererem, quo in dies vos

bed and summoned his three dear sons, who resembled him in every sort of excellence. The oldest was named Mitio, the second Acrinnus, and the youngest Trissophus.[9] Then, wiping his brow and stroking his majestic beard, he explained what he intended as his last will and testament, in roughly these words.

"My sons," he said. "Your grandfather, my father, was a worthy 5 man whom even in death we should always remember and love. The estate he left me I have to this day assiduously preserved with faith and diligence. As you can see, I now pass it on to you well maintained and improved, and I expect that you will regard it as clear proof both of my diligence in managing our property and of my moderation in every other aspect of life. I urge you, my sons, 6 to continue this same way of life, as indeed I hope you will. For I 7 have sought to raise you as very moderate and diligent men, and I plainly see that you are such. Hence you will do your best, my 8 sons. And this will be your special concern, Mitio, for as the oldest you must act like a father to your brothers. Do your utmost, my sons, to see that your children, like yourselves, laud and imitate my frugality and moderate way of life. For as best I could, I de- 9 voted whatever talent and industry I possessed to become a father of whom you may rightly be proud and may perhaps even boast. I 10 consider it your duty to continue to live as you do. In this way, if we have any awareness after death, as your father I shall have the pleasure in the next life of knowing that, by my teachings and ad-monitions, I left you desirous of praise and very fond of each other. I laud you for never failing to show me the reverence and 11 affection which have made my life as pleasant and happy as for-tune would permit. My sons, it has been my intention to take the 12 greatest care in educating you. So, when I witness your constant

factos esse meliores sentio, eo vehementius gaudeo et superis gratias habeo, quod eorum benignitate id assecuti sumus, ut opera et
diligentia nostra cum officio patris tum bonorum civium de vobis
13   expectationi satis nobis licuerit facere. Exque vita non nisi maxima
ex parte animo bene expleto decedam, cum et fortunas domesticas
minime perturbatas aut comminutas et vos bene degende vite rationibus instructos reliquero.

14   'Hec preterea apud me que facile novistis ornamenta non a
maioribus familie nostre suscepta, sed que iudicium atque consensus nostrorum concivium virtuti presertim mee esse contributa
voluere, eiusmodi quidem sunt, ut non pretio modo sed vel magis
dignitatis specie et raritate ipsa merito vos, quantum suspicer, mo-
15   veant. Atqui sic apud me quidem de his ipsis non iniuria decretum
est, insignia hec communi vestra in hereditate adscribenda non
esse sed uni huic vestrum relicta esse volo, qui vos inter sese modestia pre ceteris, prudentia, constantia, pietate veraque iustitia
16   preditum virtutisque amantissimum prestiterit. Hocque factum a
me, homine alioquin haudquaquam inconsiderato, fieri velim exis-
timetis, filii, prorsus ut vos ad mutuam concertationem virtutis, ad
17   desiderium emerite laudis excitem. Tum etiam sic visum est (neque absurda quidem hec mea vobis videbitur, si huc animum in-
tenderitis, ratio), ut que munera et perspecte virtutis premia uni
tantum patria omnium sapientissima contribuerit, maiorum patrieque exemplo eadem non pluribus a me sed uni maxime spec-
tate et prestantis virtutis commendentur.

18   'Id vos consilii siquid, filii mei, fortassis improbaritis, una et
immensum et prope nimium erga vos meum amorem improbetis
necesse est, quo quidem fit ut, dum vestrum quemvis tam splendide hereditatis compotem fieri cupiam, is ipse apud me interea
19   mortales omnes omni genere laudis multo precedere videatur. Neque ipse mihi satis mea comparatione placeo, tam longe vestrum
singulos et prestituo reliquis et in postremis locandum ex tribus
20   vobis statuo neminem. Vos id igitur inter vos pro vestra modestia

improvement, I rejoice and thank the gods whose kindness has allowed me to fulfill my paternal duty and to satisfy our citizens' expectations of you. I shall depart this life with great satisfaction, 13 for I leave our family fortune in no wise disturbed or diminished, and leave you instructed in living well.

"Now, you are familiar with these insignia, which I did not in- 14 herit from our ancestors, but which the judgment and consensus of my fellow citizens chose to award me for my personal virtue. I expect that you will be inspired not only by their value, but even more by their prestige and rarity. However, I have justly resolved 15 not to bequeath them to you in common. Instead, I wish to leave them to the one of you who has surpassed the others in prudence, moderation, constancy, piety, justice, and love of virtue. I want you 16 to know that I have not acted ill-advisedly, my sons. You will see that I am stirring you to compete in virtue and desire for praise. I 17 made the following decision, according to reasoning which, when you consider it, will seem neither unusual nor unreasonable: just as our wise homeland followed its ancestral tradition in awarding these gifts to one man as a reward for his proven virtue, so should I entrust them not to several persons, but to the one who has shown the most outstanding virtue.

"Should you perhaps object to my resolve, my sons, then you 18 must also object to the immense and nearly excessive love which I bear you. For in my love, I wish one of you to possess this splen-did inheritance, which I think will make him surpass all other mortals in every kind of praise. Nor am I content with my own 19 ability to compare you, since I regard each of you as superior to the others, and none of you inferior. Being modest and humane 20

et unanimitate equius discernetis, filii, cuinam splendida hec here-
21 ditas decernatur. Itaque quisquis ille fuerit vestrum qui se pre ceteris virtute insignem prestiterit (quod illi quieti pacique atque integre felicitati sit!) hanc sibi coronam, hanc vestem, hec denique
omnia triumphi ornamenta eo sibi desumat animo atque mente, ut
pro his promerendis neque laborem neque periculum fore sibi uspiam recusandum statuat.'

22   Hec ubi dixit Cleiodramus, iuvenes filii gravissimis dignissi-
misque patris verbis commoti, non minus et regiis et perfulgenti-
bus illis atque admodum divinis ornamentis una et caritate erga se
illa mirifica senis patris acti, qua eum intelligerent ad extremum
usque vite diem nihil de pristina incredibili erga suos cura dimi-
sisse, collachrimarunt non nihilque tristes quisque alterum con-
23 spicientes conticuere. Tandem Mitio natu inter fratres maior
huiusmodi verbis exorsus est:

'Tam quidem quod prebuisti in omni vita optimi exempli tue-
que adepte glorie memoria, ornamento atque felicitati familie nostre sit, pater, quam ipsi in nostrum animum induximus omni
opera, studio, diligentia id agere, ut tui simus, pater, non dissimil-
24 limi. Ac te quidem plane id sperasse decet, pater, perplures affuturum te annos apud nos, qui quidem pro vetere nostra consuetudine tibi cum obsequentissimi in hanc usque diem fuerimus, tum
eosdem in gradus honoris optatissimos suffragio tuo, pater, deo-
25 rumque benignitate mature conscendisse intuebere. Nam te quidem eius diligentie fructus, quam in exornandis nobis omni virtu-
26 tis cultu adhibuisti, capere superi piissimi volent.' Hoc loco et
iuvenum et patris lachrime immodice erumpere occeperant, ut iam
sermonem hortando patre protrahere longius non licuerit.

27   At cum senex e vita decessisset, etsi modestia singulari prediti
essent, iuvenes fratres hereditatis tamen huiusmodi splendidis-
sime lautissimeque cupiditate quadam angebantur, eaque cuique
gloria iam tum quidem pergrata futura esse videbatur, si id
assecuti essent, ut se hoc pacto inter fratres virtute primarium

men, you will therefore judge more equitably than I can, my sons.
Whichever of you shows himself most remarkable for his virtue   21
(may it give him peace and perfect happiness!), let him accept this
crown, this robe, and all these triumphal insignia, bearing in mind
that, to remain worthy of them, he must henceforth shun no labor
or danger."

When Cleiodramus had spoken, his young sons were moved by   22
their father's grave and noble words, and no less by his regal, re-
splendent, and quite divine insignia. And being touched by the old
man's marvelous affection when they perceived that, even near the
end, his singular care for them was not abated, they wept together,
and exchanged glances in sad silence. At length, the oldest brother   23
Mitio began to speak:

"May the memory of the noble example you have shown us and
of the glory you have attained, father, bring distinction and prosperity to our family. We are resolved to devote our efforts, zeal,
and diligence to becoming like you, father. It befits you, father, to   24
hope to remain with us for many years. For to this day, we have
been most obedient to you, and soon you will see us ascend, with
your aid and the gods' kindness, to the most coveted ranks of
honor. The gods above surely desire you to reap the fruits of the   25
diligence you have used in providing us with high standards of
virtue." At this point, the tears of the youths and their father be-   26
gan to pour forth copiously, so that it was impossible to say more
to cheer him.

When the old man had departed this life, the young brothers   27
were excited, despite their remarkable modesty, by their desire for
this splendid and sumptuous inheritance. And each envisioned the
sweet glory which he would enjoy, if he succeeded in being judged

28 diiudicassent. Sed qui et ingenue educati et optimis moribus imbuti essent, ne ulla inter eos contentio gravior exoriretur neve
etiam minime inter eos altercationes vulgarentur, seniores familie
sue viros integerrimos et severissimos convocarunt, apud quos
29 suam quisque causam pacatissime disceptarent. Constituta deinde
die, considentibus patribus, qui maior erat natu Mitio huiusmodi
orationem habere instituit:

'Ni exploratissimum apud me esset, patres, coequata vos parique in quemque nostrum benivolentia esse affectos, ut neque a
me neque a reliquis fratribus meis amplius quicquam ad amorem
30 erga nos vestrum accumulandum desiderari possit, ni item id palam cognitumque esset eam in vobis esse animi equitatem insitam
innatamque iustitiam, ut minime unquam commissuri sitis gratificando aut favendo, ut precipuas ullius partes suscepisse videamini,
fortassis hoc loco precibus apud vos in me commendando eniterer
rationesque adducerem, quibus apud vos persuasum relinquerem
non hanc esse inter nos disceptationem susceptam quo ornamenta
31 vestium et coronam a patre relictam vehementius affectemus, sed
potius ut ipsum virtutis meritorumque nostrorum iudicium de
vobis vestrum excipiamus, quo et quantum quisque nostrum ad
integram perfectamque virtutem propius accesserit et pro sua modestia quantum apud vos acceptissimus sit vestra approbatione et
32 iudicio intelligamus. Iam ne esset quidem in me recta modestia
parumque me prudentem exhiberem, patres, si preter equitatem
non medios communesque arbitros sed partium hac in nostra
causa suffragatores vos futuros exposcerem aut expectarem: quam
quidem rem, patres, cum vos moris optimi atque omnis honestatis
observantissimos et religiosissimos novi, neque peto neque impe-
33 trari posse reor. Tantum, spero, hac vestra mirifica humanitate, ut
34 facitis, dicentes nos deinceps attentissime audietis. Quod si nostra
in disceptatione aliquid fortasse dicentibus nobis exciderit, quod
quidem severitati vestre parum convenisse videatur, petimus,
patres, non id studiis immoderatis vincendi sed concertantium

the most virtuous of the brothers. Yet being educated as gentlemen 28
and imbued with the finest character, they wished to avoid any
damaging contention or any public knowledge of even their slightest disputes. So they summoned the gravest and most upright elders of the family to hear each of them plead his case. On the ap- 29
pointed day, the elders convened, and the oldest son Mitio began
the following speech.

"I am convinced, gentlemen, that your affection for each of us is
so equally divided that neither my brothers nor I could desire further proof of the love that you bestow on us. And it is clear that, 30
in your innate justice and fairness, you would never do anything
that would make you seem to favor one or the other of us. Were
this not so, I might now strive, either by commending myself to
you with entreaties, or by adducing arguments, to convince you
that we have undertaken this debate, not because we greatly desire
our father's glorious garments and crown, but rather because we 31
want to hear your judgment of our merits and virtues. For from
this debate, we may in all modesty learn how nearly we attain to
pure and perfect virtue, and how acceptable each of us is to you.
Yet I would display false modesty and insufficient wisdom, gentle- 32
men, if I were to hope or to ask that you unfairly take sides in this
case, rather than act as impartial arbiters. Knowing your scrupulous observance of moral integrity, I neither ask this nor think I
could obtain it. I only hope that you will continue to hear us, as 33
you do, with your exceptional humanity and attention. And if in 34
this debate one of us should chance to utter anything inconsistent
with your gravity, gentlemen, we ask you to attribute it, not to
an immoderate desire for victory, but to the accepted custom of

non usquequaque improbate consuetudini adscribatis, siquidem inter ingenia paulo promptiora et ad dicendum parata agitari causa perraro aliqua sine vehementia potest.

35 'Dico, patres, eum fore me non ultimum de quo apud vos eam firmasse opinionem deceat, ut non me vestra singulari erga me
36 gratia et benivolentia indignum habendum censeatis. Vobis enim apud quos etatem vixi mea omnis vita satis cognita et perspecta est, ac meministis quidem ut ipse studiis rerum difficillimarum me ab ineunte etate omni assiduitate et perseverantia dederim perque etatem elaborarim ut cultu virtutum et industrie meritis annos meos exuperarem vestreque de nobis expectationi multo satisface-
37 rem; grataque vobis fuit mea erga vos observantia perpetuaque re-verentia, et quod patri obsequentissimus semper fuerim, quod eius voluntati morem gesserim, quod dictis volens ac lubens steterim
38 sepe collaudastis. Sed non illud ausim ullo in eiusmodi virtutum genere meis me fratribus anteferre commemorando: fuere et illi per etatem simili omni in laude eque digni benivolentia et admira-
39 tione. Sed a fortuna quidem propria mihi diversaque adiecta mate-ria extitit in qua omnem ipse virtutem expromerem atque exer-cerem: hanc igitur, reliquis nostris communibus meritis, patres, posthabitis, quam potero breviter recensebo, neque diffido, asse-quar ut me unicum primarium statuatis, quem totis animis beni-volentia et gratia prosequendum amplectendumque diiudicetis.

40 'Repetite, queso, memoria, patres, quenam mihi fuerit uxor, pre aliis importuna contumacique natura, mente inconstanti ac levi, lascivo ingenio atque petulco, animo denique elato ac nimium su-
41 perbo. An non quantum illius causa animo ipse pertulerim acerbi-tatis meministis? Mulierem rixosam, malignam, obstinatam! que ut primum nostris sub tectis successit, vos, patres, partim admira-tio illius petulantie et mee patientie, partim nostri misericordia
42 plurimum habebat. Missa facio que verba immoderata, inconside-rata, quas assiduas et acres obiurgationes, quas futiles et inanes expostulationes passim totis tectis et angiportis semper habebat

disputers. For minds which are ready and eager to debate can sel-
dom argue a cause without intense emotion.

"I maintain, gentlemen, that I am not the last person whom you   35
should judge as meriting your special favor and affection. As I   36
have lived my life among you, you are familiar with every aspect of
my life. You recall how since my earliest youth I have applied myself to the most difficult studies with great assiduity and perseverance. Through the years, I have striven to surpass my age in the
practice of virtue and the merits of my industry, and to satisfy
completely your expectations of me. You have welcomed my con-   37
tinual deference and reverence toward you; and you have often
praised me for my thorough obedience to my father, for my compliance with his wishes, and for my willing adherence to his commands. Yet I would not dare to claim superiority to my brothers   38
by rehearsing such virtues. For at every age they were equally deserving of affection and admiration. But my peculiar and diverse   39
fortune gave me additional material for expressing and exercising
my virtue. So, omitting our common merits, gentlemen, I shall
recount this matter as briefly as I can. I have no doubt that it will
cause you to judge me uniquely superior, and worthy to be embraced by everyone with affection and favor.

"I ask you, gentlemen, to recall my wife's character — her trou-   40
blesome and stubborn nature, her inconstant and fickle mind, her
wanton and aggressive temperament, and her haughty and proud
spirit. Do you remember how much bitter distress I bore on ac-   41
count of this quarrelsome, spiteful, and obstinate woman, and
how, when she first entered our house, you were overcome, both
with wonder at her impudence and my patience, and with compassion for me? I say nothing of her immoderate and inconsiderate   42
words, her incessant sharp reproaches, and her vain and pointless
remonstrations, with which this querulous woman relentlessly

43   querula mulier et importuna; missaque denique reliqua huiusmodi
facio quibus, ut videre licuit, sese illa mihi assiduam, duram atque
intractabilem obiectabat: longum ea esset referre atque, ni fallor,
odiosum atque a nostro instituto alienum, qui quidem ex vituperio
44   aliorum nobis laudem excerpere non aggredimur. Hoc affirmo:
animi mei equabilitate atque modestia omnes illius muliebres
(quod pauci volunt, rarissimi novere) ineptias ferendo sustuli, et—
quod vix credibile dictu est, quod et vos admirari solebatis—dicacem ipsam, asperam furibundamque mulierem placabilem, facilem
45   mansuetissimamque reddidi miris artibus. Et qua in re nullus
ferme inventus est maritus adeo maturi et bene compositi animi,
quin illico exasperetur precepsque ad iracundiam feratur, in ea me
re ita gessi, ut quid in me sit prudentie, equitatis, modestie ani-
46   mique roboris atque firmitatis probe ac pulchre explicarim. Neque
mea quidem huc in medium verebor gesta omnia adducere, quo
liquidius mee vivendi rationes studiaque virtutis aperta vobis atque
47   explicata relinquantur. Etenim si nullum dederis usque adeo turpe
dictu facinus quod audire nequeas honeste, cum loco ac tempore
proferatur, nostra procul dubio morum institutorumque aliorum
narratio erit haudquaquam aspernanda—siquidem ea huiusmodi
futura apud vos sit, ut neque his qui defuncti sunt neque nobis qui
in vita sumus, hac presertim in re in qua a culpa soluti et liberi
sumus, molestiam possit ullam ob infamie atque dedecoris notam
attulisse—quo ea minus equissimis a vobis animis audiantur.

48   'Ego, patres, cum esse in uxore mea servandi nominis et decoris
studii cureque minus quam nuptam et bene moratam matronam
deceat nossem, dies complures pro re animo ipse mecum consul-
tabam, ac ne apud alios quidem que animis volutarentur meis explicari posse commode arbitrabar measque esse sollicitudines istiusmodi intelligebam ut in obscuro et abdito contente nihil ad
lacessendum roboris aut virium haberent, palam autem exposite
dedecus ignominiamque propere essent allature, mecumque ita
49   disceptabam: "Enim et quonam potero id pacto uxori, quam mihi

filled the public squares and buildings. And I say nothing of other   43
similar actions by which, as all could see, she assiduously, harshly,
and intractably opposed me. It would be not only tedious to recount such things, but disagreeable to you, I believe, and foreign
to my purpose, for I do not seek to win praise by vilifying others.
But I will say this: I bore with equanimity and moderation such   44
female caprices as few men would wish to endure. Even more incredibly, as even you used to marvel, I converted this sharp-
tongued fury into a quiet and docile wife. In circumstances in   45
which practically no husband possesses enough maturity and self-
control to resist sudden exasperation and outbursts of rage, my
behavior was always governed by wisdom, fairness, moderation,
and strength of character. I shall not shrink from describing my   46
actions to you openly, so that my way of life and my pursuit of
virtue will be all the more apparent to you. Since no deed is so   47
shameful that it cannot be mentioned in an honorable context, you
will certainly not refuse to hear patiently an account of my character and conduct, especially since it will not disgrace anyone living
or dead, least of all myself, whose behavior in this regard was beyond reproach.

"Now, gentlemen, when I perceived that my wife took less care   48
for honor and decency than befits a married woman, I privately
reflected for several days. I thought it inconvenient to discuss
my thoughts with anyone else, for I knew that my worries were
such that they could do nothing to harm me if kept in the dark,
but that they would soon cause shameful disgrace if exposed
to the public. public. I debated with myself as follows: 'How could   49
I show my wife how unpleasant I found her behavior? If I

sint mores eius ingrati, ostendere? sin solam, seclusis arbitris, cas-
tigaro, facta dictaque sua obscena, ut par est, vituperaro, quid
50 egero? intolerabilem illico domi rixam excitaro. Irritata mulier, ut
levis est at pertinacis iracundie, indignatione et odiis excandescet,
omnem familiam furibunda exagitabit, audientur passim querimo-
nie, deplorationes, declamationes diem primum execrantis quo
primis hymeneis ad penates nostros adiit, apud quos non veluti
nupta apud virum frugi vivat, sed veluti vilissimum mancipium me
51 unum perferat cui sit uxoris omnis voluptas gravis. Quid preterea
si suos adeam? An non id erit omni ex parte incommodum ac in-
venustum? Quid ita? nempe quia, siquid incerti attulero, affines
artibus astutie a veterana et ex subsidiis opitulante matre mulieri
edocte, nostram iniquitatem et suspitionem incusanti, plus quam
52 nobis fidei adhibebunt. Iidemque, dum suorum ac domestica infamia erit gravis et permolesta, nihil se istiusmodi posse suis in rebus uspiam suspicari ostentabunt, ac morosi affirmabunt preter
me, qui eam in sua familia immeritam nominis turpitudinem inse-
ram, alium preterea fuisse repertum neminem, qui quidem usque
53 adeo impudenter suorum mores vituperarit; suosque denique
omnes dicent perpetua pudicitie laude claruisse casteque ac religiosissime sua in familia virgines in eam diem educatas, ut in quamvis
familiam ducte sint tum ob ceteras res tum maxime ob pudicitiam
insignem celebrentur.
54   '"Quid item si meo instituto perseverarim, ut uxori alienum a se
gerere me animum pre me feram? Quid tum illa? An non ut iniurias prosequatur, obstinata in dies novam in me suspitionum vim
excogitabit atque exaggerabit nostraque cura et sollicitudine ovans
55 totis fenestris et angiportu et trivio lasciviet? Denique esto id, ut
eam certis et manifestis indiciis esse impudicam apud me compertum habeam: quid ipse consilii capiam infelix? Utrumne et serie
56 rem suis atque ordine explicaro? Quidni? Immaturum id. Nam
dicent quidem neque primum me parili in causa neque solum fore
quem alienus solicitator affecerit, eoque redibunt ut admoneant ex

chastised her without witnesses, would that justly punish her in-
decent words and deeds? What would I have accomplished? I
would have stirred up an unbearable domestic quarrel. In her irri- 50
tation, this volatile woman would burn with relentless wrath and
indignant hatred. Everywhere one would hear complaints, laments,
and tirades, and she would curse the day when she wed me and
entered this house, where, instead of living like the wife of a man
of honor, she suffered like a vile slave whose master resented her
every pleasure. What, then, if I approached her family? Wouldn't 51
that prove entirely disagreeable and unpleasant? Why, you ask?
Because, if I could give them no certain proof, her kinsmen would
lend less credence to me than to my wife. And she, aided by her
veteran mother's crafty arts, would accuse me of suspecting her
unfairly. Since the disgrace of their own family members would
trouble and vex them, they would pretend to be incapable of
suspecting such a thing. They would peevishly assert that I was 52
the only one brazen enough to speak ill of their behavior, and to
cast unwarranted aspersions on their family name. They would 53
say that their family was celebrated for chastity, and that all
their young women received such a chaste and pious upbringing
that their remarkable purity made them desirable matches for any
family.

"Still, if I persisted in my resolve to treat my wife with reserve, 54
how would she act then? Would she obstinately continue to abuse
me, adding daily to the number of my suspicions? Would she ex-
ult in my cares and anxiety by running riot at our windows and in
the streets and squares? Or, supposing I had clear proof of her 55
promiscuity, alas, what course should I take? Should I explain the
situation to her family with gravity and in detail? Of course, that
would be inopportune. They would say that in such a case I was 56
neither the first nor the only man to be wronged by a seducer.

huiusmodi feminarum inconstantia et lascivia aliud ferme nullum exoriri incommodum, quam ut rumor aliquis sinistra in plebe exoriatur: hunc idcirco sibi recte consuluisse, siquis ille sit, qui nullam in iram ob id proruperit, ut rem sibi sua ineptia graviorem

57 fecisse postea sibi penitendum sit. Postremo edicent, siquid honori suo faveam, siquid item communibus laudibus et fame nostre esse prospectum velim, maximopere caveam ne is ipse sim qui quidem plebem tanti dedecoris testem fieri velim.

58 ‘"Quid igitur consilii tunc erit ut capiam? Impudicane vivet apud me et impunita uxor, ut per ignaviam meam insolentius in dies licentia abutatur? Quid si penas desumere instituerim? Du-

59 rum. Non enim sine solicitudine gravique molestia, non absque meo et fortunarum et capitis periculo rem ex animi sententia per-

60 ficere licuerit. Hoc sentio. Denique quid postremo cum penas de-derit? quid nobis emolumenti assequar preterquam ut cum mihi ab his omnibus, quibus erat illa cara, odium et inimicitias pararim, tum liberis meis hereditatis loco a matre turpe nomen atque in-

61 signem notam relictam doleam? Prestat igitur dissimulare, que vi-deas non videre, siquidem indomitum animal, ut aiunt, mulier frenari nusquam potest. Quid proderit curiositas ubi te nimium

62 investigasse peniteat? Quare prudentis mariti esse hoc statuo: tan-tum, quoad in se sit, uxori prestare occasionis ut, siquid illa forte sinistri animo susceperit, libere et absque molesto et dicaci aliquo

63 interprete sue queat libidini obtemperare. Si erit mens impudica, minori cum fame iactura peccabit; sin pudens et honesta, facilita-tem iterum atque iterum admirabitur atque virum castius amabit: conducetque delatores confutando et obaudiendo assuefacere ut minus eos delectet posthac de rebus incertis, mihi ingratissimis,

64 historias adornare. Nam cum apud me hominem haud omnino stolidum et tardissimum uxorem meam comiter et benigne non secus quam pudicissimam et probatissimam haberi oblocutores animadvertent, quis erit qui nostra in re uxoria plus maledicos

They would repeat their admonitions that women's infidelity and lust can be harmful only when nasty rumors arise among the populace. Hence, a prudent man would refrain from angry outbursts, lest he regret later that his folly had made matters worse. Finally, they would observe that if I sought to protect their honor 57 and to safeguard our common reputations, I should be the last to call public attention to such a disgrace.

"'What course was available to me, then? Should my wife live 58 with me unchaste and unpunished, each day abusing her freedom more insolently through my negligence? What if I resolved to punish her? That would be difficult. For I couldn't act as I wished 59 without grave worries and distress or without danger to my fortune and well-being. That much is clear. But even if she were 60 punished, what gain would be mine? Only this: I would arouse the hostility of those who love her, and leave my children their mother's notoriety as an inheritance. It would be better to dis- 61 semble, and not to see what I see. For like an untamed beast, they say, woman can never be bridled.[10] What good is inquisitiveness, when you only regret finding out too much? I think a prudent 62 husband will do what he can, if his wife should feel immoral impulses, to offer her opportunity to satisfy her lust freely and with no witnesses to bear tales. In this way, if her mind is not pure, she 63 will sin with little damage to your name. But if she is pure and upright, she will admire and cherish her husband's tolerance, and obey him. It will be useful to accustom informers, by refusing to hear them, to take less delight in embellishing unreliable and unpleasant tales. For when these slanderers see that I, who am by no 64 means dull or stupid, regard my wife as chaste and honest, can

quid conveniat intellexisse quam nos, quos in reliquis rebus solertes et perspicaces admodum novere, censeat?"

65   'Itaque istiusmodi mecum ipse disceptabam. Et quam precla-
rum hoc fuit consilium meum, quam equitatis, rationis atque
omni prudentia refertissimum! Tacendo dicacem, dissimulando

66   levem, cedendo importunam mulierem tuli. Et, superi optimi,
quante utilitates ex hoc uno honestissimo omnique molestia vacuo
consilio consecute sunt! Factum enim est ut de me uxor ita senti-
ret atque predicaret, hominem esse neminem quem eque ac me

67   omni officio merito prosequeretur. Idcirco sese, ac si mecum acre
amoris benivolentieque certamen suscepisset, facilem, tractabilem,
mansuetam mitemque exhibebat atque ad omne obsequium volens
ac lubens presto aderat, suaque de me apud notos commendatione,
quoad in se esset, consequebatur ut eorum erga me studiis addi

68   aut desiderari amplius nihil posset. Quave licentia se apud me
plurimum valere intelligebat, quantum videre licuit, ita utebatur ut

69   solis amatoriis preludiis facile contenta esse videretur. Id cum pers-
picue animadvertebam, in dies, ut par fuit, dedita opera uxori me

70   minime durum, minime tristem maritum exhibebam. Nam si me
in hanc difficilem virum prebuissem quacum dies ac noctes meam
fueram etatem acturus, sive spreta coniugis gratia quippiam per-
vestigassem quod, ut futurum quidem erat, refertissimum fuisset
acerbitatis, procul dubio adscribendum id quidem foret immani-
tati atque stultitie.

71   'Ea idcirco probe prudenterque omnia repetebam, que maritis
quibusque frugi animo infixa et insculpta gerenda sunt: natura femina leve, inconstans atque idcirco pronum et proclive ad omnem

72   lasciviam animal; in omnique mulierum genere deformem nullam
adeo reperies, que non plurimum opere, studii cureque ponat ut

73   oculis vulgi placeat seque demirari vehementer gaudeat; idque mulierum est ingenium, ut eum nequeat non diligere et magni pendere a quo admiretur: expectatissimam enim, dum spectatur,

anyone believe that he knows more about my marriage than I, whose cleverness and acumen in other matters are well known?'

"Thus I debated with myself. How excellent my resolve, how fair, rational, and prudent! I would meet my wife's sharp tongue with silence, her caprices with feigned ignorance, and her demands with compliance. Gracious gods, what benefits I reaped from this honest and painless resolution! It caused my wife to sense and to say that I deserved her respect more than anyone else. As if competing keenly with me in love and affection, she became agreeable, compliant, docile, and meek, and gladly obeyed me in everything. By praising me to our friends, she won from them the greatest possible devotion. And seeing that I allowed her considerable freedom, she seemed easily contented, as far as I could tell, with the mere overtures of her lovers. When I saw this, I strove each day to act like a mild and cheerful husband, as was just. For if I had been disagreeable to the woman with whom I was to spend my life, or had rejected her love in order to discover bitter facts, my behavior could only have been attributed to cruelty or stupidity.

"I therefore wisely bore in mind what every husband should hold fixed and emblazoned in his thoughts, namely, that by nature woman is a fickle and inconstant creature, and prone to all sorts of lust. In all the female sex, you'll find no woman so unattractive that she does not take great pains to please the public eye, nor take great pleasure in being admired. By nature, a woman can't help loving and respecting whoever admires her. When a

forme gratiam mulier sibi referri arbitratur et gaudet, in partemque muneris, dum contemplamur, deputat.

74 'Quidni igitur nobis secludenda omnis severitas fuit, patres, quandoquidem ubi secus egissemus in nos quam plurima incommoda redundassent, quando item ad honestissimam fortunarum commodorumque meorum rationem id pertinuit, quando iocunditatem voluptatemque attulit eo pacto discordiam domesticam evitasse, suorum gratiam servasse, famam tutasse, capitales inimicitias

75 seclusisse? In eoque prosequendo instituto omni ex parte probatissimo, quantum integros annos dum illa vitam agebat in me perseverantia temperando mihique imperando viguerit, quis id verbis

76 possit uspiam recensere? Ob oculos versabantur caterve amantium, videbam alternis vicibus interdiu noctuque assiduos ac veluti

77 statarios veteranos pudicitie expugnatores sectari, sollicitare. Ego vultus avertebam, oculos divertebam, os opprimebam, ex animo omnem tristem eius rei umbram expurgabam, quod ferendum

78 quidem erat ferebam. Neque deerant curiosiores aliqui nostra in re quam maturos gravesque viros conveniret, qui mihi pleraque om-

79 nia referrent que iampridem apud me erant notissima. Tum et non infrequentis occurrebant, partim ut me dicendo molestia afficerent, partim ut emulum quempiam in odium adducerent, qui quidem seu fictas seu veras fabulas, tamen ex composito, accuratissime referebant.

80 'Aderant preterea astutiores aliqui qui, cum aliis de rebus sermonem instituisse videri vellent, interiectis sententiunculis atque ambiguis dicteriis instigabant, ut mea esse causa id genus stigmatis

81 atque ironie prolatum facile intelligerem. Itaque omni ex parte excitabar, trahebar, impingebar ut in iram atque inconsultam aliquam vindicandi rationem irrumperem, quo graviorem et vulga-

82 tiorem aliquam infamiam inimicitiis iunctam subirem. Ego vero constans obfirmatique consilii, placabilitati, equabilitati, lenitati animi assuescebam. Nusquam delatorum commenta aut fabule tantum apud me valuere, ut aut mecum essem aut aliis videri

woman is looked at, she thinks that you desire her beauty, and she regards your gaze as a sort of tribute.

"I had therefore to shun all severity, gentlemen, for to act other- 74 wise would have been detrimental in many respects. It was clearly in the best interests of my fortune and advantage. In this way, I insured our pleasure and gaiety, avoided domestic strife, main- tained the favor of her family, guarded my reputation, and pre- cluded dangerous enmities. Who could adequately describe what 75 perseverance, moderation, and self-control I showed in adhering to this completely honorable resolve through all the years that she was alive? Before my eyes passed hosts of lovers, and I saw suitors 76 in continual succession both day and night courting and tempting my wife, and besieging her chastity like veteran soldiers. But I 77 looked the other way, kept silent, and purged my mind of even the semblance of gloom. In short, I bore what had to be borne. There 78 were some who, being more solicitous than befits mature and seri- ous men, reported facts which were already known to me. Not 79 infrequently they related in the greatest detail stories both real and imagined, hoping to vex me with their tales, or hoping to make some rival seem odious.

"Others were more clever. While ostensibly discussing other 80 matters, they goaded me with occasional observations and ambig- uous witticisms which made it clear that their barbs and ironies were aimed at me. From all quarters, I was aroused, urged, and 81 driven to burst into angry and reckless revenge, which would have caused me a great public disgrace attended by enmity. But true to 82 my firm resolution, I accustomed myself to being conciliatory, eq- uitable, and lenient. The inventions and tales of informers never

83 voluerim turbatior atque concitatior. Malam omnino iram inuti-
lemque indignationem totis viribus a me esse seclusam studui.
Etenim profecto sancte ipse mihi consulebam dum ita proseque-
bar, nulla in re uxori mee deesse, quo illa minus libidini usque sue
84 satisfaceret. Nam quo erat amplius nihil quod ab optimo amantis-
simoque viro uxor desideraret, eo perfacile adducebatur ut nollet
erga me minus esse quam cuperem modestissima.

85   'Sed iuvat pro mea vetere vite consuetudine hac in causa esse
quam remissus et parem moribus orationem habere, ut hactenus
vidistis, simplicem, sedatam nullisque lenociniis aut dicendi fuco
86 adornatam. Essent fortassis hoc loco aliqui gloriosiores qui rogarent: et ubinam maritum huiusmodi compertum dederis, ubi
tantum consilii et equitatis, mansuetudinis, placabilitatis, modestie, perseverantie, firmitudinis roborisque animi vigeat, ut iniquam,
ineptam, arrogantem insolentissimamque mulierculam domi be-
87 nigne ac comiter annos integros ferret? An facile reperiri poterit
vir huiusmodi qui constantem peremnemque in degenda vita rationem, multis adversantibus, infinitis in diversas partes suspitionum animum trahentibus, non deserat, sed ordine et modo in
suscepto instituto perseveret, neque se quoquam distrahi patiatur,
quo infamie aut rumoris ad se aditus patefiat, tacendo, ferendo,
dissimulando sibique imperando nihil commiserit, quominus pru-
88 dens aut bene consultus videretur? Ex quo plane effectum sibi sit,
ut festinum precepsque consilium aspernasse uspiam non penitue-
rit, ac dicendum quidem postea nusquam fuerit: "non fore a me
89 hoc admissum mallem." Grandia hec, patres, atque perrara. Nam
ceteri quidem, tame⟨t⟩si graves et compositi mariti, omni tamen
vel minima suspitione excrucientur: si spectat uxor, si spectant, si
gestiunt amantes—gravem et sibi et his cum quibus degunt vitam
90 agunt. Me neque levissimi uxoris gestus neque muliebris petulantia et impudentia commovere unquam, ut in animo sinistra aliqua
91 de coniuge suspitio intumesceret. A me istas omnes ineptas male
consultorum hominum curas abdicavi: putavi uxorem eiusmodi

succeeded in making me show others distress or anger. For I sum- 83
moned all my strength to refrain from baneful wrath and pointless
indignation. I religiously protected my own interest by affording
my wife every opportunity of satisfying her lust. Since my wife 84
could have asked for nothing more of such an excellent and affec-
tionate husband, she was easily led to practice as much moderation as I desired in her.

"I think it best to observe my long-standing custom of being 85
mild, and to suit my speech to my character, keeping it simple,
sedate, and unadorned by the artificial embellishments of rhetoric.
At this point, some vainglorious persons might ask: 'Where can 86
you show me a husband so prudent, fair, tolerant, moderate, and
strong-willed that he can abide for so many years a woman so unreasonable, arrogant, and insolent? Can it be easy to find a man 87
who never departs from his constant and perennial rules of conduct despite many obstacles and countless reasons for suspicion
and distress; a man who perseveres in his adopted plan and never
lets scandalous rumors distract him; or a man whose silence, for-
bearance, dissimulation, and self-control guarantee his reputation
for prudence and judiciousness? As a result, he never regrets his 88
course of action as hasty or rash, or says that he wished he had
not acted so?' These are indeed great achievements, gentlemen, 89
and most rare. Other husbands, even the most serious and sedate,
are tormented by the least suspicion. If a wife glances about, or is
glanced at, or if she acts elated, they make life miserable for themselves and for those who live with them. But I was never led by my 90
wife's fickle deeds or by her womanly impudence to harbor omi-
nous suspicions in my mind. Abjuring the foolish worries of 91
imprudent men, I thought of my wife was as I wished her to be,

esse ut volebam, et volens tuli quam habebam. Hoc qui contra fecerit delirat.

92 'Quod si maiore dicendi copia quispiam hunc locum exornasse
93 cupiat, novi quo suas dicendi vires ostentaturus sit. Mitto cetera:
eo deveniet ut affirmet castris armorumque expeditionibus, ubi
primas sibi fortuna partis vel magis quam virtus ipsa vendicat,
unam diem vel potius horam, unicum consilium, unam tantum
operam, solam unam victoriam omnem solere vitam fama nomi-
94 nisque claritate gloriosam reddere. At nobis longos annos singu-
losque per dies opere omnes, cuncta consilia perpetuaque certatio
ad virtutem fuit exposita: pro rerum enim eventu, pro fortune vo-
lubilitate, pro periculorum magnitudine consilia nobis ex tempore
innovata, impetus rerum adversarum summa vi et viribus excep-
tus, peiora siqua imminebant evitata; cara queque aderant integra
et intacta servata a me sunt summa industria, incredibili diligentia,
maximo labore plurimisque vigiliis.

95 'Qua sua propriaque in laude alius fortassis huiusmodi quis-
96 piam gloriaretur. Ad accumulandamque gloriam quam faceret
quod non manu aut presidiis multitudinis, non temporibus obse-
cundantibus, non locis iuvantibus, non favente publica urbis aut
privata cuiusquam fortuna, non extrinsecus petita virtute precla-
rum hoc facinus confecisset, sed suis auspiciis, suo ductu, sua bene
directa et deducta vite ratione, suo integro et probe acto officio,
solus unus ipse omnia hec — fortune iniquitatem, malos de se ru-
mores, surgentem increbrescentemque infamiam — suppresserit,
97 cohibuerit, extinxerit suis ingenii viribus animeque virtute! Et
haud scio an his omnibus postponendum sit quod sine imperio et
severitate mulieris ineptias coercuerit, temerarie libidinem frenarit,
98 arrogantis insolentiam atque immanitatem mitigarit. Similia his
plurima qui eloquentia delectaretur amplificande laudis sue gratia
99 suique ponendi facinoris in admirationem adduceret. Mihi autem
ita visum est plus nihil quam simplex nudumque meritum nostrum exponere in medium, quo in tota mea oratione hanc spem de

and gladly accepted her as she was. Anyone who acts otherwise is mad.

"Should someone wish to embellish this theme with greater eloquence, I know what rhetorical forces he would muster. To omit other topics, he would proceed to assert that in armed camps and expeditions, when fortune is more powerful than virtue, a single day or hour, a single deed or decision, or a single victory suffices to immortalize a man's fame. But in my case, entire years, each single day, all efforts, every decision — all were an incessant struggle devoted to virtue. Hour by hour, I renewed my resolve according to the course and extent of events, I repulsed with manly strength the onslaughts of adversity, I avoided the dangers which threatened me, and I defended all that I held dear with great industry, incredible diligence, immense labor, and countless vigils.

"Another man might perhaps boast it as his personal praise, and consider it an enhancement of his glory, that his achievements required no popular support, no favorable circumstances, no public or private fortunes, and no one else's virtues. He might say that his excellence lay in having overcome and suppressed the disgraceful scandal of unjust fortune through his own abilities and his dutiful conduct. And perhaps he would give equal importance to the fact that, even without discipline and without severity, he checked his wife's follies, bridled her lusts, and restrained her arrogant insolence and brutishness. Those who delight in rhetoric can find many similar points to swell their praise and to arouse admiration. But I have thought it best merely to expound my simple and unadorned merits. Throughout my speech, I have held the hope and

92
93

94

95
96

97

98

99

vobis habui, ut mihi ipsi persuaserim in vobis, patres, egregiam fore prudentiam mirificumque tantum ingenium ut, nullis ornamentis dicendi siquid emeritus sum, modo id palam prolatum sit, facile a vobis hoc impetrasse possim, ut honestiorem, quod expecto, vestris sententiis redditum me congratuler.'

100   Cum perorasset Mitio, tum Acrinnus inter fratres medius natu quam potuit maximis laudibus Mitionem extulit facilitatemque atque humanitatem, in qua se frater tantopere exercuisset, paci atque quieti domestice futuram accommodatissimam sperare se 101 attestatus est. Ac non dedecere quidem affirmavit ut, qui propter etatem in patris locum fratribus relictus sit, huic reliqua omnia dignitatis auctoritatisque coniuncta ornamenta commodentur; verum oratum a se fratrem velle esse secum usque consideret istorum utrum approbet factum.

102   'Uxorem, frater, levem, elatam, contumacem atque acrem habuisti. Mihi item evenit ut coniugem insolentem, preposteram, 103 efferatam pervicacemque experirer. Ac nobis quidem, patres, defuncte quoque uxoris mee argumentandi gratia vitam moresque recensere, queso, liceat. Tametsi quid est quod hac in re, mi frater, 104 propriam nobis aliquam contigisse fortunam deputem? Commune hoc innatumque mulierum generi vitium: est lasciva, inconstans, 105 importuna, superba, querula, procax, pertinax. Tunc enim propria et a communi sorte aliena marito fortuna obtigisset, ubi congratulari superis liceret quod apud se modesta, facilis ac nequicquam in ferendis disseminandisque in familia odiis ac dedecore dedita 106 conviveret! Rarum hoc, mi frater, inauditum. Neque est mulierum moris amicitias carasque concordias animorumque coniunctiones, quoquo media consideat loco, non discidisse, disturbasse, disper-107 disse. Id itaque si pervestigasse iuvat, fortassis evenit partim quod natura est ad flagitium femina propensa, prona et percupida, partim quod equanimitatem equabilitatemque mentis illarum assiduis et percallidis insimulationibus obsessis viris servare perdifficile est.

conviction, gentlemen, that you possess such wisdom and such intelligence that, even without rhetorical ornaments, my merits will by themselves cause you to pronounce a verdict which, I expect, will ennoble me."

When Mitio had finished his peroration, the second brother 100 Acrinnus extolled him in the highest terms of praise, and voiced his hopes that the humanity and tolerance which Mitio had so fully displayed would foster the peace and tranquility of their house. He added that, since his brother had assumed the role of 101 father to them, it was fitting that he should receive the rest of their father's tokens of dignity and authority. Nevertheless, he asked his brother to consider with him whose actions merited approbation.

"You certainly had a fickle, proud, defiant, and harsh wife, my 102 brother. But I too endured an insolent, wrongheaded, fierce, and obstinate wife. Gentlemen, I ask your leave to give an account of 103 my late wife's behavior for the sake of my case. Yet is there any reason, my brother, to think that our adverse fortune was peculiar to us? Such innate vice is common to all womankind. Every 104 woman is wanton, inconstant, troublesome, proud, querulous, shameless, and stubborn. Indeed, a husband would meet with a 105 peculiar and unusual fortune if he were allowed to thank the gods that he lived with a modest and indulgent wife who was not given to creating and spreading hatred and disgrace in his family. Such a thing is rare and unheard of, my brother. The character of women 106 leads them to disjoin friendships, to disrupt cherished concord, and to disperse bonds of sympathy. If we are pleased to examine 107 the reasons for this, it may be in part that woman is by nature prone and partial to vice, and in part that it is nearly impossible to maintain our equanimity and equability when we are beset by

108 Ita fit ut, cum hec odiis disseminandis nunquam defatigatam se
exhibeat, hic tum interea concussus commoveatur et corruat.

109 'Enimvero, mi frater, tulisti vagam, futilem, ludibundam. Ego
duram, asperam, semper tristi supercilio extuantem, nunquam ad
obganniendum, ad contumelias inferendas non alacrem et arma-

110 tam pertuli. Tuo ex consilio fateor te fructus istos assecutum, mi
frater, quietem, tranquillitatem in familia gratiamque apud coniugis affines; res autem difficiles, graves molestasque, veluti discor-

111 diam familiarem, odia inimicitiasque fortassis evitasti. Apud me
autem plus fame nominisque tuendi cura quam que recensuisti —
omnia aspera et acerbissima — valuit. Primas enim voluptatum

112 mearum omnium partes dedi honori, dedi fame nominique. Atqui
apud me quid est quod me ita fecisse pigeat ne adhuc quidem
constat, neque me viri fortis officio functum fuisse parum unquam

113 delectabit. In eo tua fuit cura exposita, ut nollet, mea ut nequiret
uxor dedecore suo familie nostre candorem splendoremque conta-
minare aut offuscare.

114 'Quibus in rebus uter tandem sibi nostrum rectius consuluerit,
non est ut longius apud hos viros sapientissimos contendamus.

115 Etate enim et usu quenam sit in muliebri sexu volubilitas, quantum nequitie, quid perfidie, quantum denique temeritatis et audacie satis ipsi quidem novere; neque eos preterit a primis usque
annis eo esse ingenio preditas mulierculas eaque cum mente ado-
lescere ut omne suum studium, operam, diligentiam, omnes conatus, omnes cogitationes, omnes postremo sensus hac una in re
consumant, ut lascivie artibus et incontinentie studiis placeant.

116 Quod si illud requiras ut optatissima et maiorem in modum dul-
cissima Veneris furta ad que totis animis contendunt potiri negligat, si sapis, non tu illi peccandi potestatem et licentiam dederis,

117 sed penitus ademeris. Namque plures, que negent, mulieres offendes, dum sue obtemperare libidini nequeant, quam si queant.

118 Etenim si que asservantur id elaborant ut animum ex sententia

their continual crafty accusations. Thus, while a wife never tires of   108
spreading hatred, her husband is convulsed and collapses.

"Very well, brother. You endured an inconstant, unreliable, and   109
mischievous wife. But I endured a harsh and bitter wife who was
always seething with grim pride and was never slow to snarl insults at me. Dear brother, I grant that your resolve bore fruits such   110
as peace and tranquility in your family, and the favor of her relations, and that you avoided burdensome difficulties such as family
strife, hatred, and enmity. But I was more concerned with preserv-   111
ing my name and reputation than with the bitter unpleasantries
which you have recounted. I have never seen any reason to regret   112
my actions, and shall always delight in manly and dutiful behavior.
We both prevented our wives' disgraceful behavior from defiling or
staining the family's spotless honor. But while you took care that   113
your wife *would* not do so, I took care that mine *could* not.

"To decide which of us chose the better course, we need   114
not contend any longer before these wise judges. From their age   115
and experience, they are well aware of the volubility, baseness,
treachery, and audacity of the female sex. Nor has it escaped
them that women are disposed, from early youth and adolescence,
to direct all their zeal, diligence, and energies, all their thoughts,
and all their senses to pleasing men by their wanton charms
and promiscuity. If you seek to make them abandon Venus' sweet   116
and desirable stolen pleasures, which they strive to obtain with all
their souls, then you must not grant them license to sin, but completely take it away. You'll find more women who refuse their   117
charms when they can't obey their lust, than when they can.
If women strive to satisfy their longings even when they are   118

compleant, quarum id erit arbitrii ut queque collibuerint possint, an non loco ille ut licebit volent?'

119   Itaque huiusmodi in rebus comparandis Acrinnus pleraque accuratissime bellissimeque disseruit, que prolixum esset hoc loco

120 enumerare. Postremo, ut reliqua omittam, ab his senibus qui arbitri considebant cepit exposcere ut memorie repeterent quam illa ipsa fuerint patri ornamenta in virtutis premium a patria dedita;

121 quod si virtutem a labore, a sudore, a vigiliis nunquam fuisse seiunctam intelligerent, a re ipsa coniecturam caperent atque diiudicarent cuinam provincia laboriosior fuerit, remissone huic et cessanti, an potius sibi qui maxima vigilantia incredibilique diligentia sese custodem in ea re assiduum prestiterit, pro qua servanda tuendaque qui rem, operas, sanguinem vitamque exposuerint, opinione consensuque omnium merito collaudentur.

122   Que cum dixisset, Trissophus, natu inter fratres minor, acri ferocique ingenio adolescens, subridens patres cepit orare ne istiusmodi comptam et ornatam a se eloquentiam expectarent, qua magis ut gesta honestarent sua, quam ut ad victoriam agerent, fratres fuisse prolixiores sibi viderentur; sed non se illos multa conatos et

123 quod optarint dicendo parum assecutos laudare. Qui enim extu fluctuum exagitati maris incommoda perstrenue et animo infracto pertulisse glorientur, non hi quidem animi virtutem suam magis laudant quam consilii stultitiam vituperant, quod equoris perfidie

124 et undarum instabilitati credideri⟨n⟩t. Pari ratione qui dixerit 'coniugis cum qua mihi vivendum esset insolentiam lenis tacitusque tuli,' non is quidem suam demonstrat probitatem potius quam ut imprudentiam delaudet qua gravem isthanc sponte sua subierit sortem.

125   Itaque aiebat Trissophus gratum idcirco sibi iampridem suum fuisse consilium, quod quidem fratres dicendo effecerint ut hodierna die vehementius approbaret, a quibus id ita esse apertius intellexisset, ut esse hactenus arbitrabatur: fratribus, dum sue secum in vita uxores adfuerint, animi letitiam aut vacuitatem a

closely watched, won't they choose to do so when they are free to do as they please?"

Employing such comparisons, Acrinnus made many fine and detailed observations, which it would be tedious to recount here. To omit the rest, he began at last to entreat the elderly judges to recall the nature of the tokens which the state had awarded his father. If they reflected that virtue involved toil and tireless care, they would readily decide who had performed the more arduous task—his remiss and lenient brother or he himself? For, having proved a diligent guardian of incredible vigilance, and having risked life, limb, and property in order to protect his family, he would rightly be praised by everyone's unanimous judgment.

When he had spoken, the youngest brother Trissophus, a youth of keen and ardent intellect, smiled and asked the judges not to expect such elegant and ornate eloquence from him. Indeed, his brothers' prolixity seemed to him more intent on glorifying their past deeds than on winning victory. He could not praise them, for their speeches had attempted too much and accomplished too little. For those who boast that they have faced with indomitable courage the dangers of a tempestuous sea do not so much praise their virtue as condemn their folly in trusting themselves to the treachery of the sea and the inconstancy of the waves. By the same logic, when a man says, "I endured in mild silence the insolence of the wife with whom I had to live," he is not demonstrating his virtue, but deploring his imprudence in choosing such a miserable condition.

Trissophus said that he had always been content with his own resolve, and that his brothers' speeches today caused him to commend it even more strongly. He now understood more clearly what he had thought before. As long as their wives were alive, his

119

120

121

122

123

124

125

297

126 merore relictam fuisse nullam. Et se idcirco dignum putasse laude qui annis plus decem, non ut fratres voluntariam et sponte suscep-tam erumnam, sed procul dubio omnium laboriosissimam et pernecessariam provinciam exercuerit, a quo tamen officio, quod honestissimum fructuosissimumque esset, neque suasionibus ne-que precibus neque minis neque vi aliqua cedendum esse uspiam duxerit, ac suam quidem, quam non unica muliercula sed univer-sus prope mortalium cetus temptarit, patientiam et firmitatem

127 omnium maximam et longe incredibilem extitisse. Hinc enim pa-rentes, illinc fratres reliquique domestici suadendo, iubendo rogan-doque, ne uxorem ducere diutius recusaret, iterum atque iterum adstitisse, neque defuisse qui minitarentur, si in ea sententia sua perseveraret, fore ut intelligeret pro incognito haberi se Trisso-

128 phum a patre atque alienum. 'Accedebant affines, conveniebant cognatorum caterve, audiebantur convicini, ornabantur familiares qui et serio et mediis in iocis atque voluptatibus sermones de re uxoria introducerent.

129 'Denique et noti et ignoti omnes circum obsidebant, obstrepe-bant, contendebant ut hoc familie nostre pro patris expectatione, pro amicorum desiderio, pro meo officio boni et obtemperantis filii munus darem, ne me inexorabilem hac in re, ne durum, ne pervicacem preberem.'

130 Itaque non sibi quidem a domestica vexatione fuisse ad convi-cinos et familiares profugium tutum neque locum satis adeo sibi

131 molestia vacuum quo se abderet uspiam fuisse relictum; ita et tri-viis et angiportis et theatris et templis publicisque omnibus atque privatis diversoriis omnes ferme mortales quasi dedita opera certa-tim rem uxoriam suadendo in eaque molestia sese exercendo peni-tus dignos odio passim offendisse, offirmate tamen in eos semper

132 sese habuisse sapientie. Etenim cum et hanc marito benignissimo et amantissimo nuptam et hanc alteram mirifica inauditaque custodia observatam non usquequaque matrimonii iura et con-nubii religionem servasse animadvertisset, sed alteram inexplebili

brothers knew neither joy nor leisure. Thus, he regarded himself 126
as praiseworthy, since for more than ten years he had avoided the
voluntary misery of his brothers. Instead, he had chosen important and laborious pursuits, so honorable and rewarding that no
arguments, no entreaties, and no threats could persuade him to
abandon them. Although his patience and fortitude had been tried
not by one woman, but by all of human society, they had proved
incredibly great. His parents, brothers, and other relatives contin- 127
ually urged, ordered, and begged him to marry. Some of them had
threatened that, if he did not change his mind, his father would
consider him a stranger rather than a son. "My kinsmen ap- 128
proached me, my cousins gathered in groups, my neighbors spoke
up, and my friends exhorted me, introducing the subject of marriage amid their sports and pleasures.

"In short, friends and strangers alike besieged and deafened me, 129
pressing me to fulfill my obligation to the family, and to do what
my father expected, what my friends desired, and what my duty as
an obedient son required, without acting harshly or stubbornly."

Neither friends nor neighbors afforded Trissophus any relief 130
from his domestic vexations, and there was no place to which he
could flee from such importunities. In streets and squares, in the- 131
aters and temples, and in all public and private buildings, nearly
everyone competed in urging him to take a wife, and harassed him
odiously. But he always adhered to his unyielding wisdom. He had 132
observed that neither this wife married to a generous and devoted
husband, nor this wife subjected to extraordinary surveillance,
respected the sacred laws and obligations of marriage. For the

flagrantique libidine preditam in dies novo amatore delectari, alteram nullo posse metu coerceri quin genitale impudentia sua thorum commacularet, id se Trissophus suscepisse instituti in animum aiebat, ut quidvis a patre potius quam uxorem posset

133   perpeti; in ea tamen expostulatione parentes atque fratres sibi ferendos visos fuisse, ut plane pertulit, animo nequicquam molesto aut acerbo. Cum huiusmodi complura disputasset, tandem porrecta manu:

134   'An non, o fratres — eos contuens inquit —, me vobis eum prebui cuius modestiam lenitatemque et mansuetudinem dignam duceretis admiratione, siquidem pro tanto vestro in me tedio neque apud vos neque apud mortalium quemquam turbatior uspiam vi-

135   deri volui? Cum sat superque esse statuebam multas et prelongas conciones vestras unicis verbis refellere, "uxorem non duco," cumque ceteras complures et imprimis has ipsas quas adduxi rationes

136   consulto obticebam. Noveram quidem quenam subinde vestre future fuissent argumentationes: huiusmodi — "Non tibi quidem sortem, o noster frater, quam nobis equiorem obtigisse volumus."

137   Sic, opinor, respondissetis. Eratque et ineptum et incommodum futurum si que tu partim odisti fugistique nosse, Mitio, partim clare atque dilucide ex te didiceras et probe tenebas, enuntiassem.

138   Tibi autem omnium diligentissimo ac perspicacissimo, Acrinne, de uxore adduci nihil posse arbitrabar, quod tibi ulla esset ex parte incognitum aut non usque iampridem clarum dilucideque perspectum.

139   'At vos, patres, quidnam censetis, nostrum an potius fratrum meorum rectius fuisse consilium? Tu, Mitio, ne obtundentis muliercule ineptias domi perferres, quid egisti? Apud extraneos ingrata et iniocunda pleraque de te audire tulisti perparum moleste.

140   At Acrinnus noster, quidnam? Ne in coronis civium de te quippiam illepidum recenseretur, intra lares penates infinitam discor-

141   diam assiduosque tumultus confovisti. Videor iam nunc videre, ut illius presentia commovebar, bacchantem totis tricliniis mulierem,

former was overcome by insatiable lust and took new lovers daily, while the latter, being checked by no fear, shamelessly defiled the marriage bed. Trissophus said that he had therefore decided to obey his father in everything but in taking a wife. And he resolved 133 to bear the expostulations of his parents and brothers without annoyance or rancor. Having spoken at length in this vein, Trissophus stretched forth his hand, and, looking at his brothers, said:

"Haven't I displayed admirable moderation, mildness, and gen- 134 tleness toward you, my brothers? Despite all your wearisome objections, I never seemed vexed by you or anyone else. I thought it 135 sufficient to rebut your many lengthy speeches simply by saying 'I shall not take a wife,' and I purposely kept silent instead of offering the reasons which I have just adduced. I knew what arguments 136 you would use to counter me, such as: 'We don't want you, dear brother, to enjoy a better condition than our own.' Just so. I think, you would have answered me. As for you, Mitio, I would have 137 been a troublesome fool if I had told you what you learned so painfully and knew so clearly. And you, diligent and perceptive 138 Acrinnus, could I teach you anything about marriage which was not already familiar and clear to you?

"I ask you to judge, gentlemen: who has acted more wisely, my 139 brothers or I? What did you do, Mitio, to avoid the follies of a nagging wife? You bore the unpleasant gossip of strangers. And 140 what about our dear Acrinnus? In order to prevent disagreeable remarks in public circles, you bred infinite strife and continual tumult in your home. Even now, I seem to see how your wife, as if 141 present, runs riot in your dining room, accuses her fortune,

hominum deorumque deplorantem iniquitatem, accusantem fortunam seseque inculpantem quod diutius possit huiuscemodi in vita
superstes esse, quod lucem tantamque suam intueri miseriam non
oderit; neque se et dote et forma sua id tantisper meruisse, ut se
142   fratris uxor omni felicitatis genere exsuperet: "Vivit illa et solute et
libere, ego multo quam vilissimum mancipium conditione versor
deteriori, cui quidem nedum proloqui et confabulare, ut ceteris
ingenuis, sed nec spectare quidem nec ridere nec complorare nec
denique tussire ex arbitrio liceat."

143   'En vestras laudes, o fratres, en fructus consilii vestri! Sed non
hic insisto. Consilii autem nostri qui fuere fructus, superi boni?
144   Principio quidem id me assecutum letor ut cum mulier nulla nostra facilitate novis in dies sectatoribus se prostituerit, tum et nulla
operam ob meam duritiem dederit ut sua voluptate et mea ignomi-
145   nia de nobis vindictas sumeret. Illudque postremo a nostris laribus
longe abfuisse fortune mee congratulor, quod per me introducta
nulla est que plures infamie et libidini sue opem auxiliumque pre-
bentium familias nostro sumptu pasceret.

146   'Sed missa hec faciamus. Tandem esto, Acrinne: non patrum
istorum sententia (nunquam enim, si satis eos novi, tam iniqui
iudices erunt), sed quovis alio pacto ornamenta tibi hec occuparis
superisque volentibus tu patrem ab inferis excitatum ornatus offenderis rogatusque ut scelus honestares, ita patri ea tibi ob istas
147   quas attulisti causas fuisse adiudicata diceres. Quid censes? num
parum exclamaret, an non voce maxima pater istorum iniquitatem
148   detestaretur? "Siccine—inquiens—ornamenta hec, o patres, que
patria mee virtuti premium contribuit, que universa civitas sue
in me beneficentie meritorumque meorum quasi testificationem
quandam fore collata voluere, quibusque me senatus populusque
Lacenas, cuncti civium ordines, ob pericula, ob labores, ob vigilias,
ob propulsatum inimicorum impetum, ob libertatem, otium, quietem tranquillitatemque meis civibus a me servatam condecoravit,

bewails the injustice of gods and men, and berates herself for tolerating such a miserable life. Surely, her dowry and beauty deserved a better reward than seeing her brother's wife much happier in marriage: '*She* lives in complete license, but I am treated worse 142 than a vile slave, not free to converse, exchange glances, laugh, weep, or even cough.'

"These are your merits, my brothers, and the fruits of your 143 resolutions. I shall not dwell on them. But, good gods, what were the fruits of my wisdom? First of all, I may rejoice that no woman 144 has taken advantage of my indulgence to prostitute herself daily with new lovers, and none has avenged my severity to her pleasure and to my disgrace. I thank my fortune for sparing my home from 145 a woman who would have nourished at my expense a host of scapegraces and panders.

"But let us leave this topic. Let us suppose, Acrinnus, that 146 somehow you usurped these tokens—though not by the decision of our elders, for I know that they could not judge so unjustly— and that, with the aid of the gods above, you should be dressed in these garments and should meet our father raised from the dead. Were he to ask you to justify your crime, would you say that the tokens were awarded you for the reasons you have cited? What do 147 you think? Wouldn't he cry out and denounce the injustice of these judges? 'Gentlemen,' he would say, 'is this how you dispose 148 of the tokens which my country awarded me for my virtue, which the entire city voted me as a witness to my meritorious deeds, and which the Spartan senate and people, and every order of citizens, bestowed on me, in return for my perils and labors, for my vigilance, for repulsing enemy attacks, and for safeguarding the peace and liberty of my fellow citizens? Do you award them to a man

vosne, o patres, ea adiudicastis insignia homini huic qui suspitioni-
bus suis ineptaque et futili curiositate otium, quietem domesticam
funditus sustulit, sibique servilem quandam seque ac nostra fami-
149   lia indignam conditionem imposuit? An tu is es, fili, quem natum
arbitrabar ad glorie claritatem, ad nominis posteritatem, ad optime
150   de patria promerendum? Tune, fili, preter meam civiumque nostrorum de te expectationem operas ingeniumque tuum in servanda
huiusmodi inquieta inconstantique muliercula turpiter perdidisti?"

151   'Hec ubi longum pro rei indignitate deplorasset pater, unum
te, Acrinne, puto intueretur rogaretque et quanam virtutis laude
quibusve meritis fretus ipsa moveare petere ornamenta, siquidem
cogitationum institutorumque tuorum primos ultimosque tuos
omnes conatus inutili quadam acerbissimaque in re consumpseris.
152   Sin tua diligentia non peccavit mulier, si observando, coercendo
continendoque functus mariti officio extitisti, an tandem idcirco
153   huiusmodi te ornamenta regia promeruisse gloriabere? Sin autem
et tempora et ipsum te, dum quasi pedisequus servus muliebrem
inconstantiam sectabaris, perdere dedecebat, tunc a tua ignominia
154   exordirere! Denique uxor si peccavit, quisnam erit qui tuam in ea
re diligentiam et vigilantiam probet, aut quemnam illius probrum
et vitium quam mulierem ipsam fedasse diiudicabimus? Quid igi-
155   tur? Vanam falsamque isthanc tibi gloriam usurpas. "Ac malo quidem, filii," postremo diceret pater, "operam, ingenium, industriam
156   studiumque vestrum maioribus in rebus exponatis. Ab more est
viri presertim frugi et bene consulti, quales vos esse opto, isthic
pendere atque insistere scrutando, pervestigando, indagando quam
longum et apud quos et quo in loco, quo in tempore levis fallaxque
femina, ut sunt omnes, rideat atque confabuletur."

157   'Quid tu, Mitio? demum a patre cum hec dicta percepisses,
158   quanam auderes fronte ipsa exposcere ornamenta? Illicne hereres,
ut hactenus: "importunam, contumacem amaramque mulierem,
sedatam, affabilem mitemque effeci confecique ut omni suo in
sermone optimum esse maritum me vulgo predicaret; nulle eius

whose suspicions and foolish meddling have completely destroyed his domestic peace and quiet, and who has basely enslaved himself and his household? Are you the son whom I thought destined to   149 glorious fame, to immortal repute, and to meritorious service to our republic? Contrary to my own hopes and those of our citi-   150 zens, my son, have you ignobly wasted your time and talent in guarding this fickle and unstable wife.'

"After such lengthy and just laments, I think our father would   151 look at you alone, Acrinnus. He would ask what laudable deeds and merits had led you to claim these tokens, when in fact you had spent all your thoughts and plans on a worthless and despi- cable endeavor. If your diligence thwarted your wife's sins, and if   152 your duty as a husband lay in surveillance, restraint, and repres- sion, why do you boast that you merit these tokens? But if you   153 shamefully wasted your years in waiting on a fickle woman like a lackey, why do you begin your plea by describing your dishonor? If   154 your wife has sinned, how can we praise your untiring vigilance? Has her crime defiled anyone but herself? What then? The glory that you vaunt is vain and false. 'My sons,' our father would say, 'I   155 would rather see you devote your talents, industry, and enthusiasm to more important matters. It is inconsistent with the character of   156 an honest and prudent man to spend his time in discovering when, where, and with whom a fickle and deceitful woman laughs and talks.'

"And you, Mitio, if you heard our father speak so openly, would   157 you brazenly dare to demand his tokens? Would you stick to your   158 previous argument? 'I made my insolent and troublesome wife af- fable and gentle, so that she publicly praised me as the best of

ineptie, quanquam esset procax, apud me tantum potuere ut
159 in iram prorumperem?" "O idcirco meritum quam maximum et
admirabile! O mirificam virtutem! O civem ad gloriam, ad se, ad
familiam patriamque nobilitandam natum, qui quidem amenti in-
fandeque mulieri gratificari et in ea re mariti belli nomen nancisci
160 ad summam gloriam, ad summum viri officium ducit! Tu si cum
isthac temulenta muliere animo pacato et acclivi convixisti, profecto haud satis te habuisse stomachi declaras, aut si virum fuisse
te nondum fugerat, dum ita in eam eras affectus ut benivolentie
officiis cum ea tibi paratam certationem arbitrareris, illa prorsus
161 maligna atque adeo iniqua non erat; si autem natura fortassis facilis affabilisque illi fuerat, non ea de re id tue tu tibi adscribito,
nate, laudi atque te in ea futili et inepta re extollas, quod paulum
exasperantem coniugem levi cura tolerasti."
162 'Itaque his, ni fallor, apud vos dictis longeque gravioribus pater
uteretur. Sed non omnia prosequor. Cupio apud vos viros sanctissimos disputator videri minime immodestus, in fratres presertim
quos eque atque ipsum me amo; atque virtutis mee non minus
quam benivolentie gratia, ipsi ut me ament perpetuo, ut hactenus
163 peregi, contendam. Sed de meis meritis, ne longius provehar, hoc
tantum a me non usquequaque fore pretermissum iuvet. Etenim,
patres, siquid est quod tota isthac in re uxoria fratrum meorum
consilium comprobetis, id ipsum in me quoque probetis necesse
164 an non sit, animadvertite. Ego, patres, is sum qui neque duras
domi contumelias pertuli, neque ut in nostris matrona laribus las-
civiret sivi, neque ut ullo pacto familiam nostram mulieris cuiusvis
165 scelus dedecoraret uspiam permisi. Quod vos si in hac re perseverantia, constantia firmitasque animi delectat, si tanti interest bonum maritum fuisse habitum aut manu castam uxorem tenuisse,
in nobis quidem adversus omnium hominum turmas fuit obfir-
mata immobilisque et perennis fugiende ab uxore turpitudinis ra-
166 tio et integre de nobis fame servande cura. Cum me tot puelle
virum, tot parentes generum, tot cives affinem deposcebant meque

husbands, and I was never angered by her most shameless follies.'
'What a great and admirable achievement! What marvelous virtue! 159
What a citizen, born to bring glory and honor to his family and
country! By learning to gratify a crazed and wicked woman, you 160
won the reputation of a fine husband. If you lived in peace with an
inebriated wife, you show that you experienced far too little vexa-
tion. Or, if you did not forget that you were a man, and still strove
to rival her in acts of kindness, she cannot have been very vicious
and unjust. And if she was pleasant and courteous, your tolerance 161
of her can hardly be thought laudable.'

"Unless I am mistaken, our father would address you in these 162
terms, perhaps using even harsher reproaches. I won't pursue this
any further, gentlemen, for I wish to appear moderate in debating,
especially when I speak of my brothers, whom I love as myself. For
the sake of my virtue and affection, I shall continue to seek to win
their eternal love. But to describe my own merits briefly, I shall 163
not omit this one point. If you approve anything in my brothers'
behavior, gentlemen, consider whether I deserve the same praise. I 164
have endured no harsh abuse in my home, have allowed no wife to
run riot in my house, and have permitted no woman's sins to defile
our family. You laud perseverance and unflinching fortitude, and 165
you value a husband's good name and a wife's chastity. Clearly, I
have resisted the advice of vast hosts of men, have persistently
shunned taking a corrupt wife, and have maintained my good
name. I was considered a good match by many women, was 166

sibi habere domesticum adiunctum expedire plurimum arbitrabantur, cumque vos, fratres, hortari non desinebatis, an deerat in me
quippiam quo minus maritus ipse plane optimus diiudicarer?
167 Persuadentes tamen, trahentes vimque prope afferentes vos atque
reliquos ut connubii pestem subirem, optimo unico meo consilio
168 frustratos reddidi. Non dos opulentissima, non affinitas nobilissi-
marum prestantissimarumque familiarum, non forma puelle, non
proposite amplitudines, non magistratuum honorumque expectationes, non fortunarum ostentate copie, instituti mei firmitatem
169 atque costantiam labefactare aut uspiam convellere potuere; eoque
pacto nostros privatos lares immani monstro detestabilique omine
muliebri et publicos cetus atque fora et theatra omni sinistro ru-
more vacuos expiatosque servavi.'
170   Hec Trissophus. At patres qui arbitri considebant, consulto esse
opus pronuntiarunt. Interea apud sacerdotes dee Cybelis posita
ornamenta servantur.

sought as a son-in-law by many parents, and was desired as a kins-
man by many citizens. And you never ceased to urge me to marry,
my brothers. For what quality did I lack to be a perfect husband?
But despite your arguments, your urgings, and your pressures, I   167
resolutely thwarted your attempts to make me enter the blight of
matrimony. My firm resolve was not shaken by your promises of   168
lavish dowries, of kinship with noble families, of women's beauty,
of prestigious matches, of hopes of offices and honors, or of allur-
ing displays of wealth. In this way, I kept my private home free of   169
any savage and abominable monster of a woman, and rid the public assemblies, squares, and buildings of malicious rumors."

Thus spoke Trissophus. The elders who sat as judges declared   170
that they needed time to deliberate. In the meantime, the tokens
were deposited with the priests of Cybele.[11]

Note on the Text

※♦※

This I Tatti edition of the Latin text of the *Dinner Pieces* reproduces that found in Leon Battista Alberti, *Intercenales*, edited by Roberto Cardini, in Leon Battista Alberti, *Opere latine*, edited by Roberto Cardini (Roma: Istituto Poligrafico e Zecca dello Stato, 2010), 167–618. An account is given in the Introduction to the present volume of what is known about Alberti's redactions of the work; further details may be found in the full critical edition of the *Intercenales*, just cited, that also contains an extensive commentary to the *Intercenales* (on 223–617), also found in volume 2 of Leon Battista Alberti, *Intercenales: Editio minor*, edited by Roberto Cardini, 2 vols. (Florence: Edizioni Polistampa, 2022 = Humanistica II/5). For the present I Tatti edition, this commentary has been reduced in the Notes to the Translation.

The two principal witnesses to the final redaction are the Oxford and Pistoia manuscripts:

O   Oxford, Bodleian Library, MS Canon. Misc. 172
P   Pistoia, Biblioteca dei Domenicani, Inc. F. 19

The Oxford version antedates the Pistoia redaction: for example, it lacks Book 2's dedication to Leonardo Bruni, which begins with a paratextual apologue serving as a kind of proem; the latter was only added in the final phase of the last redaction.

A few pieces survive in manuscripts other than O and P, most notably:

Defunctus (*The Deceased*), in Vienna, Österreichisches Nationalbibliothek, MS Pal. lat. 3420, an earlier redaction that contains marginal and interlinear corrections in a second hand.

Uxoria (*Debate on Marriage*), an earlier redaction of the Latin text with a letter of presentation, in Florence, Biblioteca Nazionale Centrale, MS Panciatichiano 123.

Simie (*Monkeys*), in Florence, Biblioteca Nazionale Centrale, Naz. II IV 34, and Vatican City, Biblioteca Apostolica Vaticana, Ross. 423.

Opinio (*Opinion*), in Genoa, Biblioteca Universitaria di Genova, G IV 29.

A complete list of the manuscript and printed witnesses is found in Alberti, *Opere latine*, 173–175 and 222.

For this edition, the philological introduction of the 2010 edition (pp. 169–216) has been eliminated as has the apparatus recording the variants of earlier redactions. The apparatus of textual variants in the present text, representing the last extant redaction, has also been streamlined. The material retained is designed to give the reader a sense of the editor's choices and emendations.

Notes to the Text

ॐ

SIGLA

F   Florence, Biblioteca Nazionale Centrale, MS Panciatichiano 123

O   Oxford, Bodleian Library, MS Canon. Misc. 172

P   Pistoia, Biblioteca dei Domenicani, Inc. F. 19

Par   Paris, Bibliothèque Nationale, MS Par. lat. 6702

V   Vatican City, Biblioteca Apostolica Vaticana, MS Vat. lat. 4037

Vat   Vatican City, Biblioteca Apostolica Vaticana, MS Ottob. lat. 1424

W   Vienna, Österreichisches Nationalbibliothek, MS Pal. lat. 3420

W^{1} A second, Gothic cursive hand that adds marginal and interlinear notes in W consisting of authorial variants and minor corrections.

AUTHORITIES CITED

Bacchelli–D'Ascia   Franco Bacchelli and Luca D'Ascia, eds., Leon Battista Alberti, *Intercenales* (Bologna: Pendragon, 2003)

Biagioli   Claudia Biagioli, who has kindly communicated her editorial conjectures

Cardini   Roberto Cardini

Cardini 1978   Leon Battista Alberti, *Intercenales* (*libri III–XI*), ed. Roberto Cardini (Rome: Bulzoni, 1978)

Coppini   Donatella Coppini, who kindly communicated editorial conjectures for Cardini 1978

Garin   Leon Battista Alberti, *Intercenali inedite*, ed. Eugenio Garin (Florence: Sansoni, 1965)

Grayson   Cecil Grayson, "Una intercenale inedita di L. B. Alberti: *Uxoria*," *Italia medioevale e umanistica* 3 (1960): 291–307

Mancini	*Leonis Baptistae Alberti Opera inedita et pauca separatim impressa*, ed. Girolamo Mancini (Florence: Sansoni, 1890), 122–235 (*Intercenales*)
Mariotti	Scevola Mariotti (conjectures cited by Puccioni)
Marsh	Leon Battista Alberti, *Dinner Pieces: A Translation of the* Intercenales, trans. David Marsh (Binghamton, NY: Medieval & Renaissance Texts & Studies and the Renaissance Society of America, 1987)
Morelli	Jacobus Morelli, *Epistolae septem variae eruditionis, quarum tres nunc primum prodeunt* (Padua: ex officina sociorum titulo Minerva, 1819)
Ponte	Giovanni Ponte, "Lepidus e Libripeta," *Rinascimento*, n.s. 12 (1972): 237–65
Puccioni	Giulio Puccioni, "Note sulle nuove *Intercenali* di Leon Battista Alberti," in *Studia Florentina Alexandro Ronconi Sexagenario oblata*, 357–64 (Rome: Edizioni dell'Ateneo, 1970)
Regoliosi	Mariangela Regoliosi, who has kindly communicated her editorial conjectures
Trenti ·	Luigi Trenti, "Leon Battista Alberti e Vespasiano da Bisticci," *La Rassegna della letteratura italiana* 91 (1987): 282–89

BOOK I

PROEMIUM

1. ⟨*Prohemium ad Paulum Physicum*⟩] *suppl. Cardini*

I.I. PUPILLUS

4. iniquam] unquam O, nunquam P, *em. Mancini*

9. ac ne⟨dum⟩] ac ne OP, at nec *Mancini*, ac ne⟨dum⟩ *em. Cardini*

10. extraneis] exteris OP, *em. Cardini*

23. bi⟨s non in⟩du⟨t⟩as] biduas OP, *em. Cardini*

1.2. Religio

1. Timonis] Cimonis *OP, em. Trenti*

13. Lepidus] *om. OP (sed in O manus altera add. in mg.)*

14. Libripeta] *om. OP (sed in O manus altera add. in interl.)*

16. orassent] nossent *OP, em. Cardini*

20. eadem] iidem *P* (idem *O: prior scriptio auctoris), em. Cardini*

    utentur] utuntur *P* (utetur *O: prior scriptio auctoris), em. Cardini*

1.3. Virtus

18. omnium] hominum *OP, em. Cardini*

1.4. Fatum et Fortuna

1. *nomen eius qui cum philosopho colloquitur in codd. deest*

4. non] tum *OP, em. Mancini*

41. litus usque eiicere] lutus usque eiicere *O*, litus eiiciat *P, em. Mancini*

50. super vitreas] super in vitrias *O*, super invitreas *P*, super vitreas *em. Cardini*

54. superlabier] superlabere *OP, em. Cardini*

1.5. Patientia

1. ⟨Pat.⟩] *suppl. Mancini*

18. pharmac⟨or⟩um] farmacum *OP, em. Mancini*

23. melioris] maioribus *O*, maioris *P, em. Cardini*

34. abstulerit] attulerit *OP, em. Cardini*

40. Chroni cantione] croni concione *O*, dironite curatione *P, em. Cardini*

1.6. Felicitas

5. vos] vestros *OP, em. Mancini*

11. nostre] nostra *OP, em. Cardini*

15. ⟨pace⟩] *om. P, suppl. Cardini primae scriptionis auctoris auxilio*

20. effundemus] effundimus *OP, em. Mancini*

21. abripuit] arripuit *OP, em. tacite Mancini*

BOOK II

Prohemium

4. vocem] vocom *P, em. tacite Garin*

   pretium] premium *P, em. Cardini*

5. doctrine⟨que⟩] doctrine *P, em. Cardini*

9. iussi] misi *P, em. Mariotti*

   proinde] perinde *P, em. Cardini*

10. si, ut] sicut *P, em. Garin*

11. sint] sit *P, em. tacite Garin*

    inepte] inepti *P, em. tacite Garin*

    exposcantur] exposcuntur *P, em. tacite Garin*

12. proinde] perinde *P, em. Cardini*

    nummum] nimium *P, em. Ponte*

    oportere] oportet *P, em. Bacchelli–D'Ascia*

II.I. Oraculum

8. *Al.*] alochocratis *O*, aergocratus *P, em. Cardini*

12. *Cert.*] certopora *OP, em. Cardini*

18. comedito] commedito *O*, cedito *P, em. tacite Mancini*

21. gratis dato] *om. P*, gratis datos *O, em. Bacchelli–D'Ascia*

II.2. Parsimonia

2. se prevenirem] re pervenirem *O*, prevenirem *P, em. Mancini*

4. exa⟨u⟩ctam] exactam *OP, em. Cardini*

13. aderi⟨n⟩t] aderit *OP, em. Cardini*

II.4. VATICINIUM

9. simus] scimius *OP, em. Cardini*

23. Accedat] accede *OP, em. Mancini*

40. nosti⟨n⟩)] nosti *OP, em. Cardini*

41. omnino] omnium *OP, em. Mancini*

47. parumve] parum ne *OP, em. Cardini*

II.5. PAUPERTAS

1. Peniplusius] *hoc loco et ad calcem usque* Penplusius/Pemplusius/Pemplusi *O,* Pemplusius/Pleniplusie *P, em. Mancini*

19. largitate] etate *OP, em. Cardini*

26. damnato] damnata *OP, em. Cardini*

36. potestas] potentia *P* (licentia, *prima scriptio auctoris, O*) *em. Cardini*

44. nummularias] numularias *OP, em. Mancini*

58. velim] nolim *OP, em. Mancini*

II.6. NUMMUS

11. repperere] reperere *O,* reperiere *P,* repperere *em. Cardini*

II.8. DIVITIE

7. pertulerit] pertulerint *OP, em. Mancini*

11. bonorum] bonarum *O* (*hoc loco testis unicus*), *em. Bacchelli–D'Ascia*

    haudquaquam] haudquamquam *O* (*hoc loco testis unicus*), *em.* (*tacite*) *Mancini*

BOOK III

III.1. PICTURE

11. ostenta⟨n⟩s] ostentas *P, em.* (*tacite*) *Garin*

15. primo loco] primo in loco *P, em. Cardini*

17. radi⟨i⟩s] radis *P, em. Garin*

20. ⟨INIURIE FILIA⟩] *suppl. Cardini*

21. veste] in veste *P, em. Cardini*

24. ⟨MODESTIE FILIA⟩] *suppl. Cardini*

25. aureo] aureis *P, em. Cardini*

27. ⟨inter⟩] *suppl. Cardini*

29. ⟨e⟩laboratam] laboratam *P, em. Cardini*
    excul⟨p⟩tum] excultum *P, em. Cardini*

34. ⟨si⟩] *suppl. Cardini*

III.2. FLORES

1. delegatum] delegatus *P, em. Puccioni*

6. exorarint] exornarint *P, em. Garin*

8. coisse] cesisse *P,* ces⟨s⟩isse *Garin,* coisse *em. Cardini*

III.3. DISCORDIA

16. Terminus] termen *P, em. Cardini*

19. quo] qua *P* (qua recognita *Garin*), *em. Cardini*

III.4. HOSTIS

4. ⟨de⟩] *suppl. Cardini*

6. ⟨in⟩iuste] iuste *P, em. Cardini*

7. ac] ut *P, em. Cardini*

14. immanes] immunes *P, em. (tacite) Garin*

19. unicum] ut unicum *P,* ut *exp. (tacite) Garin*

III.5. LAPIDES

6. ignotam [. . .] alienam] ignotum [. . .] alienum *P, em. Puccioni*

III.6. HEDERA

1. intueretur] intuerentur P, *em. Garin*

III.7. SUSPITIO

1. ⟨Fama⟩] *suppl. Garin*

2. ⟨de⟩] *suppl. Cardini*

2. nec] et P, *em. Cardini*

3. ara] area P, *em. Cardini*

5. caulem] caulum P, *em. Cardini*

10. expurgatum] expergatum P, *em. Marsh*

11. fiat] fiant P, *em. Cardini*

14. manum] malum P, *em. Cardini*

16. protendebat] portendebat P, *em. Cardini*

17. vi⟨n⟩ctam] victam P, *em. Marsh*

BOOK IV
PROHEMIUM

1. ⟨in⟩] *suppl. Cardini*

3. ver⟨r⟩ucas] verucas P, *em. Cardini*

7. nos] nostrum P, nostrum ⟨ingenium⟩ *Bacchelli–D'Ascia*, nos *em. Cardini*

9. sepositis] repositis P, *em. Cardini*

12. promendo] promendis P, *em. Garin*

13. nostra] nos nostra P, *em. Garin*

    quamque] quamquam P, *em. Bacchelli–D'Ascia*

    ⟨. . .⟩] *textus mutilus in P*

IV.1. SOMNIUM

3. *Libr.* Minime] Minime. LIBRIPETA P, *em. Garin*

11. tantum] tamen P, *em. Cardini*

16. ⟨aut⟩ capillo] ⟨aut⟩ *suppl. Cardini*

17. modus] modum P, *em. Garin*

44. uterque] utrumque P, *em. Cardini*

46. strum⟨os⟩a] struma P, *em. Cardini*

IV.2. COROLLE

4. divinum] divinorum P, *em. Puccioni*

5. Eodum (*sc.* ehodum)] eo dum P, *em. Cardini*

28. studii⟨s⟩] studii P, *em. Garin*

29. confidenti] confidendi P, *em. Cardini*

31. nostris] vestris P, *em. Garin*

39. tum] tu P, *em. Cardini*

44. vidisti⟨s⟩] vidisti P, *em. Garin*

51. succensere] succenseri P, *em. Cardini*

53. ei mihi] enim P, *em. Cardini*

64. esse⟨m⟩] esse P, *em. Garin*

IV.3. CYNICUS

1. ⟨Mercur.⟩] *suppl. Garin*

2. vitam] vitium P, *em. Marsh*

8. et (omnibus)] in P, *em. Cardini*

15. dicite] digite P, *em. Garin*

20. strepitus] strepidus P, *em. Garin*

22. inexplebili] inexpiabili P, *em. Cardini*

27. recensebis] recensebo P, *em. Cardini*

28. de se] sese P, *em. Cardini*

43. libi⟨di⟩ne] libine P, *em. Garin*

55. corpori⟨s⟩] corpori P, *em. Garin*

58. ⟨et litteras⟩] *suppl. Cardini*

61. ⟨con⟩versiones] versiones P, *em. Cardini*

76. ⟨eos⟩] *suppl. Cardini*

78. ⟨cum⟩] *suppl. Cardini*

88. Adeste] adesto P, *em. Cardini*

IV.4. FAMA

7. cupio] cuipio P, *em. Garin*

8. religio⟨sis⟩simum] religiosimum P, *em. Garin*

   vivent] vivere P, *em. Cardini*

10. aberrasse⟨nt⟩] aberrasse P, *em. Cardini*

18. acclamarunt] acclamavit P, *em. Garin*

IV.5. ERUMNA

1. ***.] *nomen eius qui cum Philoponio colloquitur in P deest*

4. revocari⟨m⟩] revocari P, *em. Cardini*

16. ⟨***⟩] *lacuna in P*

    disputandi] disputanti P, *em. Cardini*

23. vix] vis P, *em. Garin*

25. ***.] Philoponius P, *em. Garin*

37. Nam sepe iam antea] nam cum sepe iam antea P, cum *exp. Cardini*

38. communi⟨s⟩que] communique P, *em. Cardini*

    arrogabant] irrogabant P, *em. Cardini*

46. affines] et affines P, et *exp. Cardini*

47. ⟨nos⟩] *suppl. Cardini*

55. miserum me] miserrime P, *em. Cardini*

61. vecordibus] verecordibus P, *em. Cardini*

    abuta⟨n⟩tur] abutatur P, *em. Garin*

65. omne] omnem P, *em. Cardini*

68. De⟨de⟩cet] decet P, *em. Cardini*

69. ⟨Philoponi⟩] *lacuna in P, suppl. Garin*

70. eosdem] eodes *P, em. Garin*

    devenerint] devenerunt *P, em. Cardini*

72. ea te] etate *P, em. Cardini*

74. moliri] emoliri *P, em. Cardini*

77–78. ⟨Philop. Non recuso.⟩ ***.] *lacuna in P, suppl. Cardini*

78. esse⟨t⟩] esse *P, em. Garin*

79. ⟨Philop. Aliorum divitias nec posco nec, si mihi commodes, volo. Peto ut mihi a cultu et studiis bonarum artium, quibus semper fui deditus, feliciora rependantur⟩] *lacuna in P, suppl. Cardini*

81. facis] facit *P, em. Garin*

83. principe] principio *P, em. Garin*

84. eum animi motum] cum animi metam *P, em. Garin*

85. prestatione] prestatiore *P, em. Cardini*

87. dicor. Quid ita?] dicor. Philoponius. Quid ita *P, em. Garin*

89. ⟨Philop.⟩] *suppl. Garin*

    freti] fieri *P, em. Garin*

91–93.] *ordinem eorum qui loquentes inducuntur pervertit P, em. Garin*

95. Triscatarus] Triscatharus *P, em. Cardini*

96. momentum] momenti *P, em. Cardini*

    ⟨tum⟩] *suppl. Marsh*

97. ipsi⟨s⟩] ipsi *P, em. Garin*

99. ⟨si⟩] *suppl. Cardini*

100. orationis] oratoris *P, em. Cardini*

101. ⟨cum⟩] *suppl. Cardini*

    ⟨negavi mutari posse sortem quam ei dedissem⟩] *suppl. Cardini*

109. iuventu⟨ti⟩s] iuventus *P, em. Cardini*

114. sed dicit] sed illud dicit *P, illud exp. Cardini*

    condonatam] condonatum *P, em. Bacchelli–D'Ascia*

115. vig⟨i⟩lias] viglas *P*, *em. Garin*

⟨ut in ea re ex sententia succederet quicquid optaverit⟩] *suppl. Cardini*

122. ⟨modo⟩] *suppl. Cardini*

126. te] se *P*, *em. Cardini*

⟨. . .⟩] *lacuna in P*

132. esset] etiam *P*, *em. Cardini*

male contenti] dum male contenti *P*, dum *exp. Cardini*

⟨in⟩] *suppl. Cardini*

rerum novarum cupiditate] in rerum novarum cupiditate *P*, in *exp.*
Cardini

IV.6. SERVUS

1. Ha ha he!] Ah ah he *P*, *em. Cardini*

14. ⟨s⟩tudio] tudio *P*, *em. Garin*

16. consilii⟨s⟩] consilii *P*, *em. Garin*

23. provideris?] perdideris *P*, *em. Garin*

25. que vitasse] quietasse *P*, *em. Garin*

30. aculeos] aculea *P*, *em. Cardini*

31. multo⟨s⟩] multo *P*, *em. Garin*

32. Utinam] utrum *P*, *em. tacite Garin*

33. necdum, primum me, ex illa legatione me domum receperam] nedum
primum me *etc. P*, nedum primum me ex illa legatione domum receperam
Garin, necdum primum ex illa legatione me domum receperam *Bacchelli–
D'Ascia*, necdum, primum me, ex illa legatione me domum receperam *em.*
Cardini

40. ut et] ut in *P*, *em. Bacchelli–D'Ascia*

47. gesti⟨culati⟩one!] gestione *P*, *em. Cardini*

55. ***. Et manus et os hominis teneo.] *haec verba innominato collocutori*
primum tribuit Cardini

56. ⟨Parm.⟩.] *suppl. Cardini*

63. nocte⟨s⟩] nocte *P*, *em. Garin*

81. Pena⟨m⟩] pena *P*, *em. Cardini*

87. isthun⟨c⟩] isthun *P*, *em. Garin*

88. pa⟨bu⟩lum] palum *P*, palam *Marsh*, pa⟨bu⟩lum *em. Cardini*

92. solutus] solutis *P*, *em. Cardini*

93. assidue] assiduam *P*, assiduum *Bacchelli–D'Ascia*, assidue *em. Cardini*

94. i⟨n⟩genium] igenium *P*, *em. Garin*

97. lente] late *P*, *em. Cardini*

105. indulseris] indulxeris *P*, *em. tacite Garin*

107. philosophus] philosophum *P*, *em. Puccioni*

     unquam] inquam *P*, *em. Garin*

108. excipit] excepit *P*, *em. Garin*

125. ignarum] ignavum *P*, *em. tacite Garin*

BOOK VII

PROHEMIUM

2. ⟨modo obscuris in nubibus latitabat⟩] *suppl. Cardini*

8. sequentem] frequentem *P*, *em. Cardini*

12. mi ⟨. . .⟩] *lacunam notat P*

15. offendas] offendam *P*, *em. Cardini*

20. ampul⟨l⟩osumque] ampulosumque *P*, *em. Cardini*

    ⟨non exquisitius atque⟩] *suppl. Cardini*

24. aspernandos] aspernendos *P*, *em. Cardini*

25. mi ⟨. . .⟩] *lacunam notat P*

    scriptorem] scriptorum *P*, *em. Marsh*

    imitaberis] miraberis *P*, *em. Coppini*

26. instruct⟨i⟩ores] instructores *P*, *em. Garin*

VII.1. Maritus

5. ⟨. . .⟩] *lacunam notat* P

6. recensuisti⟨s] recensuisti P, *em. Garin*

   perturbationes] perturbationem P, *em. Garin*

8. congratulemini] congratulamini P, *em. Bacchelli–D'Ascia*

9. ⟨. . .⟩] *lacunam notat* P

19. mechumne] meccumne P, *em. Cardini*

34. optime] optima P, *em. Cardini*

35. coadiutorem] coadiuctorem P, *em. Cardini*

38. videretur] viderentur P, *em. Garin*

   ⟨in⟩] *suppl. Garin*

48. acerbius] acerbioribus P, *em. Cardini*

60. tamen] tum P, *em. Cardini*

78–79. prona. Quod si hec una amoris vis] prona: quasi hec una amoris sui P, *em. Cardini*

80. gravitatis societatem] gravitatem societatis P, *em. Cardini; cf. Cicero, De legibus 3.1*

81. hu⟨i⟩c] huc P, *em. Cardini*

83. vultu] vulto P, *em. Bacchelli–D'Ascia*

   scivit ille] sciverit ille P, *em. Cardini*

   ⟨tolerare, at non scivit⟩] *suppl. Cardini*

   tol⟨l⟩ere] tolere (*ex* tolerare) P, *em. Cardini*

VII.2. Uxoria

4. Mitio⟨ni⟩] Mitio *codd., em. Cardini*

46. mee] meas *codd.,* mee *em. Cardini*

47. aliorum] nostrorum F, *om.* P, aliorum *em. Cardini*

50. at] ut *codd.,* at *em. Cardini*

52. vituperarit] vituperarim *codd.*, vituperarit *em. Cardini*

55. serie] serio *codd.*, serie *em. Cardini*

58. insolentius [. . .] licentia] insolentiam [. . .] licentia *F*, insolentius [. . .] licentius *P*, insolentior [. . .] licentia *Grayson*, insolentius [. . .] licentia *em. Cardini*

75. quantum] quanto *codd.*, quanta *Grayson*, quantum *em. Cardini*

89. tame⟨t⟩si] tamesi *P* (*hoc loco testis unicus*), *em. Cardini*

94. impetus] impetu *F*, impetum *P*, impetus *em. Grayson*

96. quam] que *ex* -que, *ut vid.*,*P* (*hoc loco testis unicus*), *em. Cardini*

114. uter] utrum *codd.*, *em. Grayson*

123. credideri⟨n⟩t] crediderit *codd.*, *em. Grayson*

128. caterve] caverte *F*, caterva *P*, caterve *em. Grayson*

131. in eaque] meaque *P* (*hoc loco testis unicus*), *em. Cardini*

144. nulla operam] nullam operam *F*, nulla opera *P*, nulla operam *em. Cardini*

156. longum] longos *codd.*, longe *Grayson*, longum *em. Cardini*

161. futili] futile *P* (*hoc loco testis unicus*), *em. Cardini*

Notes to the Translation

ABBREVIATIONS

Cardini 2022	*Intercenales: Editio minor,* ed. Roberto Cardini, 2 vols. (Florence: Edizioni Polistampa, 2022)
DBI	*Dizionario biografico degli Italiani* (Rome: Istituto della Enciclopedia italiana, 1960–2020). Online at www.treccani.it/biografie
ITRL	I Tatti Renaissance Library
Perry	*Babrius and Phaedrus: Fables,* ed. Ben Edwin Perry, Loeb Classical Library 436 (Cambridge, MA: Harvard University Press, 1965). Perry's standard numbering of the fables is on pages 419 to 611.

BOOK I

Preface to Paolo Toscanelli

Paolo dal Pozzo Toscanelli (1397–1482) was a Florentine physician and mathematician: see Marianne Mahn-Lot's article on him in *DBI* 32 (1986): 247–50. Alberti's choice of Toscanelli as dedicatee of the first edition in two books was by no means casual, for Toscanelli was both an astrologer (to whom Alberti sent the prophetic letters mentioned in his autobiography) and a physician who could appreciate the author's "healing" of maladies spiritual rather than physical. Alberti conceives of his own writings as a kind of psychotherapy, following the example of Cicero's *Tusculan Disputations* 3.23: "We must explain the origin of this pain, that is, the cause that occasions this grief in the mind, as if it were a sickness of the body. For as physicians think they have found out the cure, when they have discovered the cause of the distemper; so we shall discover the method of curing melancholy, when the cause of it is found out." If Alberti follows Cicero, he also follows Democritus, whose philosophy is based on laughter. In this way, the episodes of *The Deceased* personify the connection between laughter and madness that is posited in the letters of pseudo-Hippocrates (see Introduction). In the prefaces of the last known redaction, Alberti generally summarizes the themes of the book introduced, as he does here; but here he omits the Aesopic fable that often characterizes later prefaces.

1. Alberti explains the neologism of his title *Intercenales* by the phrase "over dinners and drinks" (inter cenas et pocula).

2. The metaphor of a physician's bitter medicine is traditional: see, for example, Lucretius, *De rerum natura* (*On the Nature of Things*) 1.936–42.

3. As in the prefaces to later books, Alberti outlines the topics of the pieces that follow, most often in lapidary single sentences. Sentences 6 to 10 refer in order to *The Orphan, Religion, Virtue, Fate and Fortune, Patience,* and *Happiness*. Sentence 10 alludes to Cicero, *Tusculan Disputations* 3.24.

THE WRITER

The short dialogue called *The Writer* is a paratext rather than an integral part of Book 1, as may be inferred from its absence in paragraphs 5 to 6 of the preface. "The Writer" is Alberti himself, under his pseudonym Lepidus (witty), who is said to have worked on the *Intercenales* uninterruptedly for a month. His interlocutor, Libripeta, incarnates the envious and sterile *literatus* who dissuades Lepidus-Battista from publishing the *Dinner Pieces* in Florence, because in that city of ignoramuses and slanderers it will be sharply criticized and torn to shreds. The character of Libripeta has always been identified with the famous Florentine book collector Niccolò Niccoli, but the present writer has argued (in Cardini, "Cosa è Libripeta") that the name should be understood to have a wider reference, sometimes indicating a personification of humanist bibliomania and sometimes performing other satiric functions in Alberti's poetics — sometimes even voicing Alberti's own sharp critiques of humanist ideals. The name itself is taken from Lucian, *Adversus indoctos* 22.

In *The Oracle* (2.1.10) Libripeta thought that, without study and labor, the mere possession of books would make him a man of letters, but Apollo predicted his destiny by saying, "Then be a detractor of all men of letters." This fate is exactly realized here in *The Writer*, which as a paratext clearly postdates the two books of the first version of the *Dinner Pieces* (cf. the dedication to Toscanelli).

1.1. The Orphan

If we recognize The Orphan as its first piece, we appreciate how Alberti structured Books 1 and 2 by "ring composition," or the symmetry between the initial and final works, which are both autobiographical: in *The Orphan* (1.1.1) Alberti describes himself, and in *Wealth* (2.2.8) he portrays his grandfather Benedetto. This dinner piece begins precisely where his essay *De commodis et incommodis litterarum* (*On the Advantages and Disadvantages of Literature*) (published with a translation in ITRL 96) had ended, with the author's vow to study the humanities despite all personal and public obstacles. In other words, *The Orphan* dramatizes the plight of the author, who in this essay speaks in first person. Here Philoponius replaces the comic figure of Lepidus, representing the author's struggles in a tragic light.

4. Under the name Philoponius (Greek for "fond of labor" or "industrious"), Alberti dramatizes his tribulations as a student and an illegitimate orphan.

5. A maxim of Publilius Syrus ("furor fit laesa saepius patientia," fragment 13), preserved in Aulus Gellius 17.14.4 and Macrobius, *Saturnalia* 2.7.11.

6. For Mark Antony, see Cicero, *Philippics* 2.6; Plutarch, *Antony* 9 (a work translated into Latin by Leonardo Bruni before 1405); for Dionysius, see Plutarch, *Dion* 7.7 (a work translated into Latin by Guarino of Verona in 1414); for Vitellius, see Suetonius, *Vitellius* 13.2. For Cimon, see Plutarch, *Cimon* 19; for Nero, Suetonius, *Nero* 30.3 (used here also to emend Alberti's text).

7. For Crassus, see Valerius Maximus, *Memorable Deeds and Sayings* 6.9.12, and Plutarch, *Crassus* 2; for Lucullus, see Plutarch, *Lucullus* 39–41. Alberti probably derived the figure of 400,000 volumes for the library of Alexandria from Petrarch, *De remediis* 1.43. For Darius' wealth and crystal compare Quintus Curtius, *History of Alexander* 3.3.8.

8. For Lucius Sicinius Dentatus, see Pliny, *Natural History* 7.101–2 and 22.9; Valerius Maximus 2.2.4; and Aulus Gellius 2.11. For Marcus Servilius, see Plutarch, *Aemilius Paulus* 31 (a work translated by Leonardo Bruni before 1410).

9. For Ventidius Bassus, see Aulus Gellius 15.4; for the barber's son Aggrames, see Quintus Curtius, *History of Alexander* 9.2; Perseus' ship, see Plutarch, *Aemilius Paulus* 30.1–2; Marcellus' battle fanfare, see Plutarch, *Marcellus* 18; for a huge fleet sent against Attalus, see Orosius, *History* 7.42 (who says there were 3,700 ships).

1.2. RELIGION

Ever since it was first printed in 1890, this piece has been the object of intense study. The dialogue questions the efficacy of prayer. Lepidus, who has just come from church, tends to believe in divine involvement in human affairs, whereas Libripeta believes in gods who are too busy with the entire universe to pay attention to individual prayers. The subtext is Seneca, *Natural Questions* 2.35–38, where the Stoic philosopher contrasts two schools of viewing prayers: a more rigid skepticism (Libripeta in Alberti), and a less rigid acceptance (Lepidus). The work contains many parallels as well with Alberti's satiric presentation of impetrative prayer in the *Momus*. For a more elaborate analysis of this text, see Cardini 2022, 2:543–45.

10. For Lepidus and Libripeta, see the headnote to *The Writer*, above. The Athenian misanthrope Timon offered his fig tree as a gallows: see Plutarch, *Antony* 70.4–5 (a work translated into Latin by Leonardo Bruni before 1405).

11. An echo of Thales, quoted by Cicero, *De legibus* (*On Laws*) 2.26: "omnia . . . deorum esse plena." The dictum could also be found in Diogenes Laertius' *Lives of the Philosophers* 1.1.27 (a work translated into Latin by Ambrogio Traversari by 1433).

1.3. VIRTUE

Book 1 is open to two interpretations. The first, explicit one is found at the end of the dedication and outlines a sort of *Bildungsroman*, or novel of education. The second, implicit one amounts instead to a sort of religious tract with a Stoic orientation. *Virtue* is a desperate and despairing drama that reveals the Deity as powerless against the overwhelming power of Fortune—not because the Deity is malign, but because it is subject to omnipotent Fortune. This is a frankly scandalous proposition, which explains why Alberti published *Virtue*—twice, and in different versions—not as his own work but as a Latin translation of Lucian. This prank and the adoption of Lucian as a useful lightning rod met with great success, as is demonstrated by the vast circulation, in both manuscript and print, of the dinner piece with this attribution.

12. The portrayal of Mark Antony recalls various passages in Cicero's *Philippics;* compare in particular 2.63: "Tu istis faucibus, istis *lateribus,* ista *gladiatoria* totius corporis firmitate" (You, with those jaws of yours, and those *sides* of yours, and that strength of body *suited to a gladiator*).

13. This passage inspired Dosso Dossi's painting *Jupiter Painting Butterflies, Mercury, and Virtue* (Ferrara, ca. 1535).

1.4. FATE AND FORTUNE

Fate and Fortune continues the examination of Fortune begun in *Virtue.* Alberti also uses a dream as a vehicle in *The Dream;* and in his Italian dialogue *De iciarchia (Ruling the Household)* (ca. 1470) he relates that his lucubrations were often followed by dreams offering valuable ethical lessons. Such visual allegories are also present in *Rings,* and at the end of the dialogue the author awakes to behold the eternal concatenations of nature (see Cicero, *De divinatione* [*On Divination*] 1.125; Seneca, *Letters to Lucilius* 107.8). All the same, unlike Cicero, *On Divination* 2.42–47, 87–99, Alberti seems to countenance both astrology and determinism.

14. See Cicero, *On Divination* 1.129 and 2.100.

15. Alberti's dream here seems to reveal that human souls preexist their birth, a view compatible with Pythagorean and Platonic philosophy but not orthodox Christian theology.

16. The idea that human beings develop from sparks (or "little fires") and seeds of virtue is based on Stoic teaching, explained in Cicero's *On Laws* 1.33, and is also found in his *De finibus* (*On Ends*) 5.18 and *Tusculan Disputations* 3.2.

17. Bios: Greek for "life." In the manuscripts, the noun is written *Vios* in accordance with the medieval and modern pronunciation of Greek.

18. Literally, princes of ships, i.e., political leaders. The comparison of ships to the state is an ancient one.

19. The question whether public or private life was a greater source of happiness was an important issue in humanist literature of the 1430s, for example, in Poggio's *On the Infelicity of Princes*, set in Florence in 1434 but not published until 1440.

20. Glass floats: that is, fragile flotation devices. The word for a float, *vesica*, can also mean rhetorical bombast, corresponding to inflated claims of flatterers.

21. Winged souls recall Plato's *Phaedrus* 246c, a text translated in part by Leonardo Bruni in 1424.

1.5. Patience

The dialogue offers an antithesis to *Fate and Fortune* by proposing a strategy of resistance to misfortunes caused by circumstance, or, as in *Shipwrecked* (9.1), by the unpredictable. It anticipates lessons taught in Alberti's Italian dialogues *Theogenius* and *Profugiorum ab erumna libri* (*Remedies for Affliction*). But above all, *Patience* is a further coherent link in the chain that begins with *The Orphan* and extends through all of Book 1. If we are forced to give into Necessity, we can resist by cultivating the virtue of Patience, but should do so only so long as Necessity rules. Patience is not supine resignation but a form of resistance, requiring calculation, intelligence, a strong will, and hope; it means treasuring up ones forces to be ready when the situation changes, as in the River of Life it inevitably will. The piece can be dated after 1438 because in that year Alberti first read the recently discovered *Miles Gloriosus* of Plautus.

22. Chronus (Kronos) in Greek mythology was the youngest of the Titans, son of Uranus and Gaia. From his marriage to his sister Rhea the Olympian gods were born. The Romans identified him with Saturn.

23. Dromo is the name of a Greek slave in Terence's plays *Eunuch* and *Brothers* (*Adelphoe*).

24. Earthenware from the Greek island of Samos was famous in antiquity for its fine quality and fragility.

25. The *Aphorisms* is the name of a text preserved in the Hippocratic Corpus, but the words quoted are not found there. In fact, this *medendi ratio*, or healing system, has all the marks of a semi-serious parody of the "remedies" recommended by magic and superstition. A person suffering

unbearable pain will welcome any healing system, including charms and amulets, as we read in Book 2 of *Profugiorum ab erumna libri* (*Remedies for Affliction*): see Alberti, *Opere volgari*, II, 73.

1.6. HAPPINESS

In his preface to Paolo Toscanelli, Albert summarizes this piece in language that echoes Cicero, *Tusculan Disputations* 3.24: "What is imagined to be the greatest evil is by no means so great as to defeat the happiness of life." Happiness and misery are conditions measured and controlled by our belief (*opinio*) about them. See also Appendix 3.2, *Opinion*. This Stoic sentiment not only links all the pieces of Book 1 but underlies the whole work. *Happiness* recapitulates themes of the preceding pieces in Book 1 but does so in a narrative rather than a dialogic form: see Cardini 2022, 2:554–55.

26. The career of the Mongol conqueror Tamerlane (1336–1405) will be narrated by Poggio Bracciolini in Book 1 of his dialogue *De varietate fortunae* (*On the Vicissitudes of Fortune*) of 1448, where Tamerlane's army is said to have numbered 400,000 cavalry and 600,000 infantry. It was common in humanist literature to identify the Tartars with the ancient Scythian peoples.

27. The phrase *veneres cupidinesque* recalls Catullus 3.1. The laments of the young here echo language from both Catullus and Propertius (for the latter see 3.21.15–16).

BOOK II

PREFACE TO LEONARDO BRUNI

Strikingly, Alberti dedicates his works not to powerful contemporaries, as was most common for humanists, but to friends and mentors, sometimes also to disciples. Alberti characterizes Leonardo Bruni (1370–1444) as the most learned man of the age, an ironic echo, perhaps, of Pliny's description of Homer. At the same time, Alberti's *On the Advantages and Disadvantages of Literature* had already distanced the aspiring humanist from the hostile inner circles of humanist Florence. These included Bruni, who was born in Arezzo in 1370 but became a citizen of Florence in 1415. The most widely circulated humanist author of the fifteenth century before the invention of printing, Bruni was noted for his translations from Greek, his elegant writings in both Latin and Italian, and his role as chancellor and official historian of Florence. A subtle needling of Bruni may be implied in the focus of Book 2 on wealth and frugality, as Bruni, a wealthy man, also had a reputation for avarice, noted by Piovano Arlotti (Motto e facezie del Piovano Arlotto, ed. Mori [Bolzano: no primter, 2017], Facezie XXX, 54), and Paolo Giovio, Portraits of Learned Men IX (ed. Kenneth Gouwens, ITRL 95 [Cambridge, MA: Harvard University Press, 2023], 89).

1. A Greek verse cited in Plutarch, Antony 80, which Alberti quotes in Bruni's translation, his source also for the erroneous name "Sostratus" in place of "Philostratus." Sostratus is also the name of a lost work of Lucian mentioned in Lucian's Demonax.

2. As in Book 1, Alberti outlines the topics of the seven pieces in Book 2.

II.1. THE ORACLE

Alberti also alludes satirically to oracles in his Momus, a novel published with an English translation in ITRL 8 (see Bibliography). The names of the interlocutors are symbolic. They are Philargirius, "money lover"; Procer, "nobleman"; Philotimus, "ambitious"; Scurra, "buffoon"; Zelotipus, "jealous"; Alochocratus, "wife ruler"; Libripeta, "book collector"; Ypolochus, "henpecked"; Certomopora, "mordant and offensive"; Megalophronus, "overweening"; Erastus (i.e., Erastēs), "lover"; Philodoxus, "glory seeker"; Ethiconomus, "moralizer"; Bardus, "dimwitted"; Penus, "pauper." The fundamental source for all of Book 2 is Cicero, Tusculan Disputations 3.24, as noted above. A specific intertext of The Oracle may be found in Cicero, Laelius 7 ("It is wisdom to consider everything to be within yourself": hanc esse in te sapientiam existiment, ut omnia tua in te posita esse ducas), an idea Alberti applies to fifteen human "types."

3. The venality of religion is a theme Alberti also explores in the Momus, and in The Coin in the present book.

4. Alberti's misogyny is more fully exposed in Book 7.

5. For the character Libripeta, see the notes to the paratext of Book 1, The Writer. Libripeta, who "would rather seem than be," reverses the

maxim *esse, non videri* — that one should be truly what one claims to be, and not merely seem to be. This maxim is ubiquitous in ancient Greek moral literature, but best known in Latin from Sallust, *The War against Catiline* 54.6 ("Cato preferred to be good rather than to seem so"). Cf. the Socratic maxim cited by Cicero, *On Duties* 2.43: "to be exactly as we wish to seem."

6. Whether it is better for princes to be loved or feared was a famous question raised by Cicero in *On Duties* 2.23.

7. Philodoxus is the protagonist of Alberti's first work, the comedy *Philodoxeos fabula*, written around 1424. It is published with an English translation in ITRL 19 (see Bibliography). Philodoxus, like Lepidus, is one of Alberti's masks.

II.2. FRUGALITY

Keys to this piece include Alberti's summary in his preface to Bruni, his remarks on avarice in *On the Family*, and Aristotle's *Nicomachean Ethics* 4.1–3 (on prodigality and liberality). Of the three interlocutors — Periphronus, "most prudent"; Micrologus, "penny-pincher"; and Philocerdus, "profit loving, greedy" — Alberti seems to identify with the first.

8. As in Book 3 of the *Momus*, and like his model Lucian, Alberti here (2.2–11) mimics the brief cross-examination of Socratic dialogue.

9. Albert in these paragraphs (2.11–23) falls into the *macrologia*, or longer speeches, characteristic of Ciceronian dialogue.

10. This Albertian version of the "non nobis" topos (we are not born for ourselves alone) derives ultimately from [pseudo] Plato's *Letters* via Cicero, *On Duties* 1.22.

II.3. THE COCK

The apologue, or Aesopic fable, is an important genre in Alberti's writings, which first appears in this book, and occupies all of Book 10. Apologues in the *Dinner Pieces* typically end with a moral, and thus differ from his *Apologi centum* (*One Hundred Fables*) composed in December 1437. As in *The Writer*, the reference to "our city" clearly means Florence.

The fable transforms into an apologue the description of avarice in Aristotle, *Nicomachean Ethics* 4.1 (1121b).

11. The fable concludes with an Aesopic moral that explicitly refers to Florence.

II.4. SOOTHSAYING

Like *The Oracle* and *The Dream*, this one-act comedy reveals the character of its actors, here through descriptions of their physiognomy. The Greek names — Philargirius, "greedy"; and Assotus, "dissolute" — are variants of the classical forms.

12. Xerxes is the name of a Persian king who invaded Greece in 480 BCE. Here the name is presumably used for its exoticism, or perhaps in allusion to the origins of astrology in ancient Babylon.

13. The meaning of the name Factiopora is obscure. It may be a Latin-Greek composite word from *factio* and *poreuo*, signifying "a bringer of factionalism," hence "factious" or "seditious."

14. Bacchis is a prostitute's name in Plautus' *Bacchides* (which features two sisters with that name) and Terence's *Mother-in-Law* and *Self-Tormentor*. *Meum mel*, my sweet, is an epithet taken from Plautus' *Bacchides* 18.

15. The ending, "Farewell, spectators," etc., is a typically theatrical ending.

II.5. POVERTY

The discussion of wealth here advances the paradox that seeming avaricious is preferable to seeming poor — an especially paradoxical theme in an author who often favors being over seeming. In his Italian dialogue *Theogenius*, Alberti alludes to the satirical version of this theme in Juvenal 3.143–301.

16. Peniplusius, an oxymoron, also used in Book 4 of *Momus*, made of two words, meaning "a poor wealthy man," a man who lives beyond his means, or a poor man pretending to be wealthy. Paleterus means "older (and wiser)."

17. By citing tapestries, Peniplusius refutes the charge that his home is drab (19); and by citing studs and bosses, he refutes the charge that he neglects his horses.

II.6. THE COIN

Since some of the *Dinner Pieces* were written during the Council of Ferrara-Florence (1438–45), scholars have suggested that this tale parodies that ecumenical assembly, which here worships a trinity of gods: Venus, Bacchus, and Hypocrisy. The avarice of the clergy, however, is a common theme in medieval and Renaissance literature. Alberti discussed the ethos of priests in his Latin dialogue *Pontifex*, but here the tone is closer to Lucian, the Greek satirist notorious for irreligiosity. The tale is an etiological apologue, with debts to texts like Juvenal, *Satires* 1.114, "nullas nummorum ereximus aras" (we have built no altars to money), and Persius, *Satires* 2.69, "dicite pontifices in sancto quid facit aurum?" (tell us, priests, what is gold doing in the temple?). See also Augustine, *City of God* 7.12 (on the avatar of Jupiter called Jupiter Pecunia). See also the headnote to the next piece, *Pluto*.

18. Olympiads constituted the ancient Greek dating system, indicating four-year intervals between the Olympic Games, first held in 776 BCE. Delphi was the most important cult center of ancient Greece, the home of its famous oracle, which gave responses from the god Apollo.

19. Apollo's response is given in hexameters.

20. Monopus, a Grecism from *mono* and *pous*, meaning "one-footed" or "lame." Since a one-legged man is severely crippled, and since this priest is "the most intelligent of all" (13), it follows that Monopus possesses both characteristics of the Devil. Hence, it is the Devil disguised as a priest who counsels the assembled priests to worship the god Money as the highest deity. Significantly, the priests, who initially wavered between atheism and the cult of money, at last choose money, and from the first Olympiad "to the present day" have never changed their minds (15).

II.7. PLUTO

The Coin and *Pluto* resemble two panels of a diptych. By Pluto, Alberti means Plutus, the Greek god of wealth; but he assigns this god a verbal rebuff to Hercules not found in its classical sources, Aesop's "Hercules and Plutus" (III Perry), related in Latin verse in the *Fables* of Phaedrus 4.12. If we reflect on *The Coin*, we infer that priests follow Pluto rather than Hercules. But Alberti departs from those sources by shifting the fable to a religious context and by assigning a disturbing reply to Plutus, who is silent in both Aesop and Phaedrus: namely, that Plutus, and not Hercules, is the most important god for religion, because worship is served by money and not by virtue. This rebuff reduces Hercules to silence.

21. We have seen that contemporaries often accused Leonardo Bruni of avarice. Dedicating a book to him in which the god of wealth continually and exclusively frequents slothful and indolent men (2) clearly signals an overt provocation.

II.8. WEALTH

As noted above, *The Orphan* and *Wealth*, with their tributes to the Alberti clan, form a symmetrical frame to the pieces in Books 1 and 2. In his dedication to Bruni, Alberti summarizes the moral of this piece: "It is in the use of his wealth, rather than in its abundance, that the wise man should rejoice." (In Book 1 of *On the Family*, Leonardo likewise comments: "Né sia chi stimi le ricchezze se non faticose e incommode a chi non sa bene usarle.") Alberti takes some liberty with the historical figure of his grandfather Benedetto, who in fact did dictate his last will and testament. Where Benedetto here appears as a virtuous and selfless citizen, Book 9 of Bruni's *History of the Florentine People* — published on February 6, 1439 — portrays him as an ambitious and seditious magnate whose exile was fully justified. (An edition with English translation of Bruni's *History* in three volumes is found in ITRL 3, 16, and 27.) When in 1443 Alberti dedicated his Book 2 to the chancellor and the historian, he would have been aware that their views of Benedetto were vastly different. The funeral discourse was a favorite device of Alberti, used also in *Debate on Marriage* (Appendix 1).

22. Alberti's grandfather Benedetto (ca. 1320–89) was a wealthy merchant and an important politician who was exiled from Florence after the Ciompi revolt of 1378. He died in Rhodes while returning from a pilgrimage to the Holy Sepulcher in Jerusalem.

BOOK III

III.1. PAINTINGS

An example of *ekphrasis*, or the literary description of visual artworks, *Paintings* adapts the traditional iconography of virtues and vices. As the first piece in Book 3, and hence a symbolic introduction, it provides thematic clues for interpreting the pieces that follow. It also embodies Alberti's penchant for symbolic moral reflections and stylistic *brevitas*. In three places (4, 8, and 34), Alberti implies that this piece is both a dinner piece and a paratext, comparable to his prefaces in other books. Further connections with later pieces in this book and possible literary sources for Alberti's images are explored in Cardini 2022, 2:593–601.

1. The gymnosophists (literally, "naked sages") were Indian ascetics, Hindu sages of the Brahman priestly caste, about whom Alberti may have read in Plutarch, *Alexander* 64, and Lucian, *Runaways* 6–7. He refers to them also in his dialogues *On the Family*, in *Pontifex* (dated 1437), and in the tenth book of the present work.

2. Alberti's use of technical terminology reminds us that he was an expert on ancient architecture. See his *De re aedificatoria* 9.5, 9.7.

3. The figure of Calumny is derived from Lucian's description of Apelles' painting, *Calumny*, summarized by Alberti in Book 3 of his treatise *On Painting* (1435).

4. In antiquity, the Greek island of Cos was noted for producing fine silk. A few lines below, Beneficence holds a vase from Samos, on which see *Patience*, 1.5.28, above.

III.2. FLOWERS

Flowers begins a series of pieces in Book 3 that can be related to *Paintings*: in this case, to the symbolic figures of Contention and Ambition. In Ovid, *Metamorphoses* 1.116–18, it is Jupiter who divides the seasons; here it is Phoebus Apollo. On the theme of ambition punished, we may compare the descent of Calamity from Ambition in *Paintings*; the observation of Philoponius in *Affliction*, 4.5.132 ("men who . . . perished in their desire for revolutionary change"); and Book 1 of Alberti's *Theogenius*, "Molti, per volere soprastare gli altri, perirono" ("Many who perished wishing to dominate others"). See Cardini 2022, 2:602–3.

III.3. DISCORD

Like *Flowers*, *Discord* is linked to the figure of Contention in *Paintings*; and Honor here seems the double of Ambition. The confusion of the Olympian gods recalls Lucian, and the absence of Justice parallels that of Virtue in Book 3 of Alberti's *Momus*. The fable reveals the degeneration of all values in all three realms of creation: the heavens, the earth, and the underworld. The failed search for Justice reveals her to be the daughter of Honor and Discord, a disenchanted view of contemporary morality typical of Alberti.

5. Argos, the guardian god with a thousand eyes, has looked in vain for Justice in Florence (the beautiful city below Fiesole) and Rome. According to Vergil and Livy, Rome was founded on the site of a mythical settlement known as Pallantium on the Palatine Hill, founded by Evander ("good man"), an Arcadian Greek before the Trojan War.

6. Possibly an allusion by way of contrast to a famous dictum from Sallust's *War against Jugurtha*: "Harmony makes small states great, while discord undermines the mightiest empires" (10.6). The dictum was painted on the walls of the chapel of the Signoria in the Palazzo Vecchio.

7. To grasp the relationship between Pluto and the usurers, one must remember that Alberti conflates Pluto, the ruler of the underworld, with Plutus, the god of wealth.

8. Terminus was the ancient Roman god of boundaries, protected by soldiers and by law.

9. Honor, or Honos, was the Roman god personifying honor, frequently worshipped in tandem with Virtus, goddess of Virtue. An honor in Latin can also signify an office of state or *dignitas*, social rank. Here, Honor summons an inquest of kings, princes, and gods to witness his claims as to the time and the place when he fathered Discord upon Justice.

III.4. THE ENEMY

Alberti's source for this historical anecdote-apologue has been lost, but a record is preserved in the *Cronica historiale* of the sixteenth-century Dominican friar Lorenzo Taiuoli da Pistoia. The work is more fully explicated in Cardini, *Mosaici*, 1–50. The piece can be linked back to *Pictures* via the figure of Vengeance, daughter of Injury and mother of Calamity. The question of how to treat prisoners of war — exercise the right of war to execute them, show them mercy, or take them hostage as security against future wars — was a fundamental issue in legal debates about *ius in bello* (what is right in war). Alberti's text looks back to a similar debate during Rome's Samnite Wars described in Livy 9.3–4 and to passages in Cicero's *On Duties*.

10. In 1284, the Genoese fleet routed the Pisans near the islet of Meloria in the Ligurian Sea.

11. The source is Plutarch, *Pompey* 77, where the correct form of the name is Theodotus.

III.5. STONES

The great Renaissance scholar Eugenio Garin interpreted this piece as contrasting the active and the contemplative life and linked it to a fable (number 30) by Leonardo da Vinci. In fact, the theme of this short piece is the folly of abandoning one's proper place in life and engaging in revolutionary recklessness, hoping, against the law of nature, to learn how to swim in a foreign environment. The theme of ambition punished recalls that of *Flowers* and looks forward to Alberti's dictum in *Affliction*, 4.5.131: "Hence, in my opinion, a wise man will choose to be himself."

III.6. IVY

This "apologue of protest" continues the theme running from *The Coin* to *The Cynic*, which charges the clergy with favoring those whose activities harm the Church. Ivy is also personified in a negative way in Book 1 of *Momus*, when the character Momus transforms himself into an ivy plant to break into a temple and rape Praise, the daughter of Virtue. A precedent for this apologue is found in Aesop's tale "The Walnut" (250 Perry).

III.7. SUSPICION

Suspicion and Truth are allegorical figures in Lucian's "Calumny (or Slander) of Apelles," and the destructive power of Suspicion is evoked by the figures of Envy and Calumny in *Paintings* (see note to 3.1.11). The theme of suspicion is recurrent in Alberti's works: *Amator, De amore, Deifira, Ecatonfilea, Agilitta, Uxoria, De Familia, Theogenius, De iciarchia*. The personification Rumor plays a major role in *Momus*.

12. The augurs were a Roman priesthood charged with reading the auspices, interpreting natural signs such as the flights of birds or the entrails of animals. The Sibylline Books were a collection of oracles attributed to the Sibyl, a Greek prophetess, who was regularly portrayed as both divinely inspired and raving mad.

13. Mnimia is Alberti's Greek coinage for "memory," a goddess who also appears in his Latin comedy *Philodoxus* (ca. 1424), published with an English translation in *Humanist Comedies*, ITRL 19.

14. The Vestal Virgins, an ancient Roman priesthood of Vesta, goddess of the hearth.

15. Janus, the Roman god of public gates and the eponymous deity of January, was given the cult title Pater (father). Alberti associates him with the virtue of Prudence, or practical wisdom, in his vernacular dialogue *Ecatonfilea* (1438), where it says that to block suspicion one needs prudence and understanding, or the qualities of Janus, who faces both forward and backward precisely for this reason (Macrobius, *Saturnalia* 1.7.20).

BOOK IV

PREFACE TO POGGIO BRACCIOLINI

This dedication represents one of Alberti's principal texts on poetics. Its basic motif, zeal for research into what is difficult and rare, is entirely characteristic of him; one finds it also in his works *The Dog* (edited by McLaughlin with an English translation in ITRL 96), in the dedication to the *Elementa picturae* (Elements of Painting), and in the preface to *Momus*. Here and elsewhere, Alberti uses food and nourishment as traditional metaphors for intellectual nutrition: the *Dinner Pieces* are to be read at table, and the *Momus* is said to provide humor as a condiment. Symbolically, the solitary goat scales the ruins of an ancient mountainside temple in search of rare sustenance, instead of (like most humanists, here, "buffalo") seeking nourishment in the "swamp grass" of eloquence, where food is more easily found and more richly rewarded. As an example of studies that are more rare, he gives the example of mathematics, a subject Alberti cultivated in the *Ludi matematici* (Mathematical Exercises). Poggio Bracciolini (1380–1459) was a celebrated secretary in the papal Curia, best remembered as a discoverer of Latin manuscripts, as the author of dialogues and letters, and as the chancellor of the Florentine Republic from 1453 to 1458.

1. The goat is obviously a symbol for Alberti himself, while the temple signifies classical culture.

2. The text breaks off in midsentence in the only surviving manuscript.

iv.1. THE DREAM

The fantastic trips to another world featured in Lucian's *Icaromenippus* and *Vera Historia* here inspire Alberti's entertaining dialogue, which seems to date from 1442–43, or at the earliest from 1438, because in that year Alberti first read the recently discovered *Mostellaria* of Plautus, from which he borrows the expression *cerebrum emungere* (23: "to clean out a brain"). On Alberti and Plautus, see Cardini, "Quando e dove l'Alberti conobbe il nuovo Plauto." Alberti's allegory of the valley of lost objects inspired Ariosto's episode of Astolfo on the moon in *Orlando Furioso* 34.72–86: see Segre, "Leon Battista Alberti e Ludovico Ariosto." For the interlocutors Lepidus and Libripeta, see the headnote to *The Writer*, above in Book 1.

3. Compare the River of Life, Bios, in *Fate and Fortune* (1.4).

4. Rocks tumbling downhill: compare *Stones* (3.5).

5. River of tears: compare Dante, *Inferno* 14.112–20.

IV.2. GARLANDS

This piece is formally an allegorical comedy. The contest for a garland recalls the famous *Certame coronario* (coronet competition), sponsored by Alberti in 1441, that offered a reward for the best poetic composition in Italian. In the event, the jury, made up of Latin-writing humanists, spitefully refused to pick a winner; see Gorni, "La storia del Certame Coronario." In the figures of the Poet and Rhetorician, Alberti parodies the vapid pastiches of ancient authors written by some humanists. For the figure of Lepidus, see the headnote to *The Writer*, in Book 1.

6. Praise and her mother Virtue are also personified characters in Book 1 of the *Momus*.

7. A defective hexameter verse that begins with a borrowing from Vergil's *Aeneid* 1.1 and ends with a borrowing from *Aeneid* 4.659.

8. In sentences 28 and 34–44, Alberti mimics the complex periodic style of Ciceronian oratory affected by Renaissance humanists.

9. Pronoia, the Stoic term for divine providence.

IV.3. THE CYNIC

This dialogue presents a sort of last judgment organized by Apollo, Mercury, and the Cynic, who unmasks the pretensions of souls in the underworld. The Cynic is largely a projection of the author. As often in Alberti, judgment is not of individuals but collective. The dead are divided into professional categories, and the categories are examined and condemned *en bloc*. The role of the Cynic is the same role that, from Alberti to Luigi Pirandello, is assigned to the humorist. The souls are interrogated and systematically lie: they say that they were motivated by their own duties, by what they "had to be." The Cynic, equally systematically, strips off their masks and reveals their true being, their habitual ways of life. Thus, naked, they are sent away and reincarnated as the animal most suited to their real nature.

10. Centuries and maniples, i.e., tactical subdivisions of legions in the ancient Roman army.

11. Miters are caps worn by bishops; Alberti is once again attacking the clergy.

12. The sentence is incomplete, indicating the Cynic has either broken off his remarks in fear or is whispering them so that the magistrates cannot hear what he is saying.

13. In sentences 54–55 and 79–88, compare the criticism of the philosophers in Book 4 of the *Momus*.

14. The writers in sentences 61–64 are historians, recalling Lucian's critique of this class of writers in *De historia conscribenda* (How history must be written).

15. The rhetoricians launch into an oration but are stopped by the Cynic.

16. Alberti here is sending up the astrologers, following a critical optic found in Cicero's *On Divination*.

17. The litigiousness of the philosophers and their failure to agree with each other is a topos of the ancient skeptical tradition, embraced in Cicero's *Academica* and *On Laws* 153, and in Lucian—a key author for Alberti.

IV.4. FAME

The opening of the dialogue echoes that of *The Dream*, which suggests that the two pieces were composed around the same time as the dedication to Poggio, or 1442–43. Fame here, as often in Alberti, is a negative value. Libripeta's thirst for fame represents the opposite of Alberti's view of the purpose of literary studies.

18. In 216 BCE, during the Second Punic War, Hannibal mounted torches on the horns of cattle and sent them wandering toward his Roman adversaries in order to confuse them. The incident is described in Livy 22.16–17; Cornelius Nepos, *Hannibal* 5.2; Silius Italicus 7.328–76; Plutarch, *Fabius Maximus* 6–7.

19. The cow dragged by the tail into the Temple of Fame is probably parody. Livy (1.7) in order to explain the Roman cult of Hercules and the origin of the *Ara maxima* (Greatest Altar), tells how one fine day Hercu-

les arrived with a herd of cattle on the banks of the Tiber. He fell asleep, and Cacus robbed him of his best cattle, "dragging them by the tail" into his own cave. Literati conduct themselves just like the thief Cacus, except that, crazed by the act of dragging, they keep the tail in their hands. With respect to the allusion to cattle, note that in Tuscany, according to *On the Advantages and Disadvantages of Literature* (5.45), a literatus is defined as a "marble cow."

IV.5. AFFLICTION

As a consolatory (or self-consolatory) piece, the dialogue, written before October 1437, bears an affinity to Alberti's Italian dialogues *Theogenius* and *Profugia ab erumna*. The former features the contrast between a rich man and a scholar, while the latter shares with this piece the theme of *erumna* (affliction). In the course of the dialogue, Philoponius learns that "the wise man will choose to be himself" (131), and not envy other people the lot chosen for them by Fortune. Philoponius is one of Alberti's masks: see *The Orphan*, 1.1. Much of the piece is, for Alberti, unusually convoluted and declamatory in style, far from the conversational tone dominant elsewhere in the *Dinner Pieces*. Philoponius' interlocutor is unnamed in the single manuscript witness; the indication [*Friend*] has been supplied for the reader's convenience. For parallel treatments in other works of Alberti to the themes discussed here, see Cardini 2022, 528–632.

20. The bad behavior of his own family, despite its antiquity and wealth, is an obsessive theme in Alberti's writings.

21. The manuscript leaves blank the name of the philosopher.

22. Here credulity, or *superstitio*, signifies "scrupulous observance," thus "Cynic credulity" alludes to the comportment of the Cynic school, beginning with Diogenes, above all the neglect of good manners and any sort of convention as well as verbal violence. This is the comportment that the Cynic of *Affliction* has scrupulously observed. For criticism of the Cynic doctrine, see (for example) Cicero, *De officiis* 1.148.

23. For the rest of the piece, Philoponius' friend speaks under the persona of Fortune.

24. The name Triscatarus (sometimes mistakenly written Triscatharus, "thrice cleansed," which makes no sense) is a Greek compound of *tris* (thrice) and *catára* (curse), meaning "thrice cursed": see Cardini, "Onomastica albertiana," 149–51.

25. *That man* is Philoponius; see sentence 113, where Fortune reports Triscatarus' opinion of Philoponius.

26. The ellipsis in this sentence represents a lacuna in the manuscript.

27. Rejection of revolutions both moral and political is a constant in Alberti's thought, represented in this work in Book 3, in *Stones*, and in Book 10, in *The Owl*, *The Temple*, and *The Lake*.

IV.6. THE SLAVE

The humorous elements of this dialogue and its comic style offset the gravity and philosophical eloquence of the preceding piece, *Affliction*. Like *Affliction*, *The Slave* contains a philosophical dialogue within the principal dialogue, although the philosophy in this case is more Stoic than Cynic. Alberti borrows from Terence's *Mother-in-Law* (with the characters Parmeno, Pamphilus, Charidemus, and Sostrata). The name Birria is used in Terence's *The Woman of Andros*. Slaves are also frequent interlocutors in Roman satires: see, for example, Horace, *Satires* 2.7; Persius 5; and Juvenal 9. Parmeno's interlocutor is not named in a single manuscript source; the name [SPEAKER] is provided for the reader's convenience.

28. The name Laches comes from the *Hecyra* of Terence.

29. Pamphilus, a Greek name meaning "loved by all."

30. C(h)aridemus, a Greek name meaning "joy of the people," a mangling, perhaps intentional, of Terence's character Callidemides. Both the name Caridemus and the scene are taken from Terence, *Hecyra* 431–44.

31. Again, the conclusion that it is best to be satisfied with what one is rather than long to be someone else, the lesson of the previous piece, *Affliction*.

BOOK VII

PREFACE

The moral of the delicious story told by Alberti in the first two paragraphs of this preface is drawn in the paragraphs that follow. Those who seek to model their style on single authors like Cicero are wasting their time; there was only one Cicero. Orators should set aside such impossible tasks as imitating Cicero, which are like trying to capture the moon with nets, and seek variety in their literary style, going beyond formulaic and traditional approaches to literary composition. Alberti's fable of the fauns and satyrs was adapted by Ariosto in his third Italian satire: see Segre, "Leon Battista Alberti e Ludovico Ariosto." Alberti's *One Hundred Fables* also features fauns (67) and satyrs (70).

1. "my dear X." The sole manuscript has a lacuna after *mi* for a name to be inserted. It is not known whether Alberti had a dedicatee in mind for this book.

VII.I. THE HUSBAND

After citing Cato the Elder—"a man who acts like a good husband is worthy of praise"—Alberti, adapting Martial, offers this maxim: "A husband should neither show indulgence, which breeds contempt, nor severity, which arouses hatred." This is the principle of the just mean that Quintilian recommends for a teacher (*Institutes of Oratory* 2.2.5) and that Alberti also formulates in his treatise *On Law*. But these noble moral, pedagogical, and juridical principles are applied to the unlikely category of conjugal infidelity. By reconciling the severity and indulgence suggested by these venerable principles, the husband causes the death of his unfaithful wife, not only without his remorse, but with her approval. The plot of the discovered lover has some affinities with Apuleius, *Metamorphoses* 9.14–31, and Boccaccio, *Decameron* 5.10.

2. Plutarch, *Cato the Elder* 20, a work translated into Latin by Francesco Barbaro around 1417.

3. Martial, *Epigrams* 1.57.

4. The black humor of the old man "triumphant" over the three wives he has buried is taken from Martial; compare his epigram 8.43. For the modern reader, the humor of Alfred Hitchcock may come to mind.

5. An echo of Juvenal, *Satires* 6.285: "animos a crimine sumunt" (they take courage from their crime).

6. The comment on Plato is taken from Cicero, *On Laws* 3.1.

7. When the Roman general Lucius Aemilius Paullus divorced his wife Papiria, mother of Scipio Aemilianus, his friends wondered why; and pointing to his shoe, he asked them: "Can you tell me where it pinches my foot?" The anecdote is from Plutarch, *Aemilius Paulus* 5, a work translated into Latin by Leonardo Bruni before August 1409.

8. Socrates was declared the wisest of men by the oracle of Apollo at Delphi: see Plato, *Apology* 21A, a work translated into Latin by Leonardo Bruni ca. 1404–9. Socrates' unvarying expression was noted by his shrewish wife Xanthippe: see Cicero, *Tusculan Disputations* 3.31.

VII.2. DEBATE ON MARRIAGE

The sardonic discussion of wives seems to be a covert response to the praise of marriage found in Leonardo Bruni's *Vita di Dante* (1436) and Poggio Bracciolini's *An seni sit uxor ducenda* (1436). The oratorical contest between the three brothers turns on the issue of marriage: whether one should marry and how one should conduct oneself in marriage. The contest has an irresistibly comic quality, given the implicit contrast with the great public achievements of the father, Cleiodramus, who is imagined as a Spartan king who has won glory in battle. As Alberti and his learned readers would know from Filelfo's recent translations (1430) of Xenophon's *Spartan Constitution* and *Agesilaus* and Plutarch's *Lycurgus*, celibates in Sparta were subject to severe penalties, and wives were accorded unusual freedoms, including, under certain circumstances, polygamous relations.

The misogyny of the piece has precedents in Juvenal's sixth satire, in Jerome's *Adversus Iovinianum*, Walter Map's *Dissuasio Valerii* (which Alberti translated), and Boccaccio's *Corbaccio*. The spirit of the piece might be formulated as "in tristitia hilaris, in hilaritate tristis" (cheerful in sadness; sad amid cheer), the motto of Giordano Bruno; and its humorism anticipates works by Luigi Pirandello. The Latin piece was originally published as a separate work, with a preface to an unknown dedicatee (reproduced in Appendix 1). Together with *Shipwrecked*, it is one of two pieces that Alberti translated into Italian: the Italian version, not translated here, is dedicated to Piero de' Medici (1416–69), the father of Lorenzo il Magnifico.

9. The characters have names invented by Alberti: from Greek, Cleiodramus ("glory seeking") and Trissophus ("thrice wise"); and from Latin, Mitio ("mild, tolerant") and Acrinnus ("harsh, severe"). The character Trissophus is clearly a projection of Alberti himself, a ferocious misogynist. See also Aulus Gellius 1.17.

10. Alberti's misogyny was fed from traditional sources. In addition to the sources in the headnote, note that "indomitum animal, ut aiunt, mulier frenari nusquam potest" here echoes Cato the Elder's ironic words censuring the Roman women who were protesting sumptuary laws in Livy, *History of Rome* 34.2.13: "date *frenos* impotenti naturae et *indomito animali* et sperate ipsas modum licentiae facturas" (Give loose *rein* to their uncontrollable nature and to this *untamed creature* and expect that they will themselves set bounds to their license).

11. Like the "Tale of the Three Rings" (related in Boccaccio, *Decameron* 1.3), Alberti's Spartan debate has no resolution. The judges deliver no verdict and remand the decision and the custody of Cleiodramus' military insignia to the priests of Cybele, or eunuchs, who have by castrating themselves cut away the root, one might say, of the problem of women and marriage. This conclusion entails a similarly abrupt unmasking: in this case, exposing the misogynist Trissophus, and hence Alberti, whom he symbolizes.

Bibliography

꽃♡꽃

EDITIONS

Opera inedita et pauca separatim impressa. Edited by Girolamo Mancini. Florence: Sansoni, 1890. The *Intercenales* are printed on pp. 122–235. *Editio princeps* of the first two books, based on the Oxford manuscript, with the *Defunctus* and *Anuli.*

Intercenali inedite. Edited by Eugenio Garin. Florence: Sansoni, 1965. *Editio princeps* of the twenty-five *intercenali* and five prefaces preserved in the Pistoia manuscript.

Intercenales (libri III–XI). Edited by Roberto Cardini. Rome: Bulzoni, 1978. A critical revision of the Garin edition.

Intercenales. Edited by Franco Bacchelli and Luca D'Ascia, with a preface by Alberto Tenenti. Bologna: Pendragon, 2003. Based on the Oxford and Pistoiese manuscripts. With an Italian translation.

Intercenales. Edited with a commentary by Roberto Cardini. In Leon Battista Alberti, *Opere latine,* edited by Roberto Cardini, 167–618. Rome: Istituto Poligrafico e Zecca dello Stato, 2010. With an Italian translation by Maria Letizia Bracciali Magnini.

Intercenales: Editio minor. Edited by Roberto Cardini. 2 vols. Florence: Edizioni Polistampa, 2022. = Humanistica II/5. With a facing Italian translation by Maria Letizia Bracciali Magnini.

TRANSLATIONS

Dinner Pieces. Translated with notes by David Marsh. Binghamton, NY: Medieval & Renaissance Texts & Studies — The Renaissance Society of America, 1987.

Le intercenali. Translated and introduced by Ida Garghella. Naples: Edizioni Scientifiche Italiane, 1998.

Propos de table / Intercenales. Critical edition, introduction, and commentary by Roberto Cardini. Translated by Claude Laurens. 2 vols. Paris: Les Belles Lettres, 2018. (Les classiques de l'humanisme.)

351

OTHER WORKS OF ALBERTI CITED

Biographical and Autobiographical Works. Edited by Martin McLaughlin. I Tatti Renaissance Library 96. Cambridge, MA: Harvard University Press, 2023.

Momus. Edited and translated by Sarah Knight and Virginia Brown. I Tatti Renaissance Library 8. Cambridge, MA: Harvard University Press, 2003.

Opere volgari. Edited by Cecil Grayson. 3 vols. Bari: Laterza, 1960–73.

Philodoxeos fabula. In *Humanist Comedies,* edited by Gary Grund. I Tatti Renaissance Library 19. Cambridge, MA: Harvard University Press, 2005.

SECONDARY LITERATURE

Acocella, Mariantonetta. "Appunti sulla presenza di Luciano nelle *Intercenales.*" In *Alberti e la tradizione. Per lo "smontaggio" dei "mosaici" albertiani: Atti del Convegno internazionale di Arezzo, 23–25 settembre 2004,* edited by Roberto Cardini e Mariangela Regoliosi, 1:81–139. 2 vols. Florence: Edizioni Polistampa, 2007.

Boschetto, Luca. *Leon Battista Alberti e Firenze. Biografia, storia, letteratura.* Florence: Leo S. Olschki Editore, 2000.

Cardini, Roberto. "Alberti e Firenze." In *Alberti e la cultura del Quattrocento. Atti del Convegno internazionale di Firenze, 16–18 dicembre 2004,* edited by Roberto Cardini and Mariangela Regoliosi, 2:223–66. 2 vols. Florence: Edizioni Polistampa, 2008.

———. "Alberti o della nascita dell'umorismo moderno." *Schede umanistiche* 1 (1993): 31–85.

———. "Enigmi albertiani." In *Nel cantiere degli umanisti. Per Mariangela Regoliosi,* edited by Lucia Bertolini, Donatella Coppini, and Clementina Marsico, 1:221–73. 3 vols. Florence: Edizioni Polistampa, 2015.

———. "Un *Exemplum ad rem uxoriam pulchre agendam: Maritus* di Leon Battista Alberti." In *Exempla fidem faciunt,* edited by Maria Luisa Harto Trujillo and Joachím Villalba Álvares, 241–62. Madrid: Ediciones Clásicas, 2013.

———. "Le *Intercenales* di Leon Battista Alberti. Preliminari all'edizione critica." *Moderni e Antichi* 1 (2003): 98–142.

———. "Leonardo Dati e il Certame coronario." *Moderni e Antichi*, ser. 2, 3 (2021): 183–200.

———. *Mosaici. Il "nemico" dell'Alberti*. Rome: Bulzoni, 1990. 2nd ed., 2004.

———. "Onomastica albertiana." *Moderni e Antichi* 1 (2003): 143–75.

———. "Onomastica albertiana. Cosa è Libripeta." *Moderni e Antichi*, ser. 2, 3 (2021): 45–69.

———. *Ortografia e consolazione in un* corpus *allestito da Leon Battista Alberti. Il codice Moreni 2 della Biblioteca Moreniana di Firenze*. Florence: Olschki, 2008.

———. "Paralipomeni all'Alberti umorista." *Moderni e Antichi* 1 (2003): 73–86.

———. "Per lo smontaggio e l'interpretazione di *Religio*." In Wulfram, *Leon Battists Alberti, Intercenales*, 49–74.

———. "Quando e dove l'Alberti conobbe il nuovo Plauto." In *Itinerari del Testo per Stefano Pittaluga*, edited by Cristina Cocco and others, 1:141–94. 2 vols. Genoa: University of Genoa, 2018.

———. "Smontaggio e umorismo. *Uxoria* dell'Alberti." *Moderni e Antichi*, ser. 2, 1 (2019): 125–54.

Edizione Nazionale delle Opere di Leon Battista Alberti, which since 2003, in addition to critical annotated editions of Alberti's works, publishes also the two series of Strumenti and Studi. Florence, Edizioni Polistampa. See info@leonardolibri.com — www.leonardolibri.com

Fubini, Riccardo, and Anna Menci Gallorini. "L'autobiografia di Leon Battista Alberti: Studio e edizione." *Rinascimento*, n.s. 12 (1972): 21–78.

Furlan, Francesco, and Sylvain Matton. "Abrasae nates: Autour des *Intercenales* inconnues." In Furlan, *Studia albertiana*, 195–206. A revised and expanded version of the following article.

———. "Baptistae Alberti *Simiae* et de nonnullis eiusdem Baptistae apologis qui nondum in vulgus prodiere: Autour des *Intercenales* inconnues de Leon Battista Alberti." *Bibliothèque d'Humanisme et Renaissance* 55 (1993): 125–35.

———. *Studia albertiana: Lectures et lecteurs de L. B. Alberti*. Turin: Nino Aragno/Paris: J. Vrin, 2003.

Garin, Eugenio. *Studi su Leon Battista Alberti*. In idem, *Rinascite e rivoluzioni: movimenti culturali dal XIV al XVIII secolo*, 131–96. Rome-Bari: Laterza, 1975.

Gorni, Guglielmo. "La storia del Certame Coronario." *Rinascimento*, n.s. 12 (1972): 135–81.

Grafton, Anthony. *Leon Battista Alberti: Master Builder of the Renaissance*. New York: Hill and Wang, 2000.

Grayson, Cecil. *Studi su Leon Battista Alberti*. Edited by Paola Claut. Florence: Leo S. Olschki Editore, 1998.

Leon Battista Alberti, Intercenales. Eine neulateinische Kurzprosasammlung zwischen Antike und Moderne. Edited by Hartmut Wulfram. Stuttgart: Franz Steiner Verlag, 2021.

Mancini, Girolamo. *Vita di Leon Battista Alberti*. 2nd ed. Florence: G. Carnesecchi Editore, 1911. Reprint, Rome: Bardi Editore, 1971.

Margolin, Jean-Claude. "L'influence de Lucien sur les *Propos de table* d'Alberti." *Revue Belge de Philologie et d'Histoire* 15 (1973): 582–604.

Marsh, David. "Alberti, Scala, and Ficino. Aesop in Quattrocento Florence." *Albertiana* 3 (2000): 105–18.

——— . *Lucian and the Latins: Humor and Humanism in the Early Renaissance*. Ann Arbor: University of Michigan Press, 1998.

——— . *Studies on Petrarch and Alberti*. Farnham, UK, and Williston, VT: Ashgate, 2012.

Marsh, David, and Paolo D'Alessandro. "Girolamo Massaini trascrittore dell'Alberti." *Albertiana* 11–12 (2008–9): 260–66.

Mattioli, Emilio. *Luciano e l'Umanesimo*. Naples: Istituto Italiano per gli Studi Storici, 1980.

McLaughlin, Martin. *Leon Battista Alberti: La vita, l'umanesimo, le opere letterarie*. Florence: Leo S. Olschki Editore, 2016.

Segre, Cesare. "Leon Battista Alberti e Ludovico Ariosto." In idem, *Esperienze ariostesche*, 85–95. Pisa: Listri-Nischi, 1966.

Société Internationale Leon Battista Alberti (SILBA), publisher of *Albertiana* (1998–) and the ongoing series of his *Opera omnia*. Website: http://www.silba.msh-paris.fr

Index

꽃옹?옹

Acrinnus (char.), 269, 293–97, 301, 303, 305, 350n9
Aemilius Paullus, Lucius, 265, 349n7
Aesop, xiv, xxix, 328n, 335n, 336n11, 341–42n; "Hercules and Plutus," 337n
Aggrames, 11, 330n9
Alberti family, xxv, xxvi, 109–11, 338n, 346n20
Alberti, Benedetto (grandfather of LBA), xiii, xxiii, 109–11, 329n, 338n, 338n22
Alberti, Carlo (brother of LBA), xxvi
Alberti, Leon Battista, vii, ix–x, xiii, xviii–xix, xxiii, xxv–xxx, 329n, 343n1, 344n, 345n11, 345n, 350n. *See also* Lepidus
Alberti, Leon Battista, works: *Affliction (Erumna)*, 339n, 340n, 346n22, 347n, 347n31; *Agilitta*, 342n; *Amator*, 342n; *Autobiography*, xxiv, 327n; *The Bishop (Pontifex)*, xxviii, 337n, 339n1; *The Coin (Nummus)*, xvi, 341n; *De amore*, 342n; *Debate on Marriage (Uxoria)*, viii, ix, xvii, xxiv, 311, 338n, 342n; *Deifira*, xxvii, 342n; *Discord (Discordia)*, xvi, xxiii, xxiv, 340n; *The Dog (Canis)*, xxiii, 342n; *Ecatonfilea*, 342n,

342n15; *Elements of Painting*, 342–43n; *The Enemy (Hostis)*, xvi, xxiv; *Grammar of the Tuscan Language (Grammatichetta)*, xxvii, xxviii, xxix; *Mathematical Exercises (Ludi matematici)*, 343n; *Momus*, xviii, xx, xxi, xxiii, xxix–xxx, 330n, 334n, 334n3, 335n8, 336n16, 340n, 341n, 341n, 343n, 344n6, 345n13; *One Hundred Fables (Apologi centum)*, xxiii, xxviii–xxix, 335n, 348n; *On Law (De iure)*, xxviii, 348n; *On Painting*, xxviii, 339n3; *On the Advantages and Disadvantages of Literature (De commodis litterarum atque incommodis)*, xiii, xiv, 329n, 333n, 346n19; *On the Art of Building (De re aedificatoria)*, x, xvi, xxix, 339n2; *On the Family (De Familia)*, xxiv, xxv, xxviii, xxix, 335n, 338n, 339n1, 342n; *The Owl (Bubo)*, xvi, xxiv, 347n27; *Philodoxeos fabula (Philodoxus)*, x, xiv, xviii, xix, xx, xxvii, xxviii, 335n7, 342n13; *Remedies for Affliction (Profugiorum ab erumna libri)*, x, xxv, xxxi n10, 332n, 332–33n25, 347n; *Ruling the Household (De iciarchia)*, xv, 331n, 342n; *Theogenius*, 332n, 336n, 339–40n, 342n, 346n

355

Publication of this volume has been made possible by

The Myron and Sheila Gilmore Publication Fund at I Tatti
The Robert Lehman Endowment Fund
The Jean-François Malle Scholarly Programs and Publications Fund
The Andrew W. Mellon Scholarly Publications Fund
The Craig and Barbara Smyth Fund
for Scholarly Programs and Publications
The Lila Wallace–Reader's Digest Endowment Fund
The Malcolm Wiener Fund for Scholarly Programs and Publications